Charting a New Course
for Feminist Psychology

Edited by
Lynn H. Collins,
Michelle R. Dunlap, and
Joan C. Chrisler

PRAEGER

Westport, Connecticut
London

Library of Congress Cataloging-in-Publication Data

Charting a new course for feminist psychology / edited by Lynn H. Collins, Michelle R.
   Dunlap, and Joan C. Chrisler.
        p.   cm.
     Includes bibliographical references and index.
     ISBN 0–275–96952–5 (alk. paper)
        1. Feminist psychology. 2. Feminism. 3. Women—Psychology. I. Collins, Lynn H.
   II. Dunlap, Michelle R., 1965– III. Chrisler, Joan C.
     BF201.4.C43   2002
     105'.82—dc21   2001036315

British Library Cataloguing in Publication Data is available.

Library of Congress Catalog Card Number: 2001036315
ISBN: 0–275–96952–5

First published in 2002

Praeger Publishers, 88 Post Road West, Westport, CT 06881
An imprint of Greenwood Publishing Group, Inc.
www.praeger.com

Printed in the United States of America

The paper used in this book complies with the
Permanent Paper Standard issued by the National
Information Standards Organization (Z39.48–1984).

10 9 8 7 6 5 4 3 2 1

Contents

Introduction

Charting a New Course for Feminist Psychology is a collection of essays designed to suggest a new course for women's and girls' individual and collective lives and for feminist psychological theory, research, teaching, and practice. The theme of "charting a new course" is metaphorical in that it speaks to the need for psychology to be moved more toward paradigms and methodologies that are respectful and inclusive of women's experiences, voices, socialization, oppression, creativity, and resourcefulness. Likewise, the theme of "charting a new course" is also literal to some extent. Many women share historical roots that have to do with making their way to ships, pressing their way onto ships, escaping ships, surviving ships, and/or re-creating their lives after disembarking ships. Many women risked their lives for the hope that they might escape oppression, abuse, and genocide, and journey by ship (or boat, train, bus, foot, and/or their own psyches) to better spaces that might hold improved opportunities for them and their children. Others, rather than seeking the ship for themselves, were forced, beaten, and chained onto ships. A great number of these women elected to jump overboard with their children and drown rather than suffer the dehumanization that ships of various types of enslavement held for them.

As we enter a new millennium and hope for a brighter future for women, we must consider the meaning of these histories for the psychology of women. In doing so, we must chart for ourselves new directions, new journeys, new tools, diverse paradigms, and broader methodologies for articulating and understanding the psychology of today's women.

Many women in the modern world no longer have to sneak onto ships or drown themselves in oceans to escape dehumanizing experiences. However, as we enter the new millennium, women are still severely over-represented among those who, for example, experience poverty and homelessness, HIV, debilitating diseases, domestic violence and homicide, depression, eating disorders, and suicide attempts. Because of the oppression that women still experience because of their sex, sexual orientations, ethnicities, racial constructions, skin colors, socioeconomic status, marital status, physical abilities and disabilities, jobs, joblessness, homelessness, and other factors, there is a need to chart a new course both physically and psychologically, *and* both literally and metaphorically. These different approaches to charting a new course are not mutually exclusive; they overlap to varying degrees depending upon each individual's circumstances.

We must aim to chart our courses in such a way that we significantly reduce the chances of the painful, negative aspects of women's histories being repeated. An African proverb says that if we dwell on the past, we will lose an eye; but if we forget the past, we will lose both eyes. In terms of feminist psychology, if we do not examine where we have been, we will be blinded as we try to make our way to a stronger feminist psychology. Therefore, it would not be advisable to chart a course with blinders on, or without the necessary tools and wisdom that might assist us in viewing our lives, histories, and potential futures from a variety of perspectives. On a well-equipped ship, we might carry a variety of binoculars, telescopes, microscopes, compasses, and elders of wisdom who have traversed the waters before us. As each woman uses these tools, she must note and share with others her vision, perceptions, coping, and resources. As she uses these tools, she also benefits from listening to the experiences of her sisters who are also navigating waters that can at times be treacherous. By sharing our visions, tools, and other resources, we will learn mutually from one another in the tradition of feminist approaches.

The chapters of this book grew out of presentations at the 1998 23rd Annual Conference of the Association for Women in Psychology (AWP) in Baltimore, Maryland, whose theme was "Charting a New Course." That year's conference was planned and hosted by Lynn H. Collins and her colleagues; the co-chairs of the program committee were Joan C. Chrisler and Michelle R. Dunlap. AWP, an educational feminist organization that is devoted to correcting and reformulating the way psychologists study and describe women and their roles, seeks to comprehend and reflect the diversity of feminist/womanist concerns, and therefore includes in its mission the consideration of how race, ethnicity, age, social class, sexual orientation, and religious affiliation impact women's lives. Activism is one of AWP's primary purposes; its members are committed to acting responsibly and sensitively by challenging the unquestioned assumptions in research traditions, theory, and practice. Another of its goals is addressing questions about the institutional and sociocultural traditions and policies that inhibit women's growth and psychologists' understanding and support of women.

The association supports informed approaches to education about women's issues, promotes advocacy of women's concerns, encourages and facilitates collaboration among individuals and groups, and invites consequent social activism and political action.

Interest in research on the psychology of women and feminist psychology is on the rise. A recent search on the PsycINFO database by one of us revealed that the number of articles published in these areas has increased at a rate that exceeds that of the field of psychology in general. Accordingly, research and thinking in the area of the psychology of women is moving ahead rapidly. This book will provide a sample of innovative efforts to advance the knowledge of feminist psychology. It is intended to give readers an update on recent findings and a sense of anticipated directions of new lines of inquiry. The chapters of this book reflect AWP's goals by attempting to portray women's diversity and by incorporating implications and strategies for social action and opportunities for political activism in each chapter. The authors range from well-known experts who have published extensively in their area to younger psychologists who are bringing new ideas and perspectives to the field. The authors of the chapters are diverse in age, ethnicity, and sexual orientation.

The theme of "Charting a New Course" embraces the extremes and overlap of its metaphorical and literal meanings. It also tries to embrace all of the gray areas in between, as we, as women, try to keep our sanity while navigating our life journeys in environments that were not built for us—environments that traditionally have not valued or considered worthy our thoughts, psyches, and coping efforts. Instead, we have often been misunderstood and pathologized.

The chapters of this book offer both philosophical and practical tools that might assist us in examining our past, present, and future, as we attempt to look ahead and plan for an improved feminist psychology and an enhanced quality of life. As we consider and reconsider new directions and offer ideas for charting a new course, we continue to look forward to the hope of a world where women will be listened to, respected, and treated as equal, valuable citizens.

It should be noted that because the physical, cognitive, and psychosocial aspects of our being are not mutually exclusive of one another, the topics of the chapters within and between each of the book's five parts are not mutually exclusive of one another. The topics contained within each chapter overlap across the physical, cognitive, and psychosocial components of development; thus, chapters within one part of the book might have just as easily fit within another. Each part, therefore, should be regarded as having fuzzy boundaries.

Our voyage will begin with Part I, "Feminist Theory and Pedagogy," which includes four chapters. These chapters provide background on the history of feminism and feminist theory, and suggestions for ways these subjects can be taught in universities. In Chapter 1, Maureen C. McHugh and Lisa Cosgrove explore satirical methods of drawing attention to flaws in research on gender, as well as the consequences of studying or not studying gender differences. They argue convincingly that feminist research and pedagogy should be grounded in methodological and theoretical approaches that do not essentialize gender. In Chapter 2, Cosgrove and McHugh present a postmodern perspective on conceptualizing gender and feminist research on gender and gender differences. In Chapter 3, Merideth J. Tomlinson and Ruth E. Fassinger offer the historical context for feminist psychological pedagogy. In doing so, they also identify best practices of feminist pedagogy and examine the use of feminist pedagogical practices among a sample of feminist psychologists. In Chapter 4, Michelle K. Williams, Terry McCandies, and Michelle R. Dunlap assess feminist psychology with respect to its inclusion of issues of women of color, and note that although we have made many strides, we still have a long way to go. They offer suggestions to promote integration and application of feminism and womanism across groups, so that women of color have an opportunity to feel more at home with feminist philosophies and approaches.

Part II, "Psychological Development," provides four chapters that discuss different challenges to female development from birth to womanhood. In Chapter 5, Susan H. Franzblau deconstructs attachment theory and argues that it is an ethnocentric and coercive theory that legitimizes and "naturalizes" the control of women. She confronts essentialist theories of motherhood head-on, and explains the negative psychosocial implications of attachment theory. In Chapter 6, Joseph Spinazzola, Helen W. Wilson, and Vicki B. Stocking describe their use of an innovative, narrative approach to studying the silencing of adolescent girls. Through their discussion, they provide interventions to help girls feel empowered in the use of their voices and enabled to thrive during adolescence. In Chapter 7, Lynn H. Collins takes the concept of empowerment further by arguing that girls must not only be empowered, but must be provided many positive counter-messages that serve to inoculate them against the negative messages that exist in our culture about women. Borrowing from literature on African-American socialization and development, she proposes a theory for fostering healthy self-esteem development in all girls. In Chapter 8, Carole A. Rayburn and Lee J. Richmond emphasize the importance of spirituality to the development of women and our self-definitions. Through a series of arguments that build upon one another, they propose that spirituality adds to women's empowerment rather than diminishes it, as some organized religions do.

Part III, "Women's Health," provides three chapters on groups of women whose health risks often go unnoticed, unacknowledged, or are trivialized— even when their conditions or circumstances have been made explicit. In Chapter 9, Jennifer M. Hillman and Kristin J. Broderick discuss the challenge of HIV among older women whose medical conditions are often overlooked because of the age and gender status ascribed to them in our society. The negative and inaccurate stereotype of aging women as passive, asexual beings is shattered as the authors discuss their findings with regard to the participants of their study. In Chapter 10, Carolyn M. West discusses theory, research, and prevention with regard to African-American battered women. She incisively highlights racial differences without perpetuating the negative, inaccurate stereotype that African Americans are inherently more violent than other groups. In Chapter 11, Joan C. Chrisler documents the role of the media in the social construction of premenstrual women as inherently dangerous and out of control. Through a combination of scientific inquiry and historical documentation, she challenges us to abandon the stereotypes of premenstrual women that keep women from being taken seriously and receiving support when they need it.

The three chapters in Part IV, "Women's Mental Health and Feminist Therapy," further illuminate the integration of feminism and multiculturalism in the counseling and support of women. In Chapter 12, Lori M. Irving examines innovative feminist approaches for the prevention of eating disorders among girls and women. She reviews the problems and pitfalls of trying to prevent eating disorders, and then provides and evaluates various methods and approaches. In Chapter 13, Eleanor F. Gil-Kashiwabara examines the problems of body image and eating disorders for women of color. She provides alternative explanations for some of the mistaken theories that have suggested that body image is a lesser issue for women of color than it is for European-American women. In Chapter 14, Marja Booker discusses the life-changing value of women's support groups for the empowerment of Central American refugees in the United States. She addresses the value of client testimony as a useful technique for these women because of its ability to facilitate both intrapsychic healing and the public denouncement of social wrongs committed against them.

Consistent with AWP's and our own personal philosophies, this book concludes with Part V, "Feminist Activism in the Public Interest," which takes us beyond the development of an understanding of the issues to a focus on ways we can have a significant impact on how the issues are addressed in our community and the larger political system. This part also provides an explicit examination of how we as feminist psychologists become involved in our communities, how we can improve our awareness and understanding of feminist issues, and how we can make a greater impact with regard to women's issues in our communities and on a large-scale level. In Chapter 15, Ingrid Johnston-Robledo and Renee N. Saris discuss the activism among a small group of economically disenfranchised women in an urban environment. These women discuss their concerns about recent public policy changes and methods for surviving in a socioeconomic system that makes it very difficult to rise against the odds. In Chapter 16, Jeanine C. Cogan and Camille Preston provide concrete, prac-

tical guidance for engaging in social activism on a federal level. They provide step-by-step advice for lobbying and for establishing working
relationships with, and support from, congressional staff. Their advice can
help achieve real change on issues of concern to women.

Readers of this collection of chapters will find that each one is bursting
with theoretical, methodological, and/or practical material that will assist
women and men who desire either to help create and chart new paths for
the psychology of women, or to improve on the paths that already exist.
The variety of theories, methods, women's voices, and practical suggestions
will serve as valuable instruments as we take sail toward both familiar and
new horizons. Let the journey begin. Bon voyage!

Michelle R. Dunlap
Lynn H. Collins
Joan C. Chrisler

Part I

Feminist Theory and Pedagogy

Chapter 1

Gendered Subjects in Psychology: Satirical and Dialectic Perspectives

Maureen C. McHugh and Lisa Cosgrove

Differences between the sexes do descriptively exist: being a doormat is definitely different than being a man. . . . One of the most deceptive antifeminisms in society, scholarship, politics and law is the persistent treatment of gender as if it is truly a question of difference, rather than treating the gender difference as a construct of the difference gender makes.

(MacKinnon, 1987, p. 8)

Without the category women, the feminist project flounders. The category woman is essential in relation to the equally essential category man. This dualism persists in our sexed bodies and in our cultural construction of their meaning.

(Offen, 1990, p. 15)

The study of the psychology of women has traditionally involved a series of implicit or explicit comparisons of females to males. If women are not a distinct or "special" group, then is the study of or theorizing about them valid or useful? If women are the same as (or similar to) men, then why allocate a special course or status to them? Although the study of the psychology of women has been the study of sex and gender differences, many feminist psychologists and theorists have eschewed this type of research, pointing out the sociopolitical consequences of this perspective, and challenging the adequacy of our methodology to illuminate the meaning of gender and the experience of women. Further, many feminist theorists have challenged the category "woman" especially in its use relative to the category "man." In this chapter we briefly review a series of positions and arguments taken by feminist theorists and psychologists on the question of sex and gender differences, and then we chart a course for how feminist psychologists might approach the study of gendered experience.

SEX AND GENDER

Language shapes the way we see (and respond to) the world. In keeping with this perspective (Cosgrove & McHugh, this volume), we have decided to use the terms "sex differences" and "gender differences" interchangeably. Until fairly recently, many feminists (e.g., Unger, 1979) used the phrase "sex differences" to refer to anatomical or biologically caused differences, and the phrase "gender differences" to refer to the differences in behaviors and activities of women and men (see, for example, West & Zimmerman, 1987). Although there is greater concern now with using language that supports the biology/culture dichotomy (Unger & Crawford, 1996), there remains the assumption that sex differences exist a priori and that they provide the foundation (or rationalization) for gender differences.

Following Delphy (1984), MacKinnon (1987), and Kitzinger (1994), we want to challenge the dualistic assumptions that ground the seemingly natural distinction between "sex" and "gender." We do not deny that there are physiological differences between women and men; rather we want to emphasize that these physiological differences are not simple facts or "pure" differences in and of themselves. The meaning of these differences is shaped by sociopolitical and linguistic practices (see Yardley, 1997, for a related discussion of this issue). Therefore we understand "sex differences" to be mediated in the same way that convention allows us to recognize "gender differences" as mediated. The decision to use the phrases "sex differences" and "gender differences" interchangeably is meant to highlight the mediated character of the seemingly natural (i.e., seemingly unmediated female or male) body. Indeed, an exciting area for feminist research is to try to map "the ways in which the body circumscribes subjectivity, [it is necessary for feminists to] analyze the processes by which the female body is transformed into a feminine one" (McNay, 1992, pp. 23–24).

THE DEBATE ABOUT SEX DIFFERENCES WITHIN THE FEMINIST COMMUNITY

The question of difference is an "enduring paradox" in feminist scholarship (Rhode, 1990, p. 1). Some feminists have challenged sex-related differences as the basis for limitations and restrictions placed on women, whereas others have argued that women have special interests or perspectives. Arguments for the inclusion of women in psychology as researchers, research participants, and as topics of study are based on both the equivalence of women to their male counterparts, and on the differences between women's and men's experiences and perspectives. Thus, the question of gender differences is central to feminist psychology. To recommend that we abandon the study of gender differences raises fundamental questions about the purpose and aims of feminist psychology. Yet the continued study of gender differences may contribute to sexist ideologies and may even lead to discrimination against women by distributing "findings" that inevitably cast women as Other and conflate difference with deficiency (Hare-Mustin & Marecek, 1994). How to acknowledge without amplifying difference remains a dilemma of central importance to the women's movement (Rhode, 1990). Acknowledging without amplifying difference can seem like an arduous task because of the mass marketing of gender qua difference.

For example, millions of Americans have bought John Gray's (1992) position that "men are from Mars, women are from Venus." In his best-selling series, Gray argued that men and women are so different that they appear to have come from different planets. According to Gray (1992), men and women need assistance in understanding and communicating with each other. The popularity of Gray's books attests to the difficulty men and women experience in their heterosexual relationships and to the current popularity of the difference model. One feminist social psychological response to this observation is that a focus on the differences between women and men does more to create gender antagonism than to resolve conflict in female-male relations. Recently, Hyde (1999) made a similar point when she argued that the media reinforce gender stereotypes.

In their text *Brain Sex: The Real Difference between Men and Women*, Moir and Jessel (1989) reviewed the "new" biological evidence that they thought provided a comprehensive and authoritative framework for understanding sex differences. According to Moir and Jessel (1989): "Men are different from women. They are equal in their common membership of the same species, humankind. To maintain that they are the same in aptitude, skill or behavior is to build a society based on a biological and scientific lie" (p. 5).

Moir and Jessel contended that the general public is intensely interested in the degree, nature, and origin of differences between men and women and that people already intuitively "know" that men and women are different. A similar position was taken by John Stossel in a widely viewed televised "documentary" about the "real" differences between men and women (Breen, Gustafson, & Messina, 1998). Stossel's position is that if there are differences between men and women, then differential treatment of men and women is warranted and not discriminatory. Further, he depicted scientists as having "proved" that men and women are different and feminists as denying the truth. We cite these examples from popular media to demonstrate the prevalence, the politics, and the potential danger of promoting a belief in sex differences.

It is perhaps not surprising then, that throughout this century women psychologists have devoted a considerable amount of time and energy to refuting both popular and scientific conceptions about the abilities and dispositions of women (cf., Caplan & Caplan, 1994; Hollingworth, 1914; Kimball, 1995; Macoby & Jacklin, 1974; Rosenberg, 1982; Shields, 1982). Feminist scholars have argued that both popular and scientific ideas about sex differences are often based on faulty observations or interpretations. In community and classroom lectures and in their publications, feminist psychologists continue this tradition, taking on Gray (1992), Stossel (Breen et al., 1998), and others who emphasize women's and men's differences over their similarities. As Unger (1998) pointed out, questions about sex differences will not be resolved because "they are tied to a number of covert political agendas" (p. 101) that have been repeatedly documented (see, for example, Rosenberg, 1982; Sherif, 1979; Shields, 1975).

Debates about the existence and significance of sex differences continue among psychologists as well as in the popular media. Special issues of *The American Psychologist* (1995) and *Feminism & Psychology* (1994) have been devoted to the sex difference controversy. Although some feminist psychologists have abandoned the question of sex differences (e.g., Hare-Mustin & Marecek, 1994; Hollway, 1994) others continue to address the question empirically or theoretically. Some feminists (e.g., Halpern, 1994) have argued that to avoid or ignore the controversies over sex differences leaves the debate to ideological (non-feminist) alternatives. Unger (1998) has commented that although a variety of psychological and feminist positions on sex difference research have been presented, there are limited publication outlets for the more radical ideas on sex differences. A growing number of feminist psychologists have challenged the dominant paradigm in psychology by questioning the assumption that gender is best represented as dichotomous and trait-like. However, work is less likely to be published when it challenges rather than supports the status quo assumption of discrete gender categories, behaviors, and/or identities. Similarly, studies on gender differences that confirm the null hypothesis are more likely to be rejected by journal editors than are studies that support the notion of gender differences. This publication imbalance leaves both the general public and the psychological community with the erroneous impression that we have "pure," objective, scientific data to prove that gender differences "really" exist. The two sides of the debate—the "yes, gender differences are a real phenomenon" and the "no significant differences" position—will now be reviewed.

THE MINIMALIST AND MAXIMALIST POSITIONS

The views of Stossel (Breen et al., 1998), Gray (1992), and Moir and Jessel (1989) are labeled maximalist or referred to as "the difference model." Some feminists critique the difference model as a cultural perspective in which differences between women and men are viewed as more interesting, important, or numerous than the similarities (e.g., Wallston & Grady, 1985). According to Epstein (1988), an insistence on sex difference pervades most cultures; she has documented how research findings on sex differences are used to support the status quo. Other contemporary feminists look to women's lives, especially motherhood, as the basis for women's difference from men (see Kimball, 1995, for an excellent review of this literature).

For example, Chodorow (1978) argued that the mother-child relationship differs for sons and daughters and that this is the basis for the difference in women's and men's perspectives. Gilligan (1982) argued that women and men have different worldviews. The underlying premise of relational theory is that women have a distinctly different moral voice than men; they are "relationally oriented," and thus they respond to conflicts and dilemmas based on interpersonal ethics of care and responsibility in relationships (Gilligan, 1982; Miller, 1986). Similarly, Belenky and her colleagues (Belenky, Clinchy, Goldberg, & Tarule, 1986) maintained that women have a distinct and separate epistemology and that women's "ways of knowing" may be a source of empowerment. Although we will discuss this issue in more detail later, it is important to point out here that the maximalist position has been critiqued as essentialist (Bohan, 1993) because it assumes that there are inherent differences between women and men and these differences are best understood as trait-like.

In contrast to the maximalists, those feminists who critique the difference model are typically referred to as "minimalists." They argue that differences between the sexes have been exaggerated in both the popular culture and the scientific research. They seek to provide both the theoretical and empirical justification for gender equality, and they use the experimental methods of the natural sciences to achieve this goal.[1] Minimalists assume that scientific (i.e., empirical) methods are gender neutral tools that can be appropriated for feminist ends. Scholars who take a minimalist position contend that there is a bias toward confirming sex differences that is reflected in the greater tendency to publish and cite studies that find sex differences (Epstein, 1988; Hyde, 1994; Jacklin, 1981; McHugh, Koeske, & Frieze, 1986). Shields (1975), for example, argued that psychological research conducted on sex differences has never been value-free or neutral and that it has historically been used to justify the exclusion and subordination of women. Fausto-Sterling (1985/1992) challenged the "scientific evidence" for biological sex differences that has provided justification for discrimination. Deaux (1984) and other feminists have argued that empirical research on sex-related differences has been effectively used to refute the contention that differences between men and women are universal, significant, and stable. Feminist empiricists from Hollingworth (1914) to Hyde

(1986) have used the scientific method to try to convince theorists and the general public that stereotypes about women and men are inaccurate and dysfunctional.

Although feminist empiricists have spent a great deal of time refuting both popular and scientific (mis)conceptions about the nature of women, their research has not been effective in modifying either popular or scientific subscription to the difference model. Unfortunately, disconfirming data do not change gender stereotypes (Unger, 1998). Beliefs about alleged sex differences that are congruent with people's gender beliefs are difficult to change. For example, Frieze and her colleagues (1982) have not been able to convince the community of scholars that women as a group do not attribute their successes to luck. Belief in the significance of sex differences persists despite a century of feminist empiricism devoted to challenging the difference model. Unger (1979, 1998) pointed out that the sex differences summarized by Maccoby and Jacklin in 1974 continue to be cited today despite, in some cases, *decades* of disconfirming data.

In the spirit of feminist empiricism, Hubbard (1981) encouraged scientists to challenge existing research. She wrote that "We must fight with science's own tools, refuting illogical and self serving explanations, exposing unsubstantiated claims, disclaiming poorly conceived and inadequately controlled experiments" (Hubbard, 1981, p. 216). Alternatively, MacKinnon (1990) challenged the usefulness of sex difference research as a means of women's liberation: "Difference is the velvet glove on the iron fist of dominance. If a concept like difference is a conceptual tool of gender and of inequality, it cannot deconstruct the master's house, because it has built it" (MacKinnon, 1990, p. 213). Reflecting on the two different positions taken by Hubbard and MacKinnon, we ask whether the current methods and paradigms of psychology, and science more generally, are adequate tools for the study of women and gender. Can the same tools that have been used in the scientific construction of the difference model be used to deconstruct popular and scientific beliefs in sex differences? We will now explore these questions by charting a new direction for feminist empiricist research.

USING THE MASTER'S TOOLS: SATIRICAL EMPIRICISM

> Wouldn't the worst be, isn't the worst in truth, that women aren't castrated, that they have only to stop listening to men (for the Sirens were men) for history to change its meaning? You have only to look at the Medusa straight on to see her. And she's not deadly. She's beautiful and she's laughing.
>
> (Cixous, 1981, p. 255)

> Sat ire (sat'ir) n. 1. The use of sarcasm, irony, ridicule, or the like in exposing or denouncing abuses or follies.
>
> (Funk & Wagnall, 1984, p. 1118)

Irigaray (1985) has suggested that we transcend androcentrism through mimicry and laughter. Let us now take up Irigaray's challenge. Satirical empiricism, as introduced here, is an attempt to transcend patriarchal perspectives on gender by using science's own tools in laughter. Satirical empiricism may be described as an empirical method that exposes gender assumptions and reveals the "real" nature of essentialism and universalism in psychological research. Satirical empiricism is the application of satire to the research process. It is important to note that satire usually implies moral judgment and *corrective purpose* (as opposed to lampooning, which is political and/or personal and is characterized by malice). Hence satirical empiricism employs the empirical method in a manner that exposes folly through exaggeration, ridicule, sarcasm, and irony or reversal. The exaggeration involved in satire parallels the exaggeration of gender differences inherent in psychological research and exposes, through reversal or extension, the hidden assumptions in both the minimalist and maximalist traditions. By employing satirical empiricism it is possible to demonstrate that gendered behavior is determined (or elicited) by context, and it is possible to "deconstruct" (i.e., reveal the hidden assumptions in) the research project.

In published guidelines for the conduct of nonsexist research in psychology, McHugh and her colleagues (McHugh et al., 1986) addressed how we might continue to conduct research while minimizing the most glaring methodological errors. They recommended that the experimenter test for gender differences and consider whether demonstrated differences reveal gendered aspects of the research situation. They further encouraged researchers to consider how the construction of the experimental context differentially impacts the behavior or responses of male and female participants. In the lab, researchers may (unwittingly) construct a situation that will elicit the gendered response they want. In the field, psychologists may select contexts in which it is known that gendered differences will be evident. For example, Caplan and Caplan (1994) and Kimball (1995) pointed out how the research on gender differences in math performance has been carefully constructed to produce differences. The superior performance of girls on classroom tests and in graded work in the classroom during elementary school is dismissed in light of the research findings of male's math superiority on particular standardized tests. When the research paradigm is modified, gender differences are reduced, eliminated, and even reversed. For example, using smaller or more heterogeneous groups, nonstandardized math tests, and/or alternative testing contexts reduces or eliminates male superiority in math performance.

Each semester McHugh demonstrates to her students that the students like research psychologists can tailor or design the experimental context to get the gender difference they predict or want. When students are asked how they might investigate the existence of gender differences in emotionality, students inevitably produce the same experimental design. They suggest showing sad movies and systematically measuring the number of males and females in the audience that cry or otherwise respond emotionally. (The more sophisticated students consider the comparison with non-sad movies and make sure that they "randomly" assign participants to each condition.) In thinking of how to test for gender differences, they access the situations in their experience when they have observed men and women acting differently. If asked about gender similarity, they might have considered a different context. However, if asked for a situation in which men are more likely to cry, would they be able to design one? A satirical empiricist might design an experimental context in which adult men (but not women) are brought to tears. It may involve creating a situation in which they are totally frustrated by their own powerlessness in the situation or one in which they are shamed or embarrassed to the point of tears. (Of course, it might take a lot of pilot testing, but in psychology that is an acceptable way to develop a "paradigm" in order to test one's hypothesis).

It is not only in the construction (or the selection) of the context that researchers determine their results, but also in the selection of the sample. For example, male math superiority is found when the sample involves groups of White, middle-class, precocious adolescents (when they are tested on standardized tests). Male superiority is generally not found in more representative samples (i.e., more racially and ethnically diverse samples and samples with more heterogeneity in terms of academic performance) (Caplan & Caplan, 1994). Similarly, Favreau (1993) reported that only a few boys (outliers) account for gender differences in rough and tumble play; all girls and most boys engage in low to medium levels of aggressive play. A satirical empiricist approach might be to use the groups of White, middle class, precocious teens (from the math studies) as a sample to examine gender differences in aggressive play.

Another example of satirical empiricism would be to conduct research on work values using a sample of African-American, middle-aged or lesbian women. Objecting to that sample as not being representative of the general population exposes the (implied) position that if you used a predominantly white sample, whose sexual orientation is not specified, the results could have been applied to non-white or non-heterosexual individuals. Discomfort with drawing universal conclusions based on data collected from African-American women suggests there is something gendered or racial about the context or the constructs under study. Such research exposes the universalizing tendencies masked by cultural belief systems when the research "subjects" are all White and male.

Feminist satirical empiricists might deliberately choose to construct laboratory experiments in which male participants engage in decidedly less appropriate or desirable behavior than do their female counterparts. McHugh's dissertation research actually involved a series of studies in which college men demonstrated a preference for the task when the feed-back from the task was ambiguous, whereas the college women preferred the task when it provided clear performance feedback. Journal editors suggested that the three studies would have to be replicated before one could possibly conclude that men preferred situations that allowed them to mis-perceive their own ability levels! This anecdote demonstrates that we may anticipate some difficulty getting our satirical research published—despite the fact that research that demonstrates deficits in women or other minority groups is easily published and widely publicized.

However, as Tavris (1992) noted, if we lived in a world where psychol-ogists used women as the basis of comparison, we might be reading articles and books addressing "problems" such as male overconfidence, unrealistic self-assessment, aggression, and isolation rather than women's inadequa-cies. Thus one could argue that the need for satirical empiricism is great and its potential unlimited. For example, we could investigate the origins of female heterosexuality by interviewing prostitutes or women in therapy for sexual problems. Again the satirical approach would involve exagger-ation and irony. Why not investigate problematic, exaggerated or com-mercialized heterosexuality as a means of understanding heterosexuality? Here satirical empiricism exposes our previous folly of exploring the causes and meaning of homosexuality by studying lesbian patients, and lesbians from gay bars. A second example might involve exploring the difficulties or pathologies experienced by children raised by stay-at-home working-class mothers without any comparison groups, or in comparison to children adopted by professional, affluent lesbians. This line of research would sat-irize our current approach which pathologizes children of working and single mothers, and legitimizes stay at home moms and heterosexual cou-ples as parents. As these examples demonstrate, satirical empiricism could be used to deconstruct the androcentric assumptions that result in the priv-ileging of certain comparison groups over others.

CRITICISMS OF THE MINIMALIST AND MAXIMALIST APPROACHES: RECOGNIZING THE IMPORTANCE OF CONTEXT

As satirical empiricism demonstrates, the context in which gendered be-havior is studied is critically important in producing and interpreting data. Feminist critics of the empirical tradition in psychology argue that the ex-perimental paradigm does not offer the best approach for understanding gender differences because the research has been carried out almost exclu-sively in a social context of short-term interactions with strangers. Exper-imental (or laboratory) research strips behavior of context and thus distorts knowledge about sex differences (Parlee, 1979; Sherif, 1979). Sherif (1979) critiqued psychology's use of contrived and carefully controlled laboratory contexts. Findings from such research are not representative of daily life, and investigators frequently design the research situation to get the results they want or expect (McHugh et al., 1986). Even in field research, experimenters may intentionally or inadvertently select the context in which the hypothesized sex difference is most likely to occur.

Sex differences in social behaviors can be assessed in various ways, in multiple settings, and are unlikely to be consistent across studies. Because the behavior of both men and women is affected by many aspects of the context in which it occurs, many feminist psychologists have adopted an interactionist perspective on gender (Deaux, 1985). An interactionist approach is one in which differences between men and women are viewed as a gender by context interaction effect (and one that is affected by multiple variables). Some researchers describe their work as identifying the conditions under which gender is related to behavior (Linn, 1986). For example, there may be a few situations in which men are more likely than women to use profanity; in other situations men and women may be equally likely, and there may even be situations in which women are more likely to use profanity. Thus, a gender by situation explanation for differences in use of profanity is more accurate that thinking of this effect as a gender difference.

The emphasis on the context of the research leads to the realization that in our society women and men are differently distributed across settings and roles. Many aspects of our lives involve levels of sex segregation and stratification. An emphasis on sex differences perpetuates gender segregation (Epstein, 1988) which may in turn perpetuate gender differences (Canary, Emmers-Summers, & Faulkner, 1997; Eagly, 1987). Eagly (1987) argued that sex differences are the product of social roles that regulate behavior in adult life. As a result of differences in their social positions, women and men are exposed to systematically different expectations.

Structural explanations emphasize the importance of context by focusing on the fact that members of social groups experience common situational constraints because they tend to occupy similar social positions within organizations. In other words, status within hierarchical structure determines sex typed behavior (see, for example, Henley, 1977; Unger, 1979). Women and men who occupy the same role have had many of the same prior experiences in these organizations, and they may differ little in role relevant attitudes and behaviors; thus, specific organizational roles can override gender roles. However, when women and men share similar roles in other social contexts, they often arrive at these roles via different paths or sets of experiences. For example, the experience of a househusband may differ in marked ways from the experience of a housewife, just as the experience of women in engineering programs may not be identical to that of their male classmates. This is why Thorne (1990) critiqued the separate spheres approach as being androcentric. In a similar vein, Eagly (1987) acknowledged that social role explanations of sex differences oversimplify the complex realities of sex differences.

Another contextualized approach to understanding gender difference is to recognize the connection between gender and power (Hare-Mustin & Marecek, 1994). The behavior attributed to women is frequently the behavior of a person in a subordinated position. This view is expressed well by MacKinnon (1990): "Differences are inequality's post hoc excuse. Inequality comes first. Differences come after. To the extent this is true, a discourse of gender difference serves as ideology to neutralize, rationalize and cover up disparities of power" (p. 213). Despite increasing sophistication in our understanding of gender as a function of context, gender difference continues to be constructed as ahistorical and essentialist (Scott, 1986). In order to appreciate the relationships among power, gender, and context, researchers must become cognizant of the essentialist and universalist assumptions that ground psychology's dominant paradigm.

ESSENTIALIZING AND UNIVERSALIZING TENDENCIES

If we continue to study differences in men's and women's experience as gender differences (as opposed, for example, to differences in power), we risk essentializing gender, promoting a view of women as a homogeneous group, and reinforcing the very mechanisms of oppression against which we are fighting. Essentialism refers to the tendency to believe that properties, qualities, or natures reside in particular groups of people. In terms of gender research, essentialism refers to seeing masculinity and femininity as trait-like "things" that reside within women and men. The creation of bipolar constructs via the difference model results in the essentializing women's and men's qualities (Thorne, 1990). It would be more helpful to study gendered experience without assuming that gender is a trait that can be measured. Feminist theorists are increasingly rejecting essentialist perspectives on gender, and they are advocating a view of gender as a construction (i.e., gender is produced or performed in a series of interactions and activities) (Bohan, 1993; Lott, 1990). In other words, individuals do not "have" gender, they "do" gender (Bohan, 1993; West & Zimmerman, 1987). Butler (1990) theorized that gender identities are not internal essences but external performances. However, repeated performances in compliance with gender norms (e.g., smiling) or repeated associations with situations (e.g., beauty parlors) and behaviors (e.g., wearing a dress) result in the conceptualization of a set of activities with an internal essence of the individual (i.e., femininity).

Femininity is unarguably a construct; it has been constructed differently in different eras and by different segments of the culture. However, if we continue to essentialize femininity as residing within women (and men) and to dignify the construct by measuring it, then femininity will continue to be defined and measured in relation to masculinity (see, for example, Bem, 1993). Understanding femininity as a trait-like attribute that exists in women leads researchers to make universalist claims about women.

Minimalist and maximalist perspectives on gender hold us in this bifurcated, essentialized, and reified approach to gender, an approach that reinforces universalizing claims. Indeed, over 15 years ago, Lowe and Hubbard (1983) encouraged us to challenge such claims by critiquing the very notion that there exists a prototypical or normative woman whose experience is universally true regardless of a women's geographical, economic, political, and social settings.

CHALLENGING DICHOTOMIES

Avoiding essentialism and universalism simultaneously requires a commitment to challenge dichotomous thinking. Unfortunately, however, dichotomous portrayals of men and women result from the dominant research paradigm in psychology (Thorne, 1990). The sexually dimorphic view influences the way questions are raised, the methods of data collection, and the interpretation of data within psychology and other disciplines (Epstein, 1988). For example, McHugh and her colleagues (1986) reported that misinterpretation of statistically significant sex differences frequently occurs in empirical research on sex differences. Even the most statistically significant differences between women and men are not, in reality, dichotomous. Yet authors of scholarly publications (the very ones that are quickly picked up by the popular media) use language that portrays both sex and gender as dichotomous.

Both the minimalist and the maximalist positions are based on the dichotomous categories of women and men and on the dichotomy of sameness versus difference. Hare-Mustin and Marecek (1990) examined the minimalist and maximalist perspectives as the alpha bias (the exaggeration of differences) and the beta bias (the denial or minimization of difference). Their contention is that to pick a position is to pick a bias. Because each position presents problems and paradoxes for the feminist psychologist, the researcher might respond to this dilemma by focusing on the utility of the perspective for the question under study. In addition, the researcher must realize that every position taken obscures some perspectives and reveals others (Hare-Mustin & Marecek, 1990).

Clearly, the current terms of the gender difference debate are deeply wedded to dichotomous thinking and to essentialist and universalist assumptions. The implicit epistemology of both minimalist and maximalist positions assumes that individuals "have" (a) gender and that gender is best understood as a dichotomous trait or independent variable. Thus, as researchers, we feel forced to choose between using empiricist strategies to try to refute sexist stereotypes (the minimalist approach) or accepting—and emphasizing—the assumption that women and men are different (the max-imalist approach). We have yet to connect feminist critiques of gendered subjectivity (cf. Butler, 1990; Flax, 1990; Nicholson, 1990; Weir, 1996) with an epistemological and methodological framework that is robust and audacious enough to avoid those "either/or" choices.

AVOIDING EITHER/OR CHOICES: DEVELOPING DOUBLE VISIONS

Kimball (1995) argued for the practice of double visions with regard to feminist theory and research on gender. "The major goal of practicing dou-ble visions is to resist the choice of either similarities or differences as more true or politically valid than the other" (Kimball, 1995, p. 12). One might chose a particular position in a certain context, or prefer a given perspective on gender, but, as Kimball has noted, practicing double visions means that neither alternative is foreclosed; feminist psychologists would recognize the partiality of any perspective and respect theoretical diversity. This means that we actively resist making a choice and instead maintain a tension be-tween/among the alternative positions. Double visions, or a dialectic[2] ap-proach to sex /gender, describes the movement between or among positions as a sophisticated and theoretically grounded practice. Previously individ-uals who vacillated between denying gender differences and focusing on the unique experiences of women may have been labeled as contradictory, inconsistent, incoherent, or confused. Privileging the dialectic perspective legitimizes our current confusion, giving us permission to hold contradic-tory, paradoxical, and fragmented perspectives on gender and gender dif-ference.

DIALECTICAL PERSPECTIVES, IRONY, AND SATIRICAL EMPIRICISM

> Irony is about contradictions and the tensions of holding incompatible things together because both or all are necessary and true. Irony is about humor and serious play.
>
> (Haraway, 1985, p. 65)

Ferguson (1991) echoes Haraway (1985) in her suggestion that irony is a way to resolve the dichotomous tensions created by two (seemingly op-posing) projects or perspectives. In irony, laughter dissuades us from pre-mature closure, and exposes both the truth and the non-truth of each perspective. Ferguson (1991) talks about irony as "a way to keep oneself within a situation that resists resolution in order to act politically without pretending that resolution has come." (p. 338). According to Ferguson,

irony can help us resist both paralysis and legitimization of a single perspective. Satirical empiricism is such a form of irony, using humor for political purposes. "By using overstatement, irony makes otherwise ordinary
events outrageous, problematizing them through farce" (Ferguson, 1991,
p. 338). Similarly, satirical empiricism problematizes standard empirical
methods, exposing the absurdity inherent in traditional psychology, even
without overstatement or exaggeration.

Satire and irony represent one approach to the future of research by,
about, and for women. "Through the resources of irony we can think both
about how we do feminist theory, and about which notions of reality and
truth make our theories possible." (Ferguson, 1991, p 339). Taking a dialectic and/or an ironic approach can lead to a richer and more complex
picture and necessitates a re-visioning of the epistemological and methodological frameworks that underlie psychological research and feminist theory. Let Irony chart the course for feminist psychology, and her sister,
Satire, steer the Ship.

NOTES

1. However, it is important to note that not all feminist empiricists are minimalists. Eagly (1994), for example, has argued that there are some consistent and
socially significant sex differences. Over a decade ago (1987a) she refuted the analysis of the politics of sex difference research. She argued that "it is incautious to
presume that acknowledgment by social scientists of existing sex differences invites
discrimination against women or any other particular consequence" (p. 5). She suggested that sex differences documented by social scientists may be the basis for
sound social politics such as remedial education and optimistically claimed that
"the chances that societies evolve sensible and humane social policies are usually
increased by social scientists' presentation of valid, scientifically derived descriptions
of social reality" (p. 5).

2. A dialectic approach actually has its roots in Hegel, who argued that contradictions in philosophical arguments should be embraced rather than avoided because they can lead to more adequate conceptualizations and insights.

REFERENCES

Belenky, M. F., Clinchy, B. M., Goldberger, N. J., & Tarule, J. M. (1986).
    Women's ways of knowing: The development of self, voice, and mind. New
    York: Basic Books.
Bem, S. (1993). *The lenses of gender.* New Haven, CT: Yale University Press.
Bohan, J. (1993). Regarding gender: Essentialism, constructionism and feminist psy-
    chology. *Psychology of Women Quarterly, 17,* 5–21.
Breen, J., Gustafson, N., & Messina, R. (Producers). (1998). *ABC News Special:
    Men, women & the sex difference: Boys and girls are different* (Video re-
    cording). Oak Forest, IL: MPI Home Video.

Butler, J. (1990). *Gender trouble: Feminism and the subversion of identity*. New York: Routledge.

Caplan, P., & Caplan, J. (1994). *Thinking critically about research on sex and gender*. New York: HarperCollins.

Chodorow, N. (1978). *The reproduction of mothering: Psychoanalysis and the sociology of gender*. Berkeley: University of California Press.

Cixous, H. (1981). The laugh of the medusa. In E. Marks & I. De Courtivron (Eds.), *New French feminisms* (pp. 245–264). New York: Schocken Books.

Deaux, K. (1984). From individual differences to social categories: Analysis of a decade's research on gender. *American Psychologist, 39*, 105–116.

Deaux, K. (1985). Sex and gender. *Annual Review of Psychology, 36*, 49–81.

Delphy, C. (1984). *Close to home: A materialist analysis of women's oppression*. Amherst: University of Massachusetts Press.

Eagly, A. H. (1987b). *Sex differences in social behavior: A social role interpretation*. Hillsdale, NJ: Erlbaum.

Epstein, C. F. (1988). *Deceptive distinctions: Sex, gender, and the social order*. New Haven, CT: Yale University Press.

Fausto-Sterling, A. (1985/1992). *Myths of gender: Biological theories about men and women*. New York: Basic Books.

Favreau, O. E. (1993). Do the Ns justify the means? *Canadian Psychologist, 34*, 64–78.

Ferguson, K. E. (1991) Interpretation and genealogy in feminism. *Signs, 16* (21), 322–339.

Flax, J. (1990). *Thinking fragments: Psychoanalysis, feminism, & postmodernism in the contemporary west*. Berkeley: University of California Press.

Frieze, I., McHugh, M. C., & Hanusa, B. H. (Eds.). (1982). Sex differences in causal attributions for success and failure: A current assessment. [Special issue] *Sex Roles, 8* (4), 467–479.

Funk & Wagnall, Inc. (1984). *New international dictionary of the English language*. Newark, NJ: Publishers International Press.

Gilligan, C. (1982). *In a different voice*. Cambridge, MA: Harvard University Press.

Gray, J. (1992). *Men are from Mars, women are from Venus*. New York: HarperCollins.

Halpern, D. (1994). Stereotypes, science, censorship, and the study of sex differences. *Feminism & Psychology, 4*, 523–530.

Haraway, D. (1985, March–April) A manifesto for cyborgs: Science, technology, and socialist feminism. *Socialist Review, 15*, 65–107.

Hare-Mustin, R. T., & Marecek, J. (Eds.). (1990). *Making a difference: Psychology and the construction of gender*. New Haven, CT: Yale University Press.

Hare-Mustin, R. T., & Marecek, J. (1994). Asking the right questions: Feminist psychology and sex differences. *Feminism and Psychology, 4*, 531–537.

Henley, N. M. (1977). *Body politics: Power, sex, and non-verbal communication*. Englewood Cliffs, NJ: Prentice-Hall.

Hollingworth, L. S. (1914). Variability as related to sex differences in achievement: A critique. *American Journal of Sociology, 19*, 510–530.

Hollway, W. (1994). Beyond sex differences: A project for feminist psychology. *Feminism and Psychology, 4*, 538–546.

Hubbard, R. (1981). The emperor doesn't wear any clothes: The impact of feminism on biology. In D. Spender (Ed.), *Men's studies modified: The impact of feminism on academic disciplines* (pp. 214–245). Oxford: Pergamon Press.

Hyde, J. S. (1986). *The psychology of gender: Advances through meta-analysis.* Baltimore: Johns Hopkins University Press.

Hyde, J. S. (1994). Should psychologists study gender differences? Yes, with some guidelines. *Feminism & Psychology, 4*, 507–512.

Hyde, J. S. (1999, March). *Men are from earth, Women are from earth: The media versus science on gender differences.* Invited Address presented at the annual meeting of the American Psychological Association, Boston.

Irigaray, L. (1985). *Speculum of the other woman.* Ithaca, NY: Cornell University Press.

Jacklin, C. N. (1981). Methodological issues in the study of sex-related differences. *Developmental Review, 1*, 266–273.

Kimball, M. M. (1995). *Feminist visions of gender similarities and differences.* New York: Harrington Park Press.

Kitzinger, C. (1994). Should psychologists study sex differences? *Feminism and Psychology, 4*, 501–546.

Landrine, H., Klonoff, E., & Brown-Collins, A. (1992). Cultural diversity and methodology in feminist psychology: Critique, proposal, empirical example. *Psychology of Women Quarterly, 16*, 145–163.

Linn, M. C. (1986). Meta analysis of studies of gender differences: Implications and future directions. In J. S. Hyde & M. C. Linn (Eds.), *The psychology of gender: Advances through meta-analysis* (pp. 210–231). Baltimore: Johns Hopkins University Press.

Lott, B. (1990). Dual natures or learned behavior: The challenge to feminist psychology. In R. T. Hare-Mustin & J. Marecek (Eds.), *Making a difference: Psychology and the construction of gender* (pp. 65–101). New Haven CT: Yale University Press.

Maccoby, E. E., & Jacklin, C. N. (1974). *The psychology of sex differences.* Stanford, CA: Stanford University Press.

MacKinnon, C. A. (1987). *Feminism unmodified: Discourses on life and law.* Cambridge, MA: Harvard University Press.

MacKinnon, C. A. (1990). Legal perspectives on sexual difference. In D. L. Rhode (Ed.), *Theoretical perspectives on sexual difference* (pp. 213–225). New Haven, CT: Yale University Press.

McHugh, M. C., Koeske, R., & Frieze, I. (1986). Issues to consider in conducting nonsexist psychological research: A guide for researchers. *American Psychologist, 41*, 879–890.

McNay, L. (1992). *Foucault & feminism.* Boston: Northeastern University Press.

Miller, J. B. (1986). *Toward a new psychology of women* (2nd ed). Boston: Beacon Press.

Moir, A., & Jessel, D. (1989). *Brain sex: The real difference between men and women.* New York: Dell.

Nicholson, L. (Ed.). (1990). *Feminism/postmodernism.* New York: Routledge.

Offen, K. (1990). Feminism and sexual difference in historical perspective. In D. L. Rhode (Ed.), *Theoretical perspectives on sexual difference* (pp. 13–20). New Haven, CT: Yale University Press.

Parlee, M. (1979). Psychology and women: Review essay. *Signs, 1*, 119–138.

Rhode, D. L. (Ed.). (1990). *Theoretical perspectives on sexual difference*. New Haven, CT: Yale University Press.

Rosenberg, R. (1982). *Beyond separate spheres: Intellectual roots of modern feminism*. New Haven, CT: Yale University Press.

Scott, J. W. (1986). Gender: A useful category of historical analysis. *American Historical Review, 91*, 1053–1075.

Sherif, C. (1979). Bias in psychology. In J. A. Sherman & F. T. Beck (Eds.), *The prism of sex: Essays in the sociology of knowledge* (pp. 93–133). Madison: University of Wisconsin Press.

Shields, S. A. (1975). Functionalism, Darwinism, and the psychology of women: A study in social myth. *American Psychologist, 30*, 739–754.

Shields, S. A. (1982). The variability hypothesis: The history of biological models of sex differences in intelligence. *Signs, 7*, 469–497.

Tavris, C. (1992). *The mismeasure of women*. New York: Simon & Schuster.

Thorne, B. (1990). Children and gender: Constructions of difference. In D. L. Rhode (Ed.), *Theoretical perspectives on sexual difference* (pp. 100–113). New Haven, CT: Yale University Press.

Unger, R. K. (1979). *Female and male: Psychological perspectives*. New York: Harper & Row.

Unger, R. K. (1998). *Resisting gender: Twenty-five years of feminist psychology*. Thousand Oaks, CA: Sage.

Unger, R. K., & Crawford, M. (1996). *Women and gender: A feminist psychology* (2nd ed.). New York: McGraw-Hill.

Wallston, B. S., & Grady, K. E. (1985). Synthesizing the feminist critique. In V. E. O'Leary, R. K. Unger, & B. S. Wallston (Eds.), *Women, gender and social psychology* (pp. 7–33). Hillsdale, NJ: Erlbaum.

Weir, A. (1996). *Sacrificial logics: Feminist theory and the critique of identity*. New York: Routledge.

West, C., & Zimmerman, D. H. (1987). Doing gender. *Gender & Society, 1*, 125–151.

Yardley, L. (1997). *Material discourses of health and illness*. New York: Routledge.

Chapter 2

Deconstructing Difference: Conceptualizing Feminist Research from Within the Postmodern

Lisa Cosgrove and Maureen C. McHugh

STUDYING GENDER FROM A POSTMODERN PERSPECTIVE

Within the last 10 years there has been a burgeoning interest in postmodernism,[1] and many well-known feminists (e.g., Bohan, 1993; Burman, 1997, 1998; Crawford, 1997; Gergen & Davis, 1997; Hare-Mustin & Marecek, 1994a, 1994b; Hollway, 1989; hooks, 1990; Lather, 1991, 1992; Layton, 1998; Ussher, 1996, 1999; Wilkinson & Kitzinger, 1995) have described their work as being influenced by postmodern thought. It has been suggested that postmodernism and feminism are two critical perspectives on epistemology and each is needed to enrich the other. "A postmodern reflection on feminist theory reveals disabling vestiges of essentialism while a feminist reflection on postmodernism reveals androcentrism and political naiveté" (Fraser & Nicholson, 1990, p. 20). At the same time however, many feminists have voiced strong concerns, skepticism, and ambivalence about the usefulness of adopting a postmodern framework. The ambivalent relationship between feminism and postmodernism is rooted in what would seem to be their mutually exclusive projects: the former aims to end women's shared oppression by using identity politics and the later aims to deconstruct "women" as a falsely totalizing category (Fraser & Nicholson, 1990; Henwood, Griffin & Phoenix, 1998; Herbold, 1995).

Clearly, when the terms feminism and postmodernism are joined there is both promise and danger (Herbold, 1995, p. 86). Although we in no way want to minimize the danger, we believe that there are many aspects of postmodern theory that are highly congruent with the goals of feminist research. More specifically, we believe that situating feminist research within a postmodern perspective will help researchers respond to the question "How should psychology proceed in order to tell us something important about women and women's experiences?" without reifying gender or assuming that it is a trait that can be measured. Insofar as postmodernism has called into question the very assumptions that undergird psychological research and has called into question the assumptions that ground our understanding of gender, this is clearly an ambitious project. So, despite the rough seas ahead, we will now try to navigate the postmodern waters.

First, we will provide a brief description of what we mean by the term "postmodern," and we will provide support for our belief that situating feminist research within a postmodern framework offers exciting possibilities for investigating gendered experience. Next, we will provide definitions/descriptions of key terms used by postmodern scholars because we believe that the language used by postmodern scholars is often unnecessarily dense and inaccessible. The dense, heavily jargon-laden-language has the unfortunate effect of making readers who are sympathetic to these new ideas reject postmodernism out of hand. As bell hooks (1990) astutely noted, "it is sadly ironic that the contemporary discourse which talks most about heterogeneity, the decentered subject and recognition of Otherness, still directs its critical voice primarily to a specialized audience that shares a common language rooted in the very master narratives it claims to challenge" (cited in Henwood, Griffin & Phoenix, 1998, p. 3). Thus, all too often, postmodern feminists risk increasing rather than decreasing mystification (Allen & Barber, 1992). However, despite its sometimes objectionable language, we have found postmodern theory inspiring and helpful. We hope to facilitate further conversations between feminists and postmodernists so that together we might chart a new course for feminist psychology. Toward that end, we will try to translate the more esoteric and complex philosophical concepts of postmodern theory into accessible language which feminist psychologists will find useful.

In addition to translating philosophical concepts into more familiar psychological language, we will discuss the ways in which a phenomenological approach is consistent with feminist goals. We will also offer suggestions for how a phenomenological approach could be enriched by incorporating postmodern insights into its conceptual and methodological framework. It should be noted, however, that our choice to focus on a qualitative strategy is not in any way meant to imply that postmodern research inevitably entails a rejection of quantitative methods. We completely agree with Ussher (1999) that "quantitative methods can be a powerful tool in arguing for feminist principles" (p. 44). In a similar vein, our decision to focus on a phenomenological approach is not meant to imply that we believe that this approach is always the best or the only one that is useful for situating feminist research within the postmodern.[2] Although this issue will be discussed more thoroughly later, we want to take this opportunity to emphasize that we are advocating a theory driven rather than a method driven paradigm (Ussher, 1996).

WHAT IS POSTMODERNISM AND HOW IS IT RELEVANT TO FEMINIST RESEARCH?

> What is postmodernism? It has two parts: a deconstructive part that shows us that old ways of seeing things are limited or wrong and a constructive part that enables our imaginations to construct new and useful ways of thinking.
>
> (Shawver, 1996, p. 372)

Postmodernists critique the dominant paradigm in psychology as being rooted in a foundationalist perspective, that is, a belief that the search for "truths" (about personality, mental illness, gender differences, etc.) is an achievable and desirable goal of the social sciences. Therefore, although there have been many (sometimes competing) definitions of postmodernism, all hinge on the notion of anti-foundationalism. The belief in the grand narratives of science, the distinctions between subject and object and facts and values, and the hope that "truth" will set "us" free are exposed as naïve fictions. Grand narratives are authoritative definitions of how things work (Shawver, 1998a, p. 600). They provide definitive explanations, and their truth goes uncontested (Burr, 1995; Lyotard, 1984; Nicholson, 1990; Shawver, 1998a, 1998b). Because of its challenge to grand narratives, postmodernism has been described as a critique that "makes us aware that categories such as woman are used to constrict the multitude of ways that women can be, that heterosexuality and homosexuality, masculinity and femininity have been produced as discrete identities to ensure the continuance of compulsory heterosexuality and male dominance" (Layton, 1998, p. 6). Indeed, postmodernism seeks to deconstruct the very categories (e.g., sex, gender, masculine/feminine, disorder) that have achieved truth status within psychology (see for example, Hare-Mustin, 1994; Hare-Mustin & Marecek, 1990, 1994a, 1994b).

Thus, taking a postmodern perspective reveals the practices and discourses that create and sustain the authority of grand narrative explanations of phenomena such as homosexuality or the "truth" about gender differences. As Layton (1998) noted, postmodernism is a project that reveals the socially constructed nature of reality and the varied interests that are served by particular constructions. For example, situating feminist research within the postmodern encourages the researcher to ask about whose interests are being served by the construction of gender as difference (Caplan & Caplan, 1994; Hare-Mustin & Marecek, 1994a; Tavris, 1992). Or as Patti Lather (1991) asked, "What does it mean to do empirical research in an unjust world? How do our efforts to liberate perpetuate relations of dominance?" (p. 16). Although these questions may be *acknowledged* as important by researchers using traditional approaches, they are not questions that are explicitly asked throughout the research process.

Thus, taking a postmodern approach brings epistemological, methodological, and political issues to the foreground. It is an approach that calls into question the beliefs that allow social scientists to assume the validity of the categories "masculinity" and "femininity," and it emphasizes the processes by which we reify these categories. Again, Lather (1991) summed this up well; "intellectuals with liberatory intentions [must] take responsibility for transforming our own practices so that our empirical and pedagogical work can be less toward positioning ourselves as masters of truth and justice and more toward creating a space where those directly involved can speak on their own behalf" (pp. 163–164). We believe that situating feminist research within the postmodern creates a space for women to speak about their gendered experience.

HOW IS POSTMODERNISM DIFFERENT FROM FEMINIST EMPIRICISM AND STANDPOINT THEORIES?

Feminist empiricists (i.e., those who take a minimalist approach) believe in the ability of science to provide value neutral data and objective findings. Feminist standpoint theorists (i.e., those who take a maximalist approach) privilege women's ways of behaving and knowing. In contrast, feminist postmodernism calls into question the belief in an objective world and is harshly critical of the belief in privileged standpoints. However, as Ussher (1999) noted, the debate today within feminist psychology centers primarily on which *methods* will generate more valid data. She writes, "feminist researchers can appear at times to be obsessed with the issue of methods. Yet is it not epistemology that is actually at stake?" (p. 44). Feminist postmodernism recognizes that science is *never* innocent (Lather, 1991), methodology is inescapably political, and thus epistemological issues are always at stake. Therefore, we need to move beyond "methodological fetishism . . . [and address the fact that] if there is any moral high ground associated with qualitative methods, it arises from the way it is used rather than from any intrinsic features of the methodology" (Burman, 1997, p. 785). We agree with the "new paradigm pluralism" that Ussher (1999) advocated and thus rather than resolve the minimalist maximalist debate, we maintain that the direction of feminist research should be radically altered. Whereas the goal of modern feminist science is usually anchored in the "gradual accumulation of more and more data points, the goal of postmodern science is to find new ways to conceptualize the data at hand. . . . postmodern

theory can awaken our intelligence by inspiring our quest for a better conceptual framework" (Shawver, 1998a, pp. 601, 611).

Finding new ways to conceptualize the data at hand, as we have just
noted, requires researchers to enter the debate about the nature of knowledge and to re-think assumptions about the way knowledge is produced.
Because this challenge has obvious philosophical implications, let us now
briefly identify some of the main philosophical issues raised by postmodern
scholars. We will then discuss why these issues are highly relevant to the
conduct of psychological research.

LANGUAGE, REALITY, POWER, AND KNOWLEDGE

Morawski (1994) has suggested that feminist research be "released from
a language that establishes gender as a natural phenomenon, one that is
bipolar, symmetrical, stable in form" (p. 178). In order to release feminist
research in this way we must challenge the assumptions about the nature
of reality and knowledge. Postmodern theory (or social constructionism as
it is usually referred within psychology) challenges these assumptions vis-
à-vis a critique of the "realist" theory of language. A realist position is one
that assumes that there is an objective, material reality "out there" and that
language works in a straightforward way by naming or mirroring that reality. Words simply represent/ mirror/label the objects to which they refer.
(An "object" in this sense could be anything from a chair to depression to
femininity). Postmodernism, in contrast, is harshly critical of this view,
which it sees as naïve, simplistic, and grounded in an epistemology of privilege (Who, after all, gets to name this reality?). Language (the term discourse is frequently used because of its inclusive connotation) is seen as
constituting rather than *revealing* reality. Language affects what we do (and
don't) notice, what we do (and don't) experience (Layton, 1998; Shawver,
1996).

For example, a woman in 1900 may have felt some form of emotional
distress or physical discomfort prior to her menses but she did not have
the language/ discourse of PMS that her counterpart in 2000 does. Thus,
the woman in 2000 may position herself within the discourse of PMS, a
discourse that radically alters the meaning of her experience (compared to
her twentieth-century counterpart). Within a realist theory of language we
would say that progress has been made: finally the woman in the twenty-
first century has the language with which to name the "real" thing that has
existed all along but which we only recently discovered and named: PMS.
A non-realist theory of language suggests that one can not refer to what is
"real" "except in interpretive experience" (Derrida, 1972, cited in Shawver,
1996, p. 379). Moreover, we interpret our experience through the available
discourses that are dominant at any given time (a woman in 1900 might,
for example, have positioned herself as melancholic). In other words, rather

than mirroring the "real," language orchestrates our experience. As Shawver (1996), following Heidegger (1971) noted, "naming gives Being to a thing, it brings it to life" (p. 380). From this perspective, PMS is not a real thing that exists whether we label it or not. Rather, PMS is constituted through language, it is *produced* in and through our biopsychiatric discourse. Thus, a woman in the twenty-first century interprets her somatic and emotional experience within the dominant discourses of femininity and PMS. In other words, she positions herself—and is positioned by—various practices (e.g., women's magazines with articles such as "Do you have PMS?") technologies (e.g., Prozac was recently granted FDA approval for "treating" PMS) and discourses (e.g., Premenstrual Dysphoric Disorder). As Chrisler (1996) cogently argued, PMS is clearly a culture-bound syndrome.

DECONSTRUCTION: A STRATEGY FOR FEMINIST RESEARCH

A related strategy that comes from a postmodern (i.e., non-realist) theory of language is deconstruction. The unfortunate connotation of the term has suggested to some feminists that postmodern approaches are nihilistic and antithetical to the proactive political goals of a feminist agenda. Despite the connotation of the term, deconstruction is not rooted in a nihilistic desire to destroy. Rather, it is an approach that has emancipatory possibilities in that "it is a way of freeing ourselves from the trap of ineffective language patterns . . . it shows us a glimpse of a world that has not yet been. *Deconstruction lifts us out of the dominant paradigm, the dominant metaphor and invites us to dance a different dance*" (Shawver, 1996, pp. 383–384; emphasis added).

The term deconstruction, as originally developed by Derrida[3] (1976), is used to refer to an analysis of language/discourse that allows the reader to see the hidden internal contradictions contained in a text. A deconstructive reading renders explicit the implicit and repressed meanings that subtly coerce the reader into believing the "objective" truth of a text or discourse (one could do a deconstructive reading of a newspaper article, a public policy statement, the biopsychiatric discourse of the DSM, etc.). Deconstruction allows us to notice the power dynamics that are necessary for the production of certain "truths." For example, it allows researchers to examine the power relations—such as compulsory heterosexuality—that create and sustain a view of gender as difference, of femininity and masculinity as dichotomous traits that exist prior to and apart from our naming them as such.

However, it should also be emphasized that a non-realist theory of language does not deny the existence of a material world, a non-realist theory of language "gives Being to our psychological worlds . . . so that we only notice and attend to the world in ways that have been mediated by language" (Shawver, 1996, p. 383). Clearly, this is consistent with feminism; feminists have long argued that the power to name reality is the power that gives rise to oppression. Thus, taking a postmodern perspective on language provides feminist researchers with the conceptual apparatus with which to examine the relationship between ontology (being) and epistemology (knowing). Although examining this relationship may at first appear to be a discipline specific philosophical exercise, it has great significance for psychological research. Analyzing the relationship between ontology and epistemology helps us recognize the inescapable power/knowledge matrix. This matrix challenges the dualisms that ground psychological research: fact/value, truth/belief, subject/object. As Foucault (1980) astutely noted, power allows some to define what is or isn't knowledge. Thus, the power/knowledge matrix calls into question the epistemological structures that guarantee a foundationalist approach to knowledge and knowledge making.

For example, researchers interested in gendered experience should first challenge the "truth" of representing gender as difference. This anti-foundationalist challenge allows researchers to move out of the bifurcated position on gender differences (a position expressed via the minimalist/maximalist debate). In other words, it is necessary to theorize a relationship between gender and power before we can develop methodologies to assess that relationship (Hollway, 1989, p. 33). The question for feminist psychologists shifts from "what are the real gender differences and how can we most accurately study them and their effects?" to, as Hare Mustin and Marecek put it (1994a), "how is gender made to seem natural and how are the practices that produce gender rendered invisible, leaving us with the conviction that we have freely chosen who we are and that our choices express an inner self?" (p. 533).

BUT IF THERE ARE NO ABSOLUTE FOUNDATIONS FOR KNOWLEDGE, ISN'T EVERYTHING RELATIVE IN A POSTMODERN WORLD?

The main danger identified with adopting a feminist postmodern approach involves "the risk of sliding toward a depoliticized relativism where every viewpoint becomes equally valid and true" (Allen & Barber, 1992, p. 6). However, fear of lapsing into a relativism is a problem only to the degree that one succumbs to a methodological fetishism and continues to define validity in terms of objectivist notions of truth. Again, Lather (1992) summed this up well; "Fears of relativism . . . seem to me to be an implosion of Western, white male class-privileged arrogance: if we can not know everything than we can know nothing" (p. 100). We believe that postmodern research can serve feminism *precisely because* of its explicit focus on the sociopolitical grounding of experience, the very focus that denies us the fantasy of de-contextualized (i.e., "non-relative") scientific truths. Validity is thus understood in terms of a conception of knowledge as local, partial, and inevitably constituted in a complex network of power regimes (cf. Foucault, 1980). In this way, postmodern theory is rooted in an epistemological premise that is highly congruent with Kimball's (1995) double vision. Rather than succumbing to relativism, practicing double vision and using postmodern theory can help us to "find new ways to live coherently within the complexity of appreciating multiple views" (Shawver, 1998a, p. 601).

Simply put, rather than stagnating in fears of relativism, the feminist postmodernist researcher can struggle with the legitimacy of knowledge claims by constantly asking whose interests are served by a particular analysis, interpretation or conclusion? Similarly, the postmodern researcher might ask whether a methodology problematizes women's experience (Phoenix, 1994) or whether it assumes that it is both possible and desirable to discern fundamental truths about femininity from women's narrative accounts. Let us now examine one research strategy, the phenomenological approach, in terms of its helpfulness in addressing these questions. First however, we will offer a brief description of phenomenology.

WHAT IS A PHENOMENOLOGICAL APPROACH?[4]

A phenomenological approach can perhaps best be characterized by its commitment to the articulation of individuals' experience by description rather than by hypothesis testing. The advantage of a phenomenological perspective is that it does not sacrifice an empirical perspective in order to render itself relevant to human science research. Unfortunately, however, as Jennings (1986) noted, when the term phenomenological is used in contemporary psychology, it is "typically used as an interchangeable word for subjective" (p. 1231). This is particularly unfortunate because the conflation of these terms undermines not only the depth and vision of phenomenology, but also its radicality. A phenomenologically informed psychology does not simply accept the dualisms inherent in traditional psychology (e.g., subjective/objective) and argue that we should reverse the focus (i.e., privilege the "subjective" accounts of individuals rather than privileging the "objectivity" of the researcher). It disrupts—rather than simply reverses—the subject/object split. In doing so it allows for a radically different epistemological and methodological approach to research psychology (Cosgrove, 2000).

More specifically, one of the most fundamental tenets of a phenomenological approach is that consciousness (or, we could use the term "experience," which is more familiar to contemporary psychologists) is the proper subject matter of psychology. Husserl (1970, 1977) the founder of phenomenology, identified what he aptly called a crisis in psychology: psychology is rooted in the natural attitude, it treats consciousness/ experience as if it were an object in the natural world. By investigating the experiential underpinnings of knowledge, Husserl maintained that *human consciousness actively constitutes the objects of experience* (Holstein & Gubrim, 1998, p. 138; emphasis added). Giorgi (1970, 1985) was one of the earliest proponents of an empirical phenomenological psychology. Following Husserl, he maintained that in so far as psychological investigations remain stuck in the natural attitude (an attitude defined by its uncritical assumption of a world that exists out there prior to and apart from our experience of it) psychology winds up privileging quantification over description/qualitative methods. This, in turn, leaves the psychologist to deal with measured behavior rather than lived experience as data (Giorgi, 1985). A phenomenological approach, on the other hand, represents a paradigm shift; it is in this sense that phenomenology is not simply another methodology that can be used by feminist researchers. The paradigm shift may be described as one that emphasizes the importance of an individual's lived experience as the proper subject matter for psychology; as such it allows researchers to investigate the descriptive differences in men and women's experience *without essentializing gender*.

Thus, a phenomenologically informed psychology is not simply a new method used to obtain an individual's unique (read: subjective) perspective; phenomenology should not be equated with qualitative research, although clearly it uses qualitative methods. Rather, a phenomenologically informed psychology asks us to revise our epistemological grounding and, as a result, develop a different approach to the research situation. Clearly, this is a far more sophisticated, complex, and thought provoking approach than simply accepting empirical psychology's assumptions but asking for participants' self-reports. Research methods are based on phenomenological principles (Giorgi, 1985, 1997), and thus there are general guidelines rather than absolute specific steps that must be taken (Reitz, 1999).

IN WHAT WAY IS A PHENOMENOLOGICAL APPROACH CONGRUENT WITH FEMINIST GOALS OF RESEARCH?

Feminism and phenomenology share a commitment to creating a space to hear women's stories. Feminist and phenomenologically grounded research allow for an examination of the ways in which gender (along with race, class, and culture) plays a key role in shaping women's experiences. In addition, both share the commitment to test theory against experience. Indeed, rather than advocate hypothesis testing, a phenomenologically informed psychology suggests instead that theory should be generated from data (i.e., individuals' experiences). Recognizing the limits of laboratory-based research, emphasizing the importance of listening to individuals' experiences (prior to and apart from one's theoretical or ideological biases), and appreciating the possibilities of a descriptive science are critical to both feminist and phenomenological projects. (See Henwood & Pidegon, 1995, for a related discussion of grounded theory). As a growing number of feminist psychologists have noted, relying, epistemologically and methodologically, on quantification and measurement to the exclusion of life-world description makes for a rather hollow science and produces alienated rather than emancipatory knowledge.

Both feminists and phenomenologists define research as "a dialogue between the researcher and the research participant" (Garko, 1999, p. 170). Giorgi (1985) could just as easily have been speaking about feminist psychology when he said the following about phenomenological psychology:

a research situation is conceived of as one in which two humans engage but relate differently to the same situation, and because they relate differently, the meanings experienced by each in the same situation differ, and one of the best ways to find out the respective meanings is by having the participants enter into a dialogue and systematically and rigorously pursue all the implications of the different perspectives on the same situation . . . a full comprehension should tap into both perspectives (experimenter and subject) as well as their interaction. (p. 78)

Insofar as a phenomenological approach emphasizes the inevitable unity among self, world, and others, it allows the researcher to hear women's experiences as contextualized within the larger social order. Phenomenology can lead the researcher "back to concrete experience in which sociopolitical meanings . . . are experienced as lived-through phenomena, rather than as mere subjective additions to experience, or conversely, as political structures removed from experience" (Nelson, 1989, p. 227).

Consistent with a feminist research perspective, a phenomenological one demands that we hear, describe, and try to articulate the meaning of women's experiences. The researcher can hear stories that have been marginalized and/or silenced. It is in this sense that a phenomenological approach demands respectful listening (Keen, 1975) and thus objectivity becomes redefined as "fidelity to phenomena" (Garko, 1999, p. 169).

SUGGESTIONS FOR MAKING A PHENOMENOLOGICAL APPROACH MORE CONGRUENT WITH POSTMODERN THEORY

Despite the consonance with feminist research goals as outlined above, phenomenology as it is currently practiced still succumbs to some unhelpful empiricist assumptions. In this section we will identify some ways in which feminist researchers might appropriate phenomenology within a postmodern framework.

1. Feminist researchers should maintain a focus on lived rather than measured behavior *while simultaneously realizing that lived experience is*

not necessarily stable, uniform, or coherent. In keeping with a postmodern theory of language, researchers must recognize that the meaning of an individual's experience cannot be "revealed" in a uniform and straightforward manner. Specifically, they should *actively pursue rather than avoid inconsistent and contradictory data.* We must stop defining meaning as an absence of contradiction, as an absence of inconsistencies. Researchers might for example, use their interpretive skills to discover where the contradictions in participants' narratives occur and what those contradictions may reveal about the material and discursive positions available to women. If (not when) a common voice seems to emerge, as researchers we must ask what this apparent commonality reveals about the shared conditions of this particular group (Cosgrove & McHugh, in press; Tavris, 1992).

2. Rather than ask the phenomenologically oriented question, "what does this data analysis reveal about the essential character" (of the phenomenon under investigation), as researchers *we should ask ourselves if our thinking belies dualistic and essentialist assumptions.* Have we avoided the trap of assuming that the "individual" and "community" (or "women" and "men") are "pre-given objects of the human sciences?" (Henriques, Hollway, Urwin, Venn, & Walkerdine, 1998, p. 100). For example, researchers might attempt to do "deconstructive" readings of interview based data. A deconstructive reading would encourage researchers to examine the power relations that guarantee certain discourses as dominant and others as marginalized. Hollway's (1989) research on the construction of subjectivity and gender difference in heterosexual relations and Urwin's (1998) work on women's expectations and feelings about being mothers are good examples of a deconstructionist approach. Hollway's analysis attempted to clarify how power-desire relations are produced and re-produced within heterosexual couples (Henriques et al., 1998) and thus why the "doing" of femininity and masculinity are such difficult performances to stop. As Henriques and his colleagues (1998) noted, Urwin went beyond a description of the women she interviewed as seeing motherhood as a positive choice and interviewees trying to be "good mothers" (a description with which most phenomenologists—even feminist ones—would be satisfied). Instead, Urwin analyzed her data in terms of the questions: what does it mean to be a good mother and how is this desire produced by dominant discourses concerning femininity? Following Hollway and Urwin, researchers should attempt to explicate the power relations implicated in the production and re-production of women's gendered experiences. This will allow for a richer and more sophisticated appreciation of how regulatory processes work to produce gendered experience.

3. The phenomenologically oriented researcher must not assume that women's narrative accounts contain real meanings that can be uncovered by authorized individuals (i.e., by researchers). Rather, *the researcher must appreciate the impossibility of gaining access to an individual's "true" and*

unmediated experiences. Indeed, Bayer's (1998) critique of empirical psychology is relevant here. She wrote that "psychology's prevailing positivist paradigm supplies the much sought after decoder ring to translate into psychological terms the meanings of our everyday world" (p. 3). Unfortunately, by assuming that people have attributes, traits, or natures (e.g., femininity) that reside in them, interpretive phenomenological analysis substitutes for the decoder ring. More specifically, in its attempt to render the psychological aspect of an experience explicit, the phenomenologist often appeals to what the postmodern scholar calls "grand narratives." To the extent that researchers rely on grand narrative explanations (e.g., "compared to men, women respond to moral dilemmas with an interpersonal ethics of care and responsibility"), their ability to attend to the sociopolitical realm in the constitution of identity and experience is undermined.

From a postmodern point of view, it is epistemologically problematic to assume that a phenomenological approach gives us access to undistorted truths about women's experiences. The researcher cannot, simply by virtue of switching from a quantitative to a qualitative approach, uncover an experience or identity that exists "inside" the participant (i.e., that exists pre-discursively). There are no true/ real/ inner experiences or identities that somehow reside underneath the words a woman uses to describe that experience or identity. As Hare-Mustin and Marecek (1994b) have noted, postmodernists do not accord participants' words the status of veridical reports of actual events (p. 16). Rather, unlike the phenomenologically oriented researcher, the researcher working within a postmodern perspective "discounts the possibility of a single knowable reality that can be directly described in words" (Hare-Mustin and Marecek, 1994b p. 16).

In contrast to postmodernism, phenomenology is grounded in the belief that the researcher can (and should) analyze narrative data with the goal of revealing the true meaning of an experience. Thus, as it is currently practiced, phenomenologically based research falters on being able to theorize the production of meaning in terms of the relationships among power, discourse, and subjectivity. We agree with Hollway (1989) who maintained that psychologists must always grapple with complex issues of power and desire when attempting to understand the meaning of an experience. Therefore, we recommend the use of a deconstructive approach as outlined above. That is, instead of trying to find the true meaning of an experience, researchers could approach their data with an interest in identifying which—and why—certain discourses are dominant. The interview, and its concomitant analysis, is less about discovering "truths" and more about identifying current sociolinguistic practices so that people are better equipped to resist oppressive discourses (Cosgrove & McHugh, in press).

For example, a psychologist interested in studying women's experiences of Premenstrual Syndrome might begin her research from the perspective that PMS is a gendered illness category. Thus, the researcher does not view

PMS as a simple biomedical entity that could be studied apart from discourses about femininity, menstruation, and reproduction. Rather, she analyzes the data obtained in terms of how women are both positioned by and position themselves in discourses relevant to PMS. Chrisler (1996), Ussher (1996), and Swann and Ussher (1995) have studied menstruation from a sociopolitical perspective, "from the social and discursive context in which the female body is situated" (Swann & Ussher, 1995, p. 359). Ussher and Swann have examined the discursive strategies used by women (and investments in those strategies) to understand the processes by which women actively negotiate the meaning of their experience as PMS. Following Ussher, Swann, and Chrisler, we recommend that phenomenologically based researchers ask women about their lived experiences of menstruation *and* analyze the narrative data obtained in terms of the following questions: What is the relationship between PMS and female identity? In what ways does understanding one's emotional and/or physical distress as PMS reinforce a dominant model of femininity? How do women resist being positioned as PMS sufferers? Analyzing the narrative data obtained in terms of these questions can help us understand the complex power dynamics, discourses, and practices that produce women's experiences.

WHERE DO WE GO FROM HERE?

As we search for new methods with which to study gendered experience, it is critical that we also attend to the larger epistemological issues at stake. For example, we must remember that one of the emancipatory insights of feminism is that consciousness is constituted, it is "something produced rather than the source of ideas about the social world" (Henriques et al., 1998, p. 8). Therefore, instead of seeing individuals as "having" experience, researchers need to appreciate the fact that individuals are constituted through their experience (Scott, 1992). Situating phenomenological research within a postmodern epistemology can help researchers incorporate these ideas into their practice without sacrificing the liberatory goals of identity politics in the process. In other words, we believe that the promise of postmodernism can be kept alive by actively refusing to demonize postmodernism, dichotomize it against feminism, or resolve the tensions between these perspectives. Indeed, one of the most important challenges for feminists who wish to navigate this newly found course is to continue to embrace the possibilities of postmodernism without ever losing sight of the dangers that are also an inevitable part of uncharted waters.

NOTES

1. Postmodern theory has been applied to virtually all disciplines within and beyond the social and human sciences; thus there are postmodern approaches to

art, literature, film theory, and so on. Indeed the phrase postmodern theory is somewhat of a catchall, and some scholars (e.g., Burr, 1995; Hare-Mustin & Marecek, 1994b; Lyotard,1974) use it to refer to our current historical period rather than using it to refer to a theory per se. Other scholars, struggling for the most helpful descriptor use terms like "postmodern currents" (Nicholson, 1990) and others are more comfortable using the phrase "postmodern theory" (e.g., Layton, 1998). In the psychological literature, beginning with Gergen's (1985) groundbreaking paper, the phrase social constructionism is more typically used to describe the application of postmodern epistemological and methodological insights to psychological issues. Following Layton (1998) and Shawver (1996, 1998a, 1998b) we have chosen to use the phrase postmodern theory because of its inclusiveness. We recommend Burr (1995) for an excellent and concise explanation of the similarities and differences between postmodernism and social constructionism.

2. Our decision to examine one approach should not be seen as an endorsement of a monolithic research approach. We are in complete agreement with Ussher (1999) when she advocated "greater integration and cross-fertilization of different methods of analysis and increased dialogue" among feminist researchers working in different spheres. For example, we find discourse analysis an exciting methodology. Elsewhere (Cosgrove, 2000; Cosgrove & McHugh, in press) we have written about the possibilities of appropriating discourse analytic methods for a feminist research agenda. Thus, our decision to focus on phenomenology is simply a practical one—we prefer to go into greater depth about one method rather than providing an overview of many. Readers may also be interested in the 1999 special issue of *Psychology of Women Quarterly* on innovations in feminist research.

3. See Burr (1995) for an excellent and highly accessible discussion of Derrida's work.

4. The following represents a cursory analysis of the merits of a phenomenological approach; it is clearly beyond the scope of this paper to go into the detail necessary to do justice to the philosophical grounding of phenomenology and phenomenological psychology. Those readers interested in additional resources on phenomenological psychology should see Cosgrove, 2000; Davidson, 1987; Davidson & Cosgrove, 1991; Fischer, 1985; Giorgi, 1970, 1985; Husserl, 1970, 1977; Jennings, 1986; Kocklemans, 1967; Kohak, 1978. Also, for a recent example of feminist phenomenological research, we recommend Reitz's (1999) phenomenological study of batterers' experiences of being violent; she provides a very clear and detailed description of her methodology.

REFERENCES

Allen, K., & Barber, K. (1992). Ethical and epistemological tensions in applying a postmodern perspective to feminist research. *Psychology of Women Quarterly, 16*, 1–15.

Bayer, B. (1998). Introduction: Reenchanting constructionist inquiries. In B. Bayer & J. Shotter (Eds.), *Reconstructing the psychological subject: Bodies, practices and technologies* (pp. 1–19). London: Sage.

Bohan, J. (1993). Regarding gender: Essentialism, constructionism and feminist psychology. *Psychology of Women Quarterly, 17*, 5–21.

Burman, E. (1997). Minding the gap: Positivism, psychology, and the politics of qualitative methods. *Journal of Social Issues, 53* (4), 785–801.

Burman, E. (Ed.). (1998). *Deconstructing feminist psychology.* Thousand Oaks, CA: Sage.

Burr, V. (1995). *An introduction to social constructionism.* New York: Routledge.

Caplan, P., & Caplan, J. (1994). *Thinking critically about research on sex and gender.* New York: HarperCollins.

Chrisler, J. C. (1996). PMS as a culture-bound syndrome. In J. C. Chrisler, C. Golden, & P. D. Rozee (Eds.), *Lectures on the psychology of women* (pp. 106–121). New York: McGraw-Hill.

Cosgrove, L. (2000). Crying out loud: Understanding women's emotional distress as both lived experience and social construction. *Feminism & Psychology, 10,* 247–267.

Cosgrove, L., & McHugh, M. (in press). Speaking for ourselves: Feminist methods and community psychology. *American Journal of Community Psychology.*

Crawford, M. (1997). *Talking difference: On gender and language.* Thousand Oaks, CA: Sage.

Davidson, L. (1987). What is the appropriate source for psychological explanation? *Humanistic Psychologist, 15,* 150–166.

Davidson, L., & Cosgrove, L. (1991). Psychologism and phenomenological psychology revisited. Part I: The liberation from naturalism. *Journal of Phenomenological Psychology, 22,* 87–108.

Derrida, J. (1972). *Limited, Inc.* Evanston, IL: Northwestern University Press.

Derrida, J. (1976). *Of grammatology.* Baltimore: Johns Hopkins University Press.

Fischer, C. (1985). *Individualizing psychological assessment.* Monterey, CA: Brooks/Cole.

Foucault, M. (1980). *The history of sexuality: Volume I: An introduction* (R. Hurley, Trans.). New York: Vintage.

Fraser, N., & Nicholson, L. (1990). Social criticism without philosophy: An encounter between feminism and postmodernism. In L. Nicholson (Ed.), *Feminism/Postmodernism* (pp. 19–38). New York: Routledge.

Garko, M. (1999). Existential phenomenology and feminist research. *Psychology of Women Quarterly, 23,* 167–175.

Gergen, K. J. (1985). The social constructionist movement in modern psychology. *American Psychologist, 40,* 266–275.

Gergen, M., & Davis, S. (1997). *Toward a new psychology of gender: A reader.* New York: Routledge.

Giorgi, A. (1970). *Psychology as a human science: A phenomenological based approach.* New York: Harper and Row.

Giorgi, A. (1985). *Phenomenology and psychological research.* Pittsburgh: Duquesne University Press.

Giorgi, A. (1997). The theory, practice, and evaluation of the phenomenological method as a qualitative research procedure. *Journal of Phenomenological Psychology, 28,* 235–260.

Hare-Mustin, R. T. (1994). Discourses in the mirrored room: A postmodern analysis of therapy. *Family Process, 33,* 19–35.

Hare-Mustin, R. T., & Marecek, J. (Eds.). (1990). *Making a difference: Psychology and the construction of gender.* New Haven CT: Yale University Press.

Hare-Mustin, R. T., & Marecek, J. (1994a). Asking the right questions: Feminist psychology and sex differences. *Feminism and Psychology, 4*, 531–537.

Hare-Mustin, R. T., & Marecek, J. (1994b). Feminism and postmodernism: Dilemmas and points of resistance. *Dulwich Centre Newsletter, 4*, 13–19.

Heidegger, M. (1971). *On the way to language*. San Francisco: Harper and Row.

Henriques, J., Hollway, W., Urwin, C., Venn, C., & Walkerdine, V. (1998). *Changing the subject*. London: Methuen.

Henwood, K., Griffin, C., & Phoenix, A. (Eds.). (1998). *Standpoints and differences: Essays in the practice of feminist psychology*. Thousand Oaks, CA: Sage.

Henwood, K., and Pidgeon, N. (1995). Grounded theory and psychological research. *The Psychologist, 8*, 115–118.

Herbold, S. (1995). Well-placed reflections: (Post) modern woman as symptom of (Post) modern man. *Signs, 21*, 83–115.

Hollway, W. (1989). *Subjectivity and method in psychology: Gender, meaning and science*. London: Sage.

Holstein, J., & Gubrim J. (1998). Phenomenology, ethnomethodology, and interpretive practice. In N. Denzin & Y. Lincoln (Eds.), *Strategies of qualitative inquiry* (pp. 137–157). Thousand Oaks, CA: Sage.

hooks, b. (1990). *Yearning: Race, gender, and cultural politics*. Boston: South End Press.

Husserl, E. (1970). *The crisis of European sciences and transcendental phenomenology* (D. Carr, Trans.). Evanston, IL: Northwestern University Press.

Husserl, E. (1977). *Phenomenological psychology* (J. Scanlon, Trans.). The Hague: Martinus Nijhoff.

Jennings, J. (1986). Husserl revisited: The forgotten distinction between psychology and phenomenology. *American Psychologist, 41*, 1231–1240.

Keen, E. (1975). *A primer in phenomenological psychology*. Washington, DC: University Press of America.

Kimball, M. M. (1995). *Feminist visions of gender similarities and differences*. New York: Harrington Park Press.

Kocklemans, J. (1967). *Edmund Husserl's phenomenological psychology: A historico-critical study*. Pittsburgh: Duquesne University Press.

Kohak, E. (1978). *Idea & experience: Edmund Husserl's project of phenomenology in Ideas I*. Chicago: University of Chicago Press.

Lather, P. (1991). *Getting smart: Feminist research and pedagogy within the postmodern*. New York: Routledge.

Lather, P. (1992). Postmodernism and the human sciences. In S. Kvale (Ed.), *Postmodernism and psychology* (pp. 88–109). Thousand Oaks, CA: Sage.

Layton, L. (1998). *Who's that girl? Who's that boy? Clinical practice meets postmodern gender theory*. Northvale, NJ: Jason Aronson.

Lyotard, J. F. (1984). *The postmodern condition: A report on knowledge* (G. Bennington & B. Massumi, Trans.). Minneapolis: University of Minnesota Press.

Morawski, J. (1994). *Practicing feminism, reconstructing psychology: Notes on a liminal science*. Ann Arbor: University of Michigan Press.

Nelson, J. L. (1989). Phenomenology as feminist methodology: Explicating Interviews. In K. Carter and C. Spitzack (Eds.), *Doing research on women's com-*

munication: Perspectives on theory and method (pp. 221–241). Norwood, NJ: Ablex.

Nicholson, L. (Ed.). (1990). *Feminism/postmodernism*. New York: Routledge.

Phoenix, A. (1994). The relationship between qualitative and quantitative research: Lessons from feminist psychology. *Journal of Community and Applied Social Psychology, 4,* 287–298.

Reitz, R. R. (1999). Batterers' experiences of being violent: A phenomenological study. *Psychology of Women Quarterly 23,* 143–165.

Scott, J. W. (1992). Experience. In J. Butler & J. Scott (Eds.), *Feminists theorize the political* (pp. 22–40). London: Routledge.

Shawver, L. (1996). What postmodernism can do for psychoanalysis: A guide to the postmodern vision. *American Journal of Psychoanalysis, 56,* 371–394.

Shawver, L. (1998a). On the clinical relevance of selected postmodern ideas with a focus on Lyotard's concept of "differend." *Journal of the American Academy of Psychoanalysis, 26,* 599–618.

Shawver, L. (1998b). Postmodernizing the unconscious with the help of Derrida and Lyotard. *The American Journal of Psychoanalysis, 58,* 361–390.

Swann, C., & Ussher, J. (1995). A discourse analytic approach to women's experience of premenstrual syndrome. *Journal of Mental Health, 4,* 359–367.

Tavris, C. (1992). *The mismeasure of women.* New York: Simon & Schuster.

Urwin, C. (1998). Power relations and the emergence of language. In J. Henriques, W. Hollway, C. Urwin, C. Venn, & V. Walkerdine (Eds.), *Changing the subject* (pp. 264–322). London: Methuen.

Ussher, J. (1996). Premenstrual syndrome: Reconciling disciplinary divides through the adoption of a material-discursive epistemological standpoint. *Annual Review of Sex Research, 7,* 218–251.

Ussher, J. (1999). Eclecticism and methodological pluralism: The way forward for feminist research. *Psychology of Women Quarterly, 23,* 41–46.

Wilkinson, S., & Kitzinger, C. (Eds.). (1995). *Feminism and discourse: Psychological perspectives.* Thousand Oaks, CA: Sage.

Chapter 3

The Faces of Feminist Pedagogy: A Survey of Psychologists and Their Students

Merideth J. Tomlinson and Ruth E. Fassinger

Feminist pedagogy is the "neglected child of feminist psychology" (p. 179). So concluded Linda Forrest and Freda Rosenberg (1997) in a comprehensive review of the feminist pedagogy literature. These authors suggested that the prototypical definition of feminist pedagogy is "the fusion of feminist values into the process and methods of teaching" (Forrest & Rosenberg, 1997, p. 179). It is noteworthy that their comprehensive review yielded only a handful of articles or book chapters on feminist pedagogy that were written by psychologists. Our goal in writing this chapter was to contribute to the dialogue on feminist pedagogy in psychology, and consequently to facilitate movement along this relatively uncharted and potentially fruitful course in feminist psychology.

We begin this chapter with an attempt to elaborate the parameters of feminist pedagogy by detailing concepts that are commonly cited in the literature as its building blocks. Next, we describe a pilot study that we conducted to examine what a small sample of feminist psychologists actually does in the classroom. Although feminist pedagogy occurs in multiple learning contexts beyond the classroom (e.g., mentor/protégé relationships, academic advising, dissertation advising, and research teams), the focus of our study, and hence this chapter, is primarily on the classroom context. Thus, for the purposes of this chapter, feminist pedagogy is equivalent to feminist teaching.

Feminist pedagogy developed over the past 25 years primarily in the field of women's studies as an alternative approach to traditional education. Only recently has this educational approach begun to surface in the psychology literature. In their comprehensive review, Forrest and Rosenberg (1997) reported that the majority of articles and book chapters they found on feminist pedagogy were in interdisciplinary feminist or women's studies journals. This is not to imply that feminist psychologists are strangers to feminist curriculum transformation. They have created a sizable body of literature on changing course content to be more gender inclusive, particularly in psychology of women courses (DeFour & Paludi, 1991; Matlin, 1989). Feminist psychologists simply have published little scholarship specifically on the *process* and *methods* of feminist teaching. However, one need only attend a feminist or women's psychology conference in recent years and witness the burgeoning of feminist pedagogy presentations to realize that psychology is beginning to contribute to this knowledge base.

The historical genesis of feminist pedagogy was the women's movement (Fisher, 1982). For example, one common ingredient within feminist pedagogy is an intentional focus on women, women's oppression, and/or gender relations (both within and outside of the classroom). More recently, however, feminist pedagogy has evolved under the influence of the multicultural movement. Rather than speaking primarily for White middle-class women, feminist pedagogy has become more complex and nuanced, as it emphasizes the diversity among women and their experiences of oppression and privilege. In this way, feminist teachers may emphasize race, ethnicity, and sexual orientation in addition to gender (Forrest & Rosenberg, 1997).

Although the feminist pedagogy literature was derived primarily from the woman-centered curriculum of women's studies, several authors have noted that it can be implemented to some degree in any course (Ayers-Nachamkin, 1992). Therefore, though an explicit focus on gender and/or women's issues is more intuitively appealing for feminist pedagogy, it is not required. For example, even when teaching a statistics course, which seemingly mandates an expert model due to its skill-orientation and mechanistic nature, a teacher nevertheless can incorporate the feminist principles of shared leadership, attending to process, and valuing all voices. Ayers-Nachamkin (1992) described her feminist strategies for dealing with her students' math anxiety in an introductory statistics course. For instance, she disclosed her own experiences with math anxiety and invited the students to do the same. Also, to minimize competition, students were encouraged to help each other with homework, and students were permitted to retake exams and retain the higher score of the two.

Although it seems to be widely accepted that feminist pedagogy is the fusing of feminist values with the process and methods of teaching (Forrest & Rosenberg, 1997), to describe explicitly feminist pedagogy is not a straightforward task. The literature suggests two reasons for this. First, each teacher's pedagogy is unique. It will stem from her own particular feminist values, or, according to Enns and Sinacore-Guinn (1999), her feminist theoretical orientation. Commonly cited feminist theories are liberal, cultural, radical, socialist, multicultural, womanist (i.e., women of color), lesbian, and postmodern (Enns, 1997; Enns & Sinacore-Guinn, 1999; Forrest & Rosenberg, 1997), and any one feminist may adhere to several of these ideologies simultaneously. Therefore, there are a myriad of possible theoretical orientations, each of which articulates unique realities about the causes of gender oppression and goals for liberation, and each of which points to a particular form of pedagogy. In fact, Cohen and McKee (1999) concluded that "because of the diversity of feminist theoretical perspectives and academic disciplines represented in feminist scholarship, it seems unlikely to us that there will ever be a single, conclusive definition of feminist pedagogy" (p. 8). Consequently, Forrest and Rosenberg (1997) were quite accurate when they called for use of the more inclusive phrase "feminist pedagogies."

The second reason that feminist pedagogy defies universal definition is that it is born out of the unique dynamic that occurs between teacher and student (Lewis, 1990; Manicom, 1992). Consequently, feminist pedagogy varies with teacher and student characteristics, as well as with other contextual aspects of the classroom (e.g., class size, course topic, and institutional support). Patti Lather (1991) echoed this conceptualization when she stated that feminist pedagogy exists at the intersection of the teacher, the learners, and the knowledge they produce. Dunn (1993) provided a specific suggestion based on this assumption when she argued for the importance of adjusting feminist teaching methods according to students' cognitive development and barriers to learning.

One central theme that unites all feminist pedagogies is the belief that teaching is a political act. This is one way in which feminist pedagogy is set apart from traditional patriarchal pedagogy, which relies on the paternal "expert" model (The TWIG Writing Group, 1998). The expert model carries the assumption that there exists an ever-evolving base of objective knowledge about the world that is passed down from the senior veteran to the passive novice (MacDermid, Jurich, Myers-Walls, & Pelo, 1992; Maher, 1985). Feminists, in contrast, view knowledge as never being value-free. Furthermore, they recognize that decisions are made as to what to include in any curriculum. They understand that the traditional model only represents a single reality and so is inherently silencing and disempowering to a large portion of the population, particularly those who are not White, male, upper or middle class, or in positions of social power (Maher, 1985). Therefore, feminist pedagogy is a radical shift in perspective that has the potential to provide a transforming educational experience for those students who previously were silenced.

FEMINIST PEDAGOGY CONCEPTS

We next outline the core components of feminist pedagogy based on our review of the literature. First, the notion of integrating and/or balancing dichotomies refers to the practice of acknowledging and valuing both sides of opposing concepts, one of which, more often than not, has been unacceptable in the traditional classroom. We provide the examples of valuing personal experience, process (as opposed to content), and emotion. Second, the role of power and authority in the classroom is highlighted as an undeniable component of any feminist pedagogy. More specifically, we examine the authority of the teacher, non-hierarchical classrooms, and the evaluation of students. Diversity is the third component of feminist pedagogy, and refers to the influence of multiculturalism on feminist thought in general and feminist pedagogy in particular. We refer to the fourth basic component as epistemological diversity. This concept concerns the appreciation for varying ways of producing knowledge. Finally, we include social action as a standard ingredient of feminist pedagogy.

Integrating/Balancing Dichotomies

The feminist principle of integrating or balancing dichotomies refers to the efforts of feminist teachers to undo the damage created by the mainstream educational approach that has dichotomized and strictly separated certain fundamental aspects of being human: reason versus emotion, objective knowledge versus subjective knowledge, content versus process. This principle lies at the heart of feminist pedagogy because the classroom itself is situated within the academy, a traditionally "masculine" enterprise that has been characterized by the intellectual, impersonal, competitive, and objective (Bezucha, 1985; Maher, 1985; The TWIG Writing Group, 1998). Anything that has been traditionally associated with the "feminine" (e.g., emotions, intuition, cooperation, and subjectivity) has been dismissed as inappropriate for higher education and relegated to the private sphere (e.g., domestic life, romantic relationships) (Bezucha, 1985; Maher, 1985). Feminist pedagogy asserts that this is a false separation that stifles thinking and learning for all students because it discourages them from becoming wholly engaged with the course material. In addition, this devaluing of qualities traditionally associated with women inevitably leads to a silencing of female students and to labeling them as "other." Noting that this separation of personal from private, and subjective from objective, is so deeply embedded in traditional Western education, Bezucha (1985) suggested that this may account for a great deal of resistance to feminist education in the academy. In sum, feminist pedagogy attempts to resurrect that side of the polarity (e.g., personal, intuitive, emotional) that previously has been suppressed in the classroom.

After much experimentation and self-reflection, feminist teachers began to notice that reclaiming the "feminine" (e.g., emotions, intuition, cooperation, and subjectivity) sometimes led to disowning the "masculine" (e.g., reason, intellectual, objectivity). Feminists thus began to critique their pedagogy for embracing "sentimentality" at the cost of scholarly rigor and intellectual acuity (Friedman, 1985; Maher & Tetreault, 1996). It is important that women not deny their own authority and expertise and thus contribute to their own oppression. In order to capture the holistic nature of feminist discourse, many feminist teachers therefore emphasize *balancing and/or integrating* dichotomies, as opposed to privileging half of the dichotomy over the other.

Valuing personal experience. One of the most crucial dichotomies that feminist pedagogy seeks to integrate is between objective and subjective knowledges. The traditional Western pedagogy views truth and knowledge as objective and acontextual, thereby leaving no room for personal experience (Forrest & Rosenberg, 1997; The TWIG Writing Group, 1998). Students thus are expected to disconnect from any personal experiences or reactions that they may have in relation to the course material. Such subjective realties are thought to cloud their judgment and reasoning.

Feminist pedagogy, however, values personal experience. Feminist scholars know that without practice, or real experience, theory is limited. Therefore, as Shrewsbury (1993) noted, feminist teachers emphasize the importance of remaining grounded in personal experience while integrating new learning. Another positive consequence of encouraging shared personal experience in the classroom is that it brings women's often unseen experiences to the forefront. Furthermore, valuing personal experience provides a fertile context for self-reflection, an important aspect for both teacher and student in feminist pedagogy. Finally, feminist teachers often share their own relevant personal experiences, thereby modeling self-disclosure and appropriate risk-taking, as well as minimizing the hierarchy inherent in the teacher-student relationship.

One example of how the principle of *valuing personal experience* might look in practice involves teaching methods that point to the self as subject, such as writing an autobiography, creating a genogram, or keeping a journal (Maher, 1985). Another example involves inviting students to answer questions about their knowledge, attitudes, and experiences related to the daily discussion topic (Thompson, 1993). This not only encourages students to engage personally with the material, it also highlights the differences and commonalties among students—an ingredient essential for genuine reflection, discussion, and the participation of multiple voices.

Valuing process. Traditional pedagogies emphasize the dissemination and mastery of content, but they often ignore the process of how to teach. Feminist pedagogy balances this dichotomy by also valuing and attending to process in the classroom.

Feminist teachers do this in a number of different ways. Some teachers, for example (Schniedewind, 1993), have found it helpful to teach students feminist process skills (i.e., basic communication skills, group process skills, cooperation skills) so that they will know how to participate in a feminist classroom (e.g., learning how to listen and translate each others' reactions).

This is because, as Schniedewind (1993) noted, most students are not familiar with this style of learning and may be resistant simply because of their lack of knowledge and experience with a process-oriented classroom.

One consequence of a process orientation is the surfacing of complex power dynamics related to the discussion of controversial issues in a heterogeneous classroom. Indeed, feminist teachers are often faced with the difficult task of engaging with competing perspectives and/or agendas of different groups or students in the class. Feminist teachers thus may find it helpful to address power dynamics in the classroom, either teacher-student or among the students (Briskin & Coulter, 1992; Manicom, 1992). This is one way these educators may be able to transform dominant power relations, which is a central goal of feminist pedagogy (Manicom, 1992).

Valuing emotions. The combination of personal self-reflection, self-disclosure, and a process orientation invariably yields a range of emotions (e.g., Carmen & Driver, 1982). For feminist teachers, emotions are welcome in the classroom. Indeed, feelings are viewed as an important component of personal experience (Fisher, 1993; Schniedewind, 1993). Although traditionally taboo in the public sphere and accepted only in the private sphere, emotions are acknowledged, validated, and embraced within feminist pedagogy as a resource capable of initiating change. "Women's emotionality is not limiting as we've been taught to believe, but it is a source of strength" (Fisher, 1993, p. 80). Hence, emotions are integrated and balanced with reason and cognition. For feminist educators, there is room in the classroom for both.

Role of Power and Authority

Authority of the teacher. Feminist teachers are aware that in creating an egalitarian classroom they run the risk of denying their own authority (Friedman, 1985). Scholars of feminist pedagogy often refer to the paradox of attempting to empower students and disempowering themselves in the process. The literature suggests that this is not an easy balance to strike (Currie, 1992; Friedman, 1985; Lather, 1991; Manicom, 1992).

Issues of power therefore are central in feminist pedagogy. Feminist teachers strive to make conscious and analyze power issues as they arise in the classroom (Briskin & Coulter, 1992). It is now commonplace among feminist educators to recognize and honor their knowledge and experience, without disempowering the students. Practitioners of feminist pedagogy assert that denying their power is not helpful. In fact, students are more likely to claim and embrace their own power when teachers can comfortably claim their own (Currie, 1992; Friedman, 1985). Through experimentation and experience, these teachers seem to have found a middle ground: rather than viewing power as domination or power "over," it is viewed as power "with"—something that can be shared, to some degree, with students (The TWIG Writing Group, 1998).

Non-hierarchical classrooms. When feminist educators own their power and facilitate the same process in their students, the stage is set for communal classrooms. The contrast between the conventional expert model and feminist pedagogy has been described metaphorically as "transmission versus reciprocal interaction" (Cummins, 1986, as cited in MacDermid et al., 1992, p. 34) or "connected versus separate learning" (MacDermid et al., 1992, p. 32). Feminist teachers create democratic classrooms where the hierarchies are minimized and students are actively engaged in their learning process.

The literature clearly suggests that feminist pedagogy scholars promote the principle of non-hierarchy (MacDermid et al., 1992; Maher, 1985; Manicom, 1992; Schniedewind, 1993; Shrewsbury, 1993). For example, classroom goals may be open to joint negotiation. Furthermore, Bell (1993) referred to building communities in classrooms by citing the structural example of putting chairs in circles rather than rows (both a symbolic and practical practice). Other feminist teachers reported sharing power through giving students more responsibility for constructing and leading the course (MacDermid et. al, 1992; Maher, 1985).

Evaluations. The need for students' learning and progress to be evaluated and documented may present special challenges for the feminist teacher. For one, because of her unique role as the "authority," the task of evaluating students may emphasize this hierarchy. Consequently, her students may be more inclined to inhibit any reactions that run contrary to the teacher's perspective. Second, if each student's learning (both content and process) is tied to that student's own psychosocial experiences, then the traditional approach of evaluation based on some "quantifiable criteria of knowledge mastered" would appear to run counter to feminist values (MacDermid et al., 1992, p. 37). Feminist pedagogy may deal with these challenges and contradictions by involving students in the grading process. For example, students may evaluate themselves and/or each other, or they may be permitted to revise assignments until they are satisfied with their grade (Maher, 1985).

This is not to suggest that evaluation is inherently oppressive, however. For example, some feminist teachers may choose not to relinquish the power of evaluation, yet to be especially clear about their grading criteria as well as their rationale for choosing such a format. Others have suggested making evaluations a peripheral aspect of the relationship by placing more emphasis on other more collaborative aspects (The TWIG Writing Group, 1998).

Difference/Diversity

The attention to diversity within feminist pedagogy has evolved in a parallel fashion to the development of increased inclusivity in the broader feminist movement. Critiques from women of color, lesbian, and post-modern feminists contributed to the awareness that theoretical distinctions cannot be made exclusively on gender (Enns, 1997; Maher & Tetreault, 1996). Feminist pedagogy encourages multiple perspectives in the classroom and especially seeks to hear from those voices that historically have been silenced (e.g., people of color, women, sexual minorities) (Forrest & Rosenberg, 1997). In addition, feminist teachers encourage students to respect each other's differences rather than fear them and to use those differences to enrich their own perspectives (Shrewsbury, 1993). Furthermore, students are acknowledged and validated for having multiple, and sometimes contradictory, voices within themselves (Manicom, 1992). According to Thompson (1993), diversity within the classroom is an asset if the teacher "consciously builds on differences and commonalities" to engage students in the class discussion and mutual learning. Briskin and Coulter (1992) were referring to diversity in the classroom when they stated, "There is no doubt that one fundamental challenge facing us is to develop ways to think about, teach with, and theorize difference" (p. 262).

Epistemological Diversity

Feminist pedagogy expands the range of acceptable epistemologies from exclusively abstract, objective, rational ways of knowing to include contextualized, subjective, emotional ways of knowing. Historically, the positivist tradition of knowledge production has been dominated by privileged groups (generally White men), thereby effectively silencing the contributions of women and other minority groups (Briskin & Coulter, 1992; Maher, 1985; Manicom, 1992). However, feminists assume that women, racial and ethnic minorities, sexual minorities, poor people, and other marginalized groups have unique knowledges related to their personal experiences at the peripheries of academe and society. Therefore, feminist pedagogy attempts to facilitate learning from all perspectives and actively values those voices that previously have been silenced.

In the classroom, feminist teachers encourage open-ended inquiry where students search for knowledge in collaboration with the teacher. Bell (1993) described this collective knowledge production as community building. This process is marked by clarifying assumptions and questioning knowledge claims (Shrewsbury, 1993; Thompson, 1993). Students are assumed not only to have knowledge but also to create it, and knowledge itself is viewed as contextual and changing. Fisher (1993) noted, "Any conclusions we reach, even when they become the basis for action, have a contingent quality. They represent no more or less than our best understanding of ourselves and the world at that moment" (p. 77).

Social Action

A fundamental difference between traditional and feminist education is that the work of feminist educators often is inspired by a vision for social change at the individual, classroom, institution, society, and global levels (Manicom, 1993). Traditional educators view knowledge and science as "value free," thus creating distance between themselves and the impact that their scholarship (or course content) may have on society. Feminist pedagogy emphasizes the transformation of vision into social action, so that classroom discussions are never very far from the reality of oppressive social arrangements. Thompson (1993) described teaching her students to translate abstract ideas into concrete realities. For example, she provided an assignment that is geared to help her students learn to become more socially active. The assignment was to write a letter to a newspaper, friend, or organization about an issue that was discussed in class. These assignments, according to Thompson (1993), usually involve some level of risk, as do most forms of social activism.

In sum, the customary building blocks of feminist pedagogy—integrating/balancing dichotomies, power and authority, valuing diversity/difference, epistemological diversity, and social action—may be interwoven and emphasized in various fashions by different feminist teachers. One factor that may affect a feminist teacher's pedagogy is her feminist theoretical orientation (i.e., radical, liberal, socialist, women of color, lesbian, or postmodern). However, there is little empirical research to examine teaching practices among psychologists and even less to examine how their practices relate to their feminist theoretical orientations. In the next section of this chapter, we present a pilot study in which faculty and students were surveyed regarding each faculty member's feminist theoretical orientation, feminist identification, and feminist teaching practices. It was our hope that this study would serve as a starting point for further, more extensive investigation in this area.

THE SURVEY

The primary purpose of the present study was to determine what feminist pedagogical practices are employed by a small sample of feminist psychologists in the classroom and how these practices may relate to feminist theoretical orientation and identification. In order to capture a more complete picture of feminist teaching practices, we included both teachers' self-perceptions and their students' perceptions of the extent to which each teacher practiced feminist teaching. Because there is little existing empirical literature to document feminist pedagogical strategies, we used an author-created quantitative measure of specific practices and strategies. We developed two hypotheses and one research question based on this quantitative survey. First, we predicted that labeling oneself a feminist would be positively correlated with both feminist theoretical orientation and feminist teaching practices. Second, because the literature suggests that individual teachers' feminist pedagogies are a reflection of their feminist theoretical orientations (Enns & Sinacore-Guinn, 1999; Forrest & Rosenberg, 1997) we predicted that faculty's feminist theoretical orientations would be positively correlated with their feminist pedagogical practices. Our final analysis was exploratory in nature: we wondered whether there would be significant differences between faculty's and students' perceptions of the faculty's feminist theoretical orientation, feminist identification, and feminist teaching practices.

In addition to the 60-item survey, we included a small set of open-ended questions to gain a more in-depth response from participants of their experiences as feminist teachers or students of feminist teachers. We had three research questions that corresponded to each of the three survey questions: (1) "What types of issues about power relations arise in a feminist classroom?"; (2) "What types of issues about the teacher's authority arise in a feminist classroom?"; and (3) "What kinds of feedback and/or support do teachers and students receive regarding their experiences in a feminist classroom?"

PROCEDURES

We developed two versions of the same survey to measure feminist pedagogical practices in the classroom: one for faculty and one for their students. Each participating faculty person was asked to give the survey to two of their students whom they had actually taught in the classroom. The final sample included 38 faculty members and 46 students. Eleven faculty members were recruited through electronic-mail listservs that include feminist psychologists in their membership. The remaining 27 faculty members were recruited through an unannounced mailing of the survey packets to 150 female members of the Association for Women in Psychology (AWP) who identified themselves as academics or as both clinicians and researchers. From the mailing, we received 27 completed faculty surveys and 20 replies that stated that they were not eligible to participate (because they did not teach, were retired, or were not psychologists). Although the original sample included 38 faculty members and 46 students, we only included those faculty and students who were in a teacher/student relationship with each other and thus matched. Consequently, the final sample on which we based our statistical analyses included 37 matched pairs of faculty and students.

The racial composition of the sample was quite homogenous, with 35 White psychology faculty, one designated as "other," and two non-responses. Of the 46 students, 81% were White, 4% Latina or Mexican-American, and 4% designated "other." The faculty ages ranged from 33 to 65, with a mean of 46, and the student ages ranged from 19 to 55, with a mean of 28. Fifty-two percent of the students were undergraduates, 33% were graduate students, and the rest did not indicate their status. The faculty represented several different fields of psychology: 28% identified as counseling psychologists, 17% as social psychologists, 17% as clinical psychologists, 14% as developmental psychologists, 8% as experimental psychologists, and 12% as other. In terms of their faculty status, 33% were full Professors, 28% were Associate Professors, 22% were Assistant Professors, and 11% were Adjunct/Affiliate faculty.

MEASURES

Packets included a demographics form and a survey that consisted of 10 items to determine feminist orientation/identity and 50 items to measure classroom behavior. Items were developed based on the feminist pedagogy literature and categorized into one of the following a priori scales: Personal Experience, Communal/Collaborative Classes, Social Action, Feminist Course Content, and Process/Classroom Dynamics. Participants were asked to rate items on a 5-point Likert scale. An additional section included five open-ended questions about their experiences as feminist teachers or as students of feminist teachers. Packets also included a separate questionnaire on feminist mentoring that was described as optional and was not utilized in the current analysis.

Theoretical Orientation

Ten items were included on the survey to assess feminist theoretical orientation. Items were developed based on commonly cited theories in the literature: liberal, cultural, social, radical, and multicultural (Forrest & Rosenberg, 1997). Our primary research interest, however, was the difference between radical and non-radical feminists in terms of their pedagogy. This is because the literature seems largely to be written by feminists who are more radically oriented (e.g., wanting to transform the educational system itself) (Forrest & Rosenberg, 1997). Initially, we chose to investigate this hypothesis by creating two scales—one with the more radical items and one with all of the other items (which represented cultural and liberal). However, although a factor analysis on the 10 items confirmed our radical scale, it also pointed to a third factor that consisted of the two feminist multicultural items. Consequently, we created three scales: Radical, Liberal/Cultural, and Multicultural. (One radical item loaded primarily on the liberal/cultural factor according to the factor analysis, but for conceptual reasons, we chose to place it in the radical scale, even though it loaded there to a lesser degree.) An example of a radical item on the faculty survey is: "One of my primary objectives is to disrupt the ways in which patriarchal power structures permeate the classroom." An example of a liberal/cultural item on the student survey is: "I try to emphasize connection and collaboration." An example of a multicultural item on the faculty survey is: "I attempt to focus on multiple identities, not just gender."

Feminist Teaching Practices

Cronbach's coefficient alphas for each of the five a priori scales ranged from .62 to .87. Three survey items were dropped to increase scale alphas. The Personal Experience scale had 11 items (e.g., "I acknowledge personal experience as a vital source of knowledge.") The Communal/Collaborative Classes scale had 15 items (e.g., "I strive to create a non-hierarchical classroom.") The Social Action scale had five items (e.g., "It is important to me that my students participate in some form of social action.") The Feminist Course Content scale had eight items (e.g., "I integrate feminist theory into the curriculum.") The Process Scale had nine items (e.g., "I teach students to listen and to translate each other's concerns.") The sample size (N = 37) was insufficient to perform a confirmatory factory analysis on the 50 teaching practice items.

Feminist Identification

This was measured by a single item, as in Fassinger (1990). For the faculty, the item was, "I am a feminist." The equivalent item on the student scale was, "My teacher is a feminist." Like all other items, this item was rated on a 5-point Likert scale. Higher scores indicate a greater preference for use of the feminist label.

RESULTS

Quantitative Results

Descriptive information about faculty, students, and measures was generated using means and standard deviations. The faculty data follow: Radical Scale (M = 3.63; sd = .69); Liberal/Cultural Scale (M = 4.15; sd = 1.00); Multicultural Scale (M = 4.16; sd = .66); Personal Experience Scale (M = 3.57; sd = .60); Communal Scale (M = 3.29; sd = .68); Feminist Course Content Scale (M = 4.05; sd = .60); Social Action Scale (M = 3.32; sd = .69); Process Scale (M = 3.66; sd = .65). The following is descriptive information for students: Radical Scale (M = 3.69; sd = .96); Liberal/Cultural Scale (M = 4.07; sd = .91); Multicultural Scale (M = 3.96; sd = 1.04); Personal Experience Scale (M = 3.47; sd = .68); Communal Scale (M = 3.04; sd = .73); Feminist Course Content Scale (M = 3.59; sd = 1.02); Social Action Scale (M = 2.90; sd = .85); Process Scale (M = 3.37; sd = .79). We computed simple correlations to assess the relations among the feminist theoretical orientation scales, feminist identification, and the teaching practice scales. A multivariate analysis of variance (MANOVA) was calculated to investigate differences between students and faculty on feminist theoretical orientation, feminist identification, and feminist teaching practices. Before conducting any analyses, all variables were checked to verify that they met the underlying assumptions of parametric statistics, and all did meet these distribution requirements.

Hypothesis 1. Self-identification as a feminist and students' perceptions of faculty identification as a feminist are positively related to both feminist theoretical orientation and feminist teaching practices.

Among the faculty (N = 37), self-identification as a feminist was significantly correlated ($p < .01$) with three of the five teaching practices scales: Feminist Course Content ($r = .47$), Personal Experience ($r = .43$), and Process ($r = .52$). It was not correlated with Communal/Collaborative Classes or Social Action. In contrast, students' perceptions (N = 37) of their teacher as a feminist correlated significantly ($p < .01$) with all five teaching practices scales, with coefficients ranging from .51 to .65. Correlations also were obtained between feminist identification and the three theoretical orientation scales. Within the sample of faculty, feminist identification was significantly correlated with the Radical ($r = .59$) and Liberal/Cultural ($r = .55$) scales, and demonstrated no significant relationship with the Multicultural scale ($r = .28$)—an unexpected result. Again, and as predicted, the students' perceptions of their faculty as feminist were significantly correlated with all three of the theoretical orientation scales, ranging from .67 to .71.

Hypothesis 2. Feminist theoretical orientation (i.e., radical, liberal/cultural, multicultural) is significantly positively related to feminist teaching practices (i.e., personal experience, communal, social action, feminist course content, process).

As predicted, among the faculty (N = 37) the Radical orientation scale resulted in a significant positive correlation with all five of the teaching practice scales (Personal Experience, $r = .66$, $p < .01$; Communal, $r = .63$, $p < .01$; Feminist Course Content, $r = .62$, $p < .01$; Social Action, $r = .34$, $p < .05$; Process, $r = .86$, $p < .01$). A similar pattern was found with the Liberal/Cultural scale, with one exception: there was no significant correlation with the Social Action scale (Personal Experience, $r = .59$, $p < .01$; Communal, $r = .50$, $p < .01$; Feminist Course Content, $r = .59$, $p < .01$; Social Action, $r = .31$; Process, $r = .59$, $p < .01$). The Multicultural scale, however, was not related to any of the teaching practice scales except for Social Action, with which it demonstrated a significant negative correlation (Personal Experience, $r = -.01$; Communal, $r = -.20$; Feminist Course Content, $r = -.11$; Social Action, $r = -.47$, $p < .01$; Process, $r = .14$). Hence, results regarding theoretical orientation and teaching practice were not consistent with our hypothesis.

Student responses (N = 37) were all as expected. That is, each theoretical orientation was significantly positively correlated with each teaching practice scale. Correlations for the Radical Scale are as follows: (Personal Experience, $r = .54$, $p < .01$; Communal, $r = .54$, $p < .01$; Feminist Course

Content, $r = .69$, $p < .01$; Social Action, $r = .60$, $p < .01$; Process, $r = .56$, $p < .01$). Liberal/Cultural Scale correlations are the following: (Personal Experience, $r = 41$, $p < .05$; Communal, $r = .54$, $p < 01$; Feminist Course Content, $r = .60$, $p < .01$; Social Action, $r = .68$, $p < .01$; Process, $r = .53$, $p < .01$). Finally, correlations for the Multicultural Scale are as follows: (Personal Experience, $r = .63$ $p < .01$; Communal, $r = .52$, $p < .01$; Feminist Course Content, $r = . 53$, $p < .01$; Social Action, $r = .45$, $p < .01$; Process, $r = .65$, $p < .01$).

Research question. Are there differences between faculty and student perceptions of faculty identification as a feminist, general feminist theoretical orientation of faculty, and extent of feminist teaching practices?

A multivariate analysis of variance (MANOVA) was calculated to determine whether or not there were differences between faculty and students on perceptions of the faculty as being feminist, as having a feminist theoretical orientation, and as employing feminist pedagogical practices in the classroom (N = 74, 37 faculty, 37 students). MANOVA was justified because of the substantial correlations among the three dependent variables: theoretical orientation and feminist identification ($r = .71$, $p < .01$); theoretical orientation and feminist teaching practices ($r = .76$, $p < .01$); feminist identification and feminist teaching practices ($r = .60$, $p < .01$). Before conducting the MANOVA, several demographic variables—faculty status (e.g., assistant, associate, full professor), size of class (small, medium, large), and type of class (graduate or undergraduate) referred to by participants when they responded to the survey—were examined as potential covariates; however, none significantly differentiated between faculty and students.

For several reasons, we used a single total score for feminist theoretical orientation. First, a single score accommodated our small sample size. Also, a single score was justified due to the substantial correlations ($p < .01$) among theoretical orientation scales. Furthermore, we did not expect that students would be able to make fine distinctions about the various possible theoretical orientations of their professors. We also used a single combined score for feminist pedagogical practices. In addition to accommodating our small sample size, this combined score was used because our interest was less in the particular types of pedagogical practices used by the professors and more in faculty and student perceptions of whether any such practices were employed. Also, as with feminist theoretical orientation, the substantial correlations ($p < .01$) among teaching practice scales justified combining them into a total score for feminist teaching.

Results from the MANOVA indicate an overall significant difference between faculty and students, $F(3, 70) = 3.71$, $p < .01$. That is, the dependent variables, taken as a group, did significantly distinguish between faculty and students. When results were examined at the univariate level, a significant difference was found between the two groups only on one dependent variable, feminist teaching practices, $F (1, 72) = 4.68, p < .03$. A subsequent examination of the means revealed that faculty had higher scores for feminist teaching practices. In other words, students had lower perceptions than faculty of the extent to which faculty utilize feminist ped-agogical practices in the classroom.

Analysis of Open-Ended Questions

Three open-ended questions were posed for faculty and two for their students, and space for additional comments was available. The questions inquired about experiences with power relations in the classroom, experi-ences dealing with their authority in the classroom (faculty only), and types of feedback and/or support received for participating in feminist teaching. For this analysis, we categorized the data according to each question (power relations, authority, feedback), then independently identified com-mon themes within each category. Finally, these themes were discussed until consensus was reached as to which themes were most representative of our sample.

Power relations. We asked participants to describe their experiences with power relations in the classroom. Fifty-six percent of the faculty and 33% of the students responded to this question. Among the faculty, the most commonly cited difficulty was dealing with dominating or monopolizing students. The majority of these women noted resistant male students, how-ever a few mentioned politically sophisticated students and extremely rad-ical female students who were unwilling to listen to other points of view. In essence, they pointed to problems that arise when students effectively shut down dialogue by adopting a superior or intimidating stance.

Paradoxically, the majority of faculty in this sample believed that these students had to be silenced to some degree in order to encourage the voicing of all perspectives. A variety of strategies were mentioned for dealing with these dynamics, such as working in small groups, discussing resistance early in the semester, refocusing or cutting off the monopolizer by requesting to hear from others who had yet to speak, using humor, interrupting resistant students to teach them directly, encouraging resistant students to look at themselves and their reactions, and gently articulating opposing perspec-tives without putting others down. A few strategies were described as being used only in extreme situations, such as asking the difficult student to leave or directly admonishing the student whose comments were abusive. How-ever, it should be noticed that these students were not perceived merely as problems to be eradicated. In fact, one professor commented, "Over the years the students with the most resistant stance (which sometimes trans-lates into attempts to dominate through disagreements) turn out to be those most ready for transformation, and some of them (not all!) have ended up excellent students and long-term contacts." Overall, these feminist teachers conveyed the sense that there is no one way to deal with difficult students and that they, as teachers, continue to learn through experience and experimentation.

Few students responded to this question, and those who did referred primarily to their professors' strategies of dealing with power relations in the classroom. A couple of students noted that they appreciated having open discussions with their teachers about power relations and the ideal of non-hierarchical process. Several others described their instructors as mediators who ensure that all sides of an issue are heard and respected. One student noted regretfully that her professor sometimes fails to address these issues directly, thereby sending mixed messages and creating confusion. Another student spoke of her own fear of countering resistant male students and her resulting self-criticism. One student offered an alternative perspective: she expressed comfort with and appreciation for students who dominate the discussion because she believed she could learn from them.

Authority. We invited the faculty in our sample to describe briefly the issues they have encountered regarding their authority in the classroom. Sixty-seven percent of the faculty in this study responded to this question. Among these responses, one theme stood out above all others: that it is not useful to relinquish classroom authority completely. Several described a process that began with an attempt to decrease their authority, then decided that it was ineffectual, and finally returned to embrace and use their authority in the classroom. One professor stated,

I have come to believe that I have power, to deny that is to risk using power dangerously. I try to use whatever power I have responsibly by serving as a model of a strong, fair, kind teacher and mentor. To deny my power would be to deny that women can wield power . . . something I don't want to reinforce in my students.

But, they were careful to mention the importance of using their power in the service of empowering students or furthering the learning process. For some, this required a personal struggle of learning to be comfortable with their own authority. One teacher noted,

I may not be a "typical" feminist professor as I believe that it's important to acknowledge the differential power in the classroom and then try to "use it" to advance knowledge and enhance the students' learning experiences. I've learned to accept and embrace the power inherent in the position and I try to do this in a constructive manner.

These feminist teachers apparently strive to use their authority to empower rather than dominate students, but it is clear that this is not always easy to do. For example, one of the contradictions that may arise with feminist pedagogy is that while teachers strive to empower students to come to their own conclusions, they simultaneously seek their students' identification with feminist principles. For one faculty member in our study, this raised the issue of whether to use her authority against homophobia and advance non-bias against lesbians and gay men. She took the following position:

> Students used to argue from a religious standpoint. I now begin my lectures with a statement that all relevant codes of ethics state that we will respect all sexual orientations and that if they are prejudiced or uncomfortable that they have an ethical obligation to 1) refer clients until they get over it, and 2) to get educated and get over it. I thus pit my authority (ethical guidelines) against theirs, and my authority, in this environment, wins. It's a non-feminist, authoritarian approach, but I'm just not willing to argue about that anymore. I guess my commitment to my educational goals and to my own (lesbian) dignity and the dignity of my GLB students outweighs my commitment to a feminist approach to this issue.

Although the students were not directly asked this question, student responses to the first question on power relations are also relevant here. Some of the students pointed to the challenge of attempting an egalitarian relationship within the roles of teacher/student, which include an inherent power differential. One student noted that her classmates are frequently resistant to "assuming too much responsibility for the course." She thought that her teacher's approach sometimes created confusion about who would take a leadership role in the class. One student reported that her professor occasionally behaves in authoritarian ways and speculated that this was simply a more convenient role to assume.

Feedback/support. We asked participants about the feedback and/or support they have received from students, colleagues, and supervisors regarding their feminist teaching practices. Eighty-nine percent of the faculty and 76% of the students responded to this question. The faculty reported that the feedback they receive from students is almost entirely positive. Their classes tend to be very popular (e.g., they described waiting lists for enrollment). Many of the faculty noted that their students often report that their perspectives and lives were transformed by their classroom experience and that they often receive thank you notes and gifts of appreciation several years after the course. It appears that, for many students, the impact of the class may not be realized until some time has passed.

Not all feedback was positive, however. One faculty member noted that the feedback depends on the student who is giving it: she is either viewed as too radical, or as not radical enough. Another referred to the difficulty of students who expect a more personal relationship with her because of her feminist approach. Overall, however, feminist educators in this study reported that the majority of their students express gratitude for their learning experiences.

Without exception, the students in this sample spoke quite highly of their professors. Yet, it was evident that, for some, becoming comfortable with their professors' teaching methods was a gradual process. One student summed it up in the following manner,

I think that many of the students were thrown off (perhaps uncomfortable) with what they may have perceived as a lack of structure within the classroom. My experience was that although I had not experienced a classroom environment like this before, I (once used to it) enjoyed it. What I found most difficult to adjust to was that this was an environment where our opinions, experiences, and suggestions were not only allowed, but were encouraged—certainly not something I experienced as an undergraduate.

Several women mentioned that although their students' feedback is primarily positive, the students often do not label or even recognize their experiences as feminist. It was not clear whether the teachers in this study explicitly identified their classes as "feminist." However, one professor did disclose her position: "I seldom use 'the F word' in recent years because it seems to polarize students and then we lose topic-relevant class time because I stop to do some consciousness raising. I usually try to 'do it.' That is, live by example."

Student responses suggested that at least three faculty members in this sample did not explicitly identify their courses, or themselves, as feminist. Several students suggested that their classmates did not label the classroom as feminist or that their professors did not describe it as feminist either. Opinions on this subject ranged from one extreme to the other. For example, one student expressed disappointment that her professor failed to declare her class as feminist. Yet, two other respondents defended their professors as wonderful instructors, "but *not* feminist!" Finally, one other stated that she and her peers attributed their liking of the class to the professor herself, not to her feminist approach.

The students in this sample all applauded their professors (whether they perceived them as feminist or not), and they also reported on the feedback they themselves received from other students about their participation in the class. In general, the feedback was mixed. Commonly mentioned experiences included negativity, criticism, or indifference from male students or non-feminist females, and admiration and support from others.

Faculty reported experiencing feedback that ranged from supportive to resistant, unsupportive, and/or critical. When faced with unsupportive colleagues, these faculty found support elsewhere, such as in the Association for Women in Psychology or feminist colleagues in other settings. Many of these women suggested that their department colleagues do not know or understand what really occurs in their feminist classrooms. One teacher described being criticized for "teaching fluff as opposed to rigorous, hard material."

The question on feedback from supervisors or superiors also yielded a variety of answers, ranging from a highly supportive environment to being told that feminist perspectives are not to be taught in the classroom. However, the most common response was that their superiors are only concerned with positive evaluations and/or high enrollment. Otherwise, their superiors really have no idea what they actually do in the classroom.

DISCUSSION

In this chapter, we attempted to contribute to the feminist pedagogy literature (a) by conducting an empirical, quantitative survey in a field of study where scholarship is primarily theoretical or anecdotal, (b) by investigating the perspectives of the students in addition to the faculty, and (c) by examining feminist pedagogy as it is practiced specifically in the field of psychology. We discuss here the results of the study in the context of the feminist pedagogy literature.

Hypothesis I. Our first hypothesis was partially confirmed in that the faculty's feminist identification was related to three of the five Feminist Teaching Practices scales: Personal Experience, Feminist Course Content, and Process. However, it was not significantly related to the Communal/Collaborative Classroom scale or the Social Action scale. The Communal scale included items related to minimizing hierarchy and creating a collaborative learning experience (e.g., alternative methods of evaluation). Thus, these items are reflective of our previous description of the role of power and authority in feminist pedagogy. It may be that for some faculty, being a feminist does not require reducing power differentials or creating a communal atmosphere. In fact, responses to the open-ended questions suggest that many of these faculty members do not feel the need to minimize their power in their role as teacher. Rather, they find creative ways of using their power to empower students and/or to advance a feminist agenda.

Another possible explanation for the lack of correlation with the communal scale is that larger classes are much less conducive to developing communal atmospheres (MacDermid et al., 1992; Maher, 1985). When responding to the survey, a small portion of the faculty participants (13%) referred to large (> 39 students) lecture classes, and another 42% referred to classrooms with 20–40 students. Only 32% referred to classes of fewer than 20 students. Thus, 55% described their teaching practices in classes with at least 20 students.

Yet another possible reason for the lack of correlation between the faculty's identification as feminists and the scale that measures their tendency to create collaborative and communal classrooms may be due to the specific items on this scale about alternative methods of evaluation. Feminist teaching may not require alternative methods of grading (The TWIG Writing Group, 1998), and the lower means for these items may have decreased the strength of the correlation of the scale with feminist identification. This was consistent with responses to the open-ended question on the teacher's authority, which suggested that these faculty largely grade in a traditional fashion and evaluate their students themselves. On this survey, items about evaluation may have failed to reflect the possibility that some feminists might choose to assign grades, but do so in a manner that demystifies the process, thus reducing the potential power differential.

The feminist identification of faculty also demonstrated little relationship to the Social Action scale, in which high scores indicate that the professor values, encourages, or requires her students to participate in some form of social action. Again, this scale was significantly correlated only with the radical feminist scale. Thus, it may be that for non-radical feminists, social activism is not a component of their feminist pedagogy. These feminists may equate their pedagogy with transforming the student, not the system, and eschew attempts to induce the student to transform the system. Nonetheless, this does not preclude them from valuing social activism for themselves or for others. Another possibility is that they simply do not feel comfortable expecting their students to be socially active as a course requirement, as this has been traditionally absent from academic classrooms. This finding suggests that incorporating social action into feminist pedagogy in psychology may be more complicated than one would expect. Therefore, it may be helpful to begin by taking a broader perspective of social action. For example, Laura Brown (1994) pointed out that even voicing an opinion that brings some form of oppression to consciousness is a form of social activism. Furthermore, research and scholarship are forms of social action—all of which can be incorporating into feminist pedagogy. Finally, it may be useful for feminist teachers to develop and implement workshops on how to institute social action into the feminist classroom.

Of the three feminist theoretical orientation scales, only Radical and Liberal/Cultural were related as predicted to faculty feminist identification. The Multicultural scale again stood out, this time having no relationship to feminist identification. It may be that this lack of correlation reflects a lack of connection between feminism and multiculturalism—a concern that recently has moved to the forefront of feminist scholarship (e.g., Yoder & Kahn, 1993). It is important to note, however, that the faculty in this study did, on the whole, identify strongly with both feminism and the multicultural scale (Means = 4.84 and 4.16, respectively). Thus, although they apparently value both worldviews, they may not necessarily associate the two. Future researchers could address the nature of the relationship between these two constructs among feminist and multiculturalist psychologists, in an effort to clarify the factors that prevent multiculturalism from becoming more centralized in feminist psychology. Furthermore, this finding suggests that psychologists might become more self-reflective about how inclusive they are in their feminist beliefs, as well as more vigilant about the multiple ways in which multiculturalism can inform their feminist thought.

Hypothesis II. The nascent feminist pedagogy literature in psychology suggests that each teacher's feminist theoretical base, hence her feminist values and beliefs, determines her feminist pedagogy (Enns & Sinacore-Guinn, 1999; Forrest & Rosenberg, 1997). Enns and Sinacore-Guinn (1999) speculated as to the goals and strategies that would be associated with radical, liberal, cultural, socialist, women of color, lesbian, and post-modern feminisms. Yet, Forrest and Rosenberg (1997) noted that the preponderance of the feminist pedagogy literature has been written from a radical feminist perspective.

Thus, it is not surprising that we found among the faculty sample that a radical feminist theoretical orientation related to all feminist teaching practice scales (i.e., Personal Experience, Communal/Collaborative, Social Action, Feminist Course Content, Process). Also consistent with the literature, we found that our Liberal/Cultural scale was correlated with all teaching practices scales except Social Action. This suggests that encouraging their students to participate in social action may not be important to those who are primarily concerned with individual women's equality or creating collaborative classrooms. Enns and Sinacore-Guinn (1999) noted that, "In contrast to the liberal and cultural feminist values of individual autonomy and growth, radical feminism emphasizes the centrality of social transformation that can only be accomplished by the dramatic alteration of cultural values through the vehicle of social activism (p. 12)." Future researchers may further investigate the differential patterns of feminist pedagogy among feminist psychologists with varying feminist theoretical orientations, especially by using measures that make finer distinctions among all of the major theoretical camps (e.g., radical, socialist, liberal, cultural, women of color, lesbian, and postmodern). By clarifying the various manifestations of feminist pedagogy in psychology, feminist teachers will be better positioned to adhere to the call by Forrest and Rosenberg (1997) to create a systematic and coherent agenda for feminist pedagogy in psychology, "similar to feminist psychology's clearly articulated agendas" in research, theory, and therapy practice (p. 189).

The Multicultural orientation scale provided results that, although intriguing, were less clear. This scale demonstrated no relationship to feminist teaching practices, except for a negative relationship with the Social Action scale. At first glance, this negative correlation is perplexing given the close tie between women of color feminisms and activism (Enns & Sinacore-Guinn, 1999). It may be that multicultural feminists' concern about discrimination based on variables other than sex was not explicitly recognized in the survey. Furthermore, multicultural feminists, because of their focus on diversity among women, may be more aware of the fact that, for many women, social action is not an easy choice to make. That is, due to limited time, freedom, family support, or other resources, some women may not have the option of participating in social activist pursuits. Furthermore, the teachers themselves may be in more tenuous positions within the academy and thus less able to challenge the dominant power structure.

The lack of relationship between multicultural feminist orientation and the Personal Experience, Communal, Course Content, or Process scales could reflect a lack of integration between feminism and multiculturalism. Although feminist scholars have begun to respond to the critiques of multicultural feminists, it may be that true integration has yet to be realized. In fact, this may be reflected in the survey itself. We included items on the importance of hearing multiple views and attending to multiple oppressions, but we had no items that specifically mentioned women of color or lesbians. Though such items may not have had a direct effect on the correlations, their absence may reflect the larger issue of the survey's inclusivity, and thus may have contributed to an interpretation of the survey as too narrowly defined. Future researchers could investigate the relationship between multicultural feminist beliefs and social action within feminist pedagogy. Furthermore, future scholarship should pay particular attention to bringing multiculturalism to the center of feminist pedagogy, rather than simply to the periphery.

The students in this sample presented a fairly uncomplicated view of their professors' feminist theoretical orientation, feminist identification, and feminist teaching practices, in that they were all significantly related. It may be that because faculty, as opposed to students, actually experience the struggle of attempting to create feminist classrooms, their perceptions of feminist pedagogy are more complex and nuanced than the students'. Yet, the results of the exploratory research question suggest that the students perceive themselves as receiving less feminist teaching than their professors perceive they are providing. We speculate that this may be because students are less aware of it than the teacher, who is consciously working to create a specific learning environment in her classroom. Or, it may be that professors are not actually able to teach from a feminist perspective as much as they would prefer because of institutional requirements and barriers (e.g., large lecture classes, expectation to cover specific material) or limited experience beyond traditional pedagogical approaches. Future researchers may help to clarify the nature of this difference, either larger scale quantitative studies or more in-depth qualitative studies that examine students' perceptions of feminist teaching would be helpful.

Dealing with power and authority. Responses from the open-ended questions indicated that, just as there are no universal rules for feminist pedagogy (Forrest & Rosenberg, 1997; Lewis, 1990; Manicom, 1992), there are no predetermined guidelines for handling power relations in a feminist classroom. Each teacher's relationship to power is unique and complex. This is consistent with Manicom's (1992) suggestion that the notion of minimizing the teacher's authority and sharing power with the students has been at times romanticized among feminist pedagogy scholars, rather than being appropriately conceptualized as complex and variably applicable. What is clear in the current study is that these feminist teachers consciously approach and make decisions about power relations in their work as educators. Furthermore, just as issues of power are at the core of feminism (Richardson, 1982), power relations seem to be at the core of multiple areas that concern feminist teachers (e.g., evaluating students, deciding how they will use their own power, power imbalances in the classroom and the larger society, sharing power with students, minimizing the hierarchies). Thus, there are multiple faces of feminist pedagogy based exclusively on issues of power, and one common thread throughout is that feminist teachers prioritize the addressing of these issues.

Feedback. Survey responses from this study suggest that feminist teachers are highly appreciated by their students. However, participants also conveyed that students may be uncomfortable with the feminist classroom or resent the responsibility and amount of work that are inherent in it. Furthermore, some of the faculty in this sample pointed out that students often are not appreciative of their experiences until some time after the class has ended. Thus, positive feedback may be delayed and have little impact on immediate teacher evaluations. Finally, the faculty in this sample generally reported that their superiors and colleagues are unaware of what they do in class, including the amount of work involved in creating a feminist classroom. Despite this lack of acknowledgment from superiors, these faculty reported primarily positive feedback from students and conveyed a sense that they find many rewards in feminist teaching. One possible project to further a feminist pedagogy agenda in psychology would be the development of a list of psychology programs that offer feminist learning experiences. This list could then be used to inform students and faculty who are searching for programs, as well as to encourage networking among feminist teachers regarding approaches to feminist pedagogy.

Feminist identification. The majority of the participants did not indicate whether or not they publicly label themselves or their classes as feminist. But those faculty who did noted that their students often are not aware that they are experiencing feminist teaching. Furthermore, some of the students denied that their teacher was a feminist—just as their teachers suspected.

It appears that some faculty believe that they are more likely to accomplish their goals (e.g., getting students actively involved with the material, raising students' consciousness, increasing student's critical thinking) if they avoid describing their teaching methods or world view as feminist. This raises important questions for the future of feminist pedagogy. Can we achieve our goals as feminists without raising consciousness as to what feminism is and has done? Can a teacher practice feminist pedagogy without being congruent (i.e., values and expression of values not the same)? Will women be more at risk for being silenced if we choose to avoid the feminist label? Or, is using it silencing others? One student in this study clearly depicted the negative reaction that sometimes accompanies the word, feminist, "My teacher is wonderful, but she is NOT a feminist!" Clearly, this creates a difficult situation for the feminist teacher. Future research may explore these questions and future scholarship may attempt to build a dialogue about how to deal with students' resistance to feminism, without losing the student and without losing track of the course agenda.

Students' perspective. As previously noted, feminist pedagogy varies with the teacher and the students (Dunn, 1993; Lather, 1991). Indeed, student responses to the open-ended questions in this study reveal a variety of student reactions to (and subsequent needs for) feminist teaching. Although we had no selection criterion that required the students in this study to be feminist, the majority of these students seem to have positive relationships with their teachers and positive reactions to their teaching methods. Some conveyed an appreciation for focusing honestly on process and relationship issues, and others described their classmates as uncomfortable with these and other feminist pedagogical practices. However, most of the responses reflected an awareness that participation in a feminist classroom is challenging for everyone involved. Schniedewind's (1993) suggestion that some students may require specific guidance from the beginning about *how* to participate in a feminist classroom, thus may be a useful guideline for feminist teachers.

Finally, the responses from this survey suggest that students experience both positive and negative feedback for their participation in a feminist classroom. Therefore, it seems important to be aware of not only the direct impact of the feminist classroom experience, but the indirect impact that occurs beyond the classroom itself. Future researchers could explore the experiences of students in feminist classes, such as the extent and effects of feedback from peers and other professors or how they integrate their classroom experiences into the rest of their social and academic lives. Furthermore, feminist teachers could encourage students to discuss these experiences in class or write about them in journals.

CONCLUSION

To conclude, there are three themes which are woven throughout this chapter that we would like to highlight: (a) the centrality of power and authority issues in feminist pedagogy, (b) the relationship between multiculturalism and feminist pedagogy, and (c) the complexity and unique nature of each teacher's feminist pedagogy.

The first theme that we wish to review is the centrality of issues of power and authority within feminist pedagogy. Just as power relations are a primary concern of feminist and multicultural thought, these issues arise in multiple areas of the feminist classroom. For example, feminist pedagogy is a direct reaction to the oppressive instructional methods of mainstream education in which students are trained to ingest passively the knowledge and opinions of the teacher who is the "authority on the subject." Thus, feminist teachers struggle with their own authority (e.g., how to evaluate students) and strive to create non-hierarchical classrooms. Results from our survey indicate that there are a variety of opinions on how to "use their authority in the classroom." The common thread seems to be an attempt to strike the balances of minimizing the hierarchy without disempowering themselves and using their authority without disempowering their students.

A second salient theme of this chapter is the influence of multiculturalism on feminist pedagogy. Although recent scholarship on feminist pedagogy emphasizes the valuing of diversity and the integral nature of multiculturalism, our survey results raised interesting questions as to whether this integration has yet been realized. The scale that represented multicultural values was not related to the faculty's identification of themselves as feminist, nor was it related to feminist teaching practices. In fact, it yielded a negative relation to social action. This may be a reflection of limitations of the survey—the sample was primarily White, and the teaching practice items included more on sex and gender than on race, ethnicity, sexual orientation, disability, or class. However, we think it is important for feminist teachers to continue reflecting on the interactions among race, ethnicity, sexual orientation, able-bodiness, and sex/gender within their classrooms. The literature suggests that practitioners of feminist pedagogy strive to value all voices within the classroom community and are aware that for a single individual student there may be multiple voices, which stem from multiple positions of oppression and privilege (Forrest & Rosenberg, 1997).

The third and final theme is related to feminist pedagogy's complicated and elusive nature. Feminist pedagogy often is described in the literature as the fusing of feminist values into the process and methods of teaching. Stated in a different manner, the feminist teacher's feminist theoretical orientation naturally will define her pedagogy. For example, our findings suggest that social action may be incorporated only by faculty with radical feminist beliefs. Also, just as feminist values and identity change and evolve overtime, so does each teacher's pedagogy. Clearly, there is no single definition to represent feminist pedagogy adequately. Thus, feminist pedagogy in practice is an inherently personal venture, and one goal of feminist pedagogy may be to achieve congruence between one's feminist values and one's instructional style and methods.

However, our survey indicates that at least a small proportion of feminist psychologists choose to teach their classes without explicitly identifying themselves or their classes as feminist. It seems that these women foresee resistance and barriers from students and/or administration that would result from their identifying themselves as feminist. In weighing the costs of identifying with the costs of not identifying, they choose the latter. Indeed, some of these teachers in our survey stated that identifying as feminist tends to undermine their ability to make progress with their students. But, if feminist pedagogy is a means of integrating the teacher's personal experience (i.e., her values and beliefs) within the academic classroom (itself an example of balancing dichotomies), does refraining from identifying as feminist preclude that feminist teacher from being congruent in her work?

We propose that this is a question that must be answered by each individual feminist teacher. For different teachers, in different classroom and administrative environments, their positions as feminists may naturally guide them in opposing directions on this question. Practicing feminist pedagogy can be rewarding, but it can also be a complicated struggle. The previously mentioned quote of one student in our study, "My teacher is wonderful but she is NOT a feminist!" provides only one example of the catch-22s that unfortunately are not uncommon among feminist teachers. Thus, for the feminist teacher, self-reflection is an integral and essential component of creating her unique and genuine approach to education.

Despite the difficulties inherent in practicing feminist pedagogy, the literature as well as the results from our survey suggest that feminist teachers find it to be very rewarding. Also, the students in our survey overwhelmingly described their experiences in a feminist psychology classroom as positive. Thus, we highly recommend that teachers and students of psychology continue to create and/or seek out the experiences available through a feminist pedagogical approach, and thereby contribute to charting a new pedagogical course in feminist psychology.

NOTE

We are grateful to Shanda Blaylock and Helena Kwon, who assisted with data collection and data entry; Eric Marx, who provided statistical consultation; and Mark Hulbert, who provided valuable feedback on drafts of this chapter.

REFERENCES

Ayers-Nachamkin, B. (1992). A feminist approach to the introductory statistics course. *Women's Studies Quarterly, 20* (1/2), 86–94.
Bell, L. (1993). Hearing all our voices: Applications of feminist pedagogy to conferences, speeches, and panel presentations. *Women's Studies Quarterly, 21* (3/4), 107–113.
Bezucha, R. J. (1985). Feminist pedagogy as a subversive activity. In M. Culley & C. Portuges (Eds.), *Gendered subjects: The dynamics of feminist teaching* (pp. 81–95). Boston: Routledge & Kegan Paul.

Briskin, L., & Coulter, R. P. (1992). Feminist pedagogy: Challenging the normative. *Canadian Journal of Education, 17*, 247–263.

Brown, L. (1994). *Subversive dialogues: Theory in feminist therapy.* New York: Basic Books.

Carmen, E., & Driver, F. (1982). Teaching women's studies: Values in conflict. *Psychology of Women Quarterly, 7*, 81–95.

Cohen, B., & McKee, M. (1999). *An exploration of mastery learning from a feminist pedagogy perspective.* Unpublished manuscript.

Currie, D. H. (1992). Subject-ivity in the classroom: Feminism meets academe. *Canadian Journal of Education, 17*, 341–363.

DeFour, D. C., & Paludi, M. A. (1991). Integrating scholarship on ethnicity into the psychology of women course. *Teaching of Psychology, 18*, 85–90.

Dunn, K. (1993). Feminist teaching: Who are your students? *Women's Studies Quarterly, 21* (3/4), 39–45.

Enns, C. Z. (1997). *Feminist theories and feminist psychotherapies.* New York: Harrington Park Press.

Enns, C. Z., & Sinacore-Guinn, A. (1999). *Feminist theories and feminist pedagogies: Common principles, diverse interpretations.* Manuscript in preparation.

Fassinger, R. E. (1990). Causal models of career choice in two samples of college women. *Journal of Vocational Behavior, 36*, 225–248.

Fisher, B. M. (1982). Professing feminism: Feminist academics and the women's movement. *Psychology of Women Quarterly, 7*, 55–69.

Fisher, B. M. (1993). The heart has its reasons: Feeling, thinking, and community-building in feminist education. *Women's Studies Quarterly, 21* (3/4), 75–87.

Forrest, L., & Rosenberg, F. (1997). A review of the feminist pedagogy literature: The neglected child of feminist psychology. *Applied & Preventive Psychology, 6*, 179–192.

Friedman, S. S. (1985). Authority in the feminist classroom: A contradiction in terms? In M. Culley & C. Portuges (Eds.), *Gendered subjects: The dynamics of feminist teaching* (pp. 29–48). Boston: Routledge & Kegan Paul.

Lather, P. (1991). *Getting smart: Feminist research and pedagogy within the postmodern.* New York: Routledge.

Lewis, M. (1990). Interrupting patriarchy: Politics, resistance, and transformation in the feminist classroom. *Harvard Educational Review, 60*, 467–487.

MacDermid, S. M., Jurich, J. A., Myers-Walls, J. A., & Pelo, A. (1992). Feminist teaching: Effective education. *Family Relations, 41*, 31–38.

Maher, F. (1985). Classroom pedagogy and the new scholarship on women. In M. Culley & C. Portuges (Eds.), *Gendered subjects: The dynamics of feminist teaching* (pp. 29–48). Boston: Routledge & Kegan Paul.

Maher, F., & Tetreault, M. (1996). Women's ways of knowing in women's studies, feminist pedagogies, and feminist theories. In N. Goldberger, T. Tarule, B. Clinchy, & M. Belenky (Eds.), *Knowledge, difference, and power* (pp. 149–174). New York: Basic Books.

Manicom, A. (1992). Feminist pedagogy: Transformations, standpoints, and politics. *Canadian Journal of Education, 17*, 365–389.

Matlin, M. (1989). Teaching psychology of women: A survey of instructors. *Psychology of Women Quarterly, 13*, 245–261.

Richardson, M. S. (1982). Sources of tension in teaching the psychology of women. *Psychology of Women Quarterly, 7,* 45–54.

Schniedewind, N. (1993). Teaching feminist process in the 1990s. *Women's Studies Quarterly, 21* (3/4), 17–29.

Shrewsbury, C. M. (1993). What is feminist pedagogy? *Women's Studies Quarterly, 21* (3/4), 8–16.

The TWIG Writing Group (1998). A feminist perspective on graduate student–advisor relationship. *Feminist Teacher, 10* (1), 17–25.

Thompson, M. E. (1993). Diversity in the classroom: Creating opportunities for learning feminist theory. *Women's Studies Quarterly, 21* (3/4), 114–121.

Yoder, J. D., & Kahn, A. S. (1993). Working toward an inclusive psychology of women. *American Psychologist, 48,* 846–850.

Chapter 4

Women of Color and Feminist Psychology: Moving from Criticism and Critique to Integration and Application

Michelle K. Williams, Terry McCandies,
and Michelle R. Dunlap

Criticizing feminist ideology is and always has been a favorite pastime of various conservative groups; however, not all criticisms have come from the far right. Some of the most vocal critics have been women activists, writers, and scholars, many of whom have been women of color. Women such as Lucie Cheng (1984), Esther Ngan-Ling Chow (1987), Patricia Hill Collins (1991), Lillian Comas-Diaz (1991), Angela Davis (1983), Alma Garcia (1995), bell hooks (1984), Audre Lorde (1984), Barbara Smith (1998), Alice Walker (1995), and many others have actively championed women's rights but at the same time criticized feminist ideology for being narrowly focused, culturally insensitive, and non-representative of the full spectrum of women and women's issues. Traditionally, feminist theories have focused primarily on issues relevant to European-American middle-class women, such as recognizing gender inequality, advocating egalitarian gender roles, and promoting political activism for the rights of women (Hunter & Sellers, 1998). Gender, then, has become the primary, and for some feminists, the exclusive dimension on which equality and power are evaluated and ultimately redistributed in public and private domains. For many women, however, the complexity of negotiating membership in multiply oppressed groups (e.g., race, gender, class, age, physical abilities, sexual orientation) requires an integration and conceptualization of power and oppression that moves beyond a single dimension.

Although many feminists have acknowledged the lack of inclusion of ethnic minority women's issues in feminist theory, limitations remain in how these issues are addressed theoretically, empirically, and experientially (Burman, 1998; Fine, 1985; Landrine, 1995; Spelman, 1988). The goals of this chapter are to address some of the concerns of women of color[1] regarding the applicability of feminist theory and feminist psychology to diverse experiences and to offer suggestions for improving intercultural relationships between women of color feminists and European-American feminists. First, we address specific criticisms of feminist theory and feminist psychology regarding the influence of race, ethnicity, and culture. Second, we present several responses to these criticisms by feminist scholars and discuss areas of continued concern. Third, we demonstrate specific ways in which feminist beliefs that are inclusive may not always translate into culturally sensitive interactions with women of color. Last, we provide suggestions and examples for integrating cultural awareness and inclusive behaviors into feminist ideology and feminist interactions.

There have been a number of scholarly analyses of feminist psychology, and a comprehensive review and critique is beyond the scope of this chapter (for reviews see Burman, 1998; Golden, 1996; Tong, 1998). We will focus primarily on critiques of feminist psychology regarding women of color. We do, however, acknowledge that other topics such as socioeconomic status, sexual orientation and sexual identity, age, physical abilities, spirituality, and the intersection of these various categories are also important areas of concern that should be addressed and critically evaluated within current feminist psychology models.

We also recognize that women of color and European-American women represent a diversity of women with potential membership in several oppressed groups as well as a variety of individual experiences and cultural realities. Although we often refer to women of color and European-American women collectively as distinctive groups, we understand the importance of acknowledging the complexity and diversity within ethnic groups as well as the similarities and commonalities between groups. We could not write this chapter, however, without also emphasizing that race, gender, and class are constructs that are socially derived, contrived, and maintained by institutions, individuals, and organized systems of oppression; therefore individual experiences cannot be divorced from these larger sociocultural, economic, and political contexts. It is from this perspective, one of collective cultural realities, that we write this chapter.

We are each women of color who represent a diversity of experiences and training. Michelle Williams is a clinical psychologist and the daughter of an African-American father and Korean mother. Terry McCandies is an African-American clinical psychologist who specializes in childhood and developmental issues. Michelle Dunlap, the daughter of an African-American mother and biracial father, was trained as a social psychologist but incorporates multidisciplinary perspectives in her work. As women of color psychologists, we each feel personally committed to address issues of power and privilege when they take place in larger sociopolitical domains; however, we also feel compelled to address these same issues when they take place in more immediate domains, such as within our profession, within our gender, and within our respective ethnic groups.

WHAT IS FEMINIST PSYCHOLOGY?

Like the evolution of feminist theory, gender studies, and the psychology of women, feminist psychology continues to change and develop multiple identities. Feminist psychology is typically conceptualized as one of the theoretical underpinnings found in both gender studies and the psychology of women (Burman, 1998; Crawford & Unger, 2000). Although a number of different models are utilized in feminist psychology including essentialist models (e.g., Firestone, 1970), social constructionist models (e.g., Hare-Mustin & Marecek, 1990), and psychodynamic models (e.g., Chodorow, 1989), the primary goals of feminist psychology are to address and challenge the tendency of psychological research, theories, and practice to exclude, minimize, and pathologize the development and experiences of women (Collins, 1998).

Because psychology has traditionally utilized androcentric frameworks as normative models, qualities associated with female development are often perceived and interpreted as pathological and/or deficient (Bem, 1996). To exemplify this androcentric tendency, one need only look at the abundant literature on assertive communication (Bloom, Coburn, & Perlman, 1980; Butler, 1981; Phelps & Austin, 1975). The assertiveness literature has focused primarily on differences in communicative styles between men and women and the implications of these differences for women (Crawford, 1998). According to Crawford (1998), androcentric frameworks have resulted in several flawed assumptions in the assertiveness training literature. First, men's communicative styles are assumed to be the normative or preferred communicative style for both men and women. Second, when women and men do differ in communicative styles, those differences are interpreted as deficiencies on the part of women and not on the part of men. Third, the literature does not address the influence of power, status, oppression, and socialization on women's experiences and styles of communication in every day interactions.

As a result of these flawed assumptions, numerous intervention programs and self help manuals were developed and implemented in order to train women to be more assertive and directive when communicating (Crawford, 1998). Implicit in these programs is the assumption that women's communicative styles are deficient and problematic and that any differences in status between men and women can be alleviated if women, in essence, could learn to communicate more like men. Although intended to address the power differences between men and women, some of the assertiveness literature inadvertently perpetuated images of women as pathological and weak and men as normative and powerful. A similar criticism can be lodged at feminist psychologists who developed and proposed models of gender development that although intended to address the concerns of all women, promoted models that negated and/or pathologized the experiences of women of color.

WHAT ARE SOME CRITICISMS OF FEMINIST PSYCHOLOGY REGARDING WOMEN OF COLOR?

Nancy Chodorow (1978), Mary Crawford (1995), Carol Gilligan (1982), Rachel Hare-Mustin and Jeanne Marecek (1990), Jean Baker Miller (1976), Rhoda Unger (1983), and many other feminists have developed theoretical models and therapeutic interventions designed to produce paradigmatic shifts in the perceptions, treatment, and conceptualizations of women. The substantial increase in the number of psychology of women courses, women's studies programs and departments, and journals devoted to gender and women's studies is testament to their influence and contributions to the field of psychology. Despite these progressive changes, women of color remain substantially underrepresented in these same domains. For example, Fine (1985, 1997) has consistently criticized feminist psychology for being non-representative of the full spectrum of women, especially ethnic minority women, working class and poor women, and sexual minorities. She has also called upon European-American feminists to examine the role of race and privilege in their own psychological development and to approach feminist ideology and activism from a culturally grounded foundation (Fine, 1997). In this section, we will address four specific criticisms of feminist psychology and its application to women of color.

Criticism 1: "Woman" as Universal

One of the most consistent criticisms of feminist psychology has been its tendency to advocate an all-inclusive definition of "woman" (Collins, 1991; Comas-Diaz, 1991). Historically, feminist theorists minimized or ignored individual and group differences in women's experiences. Feminists called to task the profession of psychology for its use of sexist language, sexist images, and the systematic omission of female representation in psychological literature. Consequently, the exclusive use of masculine pronouns and male only images and research samples are no longer acceptable practices in psychology. Feminist scholars, nevertheless, in their own work omitted representations of women of color and promoted activist agendas that excluded the experiences of women of color. Feminist scholars often use the word "woman" unqualified implying universal images of women whereby gender is primary over other identities. Critics of feminist psychology have argued against the notion that regardless of race, class, or sexual orientation, all women share a basic biological and social bond that produces a commonality of experience, primarily gender oppression, which outweighs, overshadows, or minimizes individual and group differences (di Stefano, 1990).

Feminist psychologists criticized the androcentric bias of traditional psychology for its inadequate and inappropriate conceptualizations of women but did not initially address the Eurocentric bias of feminist theories as inadequate and inappropriate conceptualizations of women of color (Chow, 1987; Collins, 1991; Comas-Diaz, 1991; Spelman, 1988). Although "woman" in feminist psychology implied a universal woman, it did in fact refer to a very specific type of woman: European-American and middle-class (Collins, 1991; Golden, 1996; Guy-Sheftall, 1995). Patricia Hill Collins, in reference to books by Chodorow and Gilligan, stated, "while these two classics make key contributions to feminist theory, they simultaneously promote the notion of a generic woman who is white and middle class" (Collins, 1991, p. 8).

The Eurocentric bias of feminist psychology can be highlighted in the psychodynamic theories of women's development. Commonly referred to as relational or self-in-relation theories, these models were developed primarily by scholars at the Stone Center at Wellesley College (Henderson, 1997; Jordan, Kaplan, Miller, Stiver, & Surrey, 1991). The relational models conceptualize a woman's internal representation of self as inherently tied to her ability to develop, seek, desire, and maintain relationships (Miller, 1991). According to relational theories, the relationship most significant and instrumental in women's development is that of mother-daughter (Miller, 1991; Surrey, 1991). As a result of this primary relationship, women are more likely to develop relational qualities such as empathy, nurturance, emotionality, and sensitivity (Golden, 1996).

Consistent with psychodynamic theory, relational models rely heavily on attachment theory and unconscious representations of self and parents as integral in the development of gender roles and gender role socialization. Although a number of scholars have criticized and challenged relational theories for various reasons, women of color scholars have been particularly critical of the emphasis on attachment theory and the exclusivity of mother-daughter attachment as primary for gender role socialization. For many women of color, the attachment bond between mother and daughter is not necessarily the single most important relationship in a woman's development of self, identity, or gender role socialization (Collins, 1991; Spelman, 1988).

Many women of color develop multiple and interconnected relationships with immediate and extended family members, kinship networks, and community networks. Each and/or all of these various relationships can significantly impact a woman of color's self representations and gender role development. For instance, in African-American culture, many women develop intimate and critical bonds with "surrogate" mothers, such as older sisters, aunts, grandmothers, cousins, neighbors, and family friends. Similarly, the Latina concepts of *familism* and *compadrazgo*, the Confucian concept of *familial piety*, and the Native American concept of *tiospaye* (Weaver & White, 1997) also reflect a strong affective, psychological, and interpersonal connection to extended family members that can be as salient and as influential as nuclear family relationships (Falicov, 1982; Ho, 1991; Ramos-McKay, Comas-Diaz, & Rivera, 1988). These extended family relationships are easily exemplified in many collectivist cultures where familial terms are often used to refer to non-family members. For instance, in African-American culture, a female friend may be referred to as a "cousin" and other African-American women as "sisters." Similarly in Korean culture, a close female friend is referred to as *oni* (elder sister) and is afforded the same status and deference as one's own biological sister.

By not taking into account the influence of race and culture on gender role socialization, relational theories promoted a model of gender role development that assumed either all women experienced the same socialization or that the socialization experienced by European-American women was the preferred model for all women (Brown, 1990; Collins, 1991; Comas-Diaz, 1991). The androcentric bias of assertiveness training proposed by Crawford (1998) parallels the Eurocentric bias inherent in relational theories. First, mother-child attachment is assumed to be the normative or preferred attachment style for all women. Second, when women of color and European-American women differ, these differences are interpreted as deficiencies on the part of women of color and not on the part of European-American women. Third, relational theories did not address the influence of power, status, race, and oppression in the gender role socialization of diverse women. Thus, the unique experiences and development of women of color were excluded, minimized, and/or pathologized.

Criticism 2: Gender as Primary

Endorsing a unitary or universal image of women provides the basis for the second criticism of feminist theory: a hegemonic adherence to gender oppression and male privilege at the expense of other forms of oppression and privilege. There is the presumption that women, as a group, are powerless and oppressed by male dominated structures, traditions, and institutions and that men, as a group, possess greater power, status, and opportunity than women. Many feminist psychologists have ignored the differential experiences of power and privilege within gender and between various racial and ethnic groups. Because women of color experience both racism and sexism, the concepts of power and oppression often necessitate more complex conceptualizations than just gender subordination and male privilege (Griscom, 1992; Henderson, 1997; hooks, 1984, 1990). Many

European-American feminists who espouse a belief in cultural diversity often limit that interest to women of color at the exclusion of men of color. However, for many women of color, a thorough understanding and appreciation of their developmental and socialization experiences necessitates the inclusion of men of color.

Women of color not only have their own experiences with racism, but also empathize with and observe their brothers, fathers, sons, grandfathers, and husbands encounter and struggle against personal and institutional racism. Many women of color perceive men of color as allies in their struggle for equality and not as oppressors who possess greater power and status (Henley, Meng, O'Brien, McCarthy, & Sockloskie, 1998). For some women of color, race may provide a more salient sense of solidarity than gender, and racism may be experienced as a greater deterrent to equality than gender subordination. One should keep in mind that telling an African-American woman she should share a greater bond with her "White sister" than her "Black brother" could result in raised eyebrows, incredulous looks, or outright indignation. This cultural allegiance, however, does not preclude a woman of color feminist from acknowledging, challenging, and confronting sexism by men of color. It simply means that for many women of color, race, gender, sexual orientation, and class are neither hierarchical nor independent concepts. An African-American woman cannot fully experience empowerment if she is liberated as a woman but relegated to second class citizenship because of race. Likewise, a Puerto Rican woman can no more shed her "Puerto Rican-ness" when issues of gender arise than she can shed her "woman-ness" when issues of ethnicity arise.

The tendency to believe all women are indeed sisters based upon a chromosomal allegiance fails to recognize that one's ideology, attitudes, and activist agendas are filtered as much through cultural and racial lenses as they are through gendered lenses (McIntosh, 1992). Feminist psychologists have often failed to address the interplay among various forms of social, economic, and political oppression that can exist in the lives of many women. They have also failed to address the important dynamic of experiencing both oppression and privilege simultaneously; that is to say, one can lack power as a woman and yet possess privilege as a European-American woman (Fine, 1997; McIntosh, 1992).

Criticism 3: Lack of Representation in Research

A third criticism of feminist psychology has been the limited representation of women of color in psychological research and theory development. Despite an increase in research on women and gender studies, few researchers include significant numbers of ethnic minority women in their samples or specifically address issues relevant to ethnic minority women. One reason for this deficit is the continued use of college students enrolled

in psychology courses as the most frequent samples in psychological research (Sears, 1986; Walsh, 1989). Because ethnic minority women often
comprise very small percentages of these samples, many of these published
works lack external validity and may not generalize to women of color.
Community samples that include a cross-section of women by race, age,
sexual orientation, occupation, education, family configuration, and psychological outcomes are few and far between in the psychological literature.
Such samples would require substantial resources from funding institutions,
which remain limited unless the targeted group represents a public health
"problem" such as social service utilization and resource allocation. In addition, many researchers are inadequately trained to deal with issues relevant to women of color and thus limit their research to populations that
are most familiar to them.

Reid and Kelly (1994) investigated the number of articles that reported
ethnicity in two of the leading journals devoted to women's issues, *Psychology of Women Quarterly* and *Sex Roles*. From 1986–1991, 82% of
the articles in *Psychology of Women Quarterly* and 91% of those in *Sex
Roles* reported samples that were European-American only, majority
European-American, or did not provide information on ethnicity. According to Reid and Kelly (1994), many of the articles that did include ethnicity
were published in special issues devoted to women of color as opposed to
regular issues of the journals. In addition, many of these studies simply
reported the percentage of women of color in the sample but did not include any substantive analyses by ethnicity.

When research on women of color is conducted, it tends to concentrate
on specific problem areas such as poverty and teen pregnancy (Reid &
Kelly, 1994). In their review of several hundred psychological abstracts,
Reid and Kelly (1994) identified 24 areas that tended to focus on female
samples. In only four of these areas did more than 10% of the abstracts
include African-American women in the sample. These topics included marriage (17%), poverty (17.2%), teen pregnancy (17.1%), and sexism (15%).
The results were even more dismal for Latina Americans who comprised
less than 10% of all the abstracts that focused on female samples. In areas
such as therapy, self-esteem, identity, gender role attitudes, achievement,
stress, and psychological well being, less than 5% of the abstracts that
focused on women included women of color. No data were presented for
Asian-American and Native American women (Reid & Kelly, 1994).
Clearly, feminist researchers continue to focus on European-American
women despite the growing recognition by feminist psychologists that race,
ethnicity, and gender are important concepts to incorporate in psychological research (Reid & Comas-Diaz, 1990).

Criticism 4: Limited Theoretical Development

Although terms such as woman of color feminism (Henley et al., 1998), Womanism (Walker, 1995), Black feminism (Collins, 1991), and multicultural and global feminism (Tong, 1998) are becoming more common in the feminist literature, exactly how these terms apply to the individual experiences of women of color remains limited. Woman of color feminism provides a framework for understanding the importance of race and culture in women's development but additional theories and research are needed in order to distinguish between different ethnic and cultural groups as well as address the tremendous variation within ethnic groups. For example, a Mexican-American and a Chinese-American woman may both identify as women of color feminists because each recognizes the importance of culture in her development as a woman. However, they may differ drastically in the ways in which they conceptualize gender, ethnicity, feminism, and activism. These ideological variations are as salient within ethnic groups as they are between groups. For instance, an African-American feminist who endorses an Afrocentric orientation may differ considerably from one who does not endorse such an orientation, and yet both may identify as woman of color feminists. In terms of ideology and activism, feminist theorists may need to delineate more than one type of woman of color feminism.

Without additional development, woman of color feminism may be reduced to merely a label applied to women of color, and thus run the risk of becoming a marginalized form of feminism. On the surface, woman of color feminism does not appear to differ much from socialist feminism. According to Henley et al. (1998, p. 321), woman of color feminism is a response to criticisms of the women's movement by women of color and involves "the recognition of poverty, racism, and ethnocentrism as equal concerns with sexism." On the other hand, the authors define socialist feminism as "[putting] neither class nor gender nor race as the primary division between people . . . but sees oppression based on all of them as equally bad and equally in need of consideration" (Henley et al., 1998, pp. 320–321).

Conceptually, there appears to be little that differentiates women of color feminism from socialist feminism. If you believe racism, classism, and sexism are equally important and intertwined issues and you happen to be a woman of color, then you may be identified as a woman of color feminist. If by chance, you endorse these same beliefs and you are not a woman of color, then you may be identified as a socialist feminist. There are, of course, more fundamental differences between woman of color feminism and socialist feminism, such as the ways in which various forms of oppression are addressed and an adherence to Marxist beliefs; however, these more fundamental differences tend to get lost when broad and general descriptors are used to account for all women's experiences. Because women of color are very diverse, woman of color feminism should reflect and encompass a diversity of theoretical and ideological perspectives.

HOW HAS FEMINIST PSYCHOLOGY RESPONDED TO CRITICISMS OF ETHNOCENTRISM?

Women of color have always participated in and contributed to feminist theorizing and grass roots activism. Women of color along with European-American feminists have acknowledged the negative effects of racism, sexism, classism, and heterosexism, and have advocated for greater inclusion of diverse women's experiences in feminist scholarship and activism. Many feminist scholars have attempted to address the criticisms of feminist theory as ethnocentric and exclusive (Brown, 1990).

An example of changes in the field can be demonstrated by the various publications produced by the Stone Center. In 1991 the Stone Center published *Women's Growth in Connection: Writings from the Stone Center* (Jordan, Kaplan, Miller, Stiver, & Surrey, 1991) which presented a number of essays by prominent relational theorists and feminist psychologists concerning the process of gender socialization for women. None of the essays, however, discussed the importance of culture and ethnicity in women's development and gender role socialization. In fact, the topic index of the book did not even include the terms race, culture, or specific ethnic labels (i.e. African American, Chinese American). In response to the criticism that relational theories were biased, the Stone Center invited several prominent scholars to provide a more diverse and cross-cultural examination of relational theories and women's development. The result was the 1997 publication of *Women's Growth and Diversity: More Writings from the Stone Center*, which included essays on the experiences of ethnic minority women, lesbian experiences, racial identity, and the impact of racism on women's development (Jordan, 1997).

Currently, most psychology of women textbooks and feminist psychology literature routinely include sections and/or chapters devoted to cross-cultural issues (Burman, 1998; Chrisler, Golden, & Rozee, 2000; Crawford & Unger, 2000; Tong, 1998). Carla Golden's (1996) critique of the Stone Center's theories specifically addressed the criticism that feminist psychology promotes a Eurocentric image of women. Rather than leave the term woman unqualified as is the typical practice, Golden (1996) specifically titled her critique "Relational Theories of White Women's Development." In addition, organizations devoted to women's issues such as the Association for Women in Psychology and Division 35 of the American Psychological Association have increased the diversity of their governing boards as well as created caucuses, sections, and committees devoted to issues of diversity. Feminist psychology continues to evolve and present different voices, and, as a result, the literature has become more reflective of the diversity of women's experiences. Despite these changes, however, there is still room for further development as women of color remain significantly underrepresented in feminist ideology, feminist organizations, and qualitative and quantitative research (Burman, 1998).

WHERE ARE WE NOW AS FEMINIST PSYCHOLOGISTS?

The progressive changes in the ever-evolving field of feminist psychology are indicative of a greater awareness by European-American feminists that the concerns and experiences of women who are not European-American, middle-class, or heterosexual are equally valid and that the field must actively address these concerns. Feminist psychologists who endorse socialist or liberal feminism have attempted to incorporate more multicultural perspectives into their theories, research, and attitudes. However, these more inclusive beliefs and attitudes do not always translate into inclusive and culturally sensitive behavior.

To demonstrate this inconsistency between inclusive ideology and culturally sensitive behavior, we will provide an example from one of the most notable areas of feminist theory: empowerment through the use of "voice." According to D'Almeida (1994), "silence represents the historical muting of women under the formidable institution known as patriarchy, that form of social organization in which males assume power and create for females an inferior status" (p. 1). Speaking out and using one's voice challenges the historical negation of women's experiences. For a European-American woman, the use of voice may be challenged by gender power relationships, but for a woman of color, the use of voice may be challenged by both sexism and racism. Thus, the feminist value of using one's voice as a form of empowerment may be more complex in cases where power relationships are more complicated and complex. How a woman of color chooses to express her voice may be influenced by a number of factors. As an illustration, consider the following hypothetical example[2]:

June is a young African-American feminist clinical psychologist working in a clinic among a team female psychologists. June recently joined the clinic and is the only African-American on the staff. After several months at the clinic, June is having a conversation with one of her supervisors, Barbara, a European-American feminist clinical psychologist. Barbara informs June that on several occasions during staff meetings, she has observed a tendency for June to minimize her accomplishments and contributions to the treatment staff. She is concerned that June does not feel efficacious about her clinical skills, achievements, or ability to express herself in the same assertive manner as their other colleagues. Barbara suggests that June should behave more confidently and assertively in meetings by taking full credit for the ideas she has implemented.

On the surface, this example typifies a supervisor's concern that a junior colleague is not being respected and may need some directive and supportive feedback. Although well intentioned, it does not address the specific cultural and racial issues that June, as an African-American woman, may have to negotiate in this particular situation. Collins has referred to the experiences of women of color as "interlocking systems of oppression" (Collins, 1991, pp. 16, 225) whereby race, class, and gender are interconnected and holistic concepts rather than independent or additive experiences of oppression. In the hypothetical example, June's behavior may be influenced by a number of issues that are interconnected and complex. To demonstrate the complexity of these issues, we will discuss how some specific cultural issues may influence June's behavior including a communal worldview, cultural norms, cultural differences in expressive behavior, reactions to racism, and avoidance of stereotypes and labeling.

Cultural Issue: Communal Worldview

The tendency to express modesty about one's accomplishments or de-emphasize one's success is a common and normative experience in many collectivist cultures and often reflects a communal sense of achievement rather than a need for individual recognition. Because the individual exists only in relation to her connection to family, kinship networks, mentors, and respected elders, any success or achievement is a consequence of those relationships and rarely due to individual effort alone (Myers, 1988; Shade, 1989; Willis, 1998). Therefore, it is not uncommon for African Americans to acknowledge their relationship with God, ancestors, family, friends, and members of the community for minor as well as major achievements. Rather than minimizing her contributions, June may have been demonstrating reverence and respect to all those who have contributed to her development and who continue to do so, including Barbara and the rest of the treatment staff. She may perceive her success as shared by the entire treatment staff and not necessarily her sole contribution. These acknowledgements are expressed both explicitly and implicitly and reflect cultural continuity and not necessarily gender role socialization as may be the case in European-American culture (Willis, 1998).

Cultural Issue: Cultural Norms

If June had been an Asian American, she may have been expressing the cultural norm of modesty. In many Asian cultures, taking direct credit for one's success is considered improper and impolite (Chan, 1998; Sue & Sue, 1990). One of the authors recalled as a child, her Korean mother repeatedly telling her that it would be rude and improper to "brag" about her success. Taking individual credit implies that others have not worked as hard or contributed as much and would be perceived culturally as a selfish and insensitive act. A woman need not acknowledge that she has succeeded at a task; if she has done well, others (usually elders) will acknowledge her success. Thus in Korean culture, it would have been more than appropriate for Barbara, as the supervisor, to acknowledge June's contributions but inappropriate for June to do so directly.

Cultural Issue: Differences in Expressive Styles

Yet another possibility for June's behavior may be cultural differences in how women express assertive behavior. In a study conducted by Landrine, Klonoff, and Brown-Collins (1992), African-American and European-American women were asked to define the terms assertive and passive using various descriptors. According to the results, African-American women tended to interpret passive and assertive as opposite terms defining passive as "don't say what I really think" and assertive as "say whatever's on my mind." European-American women, on the other hand, tended to interpret the two terms very differently with passive defined as "laid back/easy-going" and assertive as "stand up for myself." African-American and European-American women may differ in their expression of passive and assertive behaviors because each attaches a different meaning to the words. In the example, Barbara encourages June to behave more assertively at meetings. June, on the other hand, may feel she is being assertive because she is free to speak her mind if she chooses to do so. Alternatively, June may not be sure it is safe to express herself freely and is assessing when it will be safe and appropriate to do so.

Cultural Issue: Reactions to Racism

Staying with the hypothetical example, in addition to cultural norms and differences in expression, June's behavior may also reflect the realities of racism. Calling attention to oneself—even positive attention—opens one up for greater scrutiny (Kanter & Stein, 1980). Historically, African-American women have had a greater range of people who may feel threatened by their presence and their success. A familiar "mother wit" for many African Americans is not disclosing too much information about oneself or one's feelings, especially to European Americans, until a firm foundation of trust has been established. The ability to use one's voice in a safe and trusting environment, for some women of color, may take more time to establish than it does for European-American women (Collins, 1991; Uttal, 1990). Hale-Benson (1986), Shade (1989), and Collins (1991) have all reflected on the tendency of African Americans to scrutinize nonverbal behaviors such as facial expressions and body language in order to determine a speaker's intent before deciding if a situation is interpersonally safe. This lack of disclosure in African-American women is considered a survival strategy and not a form of passivity. Uttal (1990), a woman of color, demonstrated this caution when describing her experiences in European-American feminist groups, "every time I try to verbalize my thoughts, I think over and over again in my head how to state my thoughts diplomatically. Yet even with the careful attention to words, after I speak I always end up feeling that I have breached a code of conduct" (p. 317).

Cultural Issue: Avoidance of Stereotypes and Labeling

Yet another perspective that might assist in our understanding of June's behavior is the influence of stereotypes about African-American women. Many women of color, especially academics and professionals, work in environments where they are often the only person of color or the only woman of color. As such, they may feel more isolated and sensitive to stereotypes and generalizations about their behavior and responses (Gregory, 1995; James & Farmer, 1993; Lois, 1997). Because African Americans tend to endorse more egalitarian gender roles than European Americans (Hale-Benson, 1986), African-American women are less restricted by rigid gender roles stereotypes than European-American women. However, it is this same cultural strength that has fed the stereotype of the loud, aggressive, unfeminine Black woman (Collins, 1991; Wallace, 1991; West, 1995). William Cross (1991) has described this experience as "spot light" anxiety, whereby African Americans become so overly sensitive to negative stereotypes they constantly monitor and assess their behavior in an effort to avoid validating these stereotypes. Some women of color may experience spot light anxiety to such a degree that they actively engage in efforts to not appear "too ethnic," "too Black," "too Puerto Rican," or "too Chinese." European-American women also experience similar vulnerabilities when they respond in ways inconsistent with gender role stereotypes; however, having other women available to validate one's struggle and model alternative responses can increase a woman's sense of security. When women of color are present, they are often the only woman of color in their respective professional and social environments (Lois, 1997). The experience of being the "only one" is applicable to European-American women in all male settings but may be overlooked in settings that are exclusively or predominately female represented. In predominately female settings, many women of color continue to experience being the "only one" and as result, may not take for granted the sense of female solidarity, validation, or security implied in these settings (James & Farmer, 1993).

In summary, various cultural issues may influence the hypothetical scenario involving June, Barbara, and their colleagues. At first glance, June's behavior may be interpreted as unassertive and Barbara's behavior as supportive. However, the interaction between June and Barbara may entail any number of complex issues and cultural factors. For example, Barbara's perceptions may be accurate and June really does feel less efficacious. On the other hand, June may have behaved consistent with African-American cultural norms or with a necessary degree of caution and self-protection resulting from a history of racism and discrimination. One must also consider Barbara's position as a European-American woman and supervisor and what impact this may have on the interaction between June and Barbara. Without at least considering these various factors, behaviors that are well intentioned may result in responses that are culturally insensitive. Integrating the role of culture into individual feminist interactions is an important component in charting a new course for feminist psychology. We will revisit the example of June and Barbara as we chart a new course for feminist psychology.

WHERE DO WE GO FROM HERE?

Women of color have participated in and contributed to feminist theorizing and activism since the onset of the women's movement in the United States. Sojourner Truth's poignant speech, *Ar'n't I a Woman*[3] not only addressed the inequities between men and women but also the unique challenges placed upon African-American women who must endure both racism and sexism. It is extraordinary that Truth's speech was given at a Women's Rights Convention 12 years before the Emancipation Proclamation formally ended slavery in the United States. Even at a time when African Americans, as a group, were not free citizens, women such as Sojourner Truth and Maria Stewart publicly championed the rights of both women and African Americans.

Feminist psychologists today are more likely to acknowledge the unique experiences of women of color as well as challenge the lack of diversity in feminist ideology. Awareness and acknowledgment are important steps toward progress; however, awareness and acknowledgement without subsequent action will only stifle progress. Despite a growing body of feminist literature, a considerable gap remains between our feminist ideals and our everyday realities (Comas-Diaz, 1991). Bridging this gap means transforming feminist psychology into a discipline that not only embraces diversity but challenges women to shift their cultural worldview. This transformation process will require complex solutions and conceptualizations and may be a life long process for many women. We will outline several ways in which feminist psychology as a discipline and feminist psychologists as individuals can move from awareness to integration and action.

Recommendation 1: Expect Variability and Complexity

Women of color encompass a diversity of experiences, cultures, and beliefs. Acculturation, racial identity, socialization, and cultural affiliation vary considerably across, between, and within different racial and ethnic groups. Despite having shared experiences with other women, women of color vary in their cultural values, beliefs about gender and gender roles, and family and community relationships. One of the dangers of cultural awareness is the potential to overgeneralize specific behaviors and experiences to all members of a group. Many European-American feminists have limited contact and interactions with women of color and often when those interactions do occur, they are relegated to very specific situations or environments. The experience of race and gender for any given woman is complex and typically cannot be reduced to a single issue, concept, situation, or encounter.

Many women of color are socialized within two dichotomous worldviews: communal and individualist. W.E.B. Du Bois (1903) referred to this phenomenon as "dual consciousness" whereby African Americans must live and negotiate within and between two worlds: one African-American and the other European-American. Others have referred to this same experience as biculturalism; that is, people of color often move between the dominant culture and their minority group culture (LaFromboise, Coleman, & Gerton, 1995). Biculturalism does not imply one constantly changes cultural affiliation from one context to the next but rather, that one is able to maintain a cultural identity that is cohesive and positive even when the environment does not reflect nor validate that identity. The ability to exercise this cultural fluidity can be resourceful and adaptive but at the same time, stressful and frustrating (Guy-Sheftall, 1995).

Take for example, a Japanese-American woman who is socialized within a family and culture that values interconnected and interdependent relationships. Her behavior reflects upon her family, her community, and her culture rather than simply her own individual efforts. Every achievement is a source of shared pride and every failure a source of communal shame. She defers to and respects those who are older and more experienced than she and takes personal responsibility for those who are younger and less experienced. This same woman is also socialized in a culture where individual achievement and competition are highly valued. She works in a setting where her successes and failures are a result of her individual effort and self-promotion. She is expected to speak, behave, and express herself in ways that may be less familiar to her. The two worlds in which she lives are not just different; at times, they are opposite cultural realities. Is it possible for her to be both a collectivist and a individualist at the same time? How does she resolve the different cultural and environmental expectations? Can she negotiate these issues without losing her cultural identity or suffering too great a psychological cost? Resolution of these issues will vary considerably from woman to woman and typically are not incorporated in most feminist frameworks.

Although many women of color successfully engage in this bicultural reality, doing so while maintaining a sense of individual and cultural integrity can be difficult. Situations that appear to be simple and straightforward to some may for a woman of color, encompass a great deal of internal struggle and conflict. Integrating the complex experiences of women of color into feminist psychology will require more than an intellectual acceptance of differences but a real understanding of what those differences mean in the lives of individual women. According to Uttal (1990), incorporating diversity into feminism requires "expressing disagreements, asking for clarifications and incorporating our differences in creating a shared vision together" (p. 320).

Recommendation 2: Awareness of Culture on a Personal Level

Feminists may acknowledge cultural awareness on an intellectual or ideological basis but sometimes fail to express that same cultural sensitivity and awareness on a personal or individual level. Take the hypothetical example of June and Barbara presented previously. Ideologically and intellectually, Barbara may endorse culturally sensitive beliefs, and her behavior may have been motivated by feelings of advocacy for June. However, in the interaction, it is unclear whether Barbara took into account the influence of race and culture on her own behavior and perceptions as well as those of June's. To what degree, we wonder, has Barbara contemplated and explored what it means to be a European-American woman and how being a European American woman might influence her interactions with women of color.

What if before her interaction with June, Barbara had engaged in the following internal dialogue: "I wonder what her experiences have been like with White women?" "What have been my experiences with Black women?" "How comfortable am I talking about race?" "How comfortable am I talking about race with her?" "What am I afraid to say or afraid to hear?" "What potential risks are there for her in this situation?" "Does she see me as a woman and/or a White woman?" "Do I see her as a woman and/or a Black woman?" "What would be the difference?" "What do I know about Black culture and Black women?" "Where have I learned what I know?" "What are the power relationships between us?" "How might she interpret and experience these power relationships?" "How might she interpret my behavior and my feedback?" "How does my being White influence my interpretations of her behavior?" These are complex and daunting questions that may or may not have answers, but one wonders if asking the questions would have changed the way in which Barbara approached her feedback and interaction with June. This type of dialogue is not unusual for women of color who often engage in such internal struggles as part of daily living and survival in American culture (Essed, 1991; McIntosh, 1992; Scott, 1991). One of the "privileges" of being European-

American is not *having* to consider or confront these issues if one so chooses (McIntosh, 1992). Nevertheless, it is this personal examination and application of race, culture, and gender that is necessary if feminist psychology is to move beyond awareness to true understanding and inclusion.

Recommendation 3: Woman of Color Feminism within a Multidimensional Framework

Race and gender are complex and dynamic concepts with considerable individual variability. Rather than conceptualizing these concepts as separate and distinct, taking a multidimensional approach may be more appropriate. Although a number of racial and ethnic identity models have developed, only a few conceptualize racial identity as multidimensional and none have incorporated gender as a central component of ethnic identity formation. Although Robert Sellers and his colleagues acknowledge gender as one of several important identities for African Americans, their current model does not include an integration of gender (Sellers, Rowley, Chavous, Shelton, & Smith, 1997). Utilizing the framework of Sellers et al.'s (1997) Multidimensional Model of Black Identity, we would like to propose a multidimensional model of woman of color feminism. The model we propose is preliminary at best and will undoubtedly experience substantial modification and revision over time. Sellers et al. (1997) proposed four primary dimensions in the development of African-American identity: race centrality, race salience, race regard, and race ideology. The relationship between race and gender for a woman of color will be influenced by similar dimensions including the centrality of race and gender in her overall identity, the salience of race and gender across situations and contexts, affective and evaluative beliefs about ethnicity, and ideological beliefs about feminism.

Centrality

Race and gender are only two of many potential identities in a woman's self-concept. Occupation, socioeconomic status, sexual identity, motherhood, religiosity, and age are all potential identities in a woman's sense of self. However, for any given woman, one identity may be more central to her overall self-conceptualization than another. For example, a Mexican-American woman who identifies strongly with Mexican culture may respond quite differently from a Mexican-American woman who feels little affiliation for Mexican culture. A woman who places ethnicity central to her overall identity may feel a greater connection to racial issues than gender issues, whereas a woman who places gender central to her overall identity may feel a greater connection to gender issues. Of course, both identities may be equally central and important to a given woman of color.

Consequently, the salience of each identity in a given context will influence the type of feminist behavior expressed.

Salience

Imagine, for example, an African-American woman enters a classroom. Race becomes much more salient for her if she is the only African American in the class than if she is one of several African-American students. If, however, she is the only woman in the class, gender may become more salient for her. How she responds in each of these situations will vary based on the salience of ethnicity and gender in the situation, the importance of ethnicity and gender in her overall identity, and the specific demands of the situation. Thus, an African-American woman with a strong ethnic identity who is the only African American in a classroom may feel compelled to address issues of race rather than gender. We would like to emphasize, however, that responding to the saliency of ethnicity or gender in a given context does not negate nor diminish the overall importance of both in a woman of color's identity. A woman of color may experience racism in one context, sexism in another, and both racism and sexism in yet another context. She may express herself differently in each of these situations because she is responding to and confronting different issues. However, her overall identity as a woman of color may remain firmly intact.

Regard

Affective and evaluative experiences associated with being a woman of color and a feminist will vary for individual women and will be influenced by factors, such as racial self-esteem, personal self-esteem, and adherence to stereotypes. Thus, it is important to assess for individual women, feelings about being a woman of color as well as beliefs and perceptions of other women and feminists.

Ideology

One's ideological beliefs concerning woman of color feminism will be influenced by personal experience, historical context, and the centrality of race and gender to one's identity. We propose three potential ideological frameworks for woman of color feminism. The frameworks are *nationalist, traditionalist,* and *communal* woman of color feminism. Within the nationalist framework, women of color from different ethnic groups will advocate for and emphasize the unique historical and cultural experiences of women in their respective ethnic group. Thus, an African-American feminist will address issues relevant for African-American women and a Chinese-American feminist will address issues relevant for Chinese-

American women. Within the traditionalist framework, a woman of color may espouse feminist beliefs consistent with traditional feminist thought, such as liberal, radical, and socialist feminism. The third proposed framework is the communal framework whereby the commonalties and shared experiences among various groups of women of color are emphasized. The nationalist, traditional, and communal ideologies are only three possible categories for women of color feminists. They are not mutually exclusive categories but general frameworks that shape how individual women of color approach and apply feminist theory to their research, practice, interactions, and activism. Although this model proposes a multidimensional framework for understanding the interaction of race and gender for individual women of color feminists, the complexity and diversity of women's experiences and feminist beliefs may require additional frameworks.

Our model can be demonstrated by returning to the example of June and Barbara. As the only African-American woman on the treatment staff, race may be particularly salient for June. However, the salience of race will depend on the centrality of an African-American identity in June's overall identity as a woman. If African-American culture is very central to her identity, June may respond with behaviors consistent with African-American cultural norms, expectations, and reactions to institutional and personal racism. If African-American culture is not central to June's identity, she may respond consistent with the dominant culture and behave according to traditional gender role socialization. June's responses to Barbara may also vary according to whether she espouses a nationalist, traditional, or communal woman of color feminist identity.

CONCLUSION

For more than a century women activists have stressed the importance of both race and gender in understanding the experiences of women of color. Feminist literature and feminist psychology are in the process of understanding and addressing diversity issues with greater awareness and sensitivity. We have witnessed a number of critical analyses of feminist ideology, greater acknowledgment and awareness of diversity issues in the literature, and more inclusion of diverse women's experiences and scholarship in feminist literature. Many of the progressive changes in feminist psychology, however, have only taken place in the last 10 years. Women of color as a group are still significantly underrepresented on editorial boards of journals and publishing houses, as members of governing boards of various organizations, as faculty members and administrators in academic settings, and as participants in psychological research. When we are present, we are often the only woman of color, which makes issues of race and gender particularly salient for many of us.

We titled this chapter "Women of Color and Feminist Psychology: Moving from Criticism and Critique to Integration and Application" because we wanted to address specific ways in which feminist psychology can move toward a more inclusive discipline. We presented several ways in which the field has attempted to address the concerns and experiences of women of color. We also presented the limitations of these responses, as well as suggestions for future directions. Charting a new course for feminist psychology requires more than awareness and acceptance of diversity issues, but also active integration of these issues within traditional frameworks as well as utilization of new frameworks. This integration must be incorporated in all aspects of feminist psychology and traditional psychology, including our theories, research, and day to day experiences. women of color and European-American women have different cultural identities, socialization experiences, histories, and experiences with various forms of oppression. Perhaps the first step in providing a more inclusive model of feminist psychology is to acknowledge the validity of the differences that exist among various groups of women and incorporate alternative models that address this diversity rather than attempting to fit all women into a general model of feminism. Women's lives are complex and multidimensional, and our approach to understanding the experiences and development of women should be equally complex and multidimensional.

NOTES

1. Women of color is used broadly to represent women who are members of groups identified as ethnic minorities in the United States. Throughout the chapter, however, we utilize various ethnic labels when referring to specific groups of women, such as African-American, Black, Latina, Puerto Rican, European-American, White, and so on.

2. The example presented is a fictional account construed to include a number of issues and potential issues that may influence interactions between Women of Color and European-American feminist psychologists. Any resemblance to real persons or events are purely coincidental. Our subsequent analysis of the vignette includes several potential interpretations but is by no means exhaustive or conclusive. We hope the reader continues to deconstruct the vignette by identifying elements that are personally relevant and meaningful.

3. The speech titled *Ar'n't I a Woman* is often attributed to Sojourner Truth who supposedly delivered the speech in 1851 at the Women's Rights Convention in Akron, Ohio. The speech is based loosely on the recollections of Frances D. Gage, who chaired several meetings during the convention. There is considerable controversy concerning the authenticity of the speech, whether Truth delivered it, and whether Gage accurately recorded it several years later. Although a number of scholars now believe Truth did not deliver the speech, her presence at the convention and her extraordinary contributions to the abolition of slavery and the women's suffrage movement have inextricably linked her to the spirit and content

of the speech. See Truth (1995) to read the words attributed to her on that historic day.

REFERENCES

Bem, S. L. (1996). Transforming the debate on sexual inequality: from biological difference to institutionalized androcentricism. In J. C. Chrisler, C. Golden, & P. D. Rozee (Eds.), *Lectures on the psychology of women* (pp. 8–21). New York: McGraw-Hill.

Bloom, V., Coburn, K., & Perlman, J. (1980). *The new assertive woman*. New York: Dell.

Brown, L. S. (1990). The meaning of a multiple perspective for theory-building in feminist therapy. *Women & Therapy, 9* (1–2), 1–21.

Burman, E. (1998). Deconstructing feminist psychology. In E. Burman (Ed.), *Deconstructing feminist psychology* (pp. 1–29). Thousand Oaks, CA: Sage.

Butler, P. (1981). *Self assertion for women*. San Francisco: Canfield.

Chan, S. (1998). Families with Asian roots. In E. W. Lynch & M. J. Hanson (Eds.), *Developing cross-cultural competence: A guide for working with young children and their families* (2nd ed, pp. 181–257). Baltimore: Brookes.

Cheng, L. (1984). Asian American women and feminism. *Sojourner, 10,* 11–12.

Chodorow, N. (1978). *The reproduction of mothering: Psychoanalysis and the sociology of gender*. Berkeley: University of California Press.

Chodorow, N. (1989). *Feminism and psychoanalytic theory*. New Haven, CT: Yale University Press.

Chow, E.N.L. (1987). The development of feminist consciousness among Asian American women. *Gender & Society, 1,* 284–299.

Chrisler, J. C., Golden, C., & Rozee, P. D. (2000). *Lectures on the psychology of women* (2nd ed.). New York: McGraw-Hill.

Collins, L. H. (1998). Illustrating feminist theory. *Psychology of Women Quarterly, 22,* 97–112.

Collins, P. H. (1991). *Black feminist thought*. New York: Routledge.

Comas-Diaz, L. (1991). Feminism and diversity in psychology: The case of women of color. *Psychology of Women Quarterly, 15,* 597–609.

Comas-Diaz, L., & Greene, B. (1994). An integrative approach. In L. Comas-Diaz & B. Greene (Eds.), *Women of color: Integrating ethnic and gender identities in psychotherapy* (pp. 287–318). New York: Guilford Press.

Crawford, M. (1995). *Talking difference: on gender and language*. London: Sage.

Crawford, M. (1998). The reciprocity of popular culture. In E. Burman (Ed.), *Deconstructing feminist psychology*. Thousand Oaks, CA: Sage.

Crawford, M., & Unger, R. (2000). *Women and gender: A feminist psychology* (3rd ed.) New York: McGraw-Hill.

Cross, W. E. (1991). *Shades of black: Diversity in African American identity*. Philadelphia: Temple University Press.

D'Almeida, I. A. (1994). *Francophone: African women writers destroying the emptiness of silence*. Gainesville: University of Florida Press.

Davis, A. (1983). *Women, race, and class*. New York: Random House.

di Stefano, C. (1990). Dilemmas of difference. In L. J. Nicholson (Ed.), *Feminism/postmodernism* (pp. 63–82). New York: Routledge.

Du Bois, W.E.B. (1903). *The souls of black folk*. Chicago: A. C. McClurg.

Essed, P. (1991). *Understanding everyday racism*. Newbury Park, CA: Sage.

Falicov, C. J. (1982). Mexican families. In M. McGoldrick, J. K. Pearce, & J. Giordano (Eds.), *Ethnicity and family therapy* (pp. 169–182). New York: Guilford Press.

Fine, M. (1985). Reflections on a feminist psychology of women: Paradoxes and prospects. *Psychology of Women Quarterly, 9*, 167–183.

Fine, M. (1997). Witnessing whiteness. In M. Fine, L. Weis, L. C. Powell, & L. M. Wong (Eds.), *Off white: Readings on race, power, and society* (pp. 57–65). New York: Routledge.

Firestone, S. (1970). *The dialectic of sex*. New York: Bantam Books.

Garcia, A. (1995). The development of Chicana feminist discourse. In A. Kesselman, L. D. McNair, & N. Schniedewind (Eds.), *Women images and realities: A multicultural anthology* (pp. 406–416). Mountain View, CA: Mayfield.

Gilligan, C. (1982). *In a different voice: Psychological theory and women's development*. Cambridge, MA: Harvard University Press.

Golden, C. (1996). Relational theories of European American women's development. In J. C. Chrisler, C. Golden, & P. D. Rozee (Eds.), *Lectures on the psychology of women* (pp. 229–242). New York: McGraw-Hill.

Gregory, S. T. (1995). *Black women in academia*. Lanham, MD: University Press of America.

Griscom, J. L. (1992). Women and power. *Psychology of Women Quarterly, 16*, 389–414.

Guy-Sheftall, B. (1995). *Words of fire: An anthology of African American feminist thought*. New York: The New Press.

Hale-Benson, J. (1986). *Black children: Their roots, culture, and learning styles*. Baltimore: Johns Hopkins University Press.

Hare-Mustin, R., & Marecek, J. (1990). Gender and the meaning of difference: Postmodernism and psychology. In R. Hare-Mustin & J. Marecek (Eds.), *Making a difference: Psychology and the construction of gender* (pp. 22–64). New Haven, CT: Yale University Press.

Henderson, D. (1997). Intersecting race and gender in feminist theories of women's psychological development. *Issues in Mental Health Nursing, 18*, 377–393.

Henley, N. M., Meng, K., O'Brien, D., McCarthy, W. J., & Sockloskie, R. J. (1998). Developing a scale to measure the diversity of feminist attitudes. *Psychology of Women Quarterly, 22*, 317–348.

Ho, C. K. (1991). An analysis of domestic violence in Asian American communities: a multicultural approach to counseling. In K. P. Monteiro (Ed.). *Ethnicity and psychology* (pp. 138–152). Dubuque IA: Kendall/Hunt.

hooks, b. (1984). *Feminist theory: From the margin to center*. Boston: South End Press.

hooks, b. (1990). *Yearning: Race, gender, and cultural politics*. Boston: South End Press.

Hunter, A. G., & Sellers, S. L. (1998). Feminist attitudes among African American women and men. *Gender & Society, 12*, 81–99.

James, J., & Farmer, R. (Eds.). (1993). *Spirit, space, & survival: African American women in white academia*. New York: Routledge.

Jordan, J. V., Kaplan, A. G., Miller, J. B., Stiver, I. P., & Surrey, J. L. (1991).

Women's growth and development: Writings from the Stone Center. New York: Guilford Press.

Jordan, J. V. (Ed.). (1997). *Women's growth in diversity: More writings from the Stone Center.* New York: Guilford Press.

Kanter, R., & Stein, B. (1980). *A tale of O.* New York: Harper & Row.

LaFromboise, T., Coleman, H.L.K., & Gerton, J. (1995). Psychological impact of biculturalism: evidence and theory. In N. R. Goldberger & J. B. Veroff (Eds.), *The culture and psychology reader* (pp. 489–535). New York: New York University Press.

Landrine, H. (1995). Introduction: cultural diversity, contexualism, and feminist psychology. In H. Landrine (Ed.), *Bringing cultural diversity to feminist psychology: Theory, research, and practice* (pp. 1–20). Washington, DC: American Psychological Association.

Landrine, H., Klonoff, E., & Brown-Collins (1992). Cultural diversity and methodology in feminist psychology: Critique, proposal, empirical example. *Psychology of Women Quarterly, 16,* 145–164.

Lois, B. (Ed.). (1997). *Black women in the academy: Promises and perils.* Gainesville: University of Florida Press.

Lorde, A. (1984). *Sister outsider.* Trumansburg, NY: Crossing Press.

McIntosh, P. (1992). White privilege and male privilege: A personal account of coming to see correspondences through work in women's studies. In M. L. Andersen & P. H. Collins (Eds.), *Race, class, and gender: An anthology* (pp. 70–81). Belmont, CA: Wadsworth.

Miller, J. (1976). *Toward a new psychology of women.* Boston: Beacon Press.

Miller, J. (1991). The development of women's sense of self. In J. V. Jordan, A. G. Kaplan, J. B. Miller, I. P. Stiver, & J. L. Surrey (Eds.), *Women's growth in connection: Writings from the Stone Center* (pp. 11–16). New York: Guilford Press.

Myers, L. J. (1988). *Understanding an Afrocentric world view: Introduction to an optimal psychology.* Dubuque IA: Kendall/Hunt.

Phelps, S., & Austin, N. (1975). *The assertive woman.* San Luis Obispo, CA: Impact.

Ramos-McKay, J. M., Comas-Diaz, L, & Rivera, L. (1988). Puerto Ricans. In L. Comas-Diaz & E.E.H. Griffith (Eds.), *Clinical guidelines in cross-cultural mental health* (pp. 204–232). New York: John Wiley & Sons.

Reid, P. T., & Comas-Diaz, L. (1990). Gender and ethnicity: Perspectives on dual status. *Sex Roles, 7/8,* 397–408.

Reid, P. T., & Kelly, E., (1994). Research on women of color: From ignorance to awareness. *Psychology of Women Quarterly, 18,* 477–486.

Scott, K. (1991). *The habit of surviving: Five extraordinary women share conflicts and struggles that define their lives as Black women in America.* New York: Ballantine Books.

Sears, D. (1986) College sophomores in the laboratory: influence of a narrow data base of social psychology's view of human nature. *Journal of Personality and Social Psychology, 51,* 515–530.

Sellers, R. M., Rowley, S. J., Chavous, T. M., Shelton, J. N., & Smith, M. A. (1997). Multidimensional inventory of Black identity: A preliminary investigation of reliability and construct validity. *Journal of Personality and Social Psychology, 73*, 805–815.

Shade, B.J.R. (Ed.). (1989). *Culture, style, and the educative process.* Springfield, MA: Charles C. Thomas.

Smith, B. (1998). *The truth that never hurts: Writings on race, gender, and freedom.* New Brunswick, NJ: Rutgers University Press.

Spelman, E. (1988). *Inessential woman: Problems with exclusion in feminist thought.* Boston: Beacon Press.

Sue, D. W., & Sue, D. (1990). *Counseling the culturally different: Theory & practice.* New York: John Wiley & Sons.

Surrey, J. L. (1991). The "self-in-relation": A theory of women's development. In J. V. Jordan, A. G. Kaplan, J. B. Miller, I. P. Stiver, & J. L. Surrey (Eds.), *Women's growth in connection: Writings from the Stone Center* (pp. 51–66). New York: Guilford Press.

Tong, R. P. (1998). *Feminist thought: A more comprehensive introduction.* Boulder, CO: Westview Press.

Truth, S. (1995). Ar'n't I a woman. In A. Kesselman, L. D. McNair, & N. Schniedewind (Eds.), *Women images and realities: A multicultural anthology* (pp. 39–40). Mountain View, CA: Mayfield.

Unger, R. (1983). Through the looking glass: No wonderland yet! (the reciprocal relationship between methodology and models of reality). *Psychology of Women Quarterly, 8*, 9–32.

Uttal, L. (1990). Nods that silence. In G. Anzaldua (Ed.), *Making face, making soul: Creative and critical perspectives by women of color* (pp. 41–45). San Francisco: Aunt Lute Foundation Books.

Wallace, M. (1991). *Black macho and the myth of the superwoman.* New York: Verso.

Walker, A. (1995). Womanism. In A. Kesselman, L. D. McNair, & N. Schniedewind (Eds.), *Women images and realities: A multicultural anthology* (p. 18). Mountain View, CA: Mayfield.

Walsh, R. T. (1989). Do research reports in mainstream feminist psychology journals reflect feminist values? *Psychology of Women Quarterly, 13*, 433–444.

Weaver, H. N., & White, B. J. (1997). The Native American family circle: Roots of resiliency. *Journal of Family Social Work, 2*, 67–97.

West, C. (1995). Mammy, Sapphire, and Jezebel: Historical images of Black women and their implications for psychotherapy. *Psychotherapy, 32*, 458–466.

Willis, W. (1998). Families with African American roots. In E. W. Lynch & M. J. Hanson (Eds.), *Developing cross cultural competence: A guide for working with young children and their families* (2nd ed., pp. 121–150). Baltimore: Brookes.

Part II

Psychological Development

Chapter 5

Deconstructing Attachment Theory: Naturalizing the Politics of Motherhood

Susan H. Franzblau

Motherhood has come to define the historical role of women to the extent of rejecting other aspects of women's lives. Beginning with Darwin (Darwin, 1859) and up to the present, a number of theories have been formulated to argue that mothers are primary, exclusive, and necessary for the healthy development of children (cf. Dinnerstein, 1977; Fraiberg, 1977; Freud, 1938; Klaus & Kennell, 1981). Attachment theory (Ainsworth & Bowlby, 1991) defines and normalizes the exclusivity of motherhood within a patriarchal nuclear family system via the explanatory paradigms of psychoanalytic and evolutionary theory. According to Bowlby (1973), "attachment" refers to discrete patterns of behaviors (e.g., proximity seeking, crying), based in the evolutionary need to develop a social relationship with the mother. This relationship is differentiated from other qualities of the infant's social relationships in its selectivity of the mother figure as object in its rearing environment. This selective attachment provides the infant with emotional security and creates the basis for later social relationships in childhood, adolescence, and adulthood. Bowlby (1969) viewed attachment as a class of social behaviors equivalent to mating in terms of its universality, its evolutionary significance, and its necessity (See also Franzblau, 1996).

In this chapter, I deconstruct attachment theory and argue that it is a coercive theory that legitimizes and naturalizes the control of women and contributes to divisions among women by social class, race, and sexual orientation. The following points will be made: First, attachment theory steers women into accepting motherhood as the dominant condition of their lives, by characterizing and then romanticizing woman as mother. Second, attachment theory promotes women's labor within the confines of maternity by narrowing, reducing, and mandating women's primary role as that of heterosexual mother. Third, attachment theory acts as the over-arching paradigm with which to scrutinize women to see if their behavior meets the definition of "good mother." Finally, if a woman resists the work of motherhood, either in thought or deed, attachment theory pathologizes her resistance.

ROMANTICIZING MOTHERHOOD

Romanticization is particularly important to society's compulsive heterosexual project. Romanticization has both a mystical and alienating character. It confuses us about the effects of material conditions of our lives and gives us both false consciousness and false hope about moving "beyond" these material conditions, thus alienating us from other resources that might be available to change our lives. Disney films are a good example of how romanticization obfuscates reality. Disney films are notorious for romanticizing the conditions of women's lives and for promoting and sustaining the bad mother/good mother dichotomy. They offer false hope that women can escape poverty, loneliness, or uncertainty about their future by marrying a rich/powerful man and having his baby. The heroine's unhappiness is usually associated with an evil woman (e.g., mother, stepmother, or any neighborhood woman). In fact, Disney's heroines usually have no mothers they can rely on, either because the mothers are absent, dead, or evil. The heroine thus opts to rely on men and become the idealized wife and mother (e.g., the Lion King's wife or the Little Mermaid).

Attachment theory participates in the romanticization and concealment of oppression by glorifying the mother/child relationship as primary, predetermined, determining, and ideal. Romanticization of woman as wife/mother obscures and mystifies the process by which sexist ideology works to control women's reproduction. Romanticization distorts our understanding of how racism, class exploitation, and heterosexism work to divide women against each other. Feminists are not immune from this hegemonic ideology.

Cultural Feminism as Romance

Among feminists, the idea that women's relationships to children is an essential and critical aspect of women's lives and distinguishes women from men is predominantly subscribed to by cultural feminism. Cultural feminists (e.g., Chodorow, 1978; Dinnerstein, 1977; Gilligan, 1982) argue that women's "ability" to relate to others and nurture them is the yin to the yang of male autonomy and that both are necessary for one to be fully and wholly human. For example, Nancy Chodorow (1978) has written that "women's mothering capacities and commitments, and the general psychological capacities and wants that are the basis of women's emotional work, are built developmentally into the feminine personality. Because women are themselves mothered by women, they grow up with relational capacities and needs and a psychological definition of self-in-relationship, which commits them to mothering" (p. 197). Can we generalize Chodorow's theory to all women?

We can take for granted that all women are initially birthed by women, and most are probably cared for by women. What this means needs to be explored within the context of a long history of sexism, racism, and class exploitation of women, and it begs a number of questions. What of women who become pregnant as a result of rape? Should they be committed to mothering? What about women who need to work in order to survive? Should they also be committed to mothering? And to what quantity and quality of mothering should they be committed? What about women who do not want to have children? Should they feel guilty? What about women who cannot have children? Should they exhaust every means, including fertility drugs, that could allow them to birth as many as seven children at one time? Should this anomalous event then be attributed to the natural lot of women as a breeder class? Within the individual context of these women's lives, what does the term "required commitment to mothering" (Chodorow, 1978, p. 197) mean? What are the other forces that drive home this sense of commitment? Does this mean that men have an opposing task, which renders them unable to commit themselves to care for children?

Some cultural feminist thought serves to romanticize political inequality. For example, Carol Gilligan (1982, p. 210) has suggested that "[t]he *illusive mystery* of women's development lies in its recognition of the continuing importance of attachment in the human life cycle. Women's place in man's life cycle is to protect this recognition while the developmental litany intones the celebration of separation, autonomy, individuation, and natural rights" (emphasis added). Of course she is correct! Caregiver has been women's historical role. However, the reasons for this historical role are not so mysterious or illusive. Women's relationships to men and children have been maintained as an ideological, political, economic, and social relationship of oppressed to oppressor for the purpose of reproductive control of women and children as private property. Gilligan's position romanticizes, mystifies, and removes from our consciousness the political, economic, and ideological conditions under which obligations to birth and to mother take place. These conditions do not, of course, invalidate women's desire to have and care for children. What this means, however, requires an understanding that the dominant discourse regarding women's reproductive and child-rearing tasks has rarely been presented in the absence of sexism.

Clearly, women social scientists and clinicians are not free from the political constraint imposed by the dominant discourse on mothering (cf. Bretherton, 1992; Muller, 1994). In their attempt to impose an orderly and disciplined approach to understanding changes over the lifespan from birth to death, they often allow the dominant patriarchal and capitalist message of individualism, competition for scarce resources, and the notion of hierarchical place to inform their thinking about what is normal about children's emotional and social relationships to family.

The simplistic notion that there is some inherent glue that unites mother and child and forms the crucial basis for later relationships simplifies, depoliticizes, and removes from historical review the exploitative and oppressive conditions under which most women reproduce and raise children. "Concientizacion," as Freiere (1970) stated, is a process that engages multiple frames-of-reference. Changes in consciousness emerge from the conditions of our lives. Without full consciousness of our situated lives within an imposed hierarchical class structure, we could very easily overlook questions regarding whose interest this dominant order benefits. This is a particularly important question in the context of inequality.

PROMOTING MATERNITY: JOHN BOWLBY IN CONTEXT

From the middle of the nineteenth century until the present, the relationship between infants and women has been explained by three grand narratives: evolution, psychoanalysis, and positivism; these combined in the middle twentieth century to form the overarching narrative of attachment theory (Ainsworth & Bowlby, 1991). Evoking Darwin's theory of evolution as the foundation of attachment theory, psychoanalytically trained English psychiatrist John Bowlby presented the idea that social and emotional development are biologically determined and that women are evolutionarily prepared to support them (Ainsworth & Bowlby, 1991; Bowlby, 1969). Early on, Bowlby made it very clear that it was his intention to ignore economic and social factors in children's mental development and concentrate solely on the conscious behavior and unconscious attitudes of women toward their children (Van Dijken, 1998), which he viewed as innate qualities. In Bowlby's words:

My own approach to the role of environment in the causation of neurosis has of course been from the analytic angle. For this reason I have ignored many aspects of the child's environment such as economic conditions, housing conditions, the school situation, diet and religious teaching. (Bowlby, 1940, cited in Van Dijken, 1998, p. 99)

The idea that women are evolutionarily prepared to mother, although it ignores the material conditions of women's lives, is consistent with a long historical tradition of using essentialist discourse to predetermine and con-

trol women's reproductive tasks and children's child rearing needs. Evolutionary and biological theories have been imbedded in a history of
misogynist discourse (Hubbard, 1995), and they have emerged from that
history among the dominant discourses of this period (Silverstein, 1993).
"Essentialism" means inherent or natural. In terms of women, it means
that women's reproductive abilities exist to serve biological and evolutionary purposes. Women's "natural" function, as defined by essentialist the-
oreticians, is to reproduce and provide continual care for infants and young
children. If the treatment of women differs from the treatment of men, such
treatment could be justified in terms of its biological and evolutionary purposes (cf. Trivers, 1972, in Silverstein, 1993). Essentialism, therefore, is
problematic for women who have challenged the idea that motherhood
defines them and by necessity limits other possibilities. Alcoff (1997,
p. 336) argued that any essentialist formulation of womanhood, even when
put forth by feminists, "that 'ties' the individual to aspects of her identity
as a woman . . . cannot represent a solution to sexism." Any essentialist
ideology that romanticizes inequality is incompatible with feminist goals of
bettering the conditions of women's lives.

IDEOLOGY CONFIGURED AS SCIENCE

As a theoretical construct, attachment theory has been presented as transcendent of culture, class, and historical context. Yet, as a research paradigm it has normalized a variety of methodological approaches that fall
within the historical and class exploitative tradition of overly investigating
women as objects of concern and pathology (cf. Caplan & Caplan, 1999).
Because attachment theory's focus is intrapsychic and intrafamilial, it removes from critical review the roles oppressive institutions play in path-
ologizing birth and early child care. Given that women are responsible for
birth and early child care, this focus leaves the relationship between gender
and power untheorized. Further, as Warner (1999) argued, the methods
used to inquire about something limit the question by the method used to
answer it, direct the answer within the confines of the methodology, and
predetermine the outcome. Thus, particularized Q-set questions, standardized interviews (Waters et al., 1995), as well as the Strange Situation Procedure (SSP) (Ainsworth & Wittig, 1969) reify already formulated criteria
for evaluating the absolute benefits of particular relationship styles and
family structures. These approaches define the limits of acceptability for all
families, and they may have the effect of obscuring the hidden realities of
abuse within apparently normative family structures (Warner, 1999).

In many ways the attachment paradigm has become the modern mythology. It is a mythology of individualism, wherein the fetus/child is conceived of as undifferentiated, genderless, and without race, class, culture,
or ancestry (Burman, 1994; Cleary, 1999). Within this mythos, Bowlby

assumed the etic stance that truth emanates from the perspective of the researcher, which further mystifies the process of finding truth. Bowlby's lens, however, was limited by his own cultural, historical, and class position. For example, Bowlby began thinking about mourning the loss of loved ones after he experienced the Nazi bombing of Britain during World War II. However, Bowlby's culturally biased assumptions and empiricist methods of inquiry concentrated on individualized detachment and loss as part of the normal course of mourning loss, which perpetuated the Western tradition of preserving the autonomous individual self as the normal goal of development. Bowlby's assumptions ignored other cultural practices within which a person's death does not end the relationship between the dead ancestor and the family/ community. Rather, in death the relationship is continued within another dimension (as in Mexico; Cleary, 1999).

ANIMAL MODELS CONSTRUE HUMAN MOTHERING

Bowlby's investment in primatology (the study of primates) as the basis for understanding human relationships reflects a White, Western, capitalist bias. The form that primatology has traditionally taken assumes inequality, male dominance, and female nurturance of infants (Haraway, 1989). This position remained unchallenged in Bowlby's normative approach to social and emotional development. Overreliance on mothers as research participants has generated a sex-biased and incomplete data set because one cannot investigate that which is unnamed (Silverstein, 1993). As the following deconstruction of Harry Harlow's rhesus monkey studies will show, monkey analogues for human caregiving maintain the hegemonized ideology of heterosexual gender relations.

Harry Harlow in Context

As graduate students at the State University of New York at Stony Brook in 1974, I and other Ph.D. candidates in developmental psychology learned that Harry Harlow's studies (cf. Harlow, 1971) of the surrogate mothering of separated rhesus monkeys challenged the argument that nurturers of children, by nature, could only be women. We took for granted, and accepted without question, the ethics and internal validity of the context within which these studies took place. Donna Haraway's (1989) critical analysis of Harry Harlow's studies of "mother love" in the United States after World War II illuminated the impact of hegemonized ideas on psychological research, public policy, and current wisdom. According to Haraway, Harlow designed his research to test Bowlby's theory that any mother-child separation posed a danger to the child. He proposed that his research would "free . . . white middle-class . . . mothers from the tyranny of doctrines of the infant's need for non-working, full time, 'natural' mothers" (Haraway, 1989, p. 235). These claims were deceptive. Although Harlow purported to show that the child could just as easily experience care from men/fathers as from women/mothers, Harlow's research, in practice, served to naturalize the heterosexual nuclear family. The notion that fathers could "mother," which was experienced by many women in the United States as relief from the burdens of motherhood, actually rendered women dispensable, given that their "essential" mothering (defined by Harlow as "comfort") could be extracted and duplicated in the laboratory. Woman as mother was represented in this rhesus monkey research as a caricature of women, as available 24 hours a day, within the boundaries of nuclear, heterosexual family structures. This representation was supported by the fact that rhesus monkey females "mother" within a structure that most resembles the human heterosexual nuclear family. Of course, Harlow's women-rejecting view of mother emerged from Bowlby's own story of the infant as potentially abandoned and isolated (cf. Bowlby, 1973; van Dijken, 1998), the remedy for which had to be 100% eternal "mother love" or its equivalent substitute "father love" (Haraway, 1989, p. 235). Harlow participated in the story by engineering the bonding of tortured, intentionally isolated rhesus monkeys with cyclopean-eyed cloth structures. Acceptance of this mother-as-cloth comfort metaphor relies on our willingness to forget that metaphors are imbedded in economic, political, cultural, and ideological contexts, all of which provide the context for their use. Nevertheless, the Harlow monkey stories continue to initiate developmental discussions concerning the beginnings of social relationships that rely on the metaphor of mother as providing "creature comfort" alone. This revealing story shows how important it is to embed theory, research, and practice in historical context. It also shows the role that ahistoricality plays in preserving certain gendered assumptions (Alcoff, 1997).

Psychobiologists now know that economics within human and monkey primate groups play a monumental role in the formulation of families (Silverstein, 1993). Among human and monkey primates, as economic conditions change, so do family relationships and caregiving tasks, which move fluidly across gender lines. Economic conditions refer to the organism's interaction with "its habitat primarily to exploit resources in order to sustain individual and collective life" (Berry, 1994, p. 118). For monkey primates, economic conditions may involve attempts to find food under conditions of scarcity, the need to travel short or long distances given changes in weather conditions that limit the food available for nutritional needs, or the reciprocal benefits males and females exchange within the group, including benefits of friendship (Silverstein, 1993). Thus, reliance on a fixed, gender differentiated ideology of family and work, whether in animal or human research, jeopardizes critical social policy changes that must be made in order that the needs of families under changing economic conditions be adequately addressed (Silverstein, 1993).

As was just evidenced, historical reflection is necessary to any self-conscious and self-correcting process that feminists use to challenge misogynist assumptions regarding the essential roles of women. This is particularly true for issues of reproduction because discussions of human reproduction and early child care wittingly or unwittingly contain within them a history of misogynist discourse (Alcoff, 1997). This discourse has influenced oppressive and exploitative practices directed at controlling and restricting women's reproductive and productive lives. Similarly, an historically situated process will penetrate previous discussions of reproduction and child care that have been framed by positioning women into hierarchical divisions by social class and race. We need to deconstruct the imparted wisdom of the historical narrative and question the self-interest of those who tell the tales that are remembered as "natural."

HISTORICIZING ATTACHMENT THEORY

During the period that North American historians call the Progressive Era (1901–1920), essentialist thinking and policies were driven by political and economic forces related to industrialization. The ruling classes in a number of countries, including Brazil, Mexico, Argentina, Cuba, the United States, Britain, Italy, France, and Germany, implemented restrictive reproductive and early child care strategies, which they imposed upon women. These strategies grew out of international meetings of eugenically oriented researchers and policymakers, who exchanged ideas. The question of how best to use women's productive and reproductive abilities was resolved by each country, taking into account their industrial needs, their class and ethnic makeup, and the racially motivated fears of each country's upper classes (Stepan, 1991). The commonality was that women's reproductive and early child-rearing attributes were "valorized" or romanticized within each culture (Alcoff, 1997), thus rendering them ahistorical and essentialist.

The Essentialist Ideology of Maternalism: Pre–World War II

In the United States during the Progressive Era, essentialist reproductive and early child rearing policies drew on maternalist thinking. Maternalists "targeted mothers in social policy and asserted the social and political significance of the maternal role. . . . All maternalists subscribed to the ideal of domestic motherhood" (Mink, 1995, p. 5). Within the framework of domestic motherhood, work and child care were situated in opposition to each other. Maternalist policies in the United States had an impact upon women in two ways: (1) they restricted a woman's right to determine when, how, and with whom to have or not have children; and (2) they influenced the definition of what constitutes good caregiving for the children of these women. All maternalists were steeped in the ideology of eugenics, the proposal to "bring . . . no more individuals into the world than can be properly cared for, and those only of the best stock"(Galton, 1914, p. 560). During this period and later, the enlisting of women's reproductive ability in the service of "the race" (Franzblau, 1996; Stepan, 1991) frequently served as a metaphor for the marginalization of immigrant women, poor women, and Black women (See also Children's Defense Fund, 1997).

The ideology of maternalism/essentialism, in its most subtle form, has been used to persuade women to doubt that they could do anything beyond the boundaries of wifedom and motherhood (cf. Friedan, 1963). At its most extreme, maternalist policies and implications have been devastating for women positioned as "other" than normal (i.e., Jewish and Romany women, mentally retarded women, poor women, and lesbians). For example, under fascism economic conditions provided the atmosphere for extreme forms of maternalist thinking and social policy in a number of countries, including Brazil, Argentina, the United States, Britain, and Germany. Stepan (1991) argued that the United States had the "most extensive and extreme legislation . . . in the world outside of Nazi Germany" (pp. 133–134). Under Nazi leadership, birth control was made illegal, potential marriage partners were guided to "eugenic counseling" centers, the punishment for abortion increased in severity, and arrests and convictions of people who performed or aided women in obtaining an abortion doubled (Koonz, 1987). Few Germans rebelled against these programs because breeding of "Aryan" fitness was linked with the fear that reproduction among so-called inferior groups of women might lead to "dysgenic" breeding, defined as bad breeding, as opposed to "eugenic" breeding, which refers to the encouragement of good breeding (Koonz, 1987).

In the United States, working class as well as middle class women were discouraged from any form of paid labor "through welfare stipulations, labor regulations, training for domesticity, and counseling" (Mink, 1995, p. 152). Governmental aid to families impoverished by huge increases in unemployment exchanged women's promise to stay home for financial help (Mink, 1995). Work regulations limited the kinds of jobs women could take, and high schools and colleges steered women into gender-dichotomized home economics programs. Women's paid public labor was presented as "unnatural" and antithetical to the unpaid but "natural" and privatized labor of motherhood.

During World War II

World War II brought about a new set of conditions that offered a unique challenge to maternalist policy makers. As women entered the work force to take jobs formerly held by men who had entered military service, the contradiction between materialist policies and the need for women to work in the war industries became apparent. The fluctuating needs of industry during and after the war, in both Britain and the United States, had an impact on women as mothers and as workers. Although employed women needed child care provisions, industry made its determination for child care not based on women's social needs, but "increasingly tied in with the fluctuating needs of . . . employers" (Riley, 1983, p. 135).

[W]omen as workers and women as reproductive social beings were understood in the most conservative ways. Women's war work, even in the presentations of their collective heroic capacities, was work done by *women*, marked through and through by the gender of its performers, and consequently by the especial temporariness of the work of women who were mothers. (Riley, 1983, p. 195; emphasis in original)

Denise Riley's (1983) "case study" of Bowlby's model of maternal deprivation in the context of gender/work/child care realities during and after World War II in Britain, reveals how entangled these competing interests became. "We're entering a dense tangle of labour requirements, shifts in state suppositions about the family and the care of children, the nature of terms like popularisation, propaganda, ideology, and wants and needs" (Riley, 1983, p. 150).

After World War II

The ruling classes had always remained hostile to mothers who worked outside the home. The hostility to these women increased in Britain and the United States after the war and was bolstered by ruling class fears that (upper class/White) birth rates were declining too rapidly. Further, despite women's interest in the social and financial benefits of paid public labor, the problems engendered by working for low pay for long hours without child care propelled women back into the home. Characterized as a "choice," this "homeward bound" (May, 1980) movement was supported by the various governments, whose maternalist and pronatalist ideology of the 1930s continued in the post-war period to provide a rationale for sending women home to reproduce. In this context, Riley wrote, "[t]he possibility of speaking politically about women's *needs* became obscured by a passing rhetoric of their maternal *function*" (1983, p. 152; emphasis in original). However, the choice was never women's. The needs of children, as defined by various experts, and the fact that women were positioned as exclusively responsible for those needs were translated into the fixed properties of mothers and valorized, unproblematized, and essentialized (Alcoff, 1997). Maternalism and the maternal deprivation hypothesis provided one conceptual framework for pronatal ideology as it intersected with the demands of governments and industrialists.

After the war in both the United States and Britain, government funded day care centers, which had provided some working women with day care during the war, began to close down, and the range of jobs available to women narrowed. Propagandist efforts to reorient women toward the home and away from the factory took on new forms. Through film, and the newly emerging medium of television, women were reinvented as yielding their independence for the obligation to be a good wife, mother, and hausfrau; heterosexual marriage and child rearing were extolled as a woman's patriotic duty (May, 1988), as well as her romantic inclination, and eugenicists continued to argue that the strains of education would impede a woman's ability to conceive (cf. Thompson, 1949). To this end, eugenically oriented programs and departments opened up in a number of colleges and universities throughout the United States (Franzblau, 1996).

Enter Bowlby

Although Bowlby had been working on his maternal deprivation hypothesis before World War II, after the war the maternal deprivation hypothesis was formalized into a report for the World Health Organization, which had asked him to gather information on children who had been orphaned as a result of the bombings in Britain during the war (Bowlby, 1951). As a psychoanalytically trained psychiatrist, Bowlby began with the premises that children were motivated by a strong, unconscious need for mother and that "maternal" deprivation led to orphaned children's feelings of anxiety and isolation and their later delinquency (Ainsworth & Bowlby, 1991). To this he added the argument that evolutionary survival served as both the necessary and sufficient reasons for a long, sustained, and intimate relationship between all species of mother and child. Bowlby argued that selective attachment to mother provides emotional security and creates the basis for later social relationships. Hence, any discrepancy between the infant's evolutionary need and the mother's behavioral response would necessitate reorientation so that the goal of infant survival is achieved. For example, fear of being placed with strangers is an evolutionarily adapted atypical behavior pattern that assures attachment (Bowlby, 1973) by activating the child's feelings of separation anxiety. These feelings could occur in other situations as well: if the mother separates from the child for any reason or for any length of time; if she gives her attention to someone else; or if she rejects the child outright (Ainsworth & Bowlby, 1991). According to Bowlby, *all* mother-child separations lead to immediate distress and possible long-term detrimental effects (Silverstein, 1991). Bowlby thought that the most dangerous consequence of separation was adolescent delinquency, which he defined as a psychological phenomenon of maladjustment that is rooted in infantile experiences (Van Dijken, 1998).

In the 1950s, as Bowlby's ideas moved across the Atlantic to the United

States, childbearing and childrearing ideologies took on a distinctly religious character. Ideological/religious family movements that emphasized the
need for early mother-child bonding flourished (Eyer, 1992). Organizers of
the Christian Family Movement (CFM) (established by Catholic laity in
Chicago, Illinois and South Bend, Indiana in the 1940s, and organized
nationally in 1949) became the founders of the La Leche League (LLL) in
1956. Both organizations contributed to the quasi-religious character of the
newly developing childbirth/child care movement and to the valorization
of motherhood. According to one natural childbirth advocate of the time,
"childbirth is fundamentally a spiritual as well as a physical achievement
. . . The birth of the child is the ultimate perfection of human love" (Dick-
Read, 1959, cited in Eyer, 1992, p. 171). Breast-feeding was heralded as
an extension of this spiritual connection. Out of concern that recently instituted bottle-feeding and drug-assisted births would break family bonds
(Livingston, 1990; Weiner, 1994), these early religious advocates of breast-
feeding prescribed a regimen that included suckling on demand day and
night with no pacifier substitute and feeding the child human milk for six
months at which time solid foods would be gradually introduced along
with continuation of breast-feeding until the baby reaches at least one year
of age. Any work that competed with the infant's need for continuity of
maternal care was out of the question. One La Leche League International
group leader said that she was "pretty negative to people who just want
to dump their kids off and go to work eight hours a day" (Blum & Vandewater, 1993, p. 294).

THE CURRENT CLIMATE

The subtle forms maternalist ideology took after World War II were
abandoned in the 1980s and 1990s in favor of more blatant forms. For
example, renowned North American pediatrician, T. Berry Brazelton, went
so far as to claim that low scores on intelligence and language tests and
violent crimes, including terrorism (Brazelton, 1988, cited in Eyer, 1992,
p. 4), could result from lack of close early contact between mothers and
their babies. This period was also defined by a marked increase in profi-
teering and severe cuts in social services to poor and working class people,
which opened the way for laws and public policies that blatantly supported
race and class-based control over reproduction and child rearing. Middle
class White women were encouraged to stay at home where they would
provide the essential core of the idealized nuclear family; poor women of
color meanwhile were frequently characterized as potential overpopulators
who lived in the lap of welfare luxury at taxpayers' expense.

Under the welfare "reform" bill passed in the United States in 1996, this
divisive essentialist ideology was taken to its dysgenic extreme (Children's
Defense Fund, 1997). Relying on typical blame-the-victim ideology (Ryan,

1971), the bill required that families who receive welfare no longer be guaranteed free medical (Medicaid) coverage. And if this were not Dickensian enough, the bill mandated that if a child was conceived (for whatever reason) while a family received federal assistance, the family's benefits were to be cut off. Thus, while the virtues of exclusive stay-at-home motherhood were being sold as the middle-class ideal, poor women and women of color were characterized as potentially undeserving of motherhood, particularly if they stayed at home because they were unemployed, on public assistance, mentally retarded, and/or addicted.

Legal Implications of the Attachment Paradigm

"Bad mothering" is a strong argument in a court of law for termination of parental rights (Attorney Elva Perez Trevino, personal communication, January 14, 1999). The good mother/bad mother dichotomy has been bolstered by three separate developments: (1) the granting of separate and independent status to the fetus (Rothman, 1989), (2) the legal system's push for fathers to have equal parental rights, and (3) the use of attachment theory to determine who should be awarded custody (DeAngelis, 1997).

The courts have used the attachment paradigm to take children away from marginalized women by making the women responsible for children's conjectured failure to attach. It is no longer the case that mothers might retain the one basic *privilege* of maternalism, the right to the custody of her child. Two recent U.S. lawsuits highlight how easy it is to deny a woman her right to the product of her labor.

In *Jennifer Ireland v. Steve Smith* (1995), which involved the issue of whether day care is an acceptable substitute for care by the biological mother, the lower court decided that there is "no way that a single parent attending an academic program at an institution as prestigious as the University of Michigan can do justice to her studies and the raising of an infant child" (p. 349). The court decided that the home of the father with the grandparents as caregivers during school hours was better than day care because the grandmother was "a blood relative and not a stranger" (p. 349). This ruling took place despite the fact that the grandmother's relationship to the child had consisted solely of gift giving. This decision was reversed at the appellate level. However, in *Campbell v. Campbell* (1995) custody was awarded to the father, who was defined as primary caretaker because "mother returned to work . . . only two months after the second child was born" (p. 472). The United States appellate court agreed that when she returned to work, the mother ceased to be the primary caretaker and handed that role to the father, who was also employed, but was at home temporarily because of an injury.

These cases also reveal why women who are under threat of having their children taken away would be willing to use essentialist theories to advocate *for* their essential right to mother (Johnson & Torres, 1994). The dilemma in this period of divisive woman blaming is that, because the ideological history of natalistic and maternalistic ideas has been obscured, feminist activists find ourselves arguing for reproductive and mothers' rights using the same concepts and language that divide and oppress us. The continued use of problematic language, which in the past has been used to render inferior, stigmatize, and divide groups of people has been recognized as a concern by a number of progressive psychologists (cf. Atkinson, Morten, & Sue, 1998). However, these same psychologists argued for continued usage, given that no other language is available. This is a reactionary position that helps maintain the status quo. The challenge is not just to acknowledge that we recognize that certain language is fraught with historical bias, but to change that language *so that it no longer functions to stigmatize*. Finally, continued use of a universalized language of mothering obscures the differences in how Black and White women are treated in terms of their maternal rights and responsibilities.

Racialization of Good Mothering

Ideologies of privilege bias perceptions in critical domains of power and control. For example, women-blaming ideology differentially impacts Black and White women who are caught in the legal system because of their addiction to drugs. If a pregnant woman is found through a urine test to be positive for drugs, it would not be uncommon for attachment theory to be part of the language of persuasion used before an authority figure (e.g., judge, probation officer, social worker) to argue that her infant not be taken away from her. She might argue that to deny her child total access to her nurturance would harm that child's later development. However, In the United States, women who are poor and Black are *more* likely to be tested for drug use than are middle class White women. Further, drug use by Black women is more stigmatized than drug use by White women, which means there are a priori assumptions about the abilities of Black women to mother. Children are more likely to be taken away from Black than White women (Children's Defense Fund, 1997). Loren Siegel of the American Civil Liberties Union (1990) stated that there is much evidence that "[t]he criminalization of pregnant and child-rearing [drug] users . . . is blatantly racist in its application" (p. 10).

A recent study (Jenny, Hymel, Ritzen, Reinert, & Hay, 1999) revealed that doctors are more likely to ignore obvious physical abuse if the families are heterosexual, White and middle class than if the families are single parent or comprised of persons of color. Thus, attachment theory would to work in favor of White, middle-class and heterosexual women who are already assumed to have a natural right to mother. As Alcoff (1997) reminded us, "mothering is subject of and subjected to a shifting context, a context that includes a network of elements involving others, the objective economic conditions, cultural and political institutions and ideologies" (p. 349). Under conditions of racism and sexism good mother/bad mother theories are fraught with racial bias.

CONCLUSION

Maternalist theories are currently utilized by feminist developmental and clinical psychologists to explain women's obvious and unending responsibilities for child care, the nurturance that children require for healthy development, and later problems that most of us have in relatedness and relationships (e.g., Gilligan, 1982; Ruddick, 1995). These claims, however, stand in contradiction to feminists' claim that when women are defined and understood by women, sexist discourse will end. There is nothing essential about women that implies that women are similarly situated in time and space, in relationship to power, in relationship to material conditions, in relationship to men, and in relationship to each other. Therefore, the universality assumption underlying maternalist concepts such as attachment theory is violated, which makes it useless as a general causal explanation for the success or failure of early child-parent relationships.

Any language that describes women's reproductive and child rearing duties as essentialist but ignores differences in the experiences of African-American, Latina, Asian, American Indian, poor White, and lesbian women (whose differences are influenced by the complex interaction of culture, economics, and the politics of exploitation and oppression) ignores the potential of that language to reify sexist and exploitative social class ideology and practice as it concerns motherhood. According to Fanon (1963), fascist policies are always unnecessary if people oppress themselves. This is the inherent danger in unproblematizing reproduction and motherhood.

The lessons of social history as they inform psychology present the means for tracing directions of thought and drawing relevant analogies to the period in which we live. We can use this knowledge to deconstruct and "transform the meaning" (Stefan & Gilman, 1993, p. 177) imbedded in the oppressive language that pervades our thinking. We then have greater freedom to invent a language that allows us to reconstruct our reproductive and productive lives in our best, diverse, as well as common, interests.

We have been provided a language of essentialist motherhood, biologically mandated but differentially enforced. This language was created and is maintained within the context of vast inequalities in resources for people who parent and for their children. It is my strong belief that the primary way to chart a new course is to change not only our language but also the material conditions of our lives. The Universal Declaration of Human Rights (UDHR) (1948, cited in Metzer, 1979) and the Declaration of The Rights of The Child (DTRC) (1959, cited in Metzer, 1979), which the

United States has yet to sign, sets out conditions for change. They include adequate pre- and postnatal care, "the right to adequate nutrition, housing, recreation and medical services" (DRTC, p. 180) as well as "education, which shall be free and compulsory"(DRTC, p. 181). For all humans they include the right to live in freedom and dignity "without distinction of any kind, such as race, colour, sex, language, religion, political or other opinion, national or social origin, property, birth or other status" (UDHR, p. 173). The Universal Declaration of Human Rights says very clearly that everyone should have "the right to a standard of living adequate for the health and well-being of [themselves and their family] including food, clothing, housing and medical care and necessary social services, and the right to security in the event of unemployment, sickness, disability, widowhood, old age or other lack of livelihood in circumstances beyond [their] control" (p. 177).

Only when we actively collaborate to produce the conditions for economic and social justice, will a new language of caregiving emerge to fit those conditions. Only when we shed beliefs that the reproduction of children is for private enterprise rather than for the public good will a new language of human potential be possible.

REFERENCES

Ainsworth, M. D., & Bowlby, J. (1991). An ethological approach to personality development. *American Psychologist, 46,* 333–341.

Ainsworth, M. D., & Wittig, B. A. (1969). Attachment and exploratory behavior in one-year olds in a strange situation. In B. M. Foss (Ed.), *Determinants of infant behavior* (vol. 4, pp. 111–136). London: Methuen.

Alcoff, L. (1997). Cultural feminism versus post-structuralism; The identity crisis in feminist theory. In L. Nicholson (Ed.), *The second wave: A reader in feminist theory* (pp. 330–355). London: Routledge.

Atkinson, D. R., Morten, G., & Sue, D. W. (1998). *Counseling American minorities.* Boston: McGraw-Hill.

Berry, J. W. (1994). An ecological perspective on cultural and ethnic psychology. In E. J. Trickett, R. J. Watts, & D. Birman (Eds.), *Human diversity: Perspectives on people in context* (pp. 115–141). San Francisco: Jossey-Bass.

Blum, L., & Vandewater, E. (1993). Mother to mother: A maternalistic organization in late capitalistic America. *Social Problems, 40,* 285–300.

Bowlby, J. (1951). *Maternal care and mental health: A report proposed on behalf of the World Health Organization as a contribution to the United Nations.* Geneva: World Health Organization.

Bowlby, J. (1969). *Attachment and loss: Volume 1. Attachment.* New York: Basic Books.

Bowlby, J. (1973). *Separation: Anxiety and anger* (vol. 2). New York: Basic Books.

Bretherton, I. (1992). Attachment and bonding. In V. B. Van Hasselt & M. Herson (Eds.), *Handbook of social development: A lifespan perspective* (pp. 133–155). New York: Plenum Press.

Burman, E. (1994). *Deconstructing developmental psychology*. London: Routledge.

Campbell v. Campbell, 460 S.E. 2d, 469 (W. Va. Ct. App. 1995).

Caplan, P. J., & Caplan, J. B. (1999). *Thinking critically about research on sex and gender* (2nd ed.). New York: Longman.

Children's Defense Fund. (1997). *The state of America's children—yearbook 1997*. Washington, DC: Author.

Chodorow, N. (1978). *The reproduction of mothering*. Berkeley: University of California Press.

Cleary, R. (1999). Bowlby's theory of attachment and loss: A feminist reconsideration. *Feminism & Psychology, 9*, 32–42.

Darwin, C. (1859). *The origin of species*. New York: The Modern Library.

DeAngelis, T. (1997, June). When children don't bond with parents. *American Psychological Association Monitor, 28*, 11.

Dinnerstein, D. (1977). *The mermaid and the minotaur*. New York: Harper.

Eyer, D. (1992). *Mother-infant bonding: A scientific fiction*. New Haven, CT: Yale University Press.

Fanon, F. (1963). *The wretched of the earth*. New York: Grove Press.

Fraiberg, S. (1977). *Every child's birthright: In defense of mothering*. New York: Bantam Books.

Franzblau, S. H. (1996). Social darwinian influences on conceptions of marriage, sex, and motherhood. *Journal of Primary Prevention, 17*, 47–73.

Freud, S. (1938). *An outline of psychoanalysis*. New York: Norton.

Friedan, B. (1968). *The feminine mystique*. New York: Norton. (Orig. pub. 1963.)

Freiere, P. (1970). *Pedagogy of the oppressed*. New York: Seabury Press.

Galton, F. (1914/1908). Conclusion to memories of my life. *Journal of Heredity*, 560.

Gilligan, C. (1982). Woman's place in man's life cycle. In L. Nicholson (Ed.), *The second wave: A reader in feminist theory* (pp. 198–215). London: Routledge.

Haraway, D. (1989). *Primate visions: Gender, race, and nature in the world of modern science*. New York: Routledge.

Harlow, H. F. (1971). *Learning to love*. San Francisco: Albion.

Hubbard, R. (1995). *Profitable promises: Essays on women, science and health*. Monroe, ME: Common Courage Press.

Jennifer Ireland v. Steve Smith, 542, N.W. 2d, 344 (Mich. Ct. App. 1995).

Jenny, C., Hymel, K. P., Ritzen, A., Reinert, S. E., & Hay, T. C. (1999). Analysis of missed cases of abusive head trauma. *Journal of the American Medical Association, 281*, 621–626.

Johnson, J., & Torres, L. (1994). Bonding and contested parental rights termination: The New Jersey "JC" case. *American Journal of Forensic Psychology, 12*, 37–57.

Klaus, M. H., & Kennel, J. H. (1981). *Parent-infant bonding: The impact of early separation or loss on family development*. St. Louis: Mosby.

Koonz, C. (1987). *Mothers in the fatherland: Women, the family and Nazi politics*. New York: St. Martin's Press.

Livingston, M. (1990). *Choice in childbirth: Power and impact of the modern childbirth reform movement*. Unpublished manuscript.

May, E. T. (1980). *Homeward bound*. New York: Basic Books.

Metzer, M. (1979). *The human rights book*. New York: Farrar, Straus, Giroux.

Mink, G. (1995). *The wages of motherhood.* Ithaca, NY: Cornell University Press.

Muller, M. E. (1994). A questionnaire to measure mother-to-infant attachment. *Journal of Nursing Measurement, 2,* 129–141.

Riley, D. (1983). *War in the nursery.* London: Routledge.

Rothman, B. K. (1989). *Recreating motherhood: Ideology and technology in a patriarchal society.* New York: Norton.

Ruddick, S. (1995). *Maternal thinking.* Boston: Beacon Press.

Ryan, W. (1971). *Blaming the victim.* New York: Random House.

Siegel, L. (1990). The criminalization of pregnant and child-rearing drug users. *Drug Law Report, 17* (4), 10.

Silverstein, L. (1991). Transforming the debate about child care and maternal employment. *American Psychologist, 46,* 1025–1032.

Silverstein, L. (1993). Primate research, family politics, and social policy: Transforming "cads" into "dads." *Journal of Family Psychology, 7,* 267–282.

Stepan, N. L. (1991). *The hour of eugenics, race, gender, and nation in Latin America.* Ithaca, NY: Cornell University Press.

Stepan, N. L., & Gilman, S. L. (1993). Appropriating the idioms of science. In S. Harding (Ed.), *The racial economy of science* (pp. 170–193). Bloomington: University of Indiana Press.

Thompson, D. (1949, June). Race suicide of the intelligent. *Ladies' Home Journal,* 11.

Van Dijken, S. (1998). *John Bowlby: His early life.* London: Free Association Books.

Warner, S. (1999, March). *Attachment theory and normative prescriptions: Regulating relationships.* Paper presented at the 24th Annual Conference of the Association for Women in Psychology, Providence, RI.

Waters, E., Vaughn, B. E., Posada, G., & Kondo-Ikemura, K. (1995). Caregiving, cultural, and cognitive perspectives on secure-base behavior and working models: New growing points of attachment theory and research. *Monographs of the Society of Research on Child Development, 60* (2/3; serial no. 244).

Weiner, L. (1994). Reconstructing motherhood: The la leche league in postwar America. *Journal of American History, 80,* 1357–1381.

Chapter 6

Dimensions of Silencing and Resistance in Adolescent Girls: Development of a Narrative Method for Research and Prevention

Joseph Spinazzola, Helen W. Wilson, and Vicki B. Stocking

"Joan, come here, Aunt Beth is here," came the cry from the next room. Joan wearily got up out of bed. She had had a bad day. All her friends were fighting with each other, her braces were really hurting her mouth, and the homework she had was incredibly hard. . . . When she looked in the mirror she saw every flaw about her. She quickly tied her hair and walked out of the room.

In the hallway her grandmother stopped her. "Joan," she said sternly, "at least look happy. You mustn't upset Aunt Beth. Pick up your head, that's good. Now let me see you smile."

Joan walked down the hall in her fake position, looking like a posed doll.

"How she has grown!" stated Aunt Beth. "It's amazing how happy she always is." For the next half hour Joan sat still, head up, and smiling. During that time Aunt Beth discussed how her little Billy was making the honors list and how perfect he is.

"Oh, if only my little Joan were like that. Joan, you can go now." Joan stood up, nodded her head at her female relative and walked down the hallway back into her room.

"Great," she thought, "more standards I must live up to."

This poignant story, written by a 13-year-old participant in our study, illustrates a phenomenon increasingly recognized as a problem for many adolescent girls in contemporary Western culture. Joan cannot tell her grandmother about the difficulties and concerns she must juggle, for her grandmother is not interested in how she really feels, but only in instructing her about how to mask her genuine feelings for appearances sake. To avoid potentially upsetting her aunt, Joan suppresses her true feelings and hides behind an inauthentic representation of herself that is consistent with narrow constructions of feminine identity. With a forced smile she painfully endures the weight of idealized expectations borne down upon her. In effect, Joan appears to be experiencing what has come to be referred to in feminist psychology as a "silencing of the self."

SILENCING AND THE ADOLESCENT TRANSITION FOR GIRLS

Adolescence has been widely acknowledged to be a critical period in girls' development that has important ramifications for identity formation, gender-role socialization, and mental health. Across the theoretical, clinical, and empirical literature on female development during adolescence, there has been a general consensus that this period occasions a marked increase in social, interpersonal, and emotional challenges for many girls in contemporary Western societies.[1] For instance, the early-adolescent transition has been associated with disturbances in aspects of girls' self-image as well as with increased rates of depression and eating problems (for a review of this literature, see Spinazzola, 1996, 1997). Of the numerous challenges to girls' social and emotional well-being during adolescence, "silencing of the self," alternately referred to as "loss of voice," has been increasingly recognized over the past decade by feminist and relational psychologists as a significant threat to healthy development (see, for example, Gilligan, 1991; Hart & Thompson, 1996; Spinazzola, 1999).

The basic features of the problem of silencing, however, were first recognized in feminist scholarship and clinical research with women. Early conceptualizations of women's struggles with self-representation adopted voice as a metaphor for women's attempts to establish agency in their personal and professional relationships (Belenky, Clinchy, Goldberger, & Tarule, 1986), illuminated the centrality of these relationships to women's sense of self and underscored the paradoxical self-sacrifices often made by women to maintain a sense of "being-in-relationship" (e.g., Gilligan, 1982; Jordan, Kaplan, Miller, Stiver, & Surrey, 1991). Jack (1991) used the phrase "silencing of the self" to describe the self-censoring thoughts and behaviors of depressed women and provided the first conceptual model of the silencing process. Informed by retrospective accounts of adult women, Gilligan and colleagues (Brown & Gilligan, 1992; Gilligan, 1991; Gilligan, Lyons, & Hanmer, 1990) directed their attention to the adolescent transition as the pivotal moment in the onset of silencing experiences for girls. These researchers contrasted the hesitancy, self-censorship, and false idealization they observed in the intimate relationships of adolescent girls with the agency, assertiveness, and willingness to take risks in relationships witnessed by these girls' younger counterparts (see, for example, Brown, 1991; Hancock, 1989; Rogers, 1993).

Spinazzola (1996) has since questioned the accuracy of this stage-based, dichotomous framework for the etiology of girls' silencing experiences. In a review of the developmental literature on gender socialization from a feminist psychology perspective, Spinazzola uncovered a number of precipitants and precursors to girls' silencing experiences that are embedded within differential patterns of gender socialization for girls and boys beginning during infancy. He argued that these socialization processes are likely to engender in girls a unique vulnerability to succumb to silencing pressures encountered in their social and cultural environments with heightened intensity during adolescence. On the basis of this review, Spinazzola has suggested that the apparent resiliency of pre-adolescent girls against silencing may be more accurately construed as the relative sheltering of these younger girls from gender-based cultural imperatives that become more pervasive and insistent during adolescence.

This view of girls' socialized vulnerability to engage in self-silencing when confronted during adolescence with a magnification of cultural silencing pressures has informed our research. Although we have adopted a more developmental perspective on the *origins* of silencing than has previously been assumed, we nevertheless share the more common viewpoint of Gilligan and colleagues that early adolescence represents a period of critical importance to the *emergence* of external silencing pressures and the *manifestation* of self-silencing thoughts and behaviors in girls. The heightened salience of these pressures for adolescent girls is widely evident in clinical research and practice, and it appears to be related to the intensification during adolescence of a range of identity-constraining experiences for girls, including sexual objectification and exposure to media portrayals of unrealistic and gender-role stereotyped ideals for young women (see for example, Fredrickson & Roberts, 1997; Steen & Spinazzola, & Stocking, 1997).

AN INTEGRATIVE DEFINITION OF THE SILENCING PROCESS

Published work on silencing has typically focused on women's abandonment of a sense of voice in the context of intimate relationships. This scholarship has emphasized pressures women experience to stifle authentic self-disclosure in relationships and to sacrifice personal needs and goals in order to care for others. In her work, Jack (1991) elaborated on this notion of the self-silencing processes and acknowledged the ways in which silencing can manifest itself in purely intrapsychic forms (e.g., self-doubt in relation to external standards). Ultimately, however, Jack's formulation of the silencing construct has been hindered by her insistence that silencing not only constitutes a risk factor for depression in women, but actually reflects the underlying phenomenology of women's depression itself. The problems inherent in this formulation have been illuminated and critiqued by empirical research that suggests a more complex relationship between silencing and depression and other self-concept outcomes (Page, Stevens, & Galvin, 1996; Spinazzola, 1999; Spinazzola & Stocking, 1998).[2]

Spinazzola (1996; 1999) has delineated a more comprehensive formulation of the silencing construct that appears to address many of the limitations of Jack's model. Extending Jack's observation of the discrepancy between internal (i.e., psychological) experience and external (i.e., social) demands at the core of silencing experiences, Spinazzola has conceptualized silencing as a broader process of self-monitoring and restriction. In doing so, he has suggested a mechanism of silencing that is more firmly rooted in established social and personality theories of self-concept while retaining a feminist and relational perspective on this phenomenon. Specifically, Spinazzola has argued that the silencing construct reflects a finite set of self-restrictive processes, one or more of which become enacted in response to the experience of a rift or discrepancy between private and public self-consciousness. Whereas private self-consciousness involves an awareness of and responsiveness to personal thoughts, feelings, and beliefs about self, public self-consciousness entails awareness of and responsiveness to how one is perceived by others (Scheier & Carver, 1981). Ultimately, silencing of the self occurs when individuals feel compelled in some way to subordinate aspects of their private selves to maintain public self-presentations consistent with social expectations and ideals.

Spinazzola's (1999) model of silencing accounts for the emergence of silencing on three levels: behavioral (i.e., censorship of potentially conflictual self-expression in interactions with others), cognitive (i.e., the experience of self-doubt or dissociation from former beliefs in response to environmental appraisal or unrealistic ideals) and bodily centered (i.e., the suppression of physiological cues such as hunger and sexual desire when these are inconsistent with social prescriptions for female appearance and behavior). Spinazzola's formulation of silencing also accounts for individuals' capacity to resist silencing, whether through overt public challenge of restrictive imperatives, refusal to internalize societal ideals, or satisfaction of physiological needs (e.g., hunger) despite the resulting defiance of social ideals for women.

RESEARCH ON SILENCING AND RESISTANCE

To date, there have been two major trends in research on silencing. The first has involved ethnographic/case studies, and the second, an emphasis on questionnaire-based approaches. Relying primarily on school-based ethnography, Gilligan and her colleagues have explored aspects of the emergence and impact of silencing on girls' emotional and social development (e.g., Brown & Gilligan, 1992; Gilligan, Lyons, & Hanmer, 1990; Rogers, 1993). Although clinical inquiry into the dynamics of silencing has afforded some important insights about the role of the therapist in the silencing process (Rogers, 1991), much of the clinical and anecdotal work on silencing (e.g., Hancock, 1989; Mann, 1996; Pipher, 1994) has lacked a clearly defined focus, methodological approach, or theoretical framework.

Recent attempts to examine silencing with quantitative methods have used the Silencing the Self Scale (STSS; Jack & Dill, 1992), which was developed out of Jack's clinical work with depressed adult women. This instrument was designed to measure endorsement of self-silencing practices in intimate relationships (Jack & Dill, 1992). Research using this questionnaire has been outcome-based and primarily focused on the relationship between silencing and depression in women (e.g., Page, Stevens, & Galvin, 1996; Thompson, 1995), with some attention to ethnic and/or gender differences (Carr, Gilroy, & Sherman, 1996; Cowan, Bommersbach, & Curtis, 1995; Gratch, Bassett, & Attra, 1995). Although most of this research has focused on adult or late-adolescent samples, at least one study using the STSS has concerned an early-to-middle-adolescent sample (Hart & Thompson, 1996). In our research, we have developed a modified version of Jack's scale for use with adolescents. Using this measure, we have examined the association between silencing and self-concept dimensions, and assessed gender, ethnic, and grade differences in silencing (Spinazzola, 1999; Spinazzola & Stocking, 1998; Stocking, Spinazzola, Dueker, & Pierce, under review).

Research on the resistance of silencing has been even more sparse. Nevertheless, recent efforts to illuminate this process in ethnographic research have been promising (Brown, 1998; Taylor, Gilligan, & Sullivan, 1995; Way, 1995). Despite growing interest in resistance, attempts to develop instruments to measure this construct have yet to be made.

To date, information on silencing as a multidimensional construct has stemmed from Jack's (1991) initial clinical observations of depressed women and subsequent psychometric assessment and application of the STSS (Jack & Dill, 1992). Preliminary factor analysis of this instrument has supported the multidimensional nature of self-silencing processes and found that Jack's rationally derived subscales of this measure appear to reflect four distinct underlying factors or dimensions of silencing (Steven & Galvin, 1995). The dimensions of silencing ostensibly measured by this instrument include (a) Externalized Self-Perception (i.e., self-judgment based upon external standards); (b) Divided Self (i.e., perceived discrepancies between public expression and private experience); (c) Silencing the Self (i.e., suppression of potentially conflictual self-expression in relationships); and (d) Care as Self-Sacrifice (i.e., the abandonment of personal

needs and aspirations in order to secure those of others). Of these dimensions, the first two seem to address silencing *cognitions*, or the intrapsychic
experience of self-silencing pressures. Conversely, the latter two dimensions
of silencing measured by the STSS address silencing *behaviors*, or the manifestations of self-silencing phenomena in relationships.

Findings from our empirical studies with adolescent samples have supported the notion that silencing consists of multidimensional processes of
self-monitoring and restriction. Furthermore, correlational and predictive
findings from these studies point to the differential role of individual dimensions of silencing in influencing positive outcomes across particular domains of self-concept in terms of self-worth, emotional stability, and peer
and parental relationships. Silencing cognitions appear to be of particular
importance to adolescent self-concept and mental health. For instance, in
one of our studies which examined the contribution of friendship qualities
to adolescent self-concept, a composite scale measuring silencing cognitions
emerged as the strongest independent predictor of self-worth (Stocking,
Spinazzola, Dueker, & Pierce, under review). Similarly, Hart and Thompson (1996) found Externalized Self-Perception to be more powerfully and
uniquely predictive of depression in an adolescent sample than any of the
other silencing or gender-role orientation variables that they assessed.

Related literatures suggest the likely existence of other dimensions of this
process. For instance, in their report on gender bias in the education of
girls, the AAUW (1992) noted girls development of self-doubt about their
abilities in traditionally male domains such as science and mathematics
despite objective indicators of personal competence in these areas. This
reaction would appear to constitute another cognitive form of silencing for
girls. Moreover, Brown and Gilligan (1992) have illuminated an even more
subtle cognitive manifestation of self-silencing. In their research, they describe the process by which girls become "dissociated" from former aspects
of authentic private experience as their self-knowledge becomes increasingly
supplanted during adolescence by internalized social prescriptions and cultural ideals of femininity. Finally, in their development of objectification
theory, Fredrickson and Roberts' (1997) cited considerable research to suggest that women learn to suppress and selectively ignore certain bodily cues
(e.g., hunger, sexual desire), the satisfaction of which would potentially
undermine social ideals for self (e.g., thinness, male-determined sexual behavior). These findings, along with developmental research and feminist
observation on girls' frequent efforts to hide physical manifestation of pubertal development (e.g., Petersen, Tobin-Richards, & Boxer, 1983), unwanted body fat, or physical imperfections (e.g., Halprin, 1995),
collectively support Spinazzola's (1999) assertion that silencing of the body
represents another important dimension of this process for girls.

In examining literature on women's and girls' resistance of silencing pressures, we have uncovered evidence supporting particular dimensions of si-

lencing (Pierce, Spinazzola, & Stocking, 1999; Spinazzola, 1999). The most common manifestation of resistance involves direct confrontation of silencing agents and imperatives through girls' authentic expressions of agency and voice (e.g., Way, 1995). Writers have also alluded to more internal processes of resistance that involve girls' ability to retain personal beliefs and self-perceptions by refusing to internalize gender stereotypes (Gilligan, Rogers, & Tolman, 1991; Taylor, Gilligan, & Sullivan, 1995). In addition, Brown and Gilligan (1992) have commented on a form of political resistance among adolescent girls that involves a retreat to shared, private spaces which are sheltered from others' silencing imperatives, thus enabling the more genuine expression of thoughts and feelings.[3] These authors have referred to this symbolic and literal space as a "political underground." Ultimately, the characteristics and prevalence of these and other potential dimensions of silencing and resistance await elucidation through empirical inquiry.

THE DUKE PROJECT ON SILENCING AND RESISTANCE DURING ADOLESCENCE

For a variety of reasons, it is difficult to study silencing. This is due in no small part to the insidious nature of the silencing process itself. Brown and Gilligan (1992) have commented on the challenges of this task, and girls' predisposition to view researchers distrustfully as representatives of the same public domain in which they have learned to silence themselves. In Brown and Gilligan's work, attempts to initiate explicit discourse on these issues were initially met with silence, withdrawal, and girls' self-presentations consistent with their perception of the researchers' expectations and ideals. Even when girls were willing to discuss their experiences of silencing, their struggles with uncertainty and self-doubt infiltrated their language and hindered otherwise bright, articulate girls in their self-expression. Accordingly, Gilligan and her colleagues restructured their methodological design in narrative work with adolescent girls and developed a less directive, more relational, listening-centered approach that fostered and was attentive to girls' own voices, as well as to their silences, uncertainties, and strivings for connection (e.g., Brown & Gilligan, 1992; Taylor, Gilligan, & Sullivan, 1995; Way, 1995). Their Listening Guide, however, was primarily designed to listen for voices of justice and care that emerged in girls' personal narratives in response to direct questions about moral dilemmas in relationships (e.g., Brown, Debold, Tappan, & Gilligan, 1991).

One of the principal goals of our project at Duke University on silencing and resistance during adolescence was to develop a methodology specifically designed to detect themes of silencing or resistance against silencing in narrative data. In addition, our understanding of the challenges to the assessment of silencing experiences in adolescents required us to depart from an investigator-directed approach to narrative material. Instead, we developed a less directive, more projective approach that would facilitate the spontaneous emergence and consideration of silencing and resistance themes only to the extent that these were salient in participants' reflections about adolescent identity and relationship issues. Specifically, girls constructed narratives about their perceptions of the imagined lives of same-aged girls portrayed in a series of documentary photographs. The photographs were selected by our research team from a collection of images of 12-year-old girls (Mann, 1988) for their evocativeness of elements of the adolescent transition. In contrast to Way's (1995) thematic coding system, which involved analysis of only the most prevalent narrative themes, we developed a coding system that would enable us to detect the presence of less common and more subtle themes of silencing and resistance in participants' narratives.

In this chapter we describe some of the findings from the first phase of our project, in which we were specifically concerned with dimensions of these phenomena as they emerge in girls during early adolescence. More generally, this project was initiated in part in response to the recent call for new qualitative methodologies to better understand the meaning of the early-adolescent transition for girls (Brooks-Gunn, 1996). The following are some of the empirical and methodological questions that guided this phase of our project. First, are dimensions of silencing and its resistance salient in early-adolescent girls' perceptions, imagination, and narrative construction of identities for girls their age? To address this question, we designed our initial study to assess whether themes pertaining to these dimensions spontaneously emerged in participants' written narratives when presented with a structured but nondirective opportunity to reflect on the experiences and identities of early-adolescent girls. Moreover, to the extent that issues of silencing and resistance are present in girls' stories, can a coding system be developed to identify, categorize, and describe the dimensions of these psychological processes in a reliable manner? A principal outcome of this study was the production of a manual suitable for the identification and coding of silencing and resistance themes in narrative data. Through the development and application of this coding system, we aimed to contribute to the empirical knowledge base on the multidimensional nature of self-silencing and resistance processes in adolescent girls. For complete details regarding study methodology, sample characteristics, coding manual development, analyses, and findings, refer to Spinazzola (1999).

Our participants included 60 girls aged 12–14 who were attending one of the Duke University Talent Identification Program (TIP) summer residential programs in 1995 or 1996. Students who attend TIP summer programs have demonstrated exceptional verbal and/or mathematical ability as evidenced by high scores on college entrance examinations taken out-of-level, and on the basis of this criterion are deemed to constitute an academically gifted sample.[4] TIP's research population is predominantly White, and the ethnic diversity of our participants was reflective of this distribution. Forty-four study participants (73%) were identified as European-American, six (10%) as Asian-American, five (8%) as African-American, and five (8%) as Hispanic, Native American, or Other. Consent to participate in this voluntary research study was obtained from all participants and their parents.

The research protocol was individually administered to each participant. Participants wrote stories about the imagined lives of the girls portrayed in one of two randomly assigned subsets (Set A: Photographs #1–10; Set B: Photographs #11–21) of the photographs.[5] Selected photographs included girls with expressions that range from glowing smiles to hollow, desperate looks. Their style of dress and background settings suggests variation in socioeconomic status and overall quality of life. Twelve of the photographs portray solitary girls; nine depict girls with other children or adults. For each photograph, participants were instructed to consider in their stories their impressions of the girl including her thoughts and feelings, the events transpiring in the picture, the circumstances leading to up these events, and the outcome.[6] Participants were never prompted by investigators to include references to silencing or resistance experiences in their narratives, nor did investigators ever refer to such experiences. No stylistic or time constraints were imposed. In total, 30 narratives were collected for each of the 21 photographs. In order to control for any influence of the gender of the investigator on the content or structure of the girls' narratives, participants were equally divided among male and female investigators.[7] All investigators were European-American undergraduates or psychology doctoral students.

All 630 handwritten stories were transcribed and subjected to three phases of narrative content analysis with the goals of (a) identifying thematic dimensions of silencing and resistance elicited by the study photographs and (b) developing a coding system to detect and describe these themes in narrative data. The approach used in the first phase of the content analysis, as detailed below, was comparable to that employed by Way (1995) and informed by the work of Roth and colleagues on the detection of subtle thematic material embedded within narrative data (see especially Roth & Batson, 1997; Roth, Lebowitz, & DeRosa, 1996). In the absence of an existing classification system for dimensions of silencing and voice with which to compare the present findings, analyses were guided by the definition of silencing elaborated by Spinazzola (1996) as well as by a consideration of extant theory, research, and clinical work on silencing.

In the first phase of narrative analysis, three raters independently read and summarized each narrative. Key aspects of the narratives were quoted with annotation noting thematic elements of silencing and resistance thought to be present. Raters then independently organized the identified thematic content into conceptually clustered matrices (Miles & Huberman, 1984) which formed the basis for silencing and resistance subtheme categories. After all narratives for a given photograph were independently analyzed, raters reconvened to (a) compare agreement in identification of themes, and (b) establish a thematic coding guide. This process was conducted in an incremental fashion. Disagreement in identification and interpretation of themes was resolved upon discussion. This work culminated in the development of a coding manual that contains descriptions and narrative illustrations of study themes as well as coding guidelines (Spinazzola, Wilson, & Pierce, 1999).

In the second phase of narrative analysis, two raters independently applied the developed coding system to the entire narrative data set in order to (a) establish initial interrater reliability estimates using this system; (b) determine the frequency of silencing and resistance themes in the entire set of narratives as well as by photograph; and (c) refine the coding manual. Percentage agreement was established at an overall rate of 94.0%. Cohen's Kappa, a measure of percent agreement that removes the effect of chance agreement, was 83.0%. A "master coding" was established for each narrative. Then, in the final phase of narrative analysis, the coding manual was used to train an additional coder naive to the study for the purposes of establishing blind rater reliability. Percentage agreement between ratings of the independent coder naive to the study and the master coding was established at an overall rate of 96.4%, with a Cohen's Kappa of 81.5%.

Number and Frequency of Study Themes

Themes of silencing, the resistance of silencing, or genuine self-expression were identified in 163 (25.9%) of the total 630 narratives. Specifically, 105 narratives (16.7%) contained silencing themes, 47 (7.5%) contained themes that involved resistance of silencing pressures, and 53 (8.4%) contained thematic material related to genuine self-expression. Eight subthemes addressing conceptually distinct dimensions of silencing were identified. An additional five subthemes were found that addressed dimensions of resistance against silencing. Finally, one theme was identified that concerned girls' capacity to maintain a sense of authentic voice through public forms of self-expression. Individual study themes are briefly described below.

Themes were distributed among the narratives of individual writers in the following manner: 53 (88%) participants wrote at least one story that contained thematic material related to silencing, resistance, or genuine self-expression. Specifically, silencing themes were identified in the stories of 46 (76.7%) participants, resistance themes were found in the narratives of 31

(51.7%) participants, and the theme of genuine self-expression was identified in the stories of 30 (50%) participants.

Description of Silencing Themes

Eight subthemes reflective of various dimensions of the self-silencing process were identified in the content analysis of narrative data. These subthemes were embedded in narratives that described the girls' relationships with family and friends, their encounters with societal expectations and standards, and their personality and gender role characteristics. In these contexts, girls were most frequently depicted as silencing aspects of their private selves in an attempt to meet social ideals, maintain connection in intimate relationships, or satisfy others' imperatives for self. In other instances, girls engaged in silencing behaviors as a form of self-protection against relational violence and abuse. Some narratives described girls who had come to more chronically silence aspects of their private selves as a consequence of interpersonal rejection, emotional neglect, and perceived failure to meet social ideals. The presence of these themes in study narratives was an indication of the writers' perceptions of the salience of silencing experiences in the lives of adolescent girls. The following is a brief summary of the particular self-silencing process identified by each subtheme.

Theme 1: Withholding genuine self-expression. This theme refers to the most frequently referred to form of self-silencing, namely, the process of withholding or restricting self-disclosure of aspects of one's private self in relationships in order to present a public identity consistent with others' expectations for self. As such, it constitutes a primarily behavioral form of silencing. Narratives that contained this form of silencing portrayed girls who censored authentic feelings, ideas, and desires in their intimate relationships for the sake of maintaining self-presentations of "socially acceptable" feelings and opinions. The most pervasive of all silencing subthemes found in our data, Theme 1 emerged in half of all narratives that contained themes of silencing.

Theme 2: Judging the self by external standards. This theme concerns a primarily cognitive form of silencing, namely, the internalization of externally derived (i.e., from intimate others; cultural institutions; media) prescriptions for and appraisals of self despite their inconsistency with pre-existing perceptions of self. Narratives that evoked this dimension of silencing depicted girls at various stages in the adoption of others' perceptions of themselves, or else striving to attain social ideals that were frequently unrealistic and damaging. Girls who engaged in this form of silencing were most often portrayed as attempting to achieve perfection in the eyes of intimate others or society in general. For these girls, self-evaluation in the face of inaccessible ideals was invariably associated with feelings of inferiority, negative self-image, or rage. Theme 2 was identified in 16% of all narratives that contained silencing.

Theme 3: Unreasonable doubt of ability or self-worth. Another cognitive form of silencing, this theme pertains to individuals who have come to suppress a core sense of belief in themselves. This process was typically described as driven by, or associated with, the internalization of limiting beliefs about gender. Characters who exhibited this form of silencing were frequently depicted as unrealistically doubting their competence in various traditionally male domains (e.g., baseball, rodeo) despite objective indications of their ability in these areas. Other characters were portrayed as coming to believe that they were undeserving of such basic human needs as love and friendship as a consequence of experiences of neglect, ridicule, or interpersonal rejection. Theme 3 was found in 12% of the narratives that contained silencing.

Theme 4: Care as self-sacrifice. A more pronounced manifestation of the silencing behavior described in Theme 1, this form of silencing concerns the abdication of personal needs, goals, or aspirations for the sake of attending to the needs or furthering the goals of others. Although the kind of lifestyle choices involved in this level of sacrifice are more characteristic of the silencing behaviors of some adults, narratives that contained this theme described girls who put aside personal scholastic or career goals to care for family members or enable an intimate other to achieve his/her own goals. In some instances, girls' bodies became the object of their sacrifices as they endured abuse or sexual exploitation in order to protect or provide for others. A more pervasive theme in research on adult women (e.g., Gilligan, 1982), among our early-adolescent participants this theme was identified in only 6% of the narratives that contained silencing.

Theme 5: Others' imperatives to silence the self. This theme pertains to individuals' encounters with external pressures to silence aspects of themselves directed at them from others in their immediate social worlds (e.g., family members, friends, authority figures). Narratives that contained this form of silencing depicted girls who were variously confronted with encouragement, ridicule, bribes, threats, commands, and implicit cues from intimate others to engage in self-silencing behaviors. One of the more common subthemes to emerge in the narratives that evoked themes of silencing, Theme 5 was found in 27% of these narratives.

Theme 6: Not being listened to/heard. This theme concerns the loss of public voice that occurs when repeated attempts at genuine self-expression are ignored, dismissed, or belittled. Narratives that contained this theme portrayed girls who had come to feel invisible and unacknowledged in their relationships because of such experiences. As a consequence, girls muted their voices or gave up trying to express themselves altogether. Theme 6 was identified in 13% of the narratives that contained silencing.

Theme 7: Dissociation from aspects of one's private self. A potential psychological consequence of the basic silencing process described in Theme 1, this cognitive form of silencing describes the disconnection from aspects of private experience than can occur as a result of habitual suppression. In this form of silencing, aspects of public self-presentation, initially regarded as discordant with internal experience, eventually become internalized and replace what were once core aspects of private experience. Narratives that evoked this theme described girls who had come to trivialize, dismiss, or forget feelings, beliefs, or interests that they once held as important. As this dimension of silencing by its very nature involves a denial or suppression from consciousness of what was once known, the limited presence of this subtheme in our participants' narratives was not surprising, occurring in only 2% of the narratives that contained silencing themes. This subtheme is perhaps more likely to be detected over the course of psychotherapy, or to emerge in careful prospective research with girls during the transition from pre- to early adolescence, as observed by Gilligan and colleagues (e.g., Brown & Gilligan, 1992).

Theme 8: Silencing aspects of the physical self. This theme subsumes two bodily centered manifestations of the silencing process: (a) the concealment of aspects of the physical self perceived to be inferior to social ideals for appearance; and (b) the suppression of or disconnection from bodily cues and needs, the appropriate response to which is perceived to be detrimental to social ideals for appearance. Narratives that contained examples of the former manifestation of this theme depicted girls attempting to hide body fat, blemishes, or other physical "flaws" to avoid social rejection. Stories that evoked the latter form of this theme described girls attempting to ignore hunger, fatigue, or discomfort in order to conform their bodies to social ideals of appearance (e.g., thinness) or force their bodies to meet performance-related goals (e.g., in athletics or dance). Theme 8 was found in 4.8% of the narratives that contained silencing themes. Accordingly, it may be that without assistance from parents, teachers, coaches, therapists, and other trusted adults, most girls do not acquire until later in adolescence the feminist lens necessary for critical insight into the associations between (a) their experiences of physical discomfort and body shame, and (b) cultural body image ideals and social imperatives compelling them to silence their bodies.

Description of Resistance Themes

Five subthemes reflective of various dimensions of the resistance of external silencing imperatives were identified in the content analysis of narrative data. As with the silencing themes, resistance subthemes were embedded in narratives that described the girls' relationships, encounters with societal standards, and identity development. The girls' resistance of silencing imperatives occasionally took the form of direct confrontation with the silencing agents in the girls' lives. More often, however, narratives depicted girls engaged in less direct or altogether private (i.e., cognitive) forms of resistance. Moreover, the forms of silencing resisted in these themes could themselves be either *internal* (i.e., self-silencing in response to external silencing imperatives) or *external* (i.e., others' literal attempts to silence the characters through oppression, domination, or abuse). Regardless of whether or not the characters described in these narratives were successful in their resistance of silencing pressures, their engagement in this process served as another indication of the writers' perceptions of the salience of silencing experiences in the lives of adolescent girls. The following section summarizes the various forms of resistance identified by each subtheme.

Theme 9: Resistance of silencing through agency or voice. This theme concerns direct forms of resistance through overt expression of dissent, opposition, or refusal to comply with external silencing imperatives or attempts at domination. This form of resistance can be manifested through either actions or words. Narratives that contained this theme depicted girls who, in their behaviors and statements, explicitly challenged or defied others (e.g., family members; peers) who were directing them to silence their opinions, expression of feelings, or pursuit of personal goals. Theme 9 was identified in 26% of all narratives that contained themes of resistance.

Theme 10: Resistance of silencing through demonstration of ability. An extension of Theme 9, through this form of resistance individuals not only oppose silencing imperative from others but actively endeavor to prove wrong the assumptions of their would-be oppressors. These assumptions most often involve myths and stereotypes based upon one's gender. Narratives that contained this theme portrayed girls determined to debunk limiting assumptions about female ability in traditional male domains by demonstrating outstanding performance in these areas. A less common subtheme to emerge in the narratives of our participants, Theme 10 was identified in only 7% of the narratives that contained resistance themes.

Theme 11: Resistance of silencing through refusal to internalize a narrow identity. In contrast to Themes 9 and 10, this theme concerns less direct and often internal manifestations of resistance against silencing imperatives. For individuals who engaged in this form of resistance, the act of resistance itself does not involve direct confrontation with external silencing agents (e.g., intimate others; cultural institutions). Rather, such individuals resist through their unwillingness to adopt limiting beliefs about gender, ethnicity, or other pertinent dimensions of their identities. These resisters are able to uphold personal convictions, persist with desired behaviors, and ultimately preserve authentic private selves unmarred by social prescriptions and pressures. Narratives that contained this theme depicted girls who retained their belief in their abilities and worth despite the criticism and discouragement of others on the basis of their gender, appearance, or ethnicity. These girls were also often depicted as remaining undeterred in their pursuit of activities (e.g., baseball) or personal goals (e.g., to become a doctor), despite others' attempts to silence these behaviors and aspirations. The most pervasive of all resistance subthemes, Theme 11 emerged in 45% of all narratives that contained themes of resistance.

Theme 12: Resistance of silencing through retreat to a political underground. This form of resistance involves the construction of private spaces where two or more individuals are able to communicate honestly about aspects of personal experience that are ordinarily silenced in their relationships and social roles. Narratives that contained these themes described girls who created havens and secret places where they could meet and share their thoughts, feelings, and aspirations without experiencing the criticism, interruption, or the oppression of others. Theme 12 was identified in 15% of narratives containing themes of resistance.

Theme 13: Resistance of silencing through flight. Like Themes 11 and 12, this theme concerns another indirect form of resistance, namely, the literal escape from external silencing agents. Narratives that contained this theme portrayed girls who, perceiving themselves as unable to successfully challenge or overcome others' (e.g., family members, boyfriends) attempts to silence or control them, resorted to running away to escape these unsupportive and often abusive environments. Theme 13 was found in 24% of the narratives that contained themes of resistance.

Description of Genuine Self-Expression (Theme 14)

This theme concerns the process of publicly communicating aspects of authentic private experience that may be inconsistent with the interests of others and potentially cause conflict in relationships. Manifestations of this theme can involve either verbal or behavioral forms of communication. Narratives that contained this theme depicted girls who were able to reveal feelings, opinions, and desires that exposed them to vulnerability in their relationships or were inconsistent with attributes girls have been traditionally socialized to express. The presence of this theme in the narratives functioned as an indication of the writers' perceptions of the salience of voice in the experiences of adolescent girls.

Narrative Illustrations with Thematic Coding Explanations

Through creative narratives, participants evoked the silencing and resistance themes described above. Although themes are at times readily apparent, more often they are subtly embedded within the stories. Following are examples of narrative responses to select study photographs, accompanied by brief qualitative analyses to illuminate the emergent themes.

Photo #1 (Mann, 1988, p. 50). This photograph portrays a girl dressed in western-style attire and a cowboy hat, standing with her hand on her hip. Behind her stand three men in cowboy hats and chaps.

Jessi was feeling kind of nervous about being in the rodeo—she was the youngest one there and the only girl, but she still loved the competition. Ever since she was able to walk her dad had taught her how to ride, and she loved the horses. The contest was very important to her, she wanted to do the best she could, and win. As all the other contestants did what they were supposed to do and left, she got even more nervous.

"What if I fall? What if I do awful? What if I completely choke? What if the horse messes up? What if they laugh at me?" she thought. More and more what ifs crossed her mind as she jumped up on the saddle and rode out into the ring.

All the time she was competing, she wasn't really thinking, just doing. When it was finally over she jumped off the horse and ran into the back room. Finally, about an hour later, she got the nerve to go see the final results. She walked up to the board and saw her name next to the champion spot. She had won and all of a sudden the what ifs sounded pretty stupid.

Despite the fact that she had been riding horses for most of her life and that she loved the competition of rodeo, this character began to doubt her ability (Theme 3: Unreasonable Doubt of Ability or Self-Worth) when the other contestants took their turns. She even started to question her success at such simple tasks as remaining seated on her horse; irrational insecurities were fueled by her realization that she was the youngest contestant and the sole female. She was able to put her anxieties aside for the time being, however, when her turn to compete arrived. Released from the nagging self-doubts she associated with her gender, she performed skillfully and won the competition. Realizing her victory, she recognized that her abilities were hers regardless of her age or gender, and she realized that her doubts were without foundation.

She's got sass. Katie, her name, wouldn't make you think that, but catch her out near her horses, listen to her back-talking to her mother, see her face crumple when she's skipped over in class because she's a girl, then you see it. There's strength inside of her. More than you'd find in her "friends" from the ranch her father owns. Everyday she comes out to ride, to kick loose, and let her body control the steed she gallops away on. She can feel the rocky earth beneath her and the dust in her face, and she is let loose from the world that says she can't be a cowboy because she's a nice little girl. But everyday as she returns from her wild, free adventures, she has to face them: the ranchers, the rodeo boys. They laugh to see her coming "Oh, little darlin,' they say "don't you know you ain't gonna be nothin?" After flying free on her horse away from them all, she comes back to see face to face her oppressors. But she's got sass. And she won't stay quiet.

This story relates a girl's refusal to internalize a narrow identity (Theme 11: Resistance of Silencing through Refusal to Internalize a Narrow Identity) despite the demeaning messages of the local men who mockingly insist that she is destined to be "nothin" (Theme 5: Others' Imperatives to Silence the Self). This young girl has "sass" enough to express her opinions and emotions shamelessly (Theme 14: Genuine Self-Expression) and enjoy the exhilaration of riding wild and free on her horse. Refusing to limit herself by being the "nice little girl" others expect, this character has enough strength to challenge fearlessly those who attempt to belittle her (Theme 9: Resistance of Silencing through Agency or Voice).

Photo #3 (Mann, 1988, p. 25). This photograph depicts a smiling girl with braces wearing a dress and a bow in her hair while a woman holds a hand under the girl's chin and looks at her.

The girl is in the middle of very awkward teenage years. She isn't happy, but feels that she must always be perfect for everyone else, especially her mother. Her mother seems to be showing off "her little girl" to other adults. You can tell from her pasted on smile that she feels forced to constantly be on stage; to play the part of the perfect little girl. She doesn't feel free to be herself.

The girl in this story does not feel like smiling, but she does not want to disappoint her mother and risk conflict by exposing her true emotions (Theme 1: Withholding Genuine Self-Expression). This character forces a smile in an attempt to be the "perfect little girl" she thinks her mother and the other adults will approve of and expect (Theme 2: Judging the Self by External Standards). She does not have the chance to be herself, but must live up to an artificial image consistent with what is expected for young women.

Photo #5 (Mann, 1988, p. 31). This is a photograph of two girls in shorts sitting with their legs outstretched and their backs against a tree.

Jackie and Beth were best friends. They had grown up together, only a yard apart, and had been friends since birth. They shared their secrets, and didn't keep a thing from each other. There was a spot where they always went to talk. It was in the woods so no one else could hear them. A special place, where two people had been before them. They were at their spot, but for the last time. Beth's dad had been transferred to a town over 300 miles away. Both were incredibly sad that they would be that far apart. However, they promised each other that they would write constantly and call each other as much as time and phone bills permitted. Together, they would keep their friendship strong.

Together, these two best friends have created their own private world (Theme 12: Resistance of Silencing through Retreat to a Political Underground) where they can exchange intimacies and celebrate the connection they have shared since birth. The relationship, as well as the physical space in the woods, has sheltered these girls and provided an emotional refuge. Faced with a major life change—in this case, a move away from home— these girls will lose their physical togetherness but pledge to continue sharing their valued underground world.

Photo #7 (Mann, 1988, p. 2). This is a photograph of an African-American girl, eyes closed and smiling, leaning against a white wall on which is cast the shadow of a tree.

A thinker, a wisher, a dreamer. That's what she thought of herself. Hers was the only black family in an all white neighborhood. Every day she was made fun of because of the color of her skin. At first it made her angry. She wanted to hurt those people, she hated them. But her mother said it wouldn't do anything but make things worse for her family. She had to vent her anger. She tried hitting pillows. She cried a lot. One day after being mocked once again at school she came home and started to write. She just picked up a pencil and started to put her feelings on paper. She wrote poem after poem everyday. Her mom said she should show them to someone. She gave them to her teacher who read them in class. When her classmates heard that she'd written the poems they were shocked but eventually gave her respect. Now she's treated like everyone else.

The racism this girl experiences from her schoolmates becomes the source of intense, initially overwhelming feelings that she openly expresses in her affect and behavior (Theme 14: Genuine Self-Expression). Aided by the understanding and support of her mother, this character is able to channel these feelings into a creative outlet. Ultimately, she uses this artistic medium to communicate her feelings to her peers in an open and constructive manner (Theme 9: Resistance of Silencing through Agency or Voice).

Photo #13 (Mann, 1988, p. 44). This is a photograph of a girl wearing a dress and bow and holding a doll. She is seated in front of a window while a woman leans over her, fixing her hair.

Sara sits by the window, feeling the hot Louisiana sun pounding on her fair head. Her mother is arranging her golden hair, almost one hair at a time. In her arms she holds Marianna, her doll and closest confidant. Marianna can hear her, and Marianna understands what she says. She has tried to speak to her mother in the same way, but she always simply shakes her head and smiles sadly. Mother says she can't go to school, the place where you learn things. Because they couldn't understand her. Sara hates sitting home all day; all day she sits, dressed up like Marianna for no reason in particular, almost like a doll herself, trapped in a doll house where the doors are locked, and the sun pounds on your head in the afternoon.

Dressed like her beloved doll, her sole confidante, this girl tries, repeatedly and unsuccessfully, to be heard, to make herself known (Theme 14: Genuine Self-Expression). Her restrictions are so severe that she is not even allowed to leave the physical confines of her home to attend school. Trapped in a world in which no one listens to her, this girl is left to sit inside all day, her needs and desires invisible to her mother. Taking the metaphor of loss of voice as a consequence of others' silent disregard to its extreme, this character is essentially rendered mute (Theme 6: Not Being Listened to/Heard).

Get your hand out of my hair. You're just so damn nitpicky, now, aren't you. Everything has to be oh so perfect, I'm your little angel, and everything has to be just right or else Daddy'll get mad. Well I've got news for you. I'm not your little angel. I don't care how mad Daddy gets, I don't want to be sheltered like this. I want to roll in the mud, play ball, get outside, be like a normal girl. But I have to be your little princess, always prim, always proper, always oh so well behaved. One of these days, mommy, one of these days. I'll show you. I'll rip off the dress, throw it in the mud, eat the wild strawberries, laze in the sun. But for now, I'm locked up, just waiting for daddy. But someday, mammy, someday . . .

This narrative evokes Themes 1, 5, and 11. Forced to be a "little princess," this girl silently rages (Theme 1: Withholding Genuine Self-Expression) against her parents' smothering restrictions (Theme 5: Others' Imperatives to Silence the Self), waiting for the time to come when she can break free and live as she likes, regardless of rules about how a girl should behave. Although she is not quite ready to challenge them directly, this girl nonetheless refuses to succumb to her parents' narrow expectations for her (Theme 11: Resistance of Silencing through Refusal to Internalize a Narrow Identity); she knows that she will survive their limits and eventually celebrate her own life fully, perhaps even eating "wild strawberries."

Photo #20 (Mann, 1988, p. 26). This is a photograph of a girl in loose-fitting jeans and a designer T-shirt sitting slouched on a couch.

As Theresa was walking home from school that Wednesday afternoon, she heard the same usual comments from the neighborhood guys. She tried to block them out as much as possible, but it was hard. After having such a bad day, she almost began to believe what everyone said, even though she knew it wasn't true. She couldn't help the fact that there was no healthy food in her house. Theresa's best friends always told her what a good hearted person she was, but when the same people always say it to her, she begins to doubt it.

In this story, this girl receives competing messages about the type of person she is. Although her friends provide positive affirmations about her personality, these become overshadowed by the taunts and insults with which she is bombarded by her male peers. In the midst of this negative feedback, this character begins to doubt the veracity of information furnished by those who know her best and, consequently, her value as a person (Theme 3: Unreasonable Doubt of Ability or Self-Worth).

Photo #21 (Mann, 1988, p. 30). This is a photo of a girl wearing shorts and a tank top with braided hair. She is sitting outdoors on a stone statue with her back to the camera.

A poet, an artist, a musician. A scientist, a teacher, a doctor, a lawyer. I could do any of those things. Not because the law says that a woman is allowed into any of these careers, but because being a woman will give me the strength to do what I want. I will do all these things without any help from any man. I will be able to do it by myself. Because I'm smart. Because I'm strong. Because I'm a woman.

Being a woman is not a burden. It is not a punishment nor a handicap. The things that we must do are not things that we must suffer through or things that we must do because we have to. They are things that make us stronger, so we may face any challenge that comes along.

There's nothing wrong with men. But I am a woman. As I sit on the steps of my house, I sit and think. Men are to love, to laugh with and to talk with, and be friends with and lovers with. But I am not a man and I'm not sorry that I'm not. Because I am a woman.

In this moving narrative, this girl celebrates her own strengths and abilities and refuses to limit herself to others' expectations based on her gender (Theme 11: Resistance of Silencing through Refusal to Internalize a Narrow Identity). She is free to be herself and to determine her own way from the full range of choices, unconcerned with the restrictions and myths some might associate with being a girl. She accepts the challenges that will face her and knows that, being a woman, she will be able to meet them successfully.

DISCUSSION

In this first phase of our project on Silencing and Resistance during Adolescence, we have attempted to address several empirical and methodological questions related to the dimensions of silencing and resistance for early-adolescent girls. Foremost, findings from the study described in this chapter revealed experiences of silencing and voice to be salient to the social worlds of early-adolescent girls as represented by our research participants. The majority of participants included reference to these issues in their writings about adolescent identities, relationships, gender roles, and confrontation with cultural prescriptions and ideals for girls. Fully one quarter of all study narratives concerned themes of silencing, resistance against silencing, or genuine self-expression. Although the findings from this phase of our project do not address the extent to which individual participants personally engage in silencing and resistance in their own lives and relationships, they do establish that girls are aware of these processes, recognize their frequent occurrence in other girls their age, and can articulate their understanding of silencing in their writing. Moreover, the frequency with which participants' narratives contained these themes would appear to suggest their central relevance to girls' experiences of early adolescence. Ultimately, findings from this phase of our project support further inquiry into the personal silencing experiences of early-adolescent girls.

Findings from the present study represent new empirical evidence supporting the multidimensional nature of self-silencing processes. Eight conceptually distinct themes reflective of behavioral, cognitive, and bodily centered dimensions of silencing were identified. The dimensions of silencing suggested by these themes were consistent with, and extended upon, those that have been observed in previous questionnaire-based and ethnographic research (e.g., Brown & Gilligan, 1992; Jack & Dill, 1992). Results from this phase of our project also contributed to the more limited clinical and ethnographic knowledge base on the resistance of self-silencing pressures and imperatives. Aside from a study by Way (1995), the present study represents the only other known systematic examination of the phenomenon of voice or genuine self-expression in adolescent girls. Moreover, this work constitutes the first empirical examination of the process of resistance against silencing. With the identification of five distinct themes, we have provided initial evidence for the multidimensional nature of resistance against silencing.

Future Research Using Our Photo-Narrative Approach to Study Silencing and Resistance

In a later phase of our work on silencing and resistance during adolescence, we employed a modified version of the photo-narrative method to examine the personal experiences of early-adolescent girls (Spinazzola, Pierce, Wilson, & Stocking, 1999). In addition, through semi-structured interviews, we explored girls' perceptions of the psychological, relational, and societal factors which function to constrain or enable silencing or resistance processes (Wilson, Spinazzola, & Stocking, 1998; Pierce, Spinazzola, & Stocking, 1999). The next step of this project will be to examine the contribution of narrative and interview data—in conjunction with more standard questionnaire data—to an understanding of the impact of silencing experiences on the self-concepts of adolescent girls. Analyses of findings from these studies are currently underway. Further research is also needed to understand how similar processes of silencing and resistance are manifest in boys' development, as well as that of girls from various ethnic and cultural backgrounds. Since boys receive different messages about appropriate forms of self-expression and social activities, the dimensions of silencing experienced by boys, as well as the *types* of private experience that they feel pressured to silence, are likely to differ in some important ways from those of girls.[8] Ultimately, it is our intent to channel knowledge gained from this research toward the development of psychoeducational, preventative, and clinical intervention strategies for both adolescent girls and boys grappling with issues of silencing and voice.

Charting Multiple Courses for Self-Expression in Adolescent Girls: Future Applications of Our Photo-Narrative Methodology in Psychoeducation and Prevention

If we truly hope to forge a future for girls in which personal agency, voice, and authentic self-expression in relationships are possible, we must first empower girls with the tools to examine critically, challenge, and, if necessary, dismantle the many obstacles to healthy development that they encounter during adolescence. Silencing is a complex and multidimensional phenomenon. As such, intervention must occur on the multiple levels and within the multiple contexts in which it is understood and experienced by adolescent girls. In helping girls to resist silencing pressures, we must recognize the various forms these pressures take and how they impact girls' ideation, behaviors, and relationships to their bodies. Then, strategies and initiatives promoting girls' resistance must be designed to intervene at the cognitive, behavioral, and bodily levels.

Through close examination of their stories, we learned that the early-adolescent girls in our study were often acutely aware not only of societal and relational silencing pressures, but also of effective ways to resist these pressures. Like silencing, resistance is a multifaceted process, suggesting that there are likely to be multiple ways for girls to challenge silencing forces and maintain authentic self-representation. Efforts at prevention and intervention of silencing by educators and clinicians need to recognize, draw upon, and enhance girls' innate and learned strategies for resistance.

We believe our photo-narrative method can be used as one psychoeducational and clinical tool in working with girls struggling with issues of silencing and voice. We suspect that encouraging girls to write and talk about the girls depicted in our study photographs could promote their ability to express and work through issues of silencing and self-representation that are otherwise difficult to articulate or even conceptualize. For example, some of our colleagues have already proposed use of this method in helping early-adolescent girls to critically examine culturally-informed ideals for female appearance and the often implicit assumptions made about the personalities, quality of relationships, and life outcomes of girls who attain or fall short of these ideals (Steen, Spinazzola, & Stocking, 1997).

Similarly, this photo-narrative approach could be incorporated into workshops and teaching modules geared towards helping girls learn to identify, challenge, and resist silencing pressures encountered during adolescence. For instance, in one such workshop, leaders could present participants with pre-written narratives in response to the study photographs that depict silenced versus agentic girls. Workshop leaders could then teach participants to identify and question various parameters of silencing (e.g., the psychological, interpersonal, and societal factors that influence girls' self-doubts and suppression of authentic thoughts, feelings, and needs in relationships) and resistance (e.g., the factors that enable girls to maintain agentic views of self and genuinely express themselves in their relationships). Next, participants could be encouraged to incorporate information gained from this exercise with personal knowledge and experience in order to work collectively to envision alternate narrative outcomes for the silenced girls in these photographs.

The narratives could thus be simultaneously used both as templates for prototypical adolescent experiences and as a medium for participants to explore ways of challenging silencing imperatives and promoting healthy resistance in their own lives. In effect, this approach could be used as a mechanism to convey to early-adolescent girls what otherwise would likely be an overly sophisticated and abstract technique: namely, the donning of a feminist psychological "lens" to "deconstruct" silencing narratives and "reconstruct" narratives of resistance. Although this represents only one of several possible applications, the creative use of this photo-narrative approach in preventative work with girls aimed at promoting resistance against silencing clearly warrants further consideration. Such workshops, if integrated into educational programs, would be beneficial for boys' as well as girls' development. First, workshops conducted with both genders could promote an atmosphere in which the multiple opportunities for self-expression available to adolescents are recognized and validated, rather than being divided into rigidly gender-stereotyped categories. Second, involving boys in this process may function to increase their sensitivity to the pressures that many adolescent girls face, along with their motivation to support girls' achievement of personal agency and voice. Finally, similar methods to our approach for girls could be developed to assist young men to work through their own difficulties with authentic self-representation and expression.

Beyond working with adolescents to foster their potential for resistance in the face of silencing pressures, findings from this study point to the need to deconstruct current societal and relational systems to clear the way for the establishment of less limiting courses for both girls and boys as they travel from childhood to adulthood. As many of the messages girls and boys receive about silencing are disseminated by significant others, we must convey in our homes, schools, and communities the importance of recognizing and fostering adolescents' unique self-expression. Furthermore, we need to advocate for institutional change in our educational system and in the media to transform narrow and often damaging images and constructions of women and men. Ultimately, findings from our study remind us of the work that remains to be done to create a world in which young people no longer feel that they must abandon vital aspects of self in order to achieve fulfillment, security, and success in their personal and professional lives.

NOTES

The research reported here was supported by the Duke University Talent Identification Program as well as by an Alison Bracey von Brock Memorial Research Fellowship awarded to the first author. Additional funding was received from a Duke University Arts & Sciences Research Council Grant awarded to Karla Fischer, Ph.D., J.D. The authors would like to acknowledge Karla Fischer for her instrumental role in helping to conceptualize and initiate the Duke Project on Silencing and Resistance during Adolescence. We would also like to thank the following undergraduate assistants for their respective contributions to the research process: Katie Anderson, Jacob Godfrey, Jamie Meyer, and Laura Weaver. We would especially like to thank Courtney Pierce and Jennifer Steen for their substantial contributions to other phases of this project, and Deanne Rhodes for her invaluable assistance throughout.

1. Clearly, not all girls succumb to these problems, and several important intrapsychic, physiological, behavioral, social, life event, and environmental risk and protective factors have been identified (see for example, Beitchman, Zucker, Hood, DaCosta, Akman, & Cassavia, 1992; Brooks-Gunn & Warren, 19889; Simmons & Blyth, 1987; Smith, Spinazzola, Stocking, Rochleau, & Dueker, 1999). Moreover, recent feminist scholarship that carefully attends to the diversity of girls' experiences during adolescence placed more equal emphasis on efforts to illuminate and draw upon girls' many manifestations of strength and resiliency during this period (Johnson, Roberts, & Worrell, 1999).

2. For one, in conceptualizing silencing as the underlying dynamic in depression, and not merely as one risk factor for depression, Jack's formulation of silencing model does not speak to the preponderance of self-silencing experiences in nondepressed women. Moreover, her model of silencing, which emphasizes psychopathology over self-consciousness, -monitoring, and -appraisal, obscures the subjective meaning making at the heart of this phenomenon by overlooking the extensive literature on the self-system. Finally, such a construction does not allow or account for transient self-silencing practices that may be engaged in for self-enhancing or ego syntonic purposes.

3. It should be noted that engagement in this form of resistance coexists along with the potential for girls' mutual enforcement of unrealistic ideals and social pressures to silence authentic experience.

4. Available research to date has indicated that academically gifted adolescent girls are at least as vulnerable to self-silencing pressures as girls who demonstrate more normative academic abilities and achievement (Olshen & Matthews, 1987; Silverman, 1986). Conversely, the possibility that superior academic achievement would better enable study participants to articulate experiences of silencing and resistance was taken into account and ultimately considered to be a potential advantage of the present study design.

5. For page citations from the original collection (Mann, 1988) for each numerically identified photograph, refer to Spinazzola (1999). All photographs used by permission of the artist.

6. Instructions were adapted from those proposed by Murray (1943) for use with the Thematic Apperception Test, a widely used image-based projective measure for narrative data collection.

7. Although no studies to date have considered whether the experimenter's gender influences the content of the girls' *written* narratives in regard to themes of silencing, Way (1995) examined whether gender of investigator influences the girls' willingness to speak openly about such themes in interviews. She found that themes of silencing and voice emerged in the girls' oral narratives irrespective of the interviewer's gender; moreover, interviewer gender had no apparent effect on the ways in which girls discussed these themes.

8. For a consideration of the impact on silencing of asymmetrical patterns of gender-role socialization in girls and boys, refer to Spinazzola (1996).

REFERENCES

American Association of University Women (AAUW). (1992). *How schools short-change girls: The AAUW report: A study of major findings on girls and education*. Washington, DC: AAUW Educational Foundation and National Educational Association.

Beitchman, J. H., Zucker, K. J., Hood, J. E., DaCosta, G. A., Akman, D., & Cassavia, E. (1992). A review of the long-term effects of child sexual abuse. *Child Abuse and Neglect, 16*, 101–118.

Belenky, M., Clinchy, B., Goldberger, N., & Tarule, J. (1986). *Women's ways of knowing: The development of self, voice, and mind*. New York: Basic Books.

Brooks-Gunn, J. (1996). *The uniqueness of the early adolescent transition: Reflections and directions*. Presidential address presented at the biennial meeting of the Society for Research in Adolescence, Boston.

Brooks-Gunn, J., & Warren, M. (1988). The psychological significance of secondary sexual characteristics in nine- to eleven-year-olds. *Child Development, 60*, 40–55.

Brown, L. M. (1991). A problem of vision: The development of voice and relational knowledge in girls ages seven to sixteen. *Women's Studies Quarterly, 19*, 52–71.

Brown, L. M. (1998). *Raising their voices: The politics of girls' anger*. Cambridge, MA: Harvard University Press.

Brown, L. M., Debold, E., Tappan, M., & Gilligan, C. (1991). Reading narratives of conflict and choice for self and moral voices: A relational method. In W. Kurtines & J. Gewirtz (Eds.), *Handbook of moral behavior and development, Vol. 2: Research* (pp. 25–61). Hillsdale, NJ: Erlbaum.

Brown, L. M., & Gilligan, C. (1991). Listening for voice in narratives of relationships. In M. Tappan & M. Packer (Eds.), *Narrative and storytelling: Implications for understanding moral development* (pp. 43–62). San Francisco: Jossey-Bass.

Brown, L. M., & Gilligan, C. (1992). *Meeting at the crossroads: Women's psychology and girls' development*. Cambridge, MA: Harvard University Press.

Carr, J., Gilroy, F., & Sherman, M. (1996). Silencing the self and depression among women. *Psychology of Women Quarterly, 20*, 375–392.

Cowan, G., Bommersbach, M., & Curtis, S. R. (1995). Codependency, loss of self, and power. *Psychology of Women Quarterly, 19,* 221–236.

Fredrickson, B., & Roberts, T. (1997). Objectification theory: Towards understanding women's lived experience and mental health risks. *Psychology of Women Quarterly, 21,* 173–206.

Gilligan, C. (1982). *In a different voice: Psychological theory and women's development.* Cambridge, MA: Harvard University Press.

Gilligan, C. (1991). Women's psychological development: Implications for psychotherapy. In C. Gilligan, A. Rogers, & D. Tolman (Eds.), *Women, girls and psychotherapy: Reframing resistance* (pp. 5–31). Binghamton, NY: Haworth Press.

Gilligan, C., Lyons, N., & Hanmer, T. (Eds.). (1990). *Making connections: The relational worlds of adolescent girls at Emma Willard School.* Cambridge, MA: Harvard University Press.

Gilligan, C., Rogers, A. G., & Tolman, D. L. (Eds.). (1991). *Women, girls, and psychotherapy: Reframing resistance.* New York: Harrington Park Press.

Gratch, L. V., Bassett, M. E., & Attra, S. L. (1995). The relationship of gender and ethnicity to self-silencing and depression among college students. *Psychology of Women Quarterly, 19,* 509–515.

Halprin, S. (1995). *"Look at my ugly face!" Myths and musings on beauty and other perilous obsessions with women's appearance.* New York: Viking.

Hancock, E. (1989). *The girl within.* New York: Fawcett Columbine.

Hart, B., & Thompson, J. (1996). Gender role characteristics and depressive symptomatology among adolescents. *Journal of Early Adolescence, 16,* 407–426.

Jack, D. (1991). *Silencing the self: Depression and women.* Cambridge, MA: Harvard University Press.

Jack, D., & Dill, D. (1992). The Silencing the Self Scale: Schemas of intimacy associated with depression in women. *Psychology of Women Quarterly, 16,* 97–106.

Johnson, N. G., Roberts, M. C., & Worrell, J. P. (Eds.). (1999). *Beyond appearance: A new look at adolescent girls.* Washington, DC: American Psychological Association.

Jordan, J. V., Kaplan, A. G., Miller, J. B., Stiver, I. P., & Surrey, J. L. (1991). *Women's growth in connection: Writings from the Stone Center.* New York: Guilford Press.

Mann, J. (1996). *The difference.* New York: Warner Books.

Mann, S. (1988). *At twelve: Portraits of young women.* New York: Aperture.

Miles, M. B., & Huberman, M. (1984). *Qualitative data analysis: A new sourcebook of methods.* Beverly Hills, CA: Sage.

Murray, H. A. (1943). *Thematic Apperception Test manual.* Cambridge, MA: Harvard University Press.

Olshen, S. R., & Matthews, D. J. (1987). The disappearance of giftedness in girls: An intervention strategy. *Roeper Review, 9* (4), 251–254.

Page, J. R., Stevens, H. B., & Galvin, S. L. (1996). Relationships between depression, self-esteem, and self-silencing behaviors. *Journal of Social and Clinical Psychology, 15,* 381–396.

Petersen, A., Tobin-Richards, M., & Boxer, A. (1983). Puberty: Its measurement and its meaning. *Journal of Early Adolescence, 3,* 47–62.

Pipher, M. (1994). *Reviving Ophelia: Saving the selves of adolescent girls.* New York: Ballantine.

Pierce, C. P., Spinazzola, J., & Stocking, V. B. (1999, March). *Catalysts for voice: Adolescent girls' perspectives on genuine self-expression and the resistance of silencing.* Paper presented at the 24th Annual Conference of the Association for Women in Psychology, Providence, RI.

Rogers, A. G. (1991). A feminist poetics of psychotherapy. In C. Gilligan, A. G. Rogers, & D. L. Tolman (Eds.), *Women, girls and psychotherapy: Reframing resistance* (pp. 5–31). New York: Harrington Park Press.

Rogers, A. G. (1993). Voice, play, and a practice of ordinary courage in girls' and women's lives. *Harvard Educational Review, 63,* 265–295.

Roth, S., & Batson, R. (1997). *Naming the shadows: A new approach to individual and group psychotherapy for adult survivors of childhood incest.* New York: Free Press.

Roth, S., Lebowitz, L., & DeRosa, R. (1996). Thematic assessment of posttraumatic stress reactions. In J. P. Wilson & T. M. Keane (Eds.), *Assessing psychological trauma and PTSD: A handbook for practitioners* (pp. 512–528). New York: Guilford Press.

Scheier, M. F., & Carver, C. S. (1981). Private and public aspects of self. *Review of Personality and Social Psychology, 2,* 189–216.

Silverman, L. (1986). What happens to the gifted girl? In C. Maker (Ed.), *Critical issues in gifted education: Defensible programs for the gifted* (pp. 43–91). Austin, TX: Pro-Ed.

Simmons, R., & Blyth, D. (1987). *Moving into adolescence: The impact of pubertal change and school context.* New York: Aldine de Gruyter.

Spinazzola, J. (1996). *The impact of gender role socialization on adolescent identity development: A silencing of girls' selves during adolescence?* Unpublished qualifying paper, Duke University Department of Psychology, Durham, NC.

Spinazzola, J. (1997, October). *A developmental perspective on the silencing of girls' selves during adolescence.* Paper presented at the Fourth Annual Conference of the Southern Regional Chapter of the Association for Women in Psychology, Wilmington, NC.

Spinazzola, J. (1999). *Dimensions of silencing and resistance for adolescents.* Unpublished doctoral dissertation, Duke University Department of Psychology, Durham, NC.

Spinazzola, J., & Stocking, V. B. (1998, March). *Psychometric properties of a revised Silencing the Self Scale (STSS) for use with adolescents.* Paper presented at the Seventh Biennial Meeting of the Society for Research on Adolescence, San Diego, CA.

Spinazzola, J., Pierce, C. P., Wilson, H. W., & Stocking, V. B. (1999, March). *Adolescent girls' narratives of silencing and voice II: Themes of resistance.* Paper presented at the 24th Annual Conference of the Association for Women in Psychology, Providence, RI.

Spinazzola, J., Wilson, H. W., & Pierce, C. P. (1999). *Themes of silencing and resistance in the social worlds of adolescent girls: A manual for narrative coding.* Unpublished manuscript, Duke University Department of Psychology, Durham, NC.

Steen, J., Spinazzola, J., & Stocking, V. B. (1997, October). *A narrative study of the psychological and relational implications of body-image archetypes for adolescent girls.* Paper presented at the Fourth Annual Conference of the Southern Regional Chapter of the Association for Women in Psychology, Wilmington, NC.

Stevens, H. B., & Galvin, S. L. (1995). Structural findings regarding the Silencing the Self Scale. *Psychological Reports, 77*, 11–17.

Stocking, V. B., Spinazzola, J., Dueker, G. L., & Pierce, C. P. (under review). *The role of silencing and best friendship qualities in predicting general self-concept.*

Taylor, J. M., Gilligan, C., & Sullivan, A. M. (1995). *Between voice and silence: Women and girls, race and relationship.* Cambridge, MA: Harvard University Press.

Thompson, J. M. (1995). Silencing the self: Depressive symptomatology and close relationships. *Psychology of Women Quarterly, 19*, 337–353.

Way, N. (1995). "Can't you see the courage, the strength that I have?" Listening to urban adolescent girls speak about their relationships. *Psychology of Women Quarterly, 19*, 107–128.

Wilson, H. W., Spinazzola, J., & Stocking, V. B. (1998, March). *Constraints against self-expression: Adolescent girls' perspectives on the causes of silencing-of-the-self.* Paper presented at the 23rd Annual Conference of the Association for Women in Psychology, Baltimore.

Chapter 7

Self-Esteem Inoculation: Protecting Girls from the Effects of Sexism

Lynn H. Collins

Despite the fact that Black girls and women face a daily barrage of both sexism and racism, often referred to as "double jeopardy" (Jeffries & Ransford, 1980; St. Jean & Feagin, 1998), they appear to have higher self-esteem than women only facing one of these challenges. Black girls and women score higher on the Rosenberg Self-Esteem Scale (Rosenberg, 1965) and other measures of self-esteem than do White girls and women (Tashakkori, 1993; Tashakkori & Thompson, 1991). Their scores are usually similar to those of White men. Are these women presenting a tough façade, or are they genuinely content and proud of who they are? After all, more than 80% of African-American adolescents in Phinney and Chavira's (1995) study reported having experienced discriminatory treatment; the actual rate was probably closer to 100% (Tatum, 1997). White women's experiences with sexism are minimal compared to the cumulative, exponential experience of combined sexism and racism that Black women face as they navigate the obstacles within Black and White cultural contexts. Black women are raised in a more egalitarian environment (Hale-Benson, 1986) and they are often stereotyped as super strong women (Chideya, 1995; West, 1995) or "mules" (Ammons, 1995), yet they also have to function in a White world where women are not expected to be strong or assertive. Their tenuous status in the White male world, which is linked to this socially constructed racial category, puts them at even greater risk of being victims of discrimination, economic disadvantage, domestic violence, and homicide compared to White women. As a group, White women are greatly privileged and have much more access to power, resources, and other privileges in White male society relative to Black women. White female feminists are themselves institutionally advantaged and more likely to be heard and protected from the problems listed above relative to Black women. Despite these realities, Black women persist and do so in a manner that results in more positive feelings about themselves and their ethnic identity.

What can European-American women and men learn from African Americans about preparing children for a sexist, racist world? How can we protect *all* girls' self-esteem from the negative, restrictive messages they face from birth to old age? Is there a way that we can help girls to determine the accuracy of feedback they receive, to separate the good and useful comments from the wrong and damaging? How can we use this information to chart a new course for us all? To answer these questions it is useful to review what is known about African-American women's self-esteem. In this chapter I will review the research on influences on self-esteem, including those related to family, community, education, attribution processes, and group dynamics. The effectiveness of these factors in ameliorating some of the impact of double jeopardy for Black women suggests they would be effective in protecting the self-esteem of White women plagued by only by sexism and the impact of sexist socialization.

THE SELF

Many theories of personality development emphasize the development of the self. Rosenberg (1979) described a conceptualization of the self that includes: the *extant self* (consisting of self-confidence related to efficacy and an affective self-acceptance); the *desired self* (what one would like to be); and the *presenting self* (aspects of self shown to others). For the purposes of this chapter Rosenberg's (1979) definition of global self-esteem will be used. According to Rosenberg, self-esteem involves personal and global feelings of self-worth, self-regard, or self-acceptance. Global self-esteem is the level of general regard one has for oneself as a person (Harter, 1993). Most studies of ethnic identity and self-esteem examine global self-esteem.

Many theories (Baumrind, 1971; Masterson, 1988; Rogers, 1951) include descriptions of a bipolar self composed of positive affect for oneself that is due in part to others' valuing of the self, balanced by a set of standards and limits for behavior. The positive affect for the self has been said to result from unconditional affection from others, or *unconditional positive regard* (Rogers, 1951), and the experience of having the attention and adoration of others, referred to as *mirroring* (Masterson, 1988). Similarly, Coopersmith (1967) believes that self-esteem is partly determined by a child's sense of whether she or he is valued. These theories of the development of the self are consistent with the sociological concept of the "looking glass self" (Cooley, 1956; Mead, 1934), which is the view of self that develops as a response to feedback from others.

A healthy self also needs a set of standards for behavior. Rogers calls the standards to which one is held *conditions of worth.* Self Psychology refers to the need for such standards for behavior *idealizing needs* (Masterson, 1988). These theoretical perspectives suggest that parents should communicate that the child is accepted, valued, and belongs, while at the same time setting appropriate limits. Baumrind (1971) and Coopersmith (1967) have advocated a balance of emotional support and appropriate limits in building a healthy, competent self. In White, middle-class families, the children who were best adjusted had parents who gave the children the freedom to be a separate individuals within reasonable behavioral limits and listened to the children's opinions and concerns (Baumrind, 1971). Self-esteem is also related to children's experiences with success and their status or position in the environment. In other societies, children may become more interdependent individuals, and the support from their community helps them to persevere. Self-esteem is moderated by children's and the communities' definition of success and failure and by their style of coping with negative feedback.

Rogers (1951) believed that problems arise when an individual is not in touch with her or his real self's values and needs, when the feedback they receive is either different than expected or not related to their own behaviors, when others block their attempts to self-actualize, and when they do not receive empathy. Given the role of feedback from others in determining our sense of self, one might predict that consequences of membership in a minority group would undermine self-esteem. Discrimination increases the likelihood of poor treatment by others, including fewer empathic responses, more negative evaluations, and the dismissal of ones opinions and concerns. Discrimination lowers status and decreases opportunities. Paradoxically, in studies of the self-esteem of adolescents and adults from a variety of backgrounds, members of oppressed or stigmatized groups have not been found to have lower self-esteem than more privileged groups (Crocker, 1999). Jensen, White, and Galliher (1982) found that the self-esteem of college students who were insulted on the basis of their race or religion did not differ from that of students who were not insulted. Furthermore, many researchers have reported that stigmatized groups actually have higher self-esteem than members of nonstigmatized groups. For example, researchers have found that on the average, Black adolescents' scores on self-esteem measures are equal to or greater than those of Whites, regardless of socioeconomic class (Bowler, Rauch, & Schwarzer, 1986; Brown, 1998; Crocker, Luhtanen, Blain, & Broadnax, 1999; Crocker & Major, 1989; Dukes & Martinez, 1994; Hughes & Demo, 1989; Martinez & Dukes, 1991; Porter & Washington, 1993; Richman, Clark, & Brown, 1985; Rosenberg & Simmons, 1972; Tashakkori, 1992). This is not to say that discrimination and the stressors mentioned do not take a toll on members of stigmatized groups, however, on the average, these groups are able to maintain self-esteem even in the face of multiple affronts (Crocker, 1999;

Crocker & Major, 1989). It is useful to examine how African Americans develop and maintain healthy self-esteem.

COMMON SOURCES OF SELF-ESTEEM

Black and White girls share many common sources of self-esteem, including peers, family, and education. Black children's self-esteem is based on reflected appraisals of friends (Hughes & Demo, 1989), parents, and teachers (Rosenberg, 1979; Rosenberg & Simmons, 1972). Family and community can support the development of self-esteem for Whites and Latinas as well (Hirsch & DuBois, 1991; Licitra-Kleckler & Waas, 1993; Luster & McAdoo, 1995; McCreary, Savin-Williams & Berdt, 1990; Slavin & Berry, 1996; Slavin & Rainer, 1990).

Peers

Supportive friends reduce the impact of stress. Positive relationships with peers have been associated with higher self-esteem (Hirsch & DuBois, 1991; Savin-Williams & Berdt, 1990), and rejection by peers has been associated with lower self-esteem (Demo & Savin-Williams, 1992) in diverse samples of adolescents. McCreary et al. (1996) studied the usefulness of stress, social support, and racial identity in predicting problem behavior in adolescent African Americans. Their participants were a church-based group (adolescents at a religious retreat) that was composed of a broader cross-section in terms of socioeconomic and geographic characteristics than is usual in self-esteem studies. The researchers found that stressful life events and lack of perceived peer support, both related to self-esteem, predicted problem behaviors. In their study, however, the relationship between problem behaviors and self-esteem was not significant. McCreary et al. (1996) found that the impact of friends on self-esteem depended on what type of friends are involved. Although the term "gang" has acquired a negative connotation, children and adolescents from all ethnic, socioeconomic status (SES), sex, and other subgroups tend to cluster together and form alliances. When structured around healthy activities, such social groups may be important to the esteem and support of ethnic minority youth who live in a challenging environment (Prothrow-Stith, 1995, 1996). Structured groups focused on constructive activities would appear to be one way to enhance support and self-esteem.

Family

Family support seems to be important to the esteem of all children (Jackson, McCullough, & Gurin, 1988; Licitra-Kleckler & Waas, 1993; Luster & McAdoo, 1995; McCreary et al., 1996; Peters, 1985; Slavin & Rainer,

1990). Family support was the best predictor of self-esteem for African American adolescents (Luster & McAdoo, 1995) and middle class European American adolescents (Licitra-Kleckler & Waas, 1993; Slavin & Rainer, 1990). McCreary et al. (1996) suggested that perceptions of parental support have even more impact on self-esteem than ethnic identity, academic achievement, or SES. A supportive family environment provides affirmation and identity enhancement which are important for health (James, 1993). African-American parents reported that they believe that providing unconditional love helps to protect their children from stress (Peters, 1985).

Education

Academic achievement is also a major predictor of self-esteem (Bachman & O'Malley, 1984; Fauce, 1984; Harter, 1993; Rosenberg, Schooler, & Schoebach, 1989; Wylie, 1979). In fact, GPA was one of the most significant predictors of self-esteem for African-American adolescents (Osborne, 1995; Phinney, Cantu, & Kurtz, 1997). African-American participants in various studies have reported stressing the value of education in opening up opportunities. The African-American families studied by Phinney and Chavira (1995) reported communicating the value of academic achievement to their children. They told their children that they'd have to work harder to get ahead, but that they could do anything they wanted if they got an education. They encouraged their children to do their best. Such encouragement may increase the chances that they will seek to achieve in school and may instill hope for the future in the face of a difficult past and present.

Inadequate family support, life dissatisfaction, and depression are related to lower achievement scores, which may lead to less confidence in this area. Spencer, Cole, DuPree, Glymph, and Pierre (1993) conducted a study of 562 African-American adolescents. They examined coping methods and academic achievement. Spencer et al. (1993) found that mother's education, negative life events, and youths' perception of family conflict predicted males' academic self-esteem. Mothers' education, parental life dissatisfaction, youths' perception of family conflict, and academic self-esteem predicted females' scores.

Thus, both singly and in combination, stress, emphasis on academic achievement, and family environment determine self-esteem. Furthermore, academic self-esteem may help increase optimism about the future. Lorenzo-Hernandez and Oullette (1998) found that their predominantly female sample of lower-SES Dominican, Puerto Rican, and African-American urban community college students was more strongly focused on the future, than the past or present. Education and an orientation toward the future may increase their optimism about improving their situation and increase their perseverance in working toward goals.

GROUP DYNAMICS INFLUENCING SELF-ESTEEM

There are several other influences that affect the self-esteem of African Americans. These influences are related to egalitarianism, multiple roles, and their status as a stigmatized group. Studies concerning power, self-complexity, social identity, and ethnic identity shed light on their self-esteem development.

Egalitarianism and Self-Complexity

Ethnic and racial issues appear to be more important than are gender issues to African-American women (Giddings, 1984; King, 1989; Slane & Morrow, 1981), perhaps because of the greater impact of racism and the smaller discrepancy between African-American women's and men's salaries. African-American families frequently reject European-American ideas about women's roles and traditional family structure (Collins, 1989; King, 1989; Lorde, 1984; Wyche, 1993). Consequently, gender roles are more flexible and complex for African-American women. African-American women often engage in both traditional and non-traditional activities (Poindexter-Cameron & Robinson, 1997). The wider range of acceptable occupations, activities, and roles associated with an egalitarian community permits African-American women more choices in how they invest their time and increases their self-complexity. Self-complexity refers is the degree to which an individual diversifies their investment of time and energy in various activities and pursuits. Self-complexity buffers and protects self-esteem (Linville, 1985) because disappointments in one area are balanced by successes in others. African Americans with greater self-complexity see themselves as having a variety of roles (e.g., athlete, entrepreneur, mother, scholar, artist) and are less likely than those with fewer roles and activities to be upset by a failure in anyone area. Consistent with this, Molloy and Herzberger (1998) found that African-American women community college students benefited from more eclectic gender roles. High self-esteem and ambitious career aspirations have also been linked to non-traditional careers for African-American college students (Bailey & Mednick, 1987; Burlew, 1982). Conversely, researchers have found that women who hold gender role stereotypic views of women's abilities and interests see themselves as having fewer options and are more likely to experience depression and low self-esteem (Eccles, Barber, Jozefowicz, Malenchuk, & Vida, 1999).

Ethnic Identity

Most of the clinical research on self-esteem has focused on individual competence (academic, athletic, and social), attractiveness, and interpersonal experiences (Harter, 1993). More attention needs to be given to the impact of group membership, such as ethnic identity, on self-esteem. To understand the importance of ethnic identity, it is useful first to understand the phenomenon of social identity. Social identity consists of those aspects of the self-image that are taken from the social categories to which one believes one belongs. People strive to enhance and maintain their self-esteem and to maintain positive social identities. According to social identity theory (Tajfel & Turner, 1986), the main function of claiming membership in a social group is the maintenance and enhancement of self-esteem (Lorenzo-Hernandez & Ouellette, 1998). Researchers have shown that there is a positive relationship between group identity (including ethnic group identity) and self-esteem (Crocker, Luhtanen, Blaine, & Broadnax, 1994; Hogg & Abrams, 1990; Hogg & Sunderland, 1991; Phinney, 1990, 1991, 1992; Stalikas & Gavaki, 1995; Wright, 1985).

Lorenzo-Hernandez and Ouellette (1998) defined ethnic identity as the perception and awareness of being a member of any national, cultural, or ethnic group. It typically includes commitment and a sense of belonging to the group, positive evaluation of the group, interest in and knowledge of the group, and participation in the activities of the group (Phinney et al., 1997). Ethnic identity makes it possible for people to differentiate themselves from other groups, and it is especially important in adolescence when individuals are developing their personal identities. Phinney (1990) conceptualized African-American racial identity as a multifaceted construct that includes positive attitudes, recognition, pride in the socioracial aspects of the self, and an awareness of the political/economic liberation struggles of African Americans.

The tendency to evaluate one's own group more positively than others is called in-group favoritism. In-group favoritism, including ethnocentrism, improves individuals' self-esteem because the group's characteristics are a reflection of its members (Lorenzo-Hernandez, 1998). Unfortunately, ethnocentrism has also been associated with rigid thinking and poor intergroup relations (Brewer, 1979; Tajfel & Turner, 1986). It may enhance self-esteem at the expense of healthy intergroup relations.

It would appear to be easier to evaluate one's group more favorably if one is part of the majority group and has better access to resources. Tajfel (1981) speculated that if one's group is viewed negatively by society, one might view oneself negatively. Researchers have found, however, that group membership enhanced self-esteem, for both minority and majority groups (Lorenzo-Hernandez & Ouellette, 1998; Phinney et al., 1997), although Phinney et al. (1997) noted that it only predicted a portion of the variance (17–27%) for Latina and African-American adolescents.

The belief that members of minority groups view themselves negatively may have been based on old studies that pre-dated the "Black is beautiful" movement and on indirect evidence of devaluation, such as doll color choice (Clark & Clark, 1947). In the mid 1960s the "Black is beautiful" movement began to enhance the way African Americans looked at themselves. It was a consciousness raising movement that provided affirmation of Black identity. Nationwide, the term "Negro" was abandoned in favor of "Black." At the end of the 1980s, African American, Jamaican American, and other more specific terms began to be used (Speight, Vera, & Derrickson, 1996) as more positive, differentiated ethnic identities emerged.

Crocker and Major (1989) concluded that members of a stigmatized or oppressed groups (i.e., a group about which others may hold negative stereotypes, which typically receives fewer positive economic and social outcomes because of discrimination) may protect self-esteem in several ways. Members of stigmatized groups may attribute negative feedback to prejudice against their group, compare their outcomes with those of other members of their group, devalue qualities not associated with their group, and value characteristics associated with their group. All of these protections require that the individual identify with a group and be aware of the biases against that group. Therefore, a strong group (ethnic or gender) identity, which includes education about discrimination, increases the likelihood that an individual is protected. Consistent with this, ethnic identity is one of the most significant predictors of self-esteem for adolescents. Ethnic identity predicts self-esteem for African-American adolescents (Lorenzo-Hernandez & Ouellette, 1998), and among European-American students, ethnic and "American" identity also predict self-esteem (Phinney et al., 1997).

Parham (1989) believed that African-American adolescents need to develop a strong African-American consciousness in order to rise above the social barriers that block their advancement. There is plenty of evidence that ethnic identity protects self-esteem and this identity may help African Americans persist in the face of adversity. Spencer, Dobbs, and Swanson (1988) found that own group cultural identity processes increase the resilience of African-American youth from a variety of socioeconomic groups who are exposed to stressful conditions. They found that African-American adolescent boys with an Afrocentric perspective had better coping skills and lower stress levels than African-American adolescent boys with a more Eurocentric perspective. Similarly, Pyant and Yanico (1991) found that more positive racial identity attitudes predict better self-esteem and well-being and lower levels of depression among lower and middle-class African-American women. Lorenzo-Hernandez and Ouellette (1998) found that ethnic identity was positively related to self-esteem in a predominantly female sample of Dominican, Puerto Rican, and African-American community college students. McCreary et al. (1996) found that positive attitudes toward African Americans predicted higher self-esteem and lower levels of problematic behaviors such as drug use and delinquency among lower and middle-class African Americans.

Social Comparison

Many people maintain self-esteem by comparing themselves to similar or less fortunate others. Within group comparison protects self-esteem, and may be a more accurate source of information about what one is likely to receive. Tashakkori (1993) suggested that African Americans use members of their own community, rather than the broader society, as a reference group. Crocker and Major (1989) found that minority group members compare themselves to other groups of similar status and focus on the areas in which they excel. While same-group and downward comparisons may be affirming or enhance sense of well-being, upward comparisons with the dominant group (whose members have more advantages) may create distress (Crocker & Major, 1989). This is one of the things that may make "token" status (i.e., being the sole minority group member in a situation) unpleasant (Crocker & Major, 1989; Taylor & Fiske, 1978).

Education About Discrimination

Although African-American parents may convey positive attitudes toward African-American culture, children are also exposed to mainstream inaccurate and negative stereotypes through the media, peers, and even the educational system (Shujaa, 1994). They inevitably become aware that their own group is viewed less favorably than others, and they could potentially develop internalized racism (Phinney & Chavira, 1995). Prior preparation for discrimination, however, may prevent them from internalizing the negative feedback and consequently protect them from potential damage to self-esteem. Bowman and Howard (1985) found that education about discrimination has a big impact upon children. They found that lower and middle-class Black parents and youths tend to discuss prejudice as a problem that involves racial barriers and blocked opportunities. Parents in their study told their children that prejudice will cause life to be difficult, and they tried to teach their children how to cope with prejudice. Children socialized to be aware of racism and taught how to behave and cope in response to it tended to have higher grades and greater personal efficacy (Bowman & Howard, 1985).

Peters (1985) studied 30 middle class African-American families over a period of two years. Mothers in Peters' study reported that they felt a sense of responsibility to teach their children how to deal with prejudice and how to acquire survival skills. The mothers stressed the importance of being role models in dealing with prejudice. Thus, the parents encouraged their children to have pride in themselves and their accomplishments, told them that they had rights, and stressed that they were entitled to good and humane treatment (Peters, 1985). Conversely, Spencer (1983) found that lower and middle-class Black children whose parents did not discuss racial discrimination and civil rights were more likely to develop racist attitudes.

The specific strategies that African-American parents and children utilized to cope with racism varied. Many parents in Demo and Hughes' study (1990) emphasized that their children need to learn to get along with and deal with all kinds of people. The parents' goal for their children was a type of mainstream socialization termed "integrative/assertive" that involves both African-American pride and getting along with European Americans (Demo & Hughes, 1990). Another group of parents in the study, however, endorsed a different variety of socialization called "cautious/defensive." This style encourages caution, social distance, and recognition of European-American prejudice.

Phinney and Chavira (1995) found a trend in which parents who themselves used a combination style of passive and active ways of coping had adolescent children who exhibited a proactive coping style. In active coping, the child recognizes racism and handles the associated discrimination without feeling defamed. Adolescents whose parents discussed prejudice as a problem were more likely either to try to ignore remarks or to disprove the stereotypes. These adolescents did not react impulsively (46.4%) and were less likely to respond with a verbal retort (3.1%). However, Phinney and Chavira (1995) found no significant relationship between specific parental socialization style and adolescents' choice of strategic approaches for coping with racism.

Some of the other strategies that African-American adolescents use to cope with prejudice include ignoring the perpetrator (65%), discussing racism with the perpetrator (53.3%), self-affirmation (15%), and proving the racists wrong (33.3%) (Phinney & Chavira, 1995). Phinney and Chavira (1995) also found trends for adolescents with higher self-esteem to use discussion and self-affirmation more frequently than those with low self-esteem. Furthermore, as ethnic identity increased, adolescents were less likely to ignore the perpetrator in response to racist incidents. Students lower in ethnic identity were more likely to respond aggressively. Of course, it is difficult to determine whether the adolescents used certain coping techniques because they felt good about themselves or whether responding in a particular way led to increased self-esteem.

Adaptive Attributional Biases

The attribution of negative feedback and consequences to external factors and positive feedback and outcomes to internal factors has long been known to protect self-esteem (Abramson, Seligman, & Teasdale, 1978; Crittenden & Lamug, 1988), decrease the risk of depression (Anderson, 1990), and increase future attempts at related tasks (Taylor & Brown, 1988). This attribution pattern is called a self-serving attributional bias, and it is a pattern common in most non-depressed people. At the group level, it is called the ethnocentric or group-serving bias (Mullen & Riordan, 1988).

Crocker (1999) argued that the "looking glass self" is too simplistic to explain the self-esteem of stigmatized groups (e.g., African-American, Latina, female, overweight). She has concluded, based on her research, that the self-esteem of stigmatized groups is grounded in the collective representations or shared meanings that people bring to a situation and the characteristics of the situation. Thus, awareness of discrimination may lead African-American women to make external attributions about negative feedback they receive. In other words, rather than take all external feedback at face value as an accurate reflection of their ability, they may attribute it to racism, thereby protecting their self-esteem (Crocker, 1999; Crocker & Major, 1989). In fact, Black students' beliefs that they have been discriminated against correlate positively with self-esteem (Crocker & Blanton, 1999). Negative feedback only seems to lower self-esteem when the evaluator is perceived as fair or unprejudiced (Crocker, Cornwell, & Major, 1989; Crocker, Voelkl, Testa, & Major, 1991). Furthermore, according to research on Kelley's (1972) augmentation principle, the perception that Black students are achieving *in spite of* prejudice may serve to bolster self-esteem (Major, Carrington, & Carnevale, 1984). Positive feedback given by people perceived to be hiding prejudice, however, did not increase the self-esteem of Black college students (Crocker et al., 1991). Thus, self-esteem following positive or negative feedback depends on the context in which it is given, such as the recipient's beliefs about prejudice and specific features of the situation (Crocker, 1999).

The drawback to discounting all feedback because it may be biased by discrimination is that one may inadvertently miss out on constructive, of non-racist, useful feedback (Goffman, 1963; Crocker & Major, 1989). African-American women may also spend extra time trying to figure out whether feedback is appropriate or racist, which detracts from the time and energy available for other activities and creates frustration. If they discount valid feedback, however, African Americans may end up feeling better, but performing less well than they might have had they made use of the feedback (Tashakkori, 1993).

Individuals with dominant status, such as European-American men, are more likely to make external attributions about failures than are European-American women (Rozell, Gundersen, & Terpstra, 1998; Maass & Volpato, 1989), which protects the men's self-esteem. European-American men's performance, however, is not scrutinized to the degree that African Americans' performance is (Crocker & McGraw, 1984; Taylor & Fiske, 1978), therefore European-American men who neglect useful, accurate feedback may suffer fewer negative consequences. Despite the loss of helpful feedback, attributing negative feedback to racism may be adaptive for

African Americans in light of the sheer number of racist messages to which they are subjected over a lifetime.

CHARTING A NEW COURSE FOR GIRLS' AND WOMEN'S SELF-ESTEEM

Although the obstacles are clearly not as numerous for White girls as Black girls, White girls' self-esteem also needs to be strong to withstand the inaccurate, negative cultural messages about women. White adolescent girls tend to experience more challenging and stressful events than do White boys, and Peterson, Sarigiani, and Kennedy (1991) suggest that they experience more depression as a result. European-American women experience less discrimination and more privilege than African American women (Fine, Weis, Powell, & Wong, 1997), and yet score lower on measures of self-esteem scores than do African-American women. There is evidence that many of the factors that contribute to Black women's self-esteem also help to enhance White women's self-esteem. It is clear that having supportive families, communities, friends, and educators is important for the development of everyone's self-esteem (Jackson et al., 1988; Licitra-Kleckler & Waas, 1993; Luster & McAdoo, 1995; McCreary et al., 1996; Peters, 1985; Slavin & Rainer, 1990).

African-American women can turn to their own culture as a source of pride and a sense of identity. European-American women would benefit from developing a source of social identity in addition to being White or American. Although the benefits reaped from the status and privileges of being European-American and associating with European-American men are significant, European-American women's identities as White, European-American *women* may not significantly enhance their self-esteem. Phinney et al. (1997) had 372 Latino/a, 232 African American, and 65 European American high school students complete measures of self-esteem, ethnic identity, American identity, attitudes toward other groups, and demographic variables. Phinney et al.'s (1997) results indicated that European-American boys' self-esteem is related to ethnic and American identity and is higher than adolescent girls' self-esteem. Although European-American boys felt empowered by identification with the dominant, European-American group (Phinney et al., 1997), White and American ethnic identity did not significantly contribute to adolescent girls' self-esteem.

European-American girls need to develop positive identities as women and could benefit from an enhanced social identity. The rest of this chapter will focus on theories of identity development. There are three main parallel models of identity formation for women (Cross, 1971, 1978; Cross, Parham, & Helms, 1991; Downing & Roush, 1984; Helms, 1990). Cross (1971, 1978) developed a model that describes changes in thinking about oneself in regard to a racial reference group for African-American women.

It is called the nigrescence model, and it includes five stages of a process of abandoning externally derived notions of Blackness and adopting a set of more empowering definitions. Downing and Roush (1984) proposed a similar model to describe feminist identity development. The model involved five stages of feminist identity development. Helms (1990) created a four-stage model of women's gender role identity development called the womanist model. It is based on Alice Walker's definition of "womanist." Walker described womanists as black feminists or feminists of color who are characteristically outrageous, audacious, courageous, or willful in behavior. She said that womanists tend to want to know more and in greater depth than is thought to be good for them and to behave as an adult, rather than a child (Walker, 1983). Helm's (1990) model describes the process of abandoning stereotypes regarding Black womanhood and adopting more empowering definitions. Ossana, Helms, and Leonard (1992) extended this model to include all women, as opposed to only Black women. The stages proposed by Downing and Roush (1984) and Ossana et al. (1992) parallel those in Cross' model. Although Cross saw these stages as a developmental sequence, Helms (1990) entertained the notion that individuals may hold simultaneously attitudes connected to any number of stages. Facilitating progress through these stages has implications for clinical interventions, which are currently based on the assumption that low self-esteem is an individual deficit. The interventions suggested in this chapter are directed at preventing, counteracting, and undoing the damage done by negative messages based on stereotypes about women, and at activism to change the stereotypes themselves. Suggestions for facilitating a womanist identity in girls are incorporated into each stage in a stage and age appropriate manner.

Stages of Acquiring a Positive Identity: Nigrescence, Feminist, and Womanist Models

Stage 1: Pre-encounter. According to Cross et al. (1991), at this stage individuals' perspectives are generally Eurocentric. Gender, race, and culture have low salience, and there is little understanding of the sociopolitical implications of group membership. Individuals at the Pre-encounter stage of the nigrescence and womanist models embrace traditional notions of Blackness and womanhood. In the Feminist model, this stage is called passive acceptance. Individuals at this stage may think and act in ways that devalue Blackness and womanhood. Women are unaware of or deny that sexism exists. They hold positive views of traditional roles.

Poindexter-Cameron and Robinson (1997) studied the relationship between African-American college women's self-esteem and their attitudes toward gender and race. They found that greater identification with the Pre-encounter stage was associated with lower self-esteem, whereas identification with a later stage, the Internalization stage, on either the Racial Identity Attitudes Scale (RIAS) (Helms, 1990) or the Womanist Identity Attitude Scale (WIAS) (Ossana et al., 1992) was associated with higher self-esteem. Others have found pre-encounter attitudes associated with poor self-concept, low self-esteem (Ossna et al., 1992; Pyant & Yanico, 1991; Smith, Burlew, & Lundgren, 1991; Speight et al. 1996), high anxiety, and depression (Parham & Helms, 1985a, 1985b). Harris (1995) found that women at this stage were very concerned about others' evaluations of their appearance. Since self-concept, low self-esteem, anxiety, and depression are the most prevalent problems among European-American women (American Psychiatric Association, 1994), it may be that many of these women are at the Pre-encounter stage of identity development.

What would it take to counteract these messages and help girls and women move beyond the Pre-encounter stage? A critical event or events that makes a girl or woman aware of attitudes towards her group is the usual propellant. Therefore, to facilitate womanist identity development, one could stage an event, provide information, or simply give examples of things that other girls experience, thereby beginning the process of educating girls and women about sexism. Another option involves providing education about discrimination and positive images of women early, before negative messages are internalized. Even very young children need to be presented with positive images of girls and women, our multiple interests and potential range of competencies, and our ability to contribute to society.

Stage 2: Encounter. This stage marks the beginning of the search for Black or womanist identity. This stage corresponds to the revelation stage of the feminist identity development model (Downing & Roush, 1984). During this stage, women become aware of sexism and/or racism, become angered by it, and start to think about related issues. At first their thinking may be dichotomous, but it becomes more sophisticated with time. Events or the proposed educational interventions mentioned above motivate the individual to reexamine her assumptions and negative feelings toward the groups to which she belongs. Encounter attitudes have been associated with increasing self-esteem and positive regard (Parham & Helms, 1985a, 1985b). Parham and Helms (1985a, 1985b) found that the further along women are in the sequence of stages, the better their self-esteem and the fewer problems they have with anxiety and depression. Harris (1995) also found that the higher African-American women's self-esteem, the more satisfied they were with their overall appearance. Racial identity attitudes were associated with measures of body satisfaction. African-American women at this stage worried more about their appearance than did women at later stages (Harris, 1995).

Enhancing girls' womanist identity development during the encounter stage. Crocker and Major (1989) have noted that in order for group-related attributions about discrimination to protect an individual, that individual must identify with the group in question, find value in the group, dismiss negative stereotypes of the group, and believe that discrimination against the group exists. How could we enhance a womanist identity? How can we encourage girls to feel good about being girls and becoming women? Cultivation of a womanist identity should begin at an early age, in an age-appropriate manner, in order to prevent inaccurate and limiting ideas about the self that are based on cultural norms. Most studies show that the critical period for the postnatal development of gender identity is from birth through 18 months (Money, 1986). After that point, further consolidation takes place up through the age of 3 or 4 years old (Basow, 1992). Sex-type labels influence the toy, activity, and career preferences of children as young as 3 years old (O'Brien, Huston, & Risley, 1983; Ruble & Ruble, 1982). At around age 3, children show signs of gender constancy. There is evidence that children show signs of gender-typing even before gender constancy is reached (Downs, 1983; Maccoby & Jacklin, 1974; Urberg, 1982). The presence of gender-typing at such an early age has implications because it may mark the time when children start to collect information about what it means to be a girl or a boy. Even if one conceptualizes gender as existing on a continuum, rather than as a dichotomy, some preferences are determined at this point. The popular culture conveys messages about normative behavior. By age 6 or 7, children may firmly state that women cannot be carpenters or doctors, and they may staunchly refuse to believe otherwise (Lips, 1993). Some concepts, such as social identity, may be difficult to grasp and therefore may remain in flux through adolescence.

Much can be learned from the way African-American families prepare their children for the world. Phinney and Chavira (1995) found that African-American families may communicate the value of African-American culture to their children early. They may tell their children about traditions, customs, and celebrations, including those involving women, and about important cultural figures. Some holidays, such as Kwanzaa, celebrate African-American heritage, pride, community, family, and culture. When parents teach children positive qualities of their ethnic culture, the children develop greater awareness, knowledge, and preference regarding their ethnic culture (Branch & Newcomb, 1986).

We need to continue to identify and rethink the messages we send girls through the stories we tell, the cartoons and television shows that we produce, the organization of toy stores, and even the clothing choices we offer. It will also be necessary to rethink and create more traditions and celebrations of milestones of female development. Rites of passage celebrations might be developed for menarche and events might be held to celebrate women who represent what each of us considers to be a valuable role, achievement, service, or other contribution to each other and to greater society.

When they reach school age, other experiences can contribute to girls' sense of worth. We need to be aware of what we teach in schools, since educational institutions play a large role in children's belief systems (Tatum, 1992). Women's roles have been largely excluded from textbooks about U.S. history, although not as much as have the roles of minority groups. Most of what is taught in schools about American heritage focuses on the identity and achievements of European-American males. Boys and girls learn about European-American *men's* history, leaders, rituals, behavior, and values. This sends the message that women and members of minority groups didn't contribute or that their contributions were unimportant. History books have yet to be revised to reflect women's roles. We need to include more information about women's history of resisting oppression, important women in history, women's achievements, women's rituals and rites of passage, and other positive images of women. Until this happens, efforts need to be made to give young girls the message that women and their contributions are valued. Some schools have begun efforts in this area and should be supported for doing so.

Education and academic achievement can be sources of self-esteem for European-American girls. Stressing the value of academic achievement and ensuring access to a good education may be protective against negative messages and may increase self-esteem. Grades on assignments and tests may serve as potential sources of relatively objective data. The results of a study of girls in a predominantly White junior high and high school indicated that girls valued intelligence as a primary source of positive feelings about themselves (Polce-Lynch, Myers, Kilmartin, Forssmann-Falck, & Kliewer, 1998). Education contributes to the sense that the future holds promise; thus it can increase girls' optimism as well.

Education about sexism. There is a tendency among European-American women to underestimate the influence of sexism on their own lives. Although most women believe that women as a group are discriminated against, individual women tend to not see themselves as victims of discrimination (Crosby, 1982). If women were made more aware of the influence of sexism in their lives, they would be more likely to develop protective external attributions. Researchers have demonstrated that women's self-esteem is not lowered by negative feedback from someone they believe to be prejudiced (Crocker et al., 1991; Dion, 1975; Dion & Earn, 1975). Furthermore, women who claim to have been discriminated against have higher self-esteem (Crocker & Blanton, 1999). It is difficult to determine the nature of the causal relationship, however. Women and girls who are not aware of the prevalence of sexism may not make similar external attributions and may therefore experience a reduction in self-esteem.

Women need to be socialized into the mainstream European-American male culture and part of that is teaching women how to deal with sexism. Sexism will not disappear overnight, and girls need to be prepared to identify and label sexist messages so that they can examine and selectively ignore or constructively challenge them. In other words, women should be "inoculated" and prepared to survive in a sexist world, especially because sexism has become more subtle and is therefore more difficult to detect now than previously (Benokraitis, 1998; Benokraitis & Feagin, 1995).

One model for this is the way African-American families' educate and socialization their children to protect them from racism. Some adaptations of the coping strategies that Phinney and Chavira (1995) found for African-American adolescents may be useful to all girls and women. For instance, such strategies as discussing sexism with the perpetrator (e.g., clarifying common misperceptions, expressing and sharing views on an issue), using self-affirmation (e.g., "I like being a girl," "I am proud to be a woman"), proving the sexist individuals wrong (e.g., doing even better than men on a task), ignoring the perpetrator (e.g., picking her battles, telling herself to overlook it for now, focusing on more pressing things, deciding not to waste energy on a jerk), or using a verbal retort (saying something snappy back) may be useful to girls as well.

Likewise, African-American women could benefit from such inoculation with regard to sexism. Racial themes are more salient for African-American women than are gender issues (Giddings, 1984; King, 1989; Slane & Morrow, 1981). Typically, Black women can make external attributions about negative feedback by attributing them to racism. However, if Black women who usually attribute negative feedback to racism are placed in a setting in which racism would be unlikely to exist, and are subjected to sexist treatment, they may not be protected unless they are also sensitive to sexism. In this situation, Black women may experience the same anxiety, depression, and reduced self-esteem as White women. Consistent with this, Poindexter-Cameron and Robinson (1997) found that Black women at Black colleges who felt respected by the faculty and administration had lower self-esteem than Black women at predominantly White universities. Although the socioeconomic status of the women at the Black college was lower and could also explain the difference, this finding is consistent with those of researchers who have found that negative feedback reduces self-esteem if it cannot be blamed on external factors (Crocker, 1999; Crocker & Major, 1989). All women's self-esteem would be better protected if they could identify sexist feedback and make appropriate external attributions about it. It should be possible to do this without necessarily dividing the men and women in ones group, a concern that is especially important to Black women.

All of the above strategies could lay a good foundation on which to build a solid womanist identity and good self-esteem, as well as protect self-esteem from assaults by negative messages from the dominant culture. Toward the end of the Encounter stage, girls and women may be more aware of the array of possible paths their lives may take, seek education, and as a result, invest their energies in a wide variety of activities. This increases their increase their self-complexity, thus protecting their self-esteem. They may also be more aware of sexism. With increasing ability to tease out sexist feedback, they may attribute some of the inaccurate, negative comments that they hear about themselves to sexism rather than to their own characteristics.

Stage 3: Immersion-emersion. This stage corresponds to the embeddedness-emanation stage of feminist identity development (Downing & Roush, 1984). In this stage, the individual becomes preoccupied with the experience of being a member of her group. She seeks out more information about the group, including role models, and becomes aware of her identity. The goal at this point would be to maintain and reinforce positive notions about women and awareness of sexism. Pyant and Yanico (1991) found that the immersion stage was related to higher self-esteem than the earlier stages. Speight et al. (1996) also found that self-esteem was positively correlated with immersion and internalization attitudes. In addition, the higher the level of educational attainment, the greater the internalization attitudes and the greater the self-esteem (Harris, 1995). Black women in the process of rejecting pro-White perspectives and incorporating Black culture reported increasing satisfaction with specific body areas and more investment in health behaviors (Smith et al., 1991). Harris (1995) also found that during this stage racial identity attitudes were positively related to body satisfaction, favorable overall evaluations of their physical appearance and health orientation.

During this stage, African Americans and White women seek out members of their group, whereas members of other groups, such as European Americans or males, respectively, may be avoided, excluded, and disparaged during this time. African American women are reluctant to create any divisions within their group, so they do not separate from African American men during this period (Collins, 1989). Such separations may not be necessary for identity development as long as the environment is affirming, or includes times and places in which members of one's group congregate.

Associating with members of one's group has several benefits. Association with similar others may offer a good chance to further consolidate and build upon the information obtained during the Encounter Stage. Functions of associating with one's group or community include the opportunity to know similar individuals, to learn to value one's group (as in the "Black is beautiful" movement), and to share experiences and information about how to cope with racism or sexism (Crocker, 1999; Crocker & Major, 1989). As individuals become more aware of being the victim of discrimination, they begin to experience disillusionment and anger related to injustices. The group may be a source of affirmation and support, as well as encourage self-esteem preserving attributions. Individuals at this stage may begin to become involved in activism that benefits their group and is an adaptive way to channel energy generated from anger towards change and to maintain a sense of efficacy.

Crocker and Major (1989) have suggested that associating with members of one's group allows for favorable social comparisons. By comparing themselves with similar others, women avoid unfavorable comparisons with those more advantaged than themselves and get more accurate information about what members of their group are likely to receive. On the other hand, such comparisons may also reduce the likelihood that an individual will strive for or request more and may reduce awareness of the discrepancy, for instance between own and advantaged groups' opportunities and salaries.

To facilitate the process of womanist identity formation we should ensure the availability of girls' and women's organizations (e.g., Girl Scouts, girls' sports teams), and other mentoring relationships. Attention should be paid to the messages about girls and women that are communicated within these contexts, however, to make sure that they don't limit girls' choices and development or reinforce negative messages about the group.

Stage 4: Internalization-commitment. Upon reaching this stage the individual establishes a particular group as her reference group and develops self-confidence about her identification with that group. At the same time, she recognizes the importance of diversity and is able and willing to interact with members of other groups. By this stage, women may have the sense of identity required to confront and address racism and sexism in their environments and the self-esteem to persist and even thrive in the face of adversity. This internalization stage parallels Downing and Roush's (1984) synthesis stage. Ossna et al. (1992), Parham and Helms (1985a, 1985b), Pyant and Yanico (1991), and Speight et al. (1996) all found that Internalization attitudes are related to high self-esteem. Internalization attitudes have been associated with high self-esteem, low anxiety, and positive regard (Parham & Helms, 1985a, 1985b). Black women who were comfortable with their Blackness and had few anti-White attitudes evaluated their body satisfaction, physical appearance, and fitness favorably and engaged in health-oriented behaviors (Harris, 1995).

This stage is characterized by continuing interest and investment in ethnic heritage, civil rights, and politics. By this stage women are acutely aware of the social injustices associated with sexism and racism. One of the challenges of being the victim of discrimination is dealing with anger in an adaptive manner. Once individuals become aware of sexism, they may be increasingly outraged at its appearance. In response, women at this stage commit themselves to working for social change related to gender and or racial issues (Downing & Roush, 1984).

Researchers have suggested that the suppression of anger in the presence of members of dominant groups results in a variety of health problems and negative life events, such as money problems, family and marriage problems, and occupational problems (Broman & Johnson, 1987, 1988). Anger and frustration with discrimination may contribute to the greater prevalence of high blood pressure among African Americans (Feagin, 1984; Feagin & Sikes, 1994; Feagin & Vera, 1995). Chambers et al. (1998) reported that African-American men and women experienced and expressed the same level of anger. African-American men in Chambers et al.'s study were more likely to keep anger in or to report controlling it than were than were African-American women. These results were consistent with that of Stoney and Engebretson (1994). Johnson and Greene (1991) found that African-American males who suppressed anger also experienced more somatic symptoms, such as cardiovascular arousal, sleep disturbance, and psychological distress, than did peers who expressed their anger. It is not surprising that African-American males are at especially high risk for high blood pressure and heart attacks. However, there are also consequences for expressing anger, such as disrupted relationships, retaliation by others, arrest, and incarceration.

European-American woman may also be expected to become angry when they become fully aware of the extent of sexism. They will also be at risk for the kinds of health problems mentioned above. The best way to reduce anger at sexism is to increase accurate ideas about women and to reduce sexism. Channeling anger toward productive efforts to end discrimination may be helpful in many cases. Activism on behalf of one's group is characteristic of those who have reached the later internalization/commitment stage. Individuals at this stage may become involved in political activism or pursue activities that otherwise benefit their group. Such action may include many of the suggestions made by other authors in this volume. For instance, one might become involved examining gender research, instituting novel intervention programs, developing relevant service learning opportunities, examining the limitations of current theories, or influencing legislation.

CONCLUSION

There is much to be learned women from African Americans' ways of protecting self-esteem in the face of discrimination. As we chart our new course, we should keep in mind that it is important that all of us to develop a positive sense of who we are, as well as an awareness of other's potential biases. Such a sense of identity allows us to balance a clear self-concept and sense of self-worth with feedback from the outside world. The effect of stressors is mediated by self-esteem and therefore self-esteem may be especially important to the adaptation and success of girls and women. We must have the self-esteem to maintain their philosophical conviction, focus, and effort in the face of obstacles (Hale-Benson, 1986; Miller & Miller, 1990). We need to make a concerted effort to help more girls form a womanist identity that values women as much as men. Socialization into a womanist identity involves enhancing girls' identity. Girls need to be socialized into mainstream culture and taught about sexism and discrimination. In addition, education about sexism teaches girls to make external attributions about some of the negative evaluations they receive, thereby enhancing the normal self-serving attributional bias and protecting self-esteem (Fletcher & Ward, 1988). Again, although it is important to respond to accurate feedback, the prevalence of negative subtle and clear sexist messages makes this an adaptive strategy.

Through the changes in curricula, boys will also be exposed to the value of women, which will contribute to the development of a more egalitarian society. A less sexist, more egalitarian society would permit women to choose to invest their energies in a wider variety of pursuits (Collins, 1989; King, 1989; Lorde, 1984; Wyche, 1993), to increase their self-complexity, and to protect their self-esteem. As a result of this womanist socialization, girls and women may feel more certain and more proud of who they are, reject undeserved criticism, and be in an even better position to navigate among the barriers, to discover new roles, and to chart a new course for women.

REFERENCES

Abramson, L. Y., Seligman, M. E., & Teasdale, J. D. (1978). Learned helplessness in humans: Critique and reformulation. *Journal of Abnormal Psychology*, *87*, 49–74.

American Psychiatric Association. (1994). *Diagnostic and statistical manual of mental disorders* (4th ed.). Washington, DC: American Psychiatric Press.

Ammons, L. L. (1995). Mules, madonnas, babies, bathwater, racial imagery, and stereotypes: The African-American woman and the battered woman syndrome. *Wisconsin Law Review*, *5*, 1003–1080.

Anderson, S. M. (1990). The inevitability of future suffering: The role of depression and predictive certainty in depression. *Social Cognition*, *8*, 203–228.

Bachman, J. G., & O'Malley, P. M. (1984). Black-White differences in self-esteem: Are they affected by response style? *American Journal of Sociology*, *90*, 624–639.

Bailey, C. R., & Mednick, M. T. (1987). Career aspiration in Black college women: An examination of performance and social self-esteem. *Women & Therapy*, *6* (3), 65–75.

Basow, S. A. (1992). *Gender: Stereotypes and roles* (3rd ed.). Pacific Grove, CA: Brooks/Cole.

Baumrind, D. (1971). Current patterns of parental authority. *Developmental Psychology*, *4*, 1–103.

Benokraitis, N. (1998). Working in the ivory basement. In L. H. Collins, J. C. Chrisler, & K. Quina (Eds.), *Career strategies for women in academe: Arming Athena* (pp. 3–36). Thousand Oaks, CA: Sage.

Benokraitis, N., & Feagin, J. (1995). *Modern sexism: Blatant, subtle, and covert discrimination* (2nd ed.). Englewood Cliffs, NJ: Prentice Hall.

Bowler, R., Rauch, S., & Schwarzer, R. (1986). Self-esteem and interracial attitudes in Black high school students: A comparison with five ethnic groups. *Urban Education, 21,* 3–19.

Bowman, P. J., & Howard, C. (1985). Race-related socialization, motivation, and academic achievement: A study of Black youths in three-generation families. *Journal of the American Academy of Child Psychiatry, 24,* 134–141.

Branch, C. W., & Newcombe, N. (1986). Racial attitude development among young Black children as a function of parental attitudes: A longitudinal and cross-sectional study. *Child Development, 57,* 712–721.

Brewer, M. B. (1979). In-group bias in the minimal intergroup situation: A cognitive-motivational analysis. *Psychological Bulletin, 86,* 307–324.

Broman, C. L., & Johnson, E. H. (1987). The relationship of anger expression to health problems among Black Americans in a national survey. *Journal of Behavioral Medicine, 10,* 103–116.

Broman, C. L., & Johnson, E. H. (1988). Anger expression and life stress among Blacks: Their role in physical health. *Journal of the National Medical Association, 80,* 1329–1334.

Brown, L. (1998). Ethnic stigma as a contextual experience: A possible selves perspective. *Personality and Social Psychology Bulletin, 24,* 163–172.

Burlew, A. K. (1982). Experiences of Black females in traditional and non-traditional professions. *Psychology of Women Quarterly, 6,* 312–326.

Chambers, J. W., Kambon, K., Birdsong, B. D., Brown, J., Dixon, P., & Robbins-Brinson, L. (1998). Africentric cultural identity and the stress experience of African American college students. *Journal of Black Psychology, 24,* 368–396.

Chideya, F. (1995). *Don't believe the hype: Fighting cultural misinformation about African Americans.* New York: Penguin & Plume.

Clark, K., & Clark, M. (1947). Racial identification and preference in Negro preschool children. In T. Newcomb & E. Hartley (Eds.), *Readings in social psychology* (pp. 169–178). New York: Holt.

Collins, P. H. (1989). The social construction of Black feminist thought. *Signs, 14,* 735–773.

Cooley, C. H. (1956). *Human nature and the social order.* New York: Free Press.

Coopersmith, S. (1967). *The antecedents of self-esteem.* San Francisco: Freeman.

Crittenden, K. S., & Lamug, C. B. (1988). Causal attribution and depression: A friendly refinement based on Philippine data. *Journal of Cross-Cultural Psychology, 19,* 216–231.

Crocker, J. (1999). Social stigma and self-esteem: Situational construction of self-worth. *Journal of Experimental Social Psychology, 35,* 89–107.

Crocker, J., & Blanton, H. (1999). Social inequality and self-esteem: The moderating effects of social comparison, legitimacy, and contingencies of self-esteem. In T. R. Tyler & R. M. Kramer (Eds.), *The psychology of the social self* (pp. 171–191). Mahwah, NJ: Lawrence Erlbaum.

Crocker, J., Cornwell, B., & Major, B. (1989). The stigma of overweight: Affective consequences of attributional ambiguity. *Journal of Personality and Social Psychology, 64,* 60–70.

Crocker, J., Luhtanen, R., Blaine, B., & Broadnax, S. (1994). Collective self-esteem and psychological well-being among White, Black, and Asian college students. *Personality and Social Psychology Bulletin, 20,* 503–513.

Crocker, J., Luhtanen, R., Broadnax, S., & Blaine, B. E. (1999). Belief in U.S. government conspiracies against Blacks among Black and White college students: Powerlessness or system blame? *Personality and Social Psychology Bulletin, 25,* 941–953.

Crocker, J., & Major, B. (1989). Social stigma and self-esteem: The self-protective property of stigma. *Psychological Review, 96,* 608–630.

Crocker, J., & McGraw, K. M. (1984). What's good for the goose is not good for the gander: Solo status as an obstacle to occupational achievement for males and females. *American Behavioral Scientist, 27,* 357–369.

Crocker, J., Voelkl, K., Testa, M., & Major, B. (1991). Social stigma: The affective consequences of attributional ambiguity. *Journal of Personality and Social Psychology, 60,* 218–228.

Crosby, F. J. (1982). *Relative deprivation and working women.* New York: Oxford University Press.

Cross, W. E. (1971). The Negro to Black conversion experience: Toward a psychology of Black liberation. *Black World, 20,* 13–27.

Cross, W. E. (1978). The Thomas and Cross models of psychological nigrescence: A review. *Journal of Black Psychology, 5,* 13–31.

Cross, W. E., Jr., Parham, T. A., & Helms, J. E. (1991). The stages of Black identity development: Nigrescence models. In R. L. Jones (Ed.), *Black psychology* (3rd ed., pp. 319–338). New York: Harper & Row.

Demo, D. H., & Hughes, M. (1990). Socialization and racial identity among Black Americans. *Social Psychology Quarterly, 53,* 364–374.

Demo, D. H., & Savin-Williams, R. C. (1992). Self-concept stability and change during adolescence. In R. P. Lipka & T. M. Brinthaupt (Eds.), *Self-perspectives across the lifespan* (pp. 116–148). Albany: State University of New York Press.

Dion, K. L. (1975). Women's reactions to discrimination from members of the same or opposite sex. *Journal of Research in Personality, 9,* 294–306.

Dion, K. L., & Earn, B. M. (1975). The phenomenology of being a target of prejudice. *Journal of Personality and Social Psychology, 32,* 944–950.

Downing, N., & Roush, K. (1984). From passive acceptance to active commitment: A model of feminist identity development for women. *Counseling Psychologist, 13,* 695–709.

Downs, A. C. (1983). Letters to Santa Claus: Elementary school-age children's sex-typed toy preferences in a natural setting. *Sex Roles, 9,* 159–163.

Dukes, R. L., & Martinez, R. (1994). The impact of ethnicity and gender on self-esteem among adolescents. *Adolescence, 29,* 105–115.

Eccles, J., Barber, B., Jozefowicz, D., Malenchuk, O., & Vida, M. (1999). Self-evaluations of competence, task values, and self-esteem. In N. G. Johnson, M. C. Roberts, & J. Worrell (Eds.), *Beyond appearance: A new look at adolescent girls* (pp. 53–83). Washington, DC: American Psychological Association.

Fauce, W. A. (1984). School achievement, social status, and self-esteem. *Social Psychology Quarterly, 47,* 3–14.

Feagin, J. (1991, February). The continuing significance of race: Antiblack discrimination in public places. *American Sociological Review, 56*, 101–116.

Feagin, J., & Sikes, M. (1994). *Living with racism: The Black middle class experience*. Boston: Beacon Press.

Feagin, J., & Vera, H. (1995). *White racism: The basics*. New York: Routledge.

Fine, M., Weis, L., Powell, L., & Mun Wong, L. (Eds.). (1997). *Off White: Readings on race, power and society*. New York: Routledge.

Fletcher, G. J., & Ward, C. (1988). Attribution theory and processes: A cross-cultural perspective. In M. H. Bond (Ed.), *The cross-cultural challenge to social psychology* (pp. 230–244). Newbury Park, CA: Sage.

Giddings, P. (1984). *When and where I enter*. New York: Morrow.

Goffman, E. (1963). *Stigma: Notes on the management of spoiled identity*. Englewood Cliffs, NJ: Prentice Hall.

Hale-Benson, J. (1986). *Black children: Their roots, culture, and learning styles*. Baltimore: Johns Hopkins University Press.

Harris, S. M. (1995). Family, self, and sociocultural contributions to body-image attitudes of African American women. *Psychology of Women Quarterly, 19*, 129–145.

Harter, S. (1993). Causes and consequences of low self-esteem in children and adolescents. In R. Baumeister (Ed.), *Self-esteem: The puzzle of low self-regard* (pp. 87–116). New York: Plenum.

Helms, J. E. (1990). *Black and White racial identity: Theory, research, and practice*. Westport, CT: Greenwood Press.

Hirsch, B. J., & DuBois, D. L. (1991). Self-esteem in early adolescence: The identification and prediction of contrasting longitudinal trajectories. *Journal of Youth and Adolescence, 20*, 53–72.

Hogg, M. A., & Abrams, D. (1990). Social motivation, self-esteem, and social identity. In D. Abrams & M. A. Hogg (Eds.), Social identity theory: *Constructive and critical advances* (pp. 28–47). New York: Springer-Verlag.

Hogg, M. A., & Sunderland, J. (1991). Self-esteem and intergroup discrimination in the minimal group paradigm. *British Journal of Social Psychology, 30*, 51–62.

Hughes, M., & Demo, D. (1989). Self-perceptions of Black Americans: Self-esteem and personal efficacy. *American Journal of Sociology, 95*, 132–159.

Jackson, S., McCullough, W. R., & Gurin, G. (1988). Family, socialization environment, and identity development in Black Americans. In H. P. McAdoo (Ed.), *Black families* (2nd ed., pp. 242–256). Newbury Park, CA: Sage.

James, S. A. (1993). Racial and ethnic difference in infant mortality and low birthweight: A psychosocial critique. *Annals of Epidemiology, 2*, 130–136.

Jeffries, V., & Ransford, H. E. (1980). Interracial social contact and middle-class White reactions to the Watts riot. *Social Problems 16*, 312–324.

Jensen, G., White, C., & Galliher, J. (1982). Ethnic status and adolescent self-evaluations: An extension of the research on minority self-esteem. *Social Problems, 30*, 226–239.

Johnson, E. H., & Greene, A. (1991). The relationship between suppressed anger and psychosocial distress in African American male adolescents. *Journal of Black Psychology, 18*, 47–65.

Kelley, H. H. (1972). Causal schemata and the attribution process. In E. E. Jones,

D. E. Kanouse, H. H. Kelley, R. E. Nisbett, S. Valins, & B. Weiner (Eds.), *Attribution: Perceiving the causes of behavior* (pp. 151–176). Morrison, NJ: General Learning Press.

King, D. K. (1989). Multiple jeopardy, multiple consciousness: The context of a Black feminist ideology. In R. M. Malson, J. F. O'Barr, S. Westphal-Wihl, & W. Myer (Eds.), *Feminist theory in practice and process* (pp. 75–105). Chicago: University of Chicago Press.

Licitra-Kleckler, D. M., & Waas, G. A. (1993). Perceived social support among high-stress adolescents: The role of peers and family. *Journal of Adolescent Research, 8*, 381–402.

Linville, P. W. (1985). Self-complexity and affective extremity: Don't put all of your eggs in one cognitive basket. *Social Cognition, 3*, 94–120.

Lips, H. M. (1993). *Sex & gender: An introduction* (2nd ed.). Mountain View, CA: Mayfield.

Lorde, A. (1984). *Sister outsider*. Trumansburg, NY: Crossing Press.

Lorenzo-Hernandez, J. (1998). How social categorization may inform the study of Hispanic immigration. *Hispanic Journal of Behavioral Sciences, 20*, 39–59.

Lorenzo-Hernandez, J., & Ouellette, S. C. (1998). Ethnic identity, self-esteem, and values in Dominicans, Puerto Ricans, and African Americans. *Journal of Applied Social Psychology, 28*, 2007–2024.

Luster, T., & McAdoo, H. (1995). Factors related to self-esteem among African American youths: A secondary analysis of the High/Scope Perry preschool data. *Journal of Research on Adolescence, 5*, 451–467.

Maass, A., & Volpato, C. (1989). Gender differences in self-serving attributions about sexual experiences. *Journal of Applied Social Psychology, 19*, 517–542.

Maccoby, E. E., & Jacklin, C. N. (1974). *The psychology of sex differences*. Stanford, CA: Stanford University Press.

Major, B., Carrington, P. I., & Carnevale, P. J. (1984). Physical attractiveness and self-esteem: Attributions for praise from an other-sex evaluator. *Personality and Social Psychology Bulletin, 10*, 43–50.

Martinez, R., & Dukes, R. (1991). Ethnic and gender differences in self-esteem. *Youth Sociology, 22*, 318–338.

Masterson, J. F. (1988). *The search for the real self: Unmasking the personality disorders of our age*. New York: Free Press.

McCreary, M. L., Slavin, L. A., & Berry, E. J. (1996). Predicting problem behavior and self-esteem among African American adolescents. *Journal of Adolescent Research, 11*, 216–234.

Mead, G. H. (1934). *Mind, self, & society*. Chicago: University of Chicago Press.

Miller, R. L., & Miller, B. (1990). Mothering the biracial child: Bridging the gaps between African-American and White parenting styles. *Women & Therapy, 10* (1–2), 169–179.

Molloy, B. L., & Herzberger, S. D. (1998). Body image and self-esteem: A comparison of African-American and Caucasian women. *Sex Roles, 38*, 631–643.

Money, J. (1986). Pediatric sexology and hermaphroditism. *Advances in Developmental & Behavioral Pediatrics, 7*, 257–274.

Mullen, B., & Riordan, C. A. (1988). Self-serving attributions for performance in naturalistic settings: A meta-analytic review. *Journal of Applied Social Psychology, 18*, 3–22.

O'Brien, M., Huston, A. C., & Risley, T. R. (1983). Sex-typed play of toddlers in a day care center. *Journal of Applied Developmental Psychology, 4*, 1–9.

Osborne, J. (1995). Academics, self-esteem, and race: A look at the underlying assumptions of the disidentification hypothesis. *Personality and Social Psychology Bulletin, 21*, 449–455.

Ossana, S., Helms, J. E., & Leonard, M. M. (1992). Do "womanist" identity attitudes influence college women's self-esteem and perceptions of environmental bias? *Journal of Counseling and Development, 70*, 402–408.

Parham, T. A. (1989). Cycles of psychological nigrescence. *Counseling Psychologist, 17*, 187–226.

Parham, T. A., & Helms, J. E. (1985a). Attitudes of racial identity and self-esteem of Black students: An exploratory investigation. *Journal of College Student Personnel, 26*, 143–147.

Parham, T. A., & Helms, J. E. (1985b). Relation of racial identity attitudes to self-actualization and affective states of Black students. *Journal of Counseling Psychology, 32*, 431–440.

Peters, M. F. (1985). Racial socialization of young Black children. In H. P. McAdoo & J. L. McAdoo (Eds.), *Black children: Social, educational, and parental environments* (pp. 33–52). Beverly Hills, CA: Sage.

Peterson, A. C., Sarigiani, P. A., & Kennedy, R. E. (1991). Adolescent depression: Why more girls? *Journal of Youth and Adolescence, 20*, 247–271.

Phinney, J. S. (1990). Ethnic identity in adolescents and adults: Review of research. *Psychological Bulletin, 108*, 499–514.

Phinney, J. S. (1991). Ethnic identity and self-esteem: A review and integration. *Hispanic Journal of Behavioral Sciences, 13*, 193–208.

Phinney, J. S. (1992). The multigroup Ethnic Identity Measure: A new scale for use with diverse groups. *Journal of Adolescent Research, 7*, 156–176.

Phinney, J. S., Cantu, C. L., & Kurtz, D. A. (1997). Ethnic and American identity as predictors of self-esteem among African American, Latino, and White adolescents. *Journal of Youth & Adolescence, 26*, 165–185.

Phinney, J. S., & Chavira, V. (1995). Parental ethnic socialization and adolescent coping with problems related to ethnicity. *Journal of Research on Adolescence, 5*, 31–53.

Poindexter-Cameron, J. M., & Robinson, T. L. (1997). Relationships among racial identity attitudes, womanist identity attitudes, and self-esteem in African American college women. *Journal of College Student Development, 38*, 288–296.

Polce-Lynch, M., Myers, B. J., Kilmartin, C. T., Forssmann-Falck, R., & Kliewer, W. (1998). Gender and age patterns in emotional expression, body image, and self-esteem: A qualitative analysis. *Sex Roles, 38*, 1025–1048.

Porter, J. R., & Washington, R. E. (1993). Minority identity and self-esteem. *Annual Review of Sociology, 19*, 139–161.

Prothrow-Stith, D. B. (1995). The epidemic of youth violence in America: Using public health prevention strategies to prevent violence. *Journal of Health Care for the Poor and Underserved, 6*, 95–101.

Prothrow-Stith, D., & Quaday, S. (1996). Communities, schools, and violence. In

A. M. Hoffman (Ed.), *Schools, violence, and society* (pp. 153–161). Westport, CT: Praeger.

Pyant, C. T., & Yanico, B. J. (1991). Relationship of racial identity and gender role attitudes to Black women's psychological well-being. *Journal of Counseling Psychology, 38*, 315–322.

Richman, C., Clark, M., & Brown, K. (1985). General and specific self-esteem in late adolescent students: Race × gender × SES effects. *Adolescence, 20*, 555–566.

Rogers, C. R. (1951). *Client-centered therapy: Its current practice, implications, and theory*. Boston: Houghton-Mifflin.

Rosenberg, M. (1965). *Society and the adolescent self-image*. Princeton, NJ: Princeton University Press.

Rosenberg, M. (1979). *Conceiving the self*. New York: Basic Books.

Rosenberg, M., Schooler, C., & Schoenbach, C. (1989). Self-esteem and adolescent problems: Modeling reciprocal effects. *American Sociological Review, 54*, 1004–1018.

Rosenberg, M., & Simmons, R. (1972). *Black and White self-esteem: The Black urban child*. Washington, DC: American Psychological Association.

Rozell, E. J., Gundersen, D. E., & Terpstra, D. E. (1998). Gender differences in the factors affecting helpless behavior and performance. *Journal of Social Behavior & Personality, 13*, 265–280.

Ruble, D. N., & Ruble, T. L. (1982). Sex stereotypes. In A. G. Miller (Ed.), *In the eye of the beholder: Contemporary issues in stereotyping* (pp. 188–252). New York: Praeger.

Savin-Williams, R. C., & Berdt, T. J. (1990). Friendships and peer relations during adolescence. In S. S. Feldman & G. R. Elliott (Eds.), *At the threshold: The developing adolescent* (pp. 277–307). Cambridge, MA: Harvard University Press.

Shujaa, M. (1994). Education and schooling: You can have one without the other. In M. Shujaa (Ed.), *Too much schooling, too little education*. Trenton, NJ: Africa World Press.

Slane, S., & Morrow, L. (1981). Race differences in feminism and guilt. *Psychological Reports, 49*, 45–46.

Slavin, L. A., & Rainer, K. L. (1990). Gender differences in emotional support and depressive symptoms among adolescents: A prospective analysis. *American Journal of Community Psychology, 18*, 407–421.

Smith, L. R., Burlew, A. K., & Lundgren, D. C. (1991). Black consciousness, self-esteem, and satisfaction with physical appearance among African-American female college students. *Journal of Black College Studies, 22*, 269–283.

Speight, S. L., Vera, E. M., & Derrickson, K. B. (1996). Racial self-designation, racial identity, and self-esteem revisited. *Journal of Black Psychology, 22*, 37–52.

Spencer, M. B. (1983). Children's cultural value and parental child rearing strategies. *Developmental Review, 4*, 351–370.

Spencer, M. B., Cole, S. P., DuPree, D., Glymph, A., & Pierre, P. (1993). Self-efficacy among urban African American early adolescents: Exploring issues of risk, vulnerability, and resilience. *Development and Psychopathology, 5*, 719–739.

Spencer, M. B., Dobbs, B., & Swanson, D. P. (1988). Afro-American adolescents: Adaptational processes and socioeconomic diversity in behavioral outcomes. *Journal of Adolescence, 11*, 117–137.

Stalikas, A., & Gavaki, E. (1995). The importance of ethnic identity: Self-esteem and academic achievement of second-generation Greeks in secondary school. *Canadian Journal of School Psychology, 11*, 1–9.

St. Jean, Y., & Feagin, J. (1998). *Double burden: Black women and everyday racism*. Armonk, NY: M. E. Sharpe.

Stoney, C. M., & Engebretson, T. O. (1994). Anger and hostility: Potential mediators of the gender difference in coronary heart disease. In A. W. Siegman, A. Wolfe, & T. W. Smith (Eds.), *Anger, hostility, and the heart* (pp. 215–237). Hillsdale, NJ: Lawrence Erlbaum.

Tajfel, H. (1981). *Human groups and social categories*. Cambridge: Cambridge University Press.

Tajfel, H., & Turner, J. C. (1986). The social identity theory of intergroup behavior. In S. Worchel & W. G. Austin (Eds.), *Psychology of intergroup relations* (2nd ed., pp. 7–24). Chicago: Nelson-Hall.

Tashakkori, A. (1992). Gender, ethnicity, and the structure of self-esteem: An attitude theory approach. *Journal of Social Psychology, 133*, 479–488.

Tashakkori, A. (1993). Race, gender, and pre-adolescent self-structure: A test of construct-specificity hypothesis. *Personality and Individual Differences, 14*, 591–598.

Tashakkori, A., & Thompson, V. D. (1991). Race differences in self-perception and locus of control during adolescence and early adulthood: Methodological implications. *Genetic, Social, and General Psychology Monographs, 117*, 133–152.

Tatum, B. (1992). Talking about race, learning about racism: The application of racial identity development theory in the classroom. *Harvard Educational Review, 62*, 1–24.

Tatum, B. (1997). *"Why are all the Black kids sitting together in the cafeteria?" and other conversations about race*. New York: Basic Books.

Taylor, S. E., & Brown, J. D. (1988). Illusion and well-being: A social psychological perspective on mental health. *Psychological Bulletin, 103*, 193–210.

Taylor, S. E., & Fiske, S. T. (1978). Salience, attention, and attribution: Top of the head phenomena. In L. Berkowitz (Ed.), *Advances in experimental social psychology* (Vol. 11, pp. 249–288). New York: Academic Press.

Urberg, K. A. (1982). The development of the concepts of masculinity and femininity in young children. *Sex Roles, 8*, 659–668.

Walker, A. (1983). *In search of our mothers' gardens*. New York: Harcourt Brace Jovanovich.

West, C. (1995). Mammy, Sapphire, and Jezebel: Historical images of Black women and their implications for psychotherapy. *Psychotherapy, 32*, 458–466.

Wright, B. (1985). The effects of racial self-esteem on the personal self-esteem of Black youth. *International Journal of Intercultural Relations, 9*, 19–30.

Wyche, K. F. (1993). Psychology and African-American women: Findings from applied research. *Applied and Preventive Psychology, 2*, 115–121.

Wylie, R. (1979). *The self concept*, Vol. 2. Lincoln: University of Nebraska Press.

Chapter 8

Women, Whither Goest Thou?
To Chart New Courses in Religiousness
and Spirituality and to Define Ourselves!

Carole A. Rayburn and Lee J. Richmond

In the scriptural account of creation, we are told that the man, Adam (Hebrew for "of the earth"), named all of the creatures brought before him by God. Whatever the man called these creatures became their name. Later, when woman was named "woman" because the man wanted it memorialized that she was made of his rib, he spoke of her being, "bone of my bones and flesh of my flesh" (Genesis 2:19–23). This was only the beginning. Men have never stopped defining Women, our roles, our thoughts and feelings, our lifestyles, our bodies, our health and illnesses, our child care duties, in short, everything about us that women ought to define about ourselves. Female persons have been enslaved by the patriarchy and male-dominated world.

Many men since Adam seem to have missed a few very significant points: God, not man, created not only man but also woman in the image of God. One of the names of God is *El Shaddai*, "the breasted one," a female image of God (Biale, 1982). The Holy Spirit, one part of the Godhead of the Christian Trinity, is *Shekinah* in Hebrew (a feminine noun) and *Pneuma* in Greek (a neuter noun) and *Ruach* (neuter in Hebrew). In the biblical parable of the widow's disproportionately large offering (Mark 12:41–43), God is pictured in female image. Jesus spoke of wanting to gather fallen Jerusalem's children together as a hen gathers her chicks under her wings (Matthew 23:37). This is another female image of God.

On the matter of Adam's rib, as used in the creation of woman, again the patriarchy has missed the significance of this part of the body. The rib is one of the paired, curved, bony or partly cartilaginous rods that stiffen the body walls and protect the viscera. The symbolic nature of the rib is that it is not by itself a vital part of the body because there are many pairs

of ribs going down the back. Physically, a rib is one of a *pair*, which symbolizes that man and woman were and are equals because each of them
are part of a pair. Both together are then "bones of my bones, and flesh
of my flesh"; both together make one complete whole (Rayburn, 1995).

Many girls and women have become increasingly intolerant of the inferior status assigned to them by the patriarchy and enforced with much
gusto by a male-dominated society in all spheres of life. These female persons, along with many enlightened male persons, have seriously questioned
the definitions of both genders and their role prescriptions. By examining
scripture, scriptural sexist language, and traditional theology in the light of
feminist thinking and analysis, women have been charting new courses in
religiousness and spirituality and defining themselves more accurately in
the process (Daly, 1973; Rayburn, 1981, 1984a, 1985, 1989, 1993; Rayburn, Natale, & Linzer, 1982; Spretnak, 1982).

DEFINITIONS OF RELIGIOUSNESS AND SPIRITUALITY

Religiousness has been viewed as a system of beliefs, doctrines, and
creedal behaviors that are shared by a group of individuals. Religion may
seek to impart and nourish spiritual life. Spirituality, on the other hand,
has been conceptualized as being involved with the transcendent, with asking ultimate questions about the meaning of life and its purposes, and with
the idea that there is more to life than that which can be fully seen or
understood (i.e., that which transcends the tangible or material). Spirituality concerns a way of living that values not only the transcendent but
also the authentic. Spirituality may be an important aspect of religious
participation, but it may also exist independently of any religious endeavor.
In the same way, an outward form of religious worship ship and doctrinal
belief system may be adopted without the involvement of a meaningful
connection to the transcendent or to the spiritual.

Craigie (1999) defined spirituality in terms of the vital center of being,
which may or may not be part of a particular religious faith and practice.
He thinks that honesty, open communication, and respect are involved in
spirituality, yet insists that it goes beyond these to embrace wholeness (i.e.,
unity, coherence, balance), groundedness (i.e., values that flow from the
sacred), and connectedness (i.e., connections to the supernatural and to
meaningful communities of people).

Historically, persons with transcendental or transpersonal leanings were
considered to be religious. Now, however, the spirituality of individuals is
recognized as well. Studies demonstrate that religion and spirituality can
operate independently of each other (Rayburn, 1996; Richmond, 1998).
Operationally, then, religion is defined as the formal system of belief in the
supernatural, a codification of creedal statements and concepts concerning
particular beliefs about God or another supernatural being, and the

shared doctrine of a group of believers. The concept "Spiritual" originally referred to the being and influences of the *pneuma* or Holy Spirit. Currently, however, spirituality is held to exist independently from religion and religiousness. Spirituality is the essence, vitality, a life force of a sense of oneness, or at least a close and intimate identity with something else— another group of people as in sisterhood, with the beauty and vastness of nature, with a movement such as the women's movement, or other spheres of life important to individuals (Rayburn, 1996).

Spirituality can, of course, exist within the context of religion. Within the Protestant tradition, spirituality has been viewed as piety or devotion (Marshall-Green & Hinson, 1990). In the Protestant view, spirituality includes Bible study, simple forms of prayer, forgiveness of sins through the unmerited favor of God or through the redemptive sacrifice of Christ, and receiving Communion. The Protestant tradition also fostered the emergence of radical or secular spirituality that arose from reflections on Dietrich Bonhoeffer's *Letters and Papers from Prison* (1971). This form of spirituality, according to Bonhoeffer, rejected other-worldly piety in favor of more interaction with the world and "going through the world to God," with prayer being not as much "for" another as "to be with" another and to be "in" the world in which God's kingdom is held to be "the beyond in the midst" of life (Hinson, 1990; Marshall-Green & Hinson, 1990.)

Besides the growing numbers of people interested in women's spirituality, with its emphasis on caring for other people, the environment, and the welfare of animals, there has been an international awareness of forms of spirituality independent of religion and religiousness. There have been several international conferences on the subject of spirituality that were not attached to any religion, and these meetings have occurred at least since 1995. Furthermore, the American Psychological Association's Division (36) on the Psychology of Religion has begun to take serious interest in spirituality and its role within religion and, though very hesitantly, its possible existence outside religion. Although religiousness and spirituality certainly do share common elements, for instance both espouse concern or caring for others, at what point do these two life views differ, follow their own paths, and attract their own adherents? Religiousness is held to concern itself with formal doctrinal beliefs, whereas spirituality has been viewed as having little or nothing to do with doctrine, creeds, or formalized beliefs. Rather, spirituality is seen as being broader in scope or outreach and including the diversity of life in all of its forms.

Furthermore, as traditional religiousness as viewed for ecclesia (the religious community) has seen far less inclusive for female persons than for male persons, women might be expected to embrace spirituality more than religiousness. There is also much interest in gender differences in religiousness across age groups. Older women may more identify with being religious or both religious and spiritual, whereas younger women may see themselves as more spiritual and far less religious. These differences may be related to a view of religion as a rigid, formalized codification of doctrines and creeds and a view of spirituality as a freeing of the force of life and a driving power that encourages fulfillment of one's potential to do the very best possible for oneself and for others. Also, rightly or wrongly, religions have been seen as exclusionary and critical of those who are outside the group of their denominational members. Spirituality, on the other hand, has been viewed as more inclusive and as showing more compassion and caring for the plight of others, even if they do not have the same religious, ethnic, gender, nationality, or age identity. Spiritual persons seek to find good in others and to help them whenever necessary. As spirituality is perceived by its practitioners, there are no doctrinal or creedal strings attached to whatever help they offer to others.

Because our theory is that spirituality can exist independently of religiousness and that people can conceivably self-identify as spiritual but not religious or as both spiritual and religious, care was taken in the development of our Inventory on Spirituality (IS) not to allude to any references to a Higher Power, as contrasted with our Inventory on Religiousness (IR), in which "Higher Power" was one of several titles used to denote supernatural being or authority. Although the IS and the IR both have subscales on Transcendence (force or being beyond the material or physical), the items in each are distinct from one another. In the IS, such items are: "I see life as having purpose beyond material, tangible, or immediate rewards" and "I feel at one with the universe." On the IR, Transcendence items include: "I believe that life has a meaning beyond the here-and-now, a transcendence to a Higher Power" and "I am comforted by the thought of a better place to dwell beyond this life, with its pain and suffering." The IR items are more theologically based than those on the IS. Similarly, both the IS and the IR have a subscale on Caring for Others; the IR subscale is being more theologically based, with items such as: "My religious beliefs lead me to act in better ways towards other people" and "My religious beliefs have led me to be compassionate for others (i.e., to care for their well-being)." The IS subscale on Caring for Others has items such as: "I care about the well-being of all others—people, animals, and plants" and "In my universe, all creatures are of great worth."

In a study by Rayburn, Osman, and our colleagues (1997), 64 college students responded to 12 items at the end of the IR and IS. These two instruments (IR & IS) were independent of each other, and the last twelve items are the same. That way, one could study any possible effects of previous responses to the IR or the IS. Further, the items measured the relative importance of mercy and justice, in both religious and spiritual persons. Different results were evidenced, even though these items were identical on both inventories. On the IR, there were no significant gender differences for considering spirituality to be different or the same as religion, for seeing oneself as spiritual but not religious, or for seeing oneself as both religious and spiritual. Nor were there any significant gender differences in viewing spirituality as not existing outside religion. However, on the IS there were highly significant gender difference on seeing spirituality as being able to exist outside religion; women significantly more often than men wrote that they never or seldom think that spirituality must exist only within religion. On the item, "I see myself as religious but not spiritual," women disagreed significantly more than did men on both the IR and IS. Therefore, women perceived themselves as more spiritual than religious than men did. However, on "I consider myself be neither religious nor spiritual," women more than men disagreed with this and at a significant level. This most probably reflected their not wanting to be seen as unspiritual rather than their not wanting to be considered irreligious. Furthermore, viewing oneself as religious but not spiritual or religious and spiritual was significantly correlated with having high scores on total IR. Similarly, viewing oneself as spiritual but not religious or both spiritual and religious was positively correlated with high scores on total IS. Women scored significantly higher than did men on spirituality. This finding is certainly not surprising because women have not had the same encouragement in leadership within ecclesiastical settings as have men. Women are seeking a new and more accepting environment in ever growing numbers, and often finding it in women's (or some other form of) spirituality.

The Roman Catholic tradition has been influenced in its concepts of spirituality by religious orders that have aimed at achieving a balance between reason and faith as well as nature and grace. Spirituality within this context has referred to specific ways of following Christ, growing in a life of faith, and communicating with God. Here spirituality is a way of making faith a matter of personal involvement as well as a prayerful and virtuous experience (Carmody & Carmody, 1990).

The traditional concept of spirituality is that it was derived from the Christian Holy Spirit of the Trinity: the Holy Spirit as the Teacher of the Godhead remained with mortals on earth to instruct them in moral living and to inspire and lead them to the holy. Jews and other non-Christians have not often been associated with the Holy Spirit or spirituality. Yet Jews and those practicing other religions are also pious and devoted to their own beliefs (in the definition from the Protestant tradition), or personally involved in a prayerful and virtuous way (as in the Roman Catholic tradition and definition), or in the sense of vital meaning of oneness with their deities or the perceived goodness of their causes. Even those not practicing the creedal codification of their belief systems, or who in fact consider themselves agnostic or even atheist, might individually hold themselves to be spiritual persons or believers in some very good or humane cause, or to be believers in the good of others or in the goodness of life itself, or have a yearning to protect nature and other inhabitants of the earth.

DOES SPIRITUALITY REPRESENT A SIXTH FACTOR OF PERSONALITY?

Piedmont (1998) studied the possibility that spirituality represents a sixth factor of personality. He reasoned that the criteria for a new factor of personality would be a factor that was independent of the agreed-upon five factors of personality (McCrae & Costa, 1987; Piedmont, 1995)—neuroticism, extraversion, openness, agreeableness, and conscientiousness, that the factor be at a comparable level of generality, and that it emerge over different information sources. He designed the Spiritual Transcendence Scale with three dimensions: Prayer Fulfillment (e.g., "I meditate and/or pray so that I can reach a higher spiritual plane of consciousness"), Universality (e.g., "I believe that on some level my life is intimately tied to all of humankind"), and Connectedness (e.g., "Although there is good and bad in people, I believe that humanity as a whole is basically good"). Studying a population of 277 women and 102 men of Judeo-Christian background, Piedmont found no significant gender differences on Universality or Prayer Fulfillment. However, women scored significantly higher than men on Connectedness. The Transcendence subscales were significantly related to subscales of the Faith Maturity Scale: Relationship with God, Frequency of Reading the Bible, and Connectedness. These were significantly related to Extraversion, Universality with Openness, and Conscientiousness. All of the Transcendence subscales were negatively related to Vulnerability to Stress. Piedmont is presently trying to ascertain whether transcendence is, as he believes, sixth factor of personality.

WHITE RACIAL CONSCIOUSNESS AND RELIGIOSITY AND SPIRITUALITY

Cohen and Boyer (1998) studied the relationship between White racial consciousness and religiosity and spirituality. White racial consciousness (WRC) referred to individuals' awareness of being White and the impact of that awareness on others. WRC was studied with various religious and spiritual motivations (i.e., extrinsic, intrinsic, quest, and phenomenological dimensions) and taking gender and socioeconomic status into account. According to Cohen and Boyer (1998), the four achieved types of racially oriented attitudes were: dominative, with a strong ethnocentric outlook that justifies dominance by the majority culture; conflictive, with opposition to clear discriminatory practices but opposition also to programs that would reduce discrimination; reactive, with awareness of inequalities and dominant culture privileges but over-identification with minority culture and thus considered paternalistic; and integrative, with the view that a pluralistic society is valuable and adherence to this belief from a moral understanding. Using the Batson and Burris (1994) Scale, Religious Orientations and Prejudicial Attitudes and Behaviors, Cohen and Boyer used categories of orientations: extrinsic (religion used as a means of providing people with social status or security; scoring high on prejudice when prejudice is forbidden by the religious community, e.g., racism); intrinsic (religion used as an end in itself and as the governing motive in life; lower scores on forbidden prejudice may indicate greater prejudice when it is not forbidden by the religious community, e.g., homophobia); quest (recognition that some religious issues such as mortality and meaning of life are complex without absolute or concrete answers or resolutions; decreased prejudice, both forbidden and allowed, is more common here); and phenomenological-humanistic spirituality or experiencing (derived from awareness of transcendent values important to the self, nature, life, and the ultimate). Those who adapted the last approach to spirituality were aware and deeply touched by others' pain and suffering, committed to social justice, and visionaries committed to the betterment of the world.

Cohen and Boyer (1998) studied 78 White students (50 women and 28 men), 61% of whom were Protestants, 26% Roman Catholics, 9% agnostics, and 4% atheists. For integrative WRC types, women scored higher on intrinsic religiosity than men, and reactive men scored higher on intrinsic religiosity than reactive women. Integrative women and men were comfortable with their Whiteness and with interacting with oppressed persons, but integrative women more often internalized their religious beliefs, than did integrative men. Reactive women and men recognized the existence of racial and ethnic discrimination and supported egalitarian values by taking paternalistic actions toward oppressed minorities; they also expressed anger toward those who espoused the status quo. Reactive men experienced religion as more personally meaningful than reactive women did. Although overall men had higher levels of extrinsic religiosity than women, dominative women and men scored high on extrinsic religiosity. Integrative women and men did not want to oppress people who are different from themselves, and they valued pluralistic society. Integrative men but not women espoused religious values as a means of obtaining approval from others and achieving high social status. Dominative women and men held strong ethnocentric views, tended to depend solely on typical negative stereotypes, and turned to religion as a means to other ends.

Those with quest religious orientation or phenomenological-humanistic spirituality showed no interaction effect between gender and WRC. Thus, to describe individuals' experience of religion and spirituality, both gender and WRC need to be taken into account. Religiosity appears to be related to a religious organization with its own rules and regulations to be explicitly or implicitly followed by its adherents. Religious organizations often take stands on issues important to religion or everyday life. Spirituality, a more individual matter with smaller groups or networks, usually espouses adherence to common ideas and more individual decision-making.

When individuals disagree with some tenets or values of religious organizations, it may cause a real schism; threat of loss of good standing, loss of membership, or even shunning from the group may result from not going along with the religious agenda. It may become a tug-of-war by the organization's and/or the member's choice (see Rayburn, Natale, & Linzer, 1982). Negative reactions to the individuals' acting as individuals and not just part of the ecclesiastical group may result in censure, disillusionment, loss of self-esteem and self-worth, distrust of oneself and the groups ideas of betrayal by the religious organization and, much worse, by God Almighty with whom the member closely associates with the organization, possible diminution of faith, and anger or rage.

The case of gender and racial discrimination within ecclesia, either by tradition or practice, is a very painful situation for many members. Those who expect an atmosphere of loving kindness, tolerance, and encouragement of all members to realize their potential and to do their utmost good in life may be repelled when they do not see these actions practiced by their religious organization. Christians may expect the fulfillment in the here-and-now rather than only in some much postponed heavenly dwelling of Galatians 3:28: "There is neither Jew nor Greek, there is neither bond nor free, there is neither male nor female: for you are all one in Christ Jesus." Although some women hold onto their memberships in patriarchal religions, they still may seek the joy, understanding, and affirmation that come from spiritual belongingness to woman-spirit, women's spirituality, or the women's spiritual movement.

SEXUALITY AND SPIRITUALITY REUNITED

Nelson (1987) noted that a more holistic understanding of people and the ways in which sexuality is present in all human experience has created a desire to reunite sexuality and spirituality. From liberation theology and from the feminist and lesbian/gay movements have come questions about ways in which experience of human sexuality and perceptions about faith interact with each other. Sexuality has been viewed as intrinsic to the connection between the divine and the human. In traditional sexual dualism, spirit has been held to be higher and superior to the lower and inferior body. Similarly, sexism or patriarchy identifies men with mind or spirit, whereas it identifies women with matter or the body and sees the need for the higher to control the lower.

"Sexual salvation" is a theory that Nelson (1987) proposed to embody the spiritual and religious. Traditionally, saints have been viewed as asexual or sexless beings who experience no sexual needs or desires, and sometimes they may even be imagined as having no genitalia. Concepts about God and the Holy Spirit have included an engendered deity, a Higher Power of both male and female genders, a completely nonsexual being, and even an ethereal being with no humanlike form. Nonetheless, humans experience the religious and spiritual through connecting the lesser known with our better known bodily experiences (Rayburn, 1995). The ecclesiastical community is currently recognized as a sexual community. Religious feminists have voiced this sexual connection and pointed out ecclesia's disempowerment of the sexually oppressed. This has included patriarchal/gender biased language, worship, imagery, ethics, and leadership roles (Nelson, 1987).

AGE INFLUENCES ON SEXUALITY AND SPIRITUALITY

Richmond (1998) studied the relationships among spirituality, religiousness, and sexuality in younger and older women. Using three inventories (Rayburn & Richmond, 1996a, 1996b, 1998) (the Inventory on Religiousness or IR, the Inventory on Spirituality or IS, and the Body Awareness and Sensitivity to Intimacy Comfort Scale or BASICS), she surveyed women from several Catholic colleges in Maryland. The younger women were 19–21 years old, and the older women were 23–62 years old. Although there were only 20 women in the younger group and 18 women in the older group, she found some interesting results. The majority of both groups considered themselves to be "almost always" spiritual, almost always thought that spirituality can and does exist independently of religion and that there certainly could be mature spirituality existing independently of religion. The older women "sometimes" and the younger women "almost always" thought that they were religious persons. Yet, the older women "almost always" turned to a Higher Power for comfort and protection when in distress, attended services once a week, and believed that the Higher Power would restore them to life after death. To the item on the IS "I believe the Almighty wants us to have a good and enjoyable life on earth," the older women responded with "sometimes," which indicates their belief that their main rewards would be in heaven. However, both the older and the younger group "usually" thought of sexual intimacy as comforting. Thus, they must see some rewards on earth. A majority of younger women considered themselves to be "almost always" spiritual and "almost always" religious. In regard to their sexual practices, 50% of the younger women were always comfortable with oral sex and 20% were never comfortable with it. Furthermore, 53% of these younger women were always comfortable with coitus, but 10% were never comfortable. For older women, the percentages were found to be about the same. All the women may have perceived religion as the formalized doctrinal and creedal organizational enterprise rather than the specific beliefs concerning the sacred personalities of the Godhead and object lessons of a divine nature.

SPIRITUALITY AND SEXUAL ABUSE

Swedlund (1998) examined the connections between spirituality and sexual abuse. She proposed that abuse survivors address issues of religion and spirituality as a vital part of the healing process. When she interviewed women who had been disillusioned with their churches, angry at God, or thought that their churches had little to offer them in dealing with abuse, Swedlund found that the religious beliefs of these women contributed to their shame. Some felt sinful, evil, and believed they had been condemned by God. When religious beliefs were used as a resource in handling sexual abuse, the women reported that something redemptive in their religion lessened the impact of the abuse, comforted them with the thought that a caring God was there for them, calmed them by the image of the church as a refuge from the chaotic home, and gave them a refuge from abuse in prayer.

SPIRITUALITY AND CONNECTEDNESS

Using spirituality as a resource in ongoing recovery might involve helping women to sense a connectedness with themselves, others, and the natural world, and to find a sense of inner strength. Theobiology, the interface of theology and biology, has been proposed to better understand where humankind fits into the world created by God (Rayburn & Richmond, 1998). Rediscovering the feminine in theology and biology can restore the balance in the big picture of life.

In her studies of the mystical union in women's sexual relationships, Ogden (1997) found that women's sexual satisfaction goes beyond biological "skin hunger" to a whole-person process that connects body, mind, heart, and soul. Women reported that peak sexual experiences gave them sensual enjoyment, partnership responses of love, commitment, romance intimacy, nurturing, and spiritual euphoria (i.e., a sense of mystical union that leads to deep and enduring wholeness, pleasure, and serenity). Using a 45-item survey, Ogden found that the majority of the 271 women (mean age = 24 years) indicated that spirituality and sexuality were more important to them than organized religion. Her population was 46% Roman Catholic, 15% Protestant, and 23% atheist, agnostic, or without religious affiliation. Over half (52%) of these women agreed that sex needs a spiritual element to be truly satisfying, and they spoke of both sexual and spiritual satisfaction as "feeling loved and accepted," "release of emotional tension," and "feeling loving and accepting." When 12 bipolar concepts were presented in a semantic differential format, spirituality and sexuality were seen as having similar levels of inner vitality and integration, honesty, caring for self, and caring for others. Furthermore, 70% of the women indicated that the conditions that contributed most to sex being a spiritual experience for them was being in love; 9% said it was feeling committed to their partner, and 9% said it was feeling safe. It is interesting that for 91% safety was not an important consideration; perhaps their youth accounts for this finding, or maybe to them safety meant stasis and comfort, whereas reaching out spiritually in relationship moves beyond their comfort zone and involves some risk. When asked what contributed least to spiritual sex, the women responded: drinking or drugs (23%), danger (16%), feeling controlled (12%), and feeling safe (10%). Actions that the women had taken most often to help make sex spiritual were sharing deep feelings, making eye contact, kissing soulfully, and laughing together with their partners. They reported that what prevented them from experiencing the sex-spiritual connection was worry about their looks; this reflects cultural values and possibly fear of rejection by their partners.

BODY IMAGES, INTIMACY, AND SPIRITUALITY

In a study of the relationships among body image, intimacy, and spirituality, Rayburn, Osman, and our colleagues (1997) recruited 127 women from four eastern U.S. states and administered the Inventory on Spirituality (Rayburn & Richmond, 1996b) and the BASICS (Rayburn & Richmond, 1996a). On the IS subscale Transcendence, designed to study that which is beyond the material and tangible, participants were asked to respond to such items as "I feel at one with the universe" and "There is a life-force beyond myself." We found that Transcendence was related significantly to the BASICS subscale Images of Sexual Intimacy ("I think sexual intimacy is frightening," "I think of sexual intimacy as inviting and joyful"). Perhaps the common link between Transcendence and Images of Sexual Intimacy is the going beyond the physical and experiencing the less tangible but more emotional and spiritual elements in sexual relationships. No significant correlation was found between the Body Comfort subscale of BASICS and the IS, but there was a strong tendency toward a negative correlation of Body Comfort (one item is "I am comfortable with the appearance of my body") in all three IS subscales. This is noteworthy because of the possibility that a spiritual frame of mind, in some cases, leads to viewing awareness or attention to the body as unnecessary or undesirable. This type of dualism would be counterproductive to holism or uniting the mind-body-spirit connection.

In a subsequent study of spirituality and sexuality, Rayburn and Osman (1998) found no significant correlations between the IS and the total BASICS or any of its subscales. Previous significant findings may have been specific to the particular population studied. The 1998 study had a smaller number of participants than the first one (Rayburn, Osman et al., 1997), and a much larger population needs to be studied in order to compare the BASICS and the IS accurately.

BODY IMAGE, SPIRITUAL EMBODIMENT, AND TRANSCENDENCE

In our study (Rayburn, Osman et al., 1997), the IS Transcendence subscale correlated significantly with Images of Sexual Intimacy (e.g., "I think of sexual intimacy as inviting and joyful") but not with Body Images (e.g., "I think of my body as bad and sinful," "I think of my body as good and wholesome"). This may have pointed to the differences between the two BASICS subscales. Sexual Intimacy involves relationships between people, whereas Body Images do not necessarily involve anyone but the individuals and their perceptions of themselves. Relationships are considered by most people to be vital. How individuals perceive their bodies, however, is not as vital to a relationships with others.

Kleinplatz (1997) studied spirituality and sex therapy as ways of celebrating erotic transcendence and spiritual embodiment. She commented that formal religious teachings tend to be viewed as antithetical to sexual fulfillment, but the specifics of which religion, which teaching, which sexuality, and ways in which the teachings are internalized and practiced have often been omitted from sex therapy literature. Often religion and spirituality are not differentiated, and the contribution and possibly enhancing effect of spirituality on sexual fulfillment or vice versa may be unappreciated. The rigidity of strict adherence to a certain set of regulations in religion, rather than religion per se, may inhibit sexuality and make it difficult to let go and give oneself fully to a divine being or to a human partner. Many may see only either-or propositions and believe that they must choose between religious or sexual fulfillment. Many believe in a taboo against seeking pleasure or lusting after sexual joy. This is what is often held to be sinful. Traditional mind-body dualism creates a schism as opposed to a union of spiritual and sexual experiences. Many people seek and long for the connection within and with one's partner that brings sexual relations into a life-affirming and spirituality enhancing experience, a feeling of being utterly alive, and a passionate, erotic experience. Many desire mind-soul expanding sex, a surrendering to passion in a sublime way in order to experience oneself as whole. Sharing a sense of harmony and being both centered in and transcending one's body seems like fulfillment of a sacred destiny. Union with the divine within and with one's partner involves heightened awareness of ultimate existential aloneness while at the same time coming together and sharing with someone else. Fulfillment of the spiritual sensation of sacred destiny, touching the divine, sensing uniqueness with universality, and embodiment of the divine are part of sex becoming transcendent. For sexuality and spirituality to be integrated, sexuality may need to be considered an element of the embodied experience of the divine, and spirituality may need to be viewed as an element of peak or ultimate erotic experience. Instead of seeing desire as sin, people may need to emphasize stagnation, fear of exposure, and hesitance to grow as sin. The biblical language of sexual relationships as "to know" may become the guide to knowing ourselves and our partners, to entering the meeting point of the sacred and the divine, and to letting go of shame as sex restores our souls and nourishes our spirits, minds, and bodies. In these ways, spirituality and sexuality may be integrated effectively.

Helminiak (1997) used a humanistic lens to study ways to integrate sexuality and spirituality. Taking the stance that "spirit is a dimension of the human mind" and that "integration of the spiritual is merely integration of the person," he defined spirit as a transcendent dimension of human experience. Spirit causes people to be self-aware, self-transcending, open-ended, and aware of our awareness. Spirituality gives meaning and value to our lives. Helminiak view is a reworking of the philosophical/theological into the psychological. This view is somewhat tongue-in-cheek, in that it seeks to resolve the issues by completely redefining the dimensions.

SPIRITUALITY AND YOUNG WOMEN

Goetz, Barkony, Gardner, Lepke, and Wager (1994) studied spiritual development in girls (ages 8–14). They used questionnaires, small group discussions, and individual interviews with 84 participants to study their socialization, sexuality, images of God, and perceptions of women's roles in their churches. All of the participants belonged to Christian churches in which there was a woman pastor or women in other significant roles. College women at a coeducational, church-related liberal arts college served as a comparison group. Most of the participants thought of God as male, but a few described God as female. After a discussion of qualities of their parents and images of God, a few participants were willing to consider God as Mother. Those from churches with women pastors did not more often spontaneously speak of God in feminine terms. College women spoke of God as loving, forgiving, good, like a father, almighty, and all knowing. Seventy-eight percent thought of God as a father, and 32% thought of God as a mother. The participants were aware that roles in their churches were divided by gender. Protestant women from churches that do not restrict roles by sex were much more likely than Roman Catholic women to express their thinking that restricting roles on the basis of gender was unfair. It was concluded that women's self-concept is affected by how they believed that God perceived them. They believed that because the church ignores physical development and sexuality, these must not be relevant to religious experience.

GENDER DIFFERENCES IN RELIGIOUSNESS AND SPIRITUALITY

Though women comprise at least 60% of most religious congregations, they have not been allowed to function in as many or as essential roles as have men. Dissatisfied girls and women often become marginalized and sense themselves as being held in less importance than are boys and men. They may then function as only nominal members of the group, and some may decide to leave the religious setting all together. When they leave, they may commit themselves to advocating for causes that would protect the welfare of others, of animals, and of the environment. Seeking to redefine their longing for their search for the ultimate, Higher Power beyond themselves, women often develop new ways of thinking, as is evidenced in woman's spirituality. In these newer endeavors, women are careful to ensure more inclusivity than they have previously experienced.

Women have often been seen as more religious than men and as having more concern about mercy than justice. Based on interviews, Gilligan (1982) concluded that women tend to make judgments based more on what is merciful than what is just, whereas men tend to make decisions based on what is just more often than on what is merciful. However, Rayburn, Goetz, Osman, Siderits, and Austria (1998) and Goetz, (1998) administered the IR and the IS, with 12 additional items at the end of each (but not figured into the total score) to 150 people. These 12 items included three items that concerned the weight given to mercy and justice in making decisions. There were no significant gender differences for any of these items. Thus, women as often as men thought that both mercy and justice were important and gave both about equal weight. This finding seriously questions Gilligan's proposal that women make judgments based more on mercy than on justice. It is possible that we reached different conclusions because the issues studied in the Gilligan interviews were specific to matters that touched the lives of women more than men, such as abortion. However, it is important to note that, when women rate the importance of mercy and justice for general issues overall, they appear to give them equal importance. Further research is needed to resolve this discrepancy.

SPIRITUALITY AND LEADERSHIP

Piedmont (1997) used the Organizational Relationships Survey (ORS) (Rayburn & Richmond, 1996b, 1999) to assess leadership styles in the work and religious environments. The ORS, the Five-Factor Model of Personality, and the Faith Maturity scale were administered to 204 undergraduate students. Correlations with spirituality and personality measures supported the construct validity of the ORS scales. Levels of personal spirituality were positively related to learning leadership skills from one's religious group and general community. Women and men who learned leadership skills from men had higher levels of power; women who learned skills from women had higher levels of purpose. Overall, more gender similarities than differences were found.

Rayburn (1997) developed the Sports, Exercise, Leadership, Friendship or SELF inventory, which was designed to investigate relationships among these variables. There are items on the SELF that involve spiritual/religious settings. When the IR and the SELF were correlated, all four of the SELF items concerned with leadership skills and the religious/spiritual setting had a highly significant correlation with IR subscales on Attendance (at religious services), Caring for Others, Forgiveness and Prayer, Transcendence, Belief, and Total IR. However, items that referred to the leadership skill of inspiring others did not significantly correlate with any of the IR subscales or Total IR. On the IS and the SELF, significant correlations were found for Total SELF and the IS subscales of Transcendence, Caring for Others, and Seeking Goodness and Truth. For the "inspiring" items, Total IS and its subscale Caring for Others were highly correlated (but Transcendence and Seeking Goodness and Truth were not significantly correlated).

Women show a positive correction on the IS and the SELF. IS Caring for Others was highly correlated with all of the various combinations of the SELF items. IS Transcendence was significantly correlated for all but the "inspiring" items for women, and this was also the case for Total IS. Seeking Goodness and Truth, however, did not have any significant relationship to any of the SELF religious/spiritual items.

Carver, Gallagher, and Richmond (1999) studied high-level women in the Maintenance Leadership Development Program of the U.S. Postal Service. The nine women in the unique and non-traditional positions of supervising and mentoring mainly men in custodial, mechanical, maintenance, and electronic/technical jobs were drawn from various sections of the country. They participated in extensive telephone interviews, were administered the Bipolar Adjective Rating Scale or BARS (Piedmont, 1995, 1999), which yields a five-factor marker of personality, the Life Choices Inventory or LCI (Rayburn, Hansen, Siderits, Burson, & Richmond, 1999), a measure of agentic versus communal values, the Inventory on the Supreme and Work (ISAW) (Rayburn & Richmond, 1999), which measure traditionally feminine and masculine approaches to both spirituality and work, and the IS (Rayburn & Richmond, 1996b, 1999). The mean age of the women was 47 years, with a range of 36 to 54 years. Five had been raised as Protestants, three as Roman Catholics, and one as an agnostic. All had some college training. All but one reported being spiritual (having some sense of the transcendent) and having a personal communication with God. Yet, only one described herself as religious. None came from well-to-do homes. Eight spoke of being "tomboys" who played baseball, war, marbles, tag, or cowboys and Indians. On the ISAW, the work satisfaction variable achievement was negatively correlated with the following concepts of the supreme: redeemer, peacemaker, rescuer, judge, and forgiver. Creator, redeemer, rescuer, and protector correlated positively with mission. Creator, redeemer, peacemaker, forgiver, and life giver correlated positively with leadership. Furthermore, all variables except lover, nurturer, sustainer, and all knowing correlated with team player. Overall, women who scored highest on the concept of the supreme on the ISAW tended to score somewhat lower on achievement, decision making, and challenging than did others. All scores were quite high on work satisfaction. Only one item of the IS was used in this study: "I see a spiritual side to my work or occupation," and this correlated positively with 9 of the 15 images of the supreme variables on the ISAW and with team playing on Work Satisfaction of the ISAW. As a group, the women "sometimes" to "usually" see a spiritual side to their occupation. The women were multi-faceted, both argentic and communal, both family and work centered, both providers and nurturers, rational and intuitive, more connected than compartmentalized, more cooperative than competitive, more achieving than relating. And they claim to be spiritual, but not religious in a formal, doctrinal, creedal way.

WOMEN'S SPIRITUALITY

Although some women hold onto their membership in patriarchal settings—perhaps in hope of facilitating needed changes—they also seek the more gender-fair affirmation, understanding, and joy that comes from taking part in woman-spirit, the women's spiritual movement, or women's spirituality. Such spirituality, as Greenfield (1982) pointed out, concerns "spirit" as the "attitude or principle that inspires, animates, or pervades thought, feeling, or action" (p. 534). Greenfield opposed hierarchical structure in women's spirituality; she saw the institutional emphasis as dangerous and confusing because such an understanding of "spirit" focuses on learned ritual instead of being a self-determined movement. The liberating factor of spirituality, according to Greenfield, must come from a woman's realization that she must determine and take control of her destiny. Ozorak (1996) suggested that women are hampered by theological pitfalls in traditions with which they must ultimately reconnect to complete their liberation.

Iglehart (1982) described the patriarchy in both religion and spirituality, as well as in political power, as oppressive and the woman spirit movement as aimed at reclaiming spiritual-political powers for women and creating new ways of being and relating. These goals have been worked on, in part, through skills sharing and consciousness-raising. A reunion of the spiritual with the political, of inner with outer, and of psychic with material is stressed by woman spirit. Intuitive powers are combined with intellectual skills, and psychological preventive medicine is practiced. The creation of a new world with conservation of energy is emphasized.

Integral to some forms of women's spirituality is the understanding of the power of women naming themselves and the rage connected with the necessity of having to create new words to replace the sexist words of a patriarchy that by such biased designations has indicated ownership of and control over female persons (Spretnak, 1982). Spretnak noted that psychic energy (creative principle, life force) is intrinsically female, and recognition of this inherent character is essential to feminist spirituality. Patriarchy is seen as a male neurosis, with male-dominated social institutions being an expression of man's womb envy and aiming to take away woman's power and usurp it, thus creating a culture that inhibits female energy and then becoming destructive and death-oriented. Morgan (1984) held that exercising healthy spirituality by showing self-love, compassion, union of self-power with group power, and emotional and psychic communication can do much to lessen oppression.

Women sometimes consider themselves to be as religious as men do. However, women are turning more and more to what is spiritual—the heart, the vitality, and the feeling of being of, caring for and reaching out to the environment, other people, animals and plants, life itself, or the maintenance of a better life. Women see themselves as effective in spiritual concerns and less hampered by restrictions of a patriarchal ecclesia. Women may continue to occupy pews in religious settings because they turn to the religious in the same way that disenfranchised ethnic groups such as African Americans have often turned to religion when deeply oppressed, but at the same time they are looking at other options such as spirituality. It was, after all, women who gave birth to the women's spirituality movement. The nurturing role has been most associated with women, and we have had a very special role in the birthing process and indeed the very engendering of creation itself. Not surprising, then, is the finding that women value caring for others and seeking peace and harmony very highly and that both spirituality and efforts toward peace are especially associated, with us. Spiritual men want peace and harmony too, and they can strive for this within their interpersonal relationships. However, they must be willing to share responsibility, power, and opportunities with female persons and do so with a respect for what women have been able to accomplish, even in times of bias against women in ecclesia and other areas of living. Patriarchal resistance to women's freedom and well-being, especially in reproductive rights, continues the repression of women's choices (Northup, 1996).

CHARTING A NEW COURSE IN RELIGIOUSNESS AND SPIRITUALITY

Women have had influence on ecclesiastical authority throughout the history of the church and synagogue. Esther, Sarah, Leah, Rachel, Miriam, Ana, Deborah, Priscilla, Dorcas, Ruth, Naomi, Jael, Junio, Rebecca, Mary—the mother of Christ, Mary Magdalene, and other women of scripture have influenced modern thinking in ecclesiastical settings and spread out from there. Discoveries or rediscoveries of roles that women have taken are now adding much for the consideration of biblical and theological scholars. For example, a woman from the House of Borgia sat on the papal seat in Rome as Pope for a short period of time, and Beruriah, an unordained rabbi rose above the limitations on women in second century Eretz Israel to become an avid student and committed teacher of Torah, a learned judge in Jewish law, and the only woman in all of Talmudic writings whose opinion was accepted as *halachah*, Jewish law (Swidler, 1977, 1979). Women served as priests and bishops in the early Christian church, one of the most outstanding of whom was Bishop Theodora, who was celebrated as a male bishop by monks or other church authorities at the Church of Saint Praxedis in Rome after her name over the door had been tampered with to read "Theodo" rather than the feminine "Theodora." A fresco of women celebrating the Eucharist in the Catacomb of Priscilla in Rome was photographed with altered features to make the figures appear to be men (Irvin, 1980; Morris 1973). The lives of Teresa of Avila and Therese of Lisieux are examples of women's reactions to religious authority and women's gender roles (Siderits, 1996).

Even traditional, conservative women who consider themselves to be religious and perhaps also spiritual cannot avoid learning about these new discoveries and taking into account what has been done to women by denying us the opportunity to be involved at all levels of ecclesia. Many are not happy with what has been done in the name of biblical writings or traditions, although they may remain faithfully—if not contentedly—in the pews of their religious settings. They rarely accept without question the interpretations of sacred writings proffered to them by the patriarchy. Instead, many are studying these matters on their own or in small study groups with other women. Although many of them do not wish to become ministers, rabbis, or priests, they desire that qualified women who want to have those roles be given the opportunity (Rayburn, 1984b).

Other women are choosing to seek other means of expressing their spiritual and even their religious leanings in the more open and accepting atmosphere of women's spirituality or other spirituality groups. Many no longer trust the male-dominated hierarchy of established religion to meet the spiritual or religious needs of girls and women. Nor do these women want their sons, husbands, or significant others to fall under the influence or authority of a less than gender-fair ecclesia. Women are seeking increasingly more bonding with other women and enlightened men in the sisterhood of women's organizations, women's networks, and community work that encompasses spiritual or religious outreach of a more inclusive nature than is found in some ecclesial settings. Women are more aware of their broader choices and of their right to determine their lives, to define themselves as women and persons and to express the various nuances of their feelings, thoughts and identities. In religiousness and spirituality, as in many other areas, women are definitely not unidimensional. They are multifaceted and evolving, not static nor stagnant. Women sense less fear, guilt, and insecurity in leaving living situations of their youth that they have depended on for their sense of security and well-being. The options for women are changing and improving. Women are taking advantage of their long-awaited and long-overdue freedoms to share power and control over areas that affect their lives and the lives of their families.

REFRAMING RELIGIOUS/SPIRITUAL ENVIRONMENTS

Both religiousness and spirituality have been important influences in the lives of many women. Nonetheless, many religious settings have not been as affirming of women and girls as they have been of men and boys. Such gender biases have been very painful to female persons and caused many of us to seek affirmation elsewhere. When women sense that they must trade self-esteem, self-worth, full religious or spiritual expression, and must deny a sense of betrayal by the very establishment and its practitioners that promised to love them and show them loving kindness, we may also realize that we are betraying ourselves and all that we could be, betraying other women, and even allowing the religious or spiritual setting itself to stagnate and to be far less meaningful than it was meant to be. In embracing spirituality, women may threaten some men who fear that such a choice is a battle cry for reform or change in what to some men may be a comfortable status quo. Some men will necessarily give up some of their power and control in order to share responsibility with women. In doing so, the ecclesial setting will become more authentic in realizing its ideals and fulfilling the teaching of Galatians 3:28: There is neither Jew nor Greek, slave nor free, male nor female, for you are all one in Christ Jesus.

WOMEN AND SPIRITUALITY, YESTERDAY AND TODAY

In the book of Ruth, the three women have come upon deplorable times; all have lost their husbands and must make their way at a time in which a woman alone could be ravaged by abusive men. Little provision was made for them to earn a living on their own. The oldest woman, Naomi, is the mother-in-law of Ruth and Orpah. The young women are not from the land of the Hebrews. In compassion, Naomi urges the two daughters-in-law to stay in Moab and return to their people and their gods, to their customs and to the probability of remarriage among their own people. Naomi thus gave them her loving consent and blessing to return to their old beliefs. Orpah reluctantly obeyed this urging, and she felt some comfort in what she had long known. Ruth, however, having seen the beautiful truths of her husband's and his family's religion, refused to be turned back to the old ways of her people. She returned to Bethlehem with her mother-in-law, and vowed that nothing but death would sever her relationship with Naomi. Ruth made her choice.

Women and girls of today are in a situation much like that of Ruth and Orpah. Orpah would represents the more traditional woman who appreciates the new insights of modern scholarship on women and ecclesia, but still feels more comfortable somehow with the old ways and among her people and family in the traditional setting. She is willing to put up with or to deny having less than full participation at every level of the ecclesial structure. She is aware, however, of what she has gleaned from being with those who have another religion and new insights, and she will be able to bring about some needed improvements at the most safe and opportune time in her own belief structure. The newer religion has touched her life and her old religion; the women's movement and women's spirituality have influenced the traditional religious thinking of many women.

Ruth, however, represents the spiritual woman who has lived with a more accepting and open family and has herself seen the light of greater freedom in which to express herself religiously and spiritually. She is unwilling to return to the more limiting ways of her people and their customs and culture, or to restrict herself in an ecclesial mold because she was born a female. She experiences more love and caring within a setting in which she is free to be a whole person and to know that her Creator fully blesses such actualization of her fulfillment. She is free to be a complete person and to refuse to cut herself off at some religious Maginot Line between the less-than-full participation and expression of religious leanings and authority and the full expression and responsibility at even the highest levels of ecclesiastical authority. Many women today choose to do away with the line of control and to level the religious field to greater and more equal participation for all members in the various religious denominations. So, the Ruth of today, when asked, "Woman, whither goest thou?" must respond, "To chart a new course in religiousness and spirituality and to define *ourselves* as women, persons, and believers . . . to make ecclesia a safe and inviting home for ourselves, our mothers, and our daughters, and to make a more authentic and loving home for our fathers, brothers, sons, and those outside our gates." This is our feminist challenge for the third millennium.

REFERENCES

Batson, C. D., & Burris, C. T. (1994). Personal religion: Depressant or stimulant of prejudice and discrimination? In M. P. Zanna & J. M. Olson (Eds.), *The psychology of prejudice* (pp. 140–169). *The Ontario Symposium*, Vol. 9. Hillsdale, NJ: Erlbaum.

Biale, D. (1982). The God with breasts: El Shaddai in the Bible. *History of Religions, 20*, 240–256.

Bonhoeffer, D. (1971). *Letters and papers from prison.* New York: Macmillan.

Carmody, J., & Carmody, D. (1990). *Christian uniqueness and Catholic spirituality.* New York: Paulist Press.

Carver, K. J., Gallagher, R., & Richmond, L. J. (1999, August). *Female spirituality, careering and the U. S. Postal Service, Maintenance Division.* Paper presented at the meeting of the American Psychological Association, Boston.

Cohen, E. A., & Boyer, M. C. (1998, March). *Unchartered cross-cultural territory: Relating White racial consciousness to religiosity and spirituality.* Paper presented at the meeting of the Association for Women in Psychology Conference, Baltimore.

Craigie, F. C., Jr. (1999). The Spirit and work: Observations about spirituality and organizational life. *Journal of Psychology and Christianity, 18* (1), 43–53.

Daly, M. (1973). *Beyond God the father: Toward a philosophy of woman's liberation.* Boston: Beacon Press.

Gilligan, C. (1982). *In a different voice.* Cambridge, MA: Harvard University Press.

Goetz, D., Barkony, B. M., Gardner, J., Lepke, G. B., & Wager, K. D. (1994, August). *Spirituality, sexuality, and socialization of girls and young women.* Paper presented at the meeting of the American Psychological Association, Los Angeles.

Goetz, D. J. (1998). *Gender and the Inventory on Religiousness and Inventory on Spirituality.* Paper presented at the meeting of the American Psychological Association, San Francisco.

Greenfield, G. (1982). Spiritual hierarchies: The Empress' new clothes? In C. Spretnak (Ed.), *The politics of women's spirituality* (pp. 531–534). Garden City, NY: Anchor Press.

Helminiak, D. A. (1997, August). *Sexuality and spirituality: A humanist account.* Paper presented at the meeting of the American Psychological Association, Chicago.

Hinson, E. G. (1990). Jubilee of the Ecumenical Institute of Spirituality. *Ecumenical Trends, 19,* 169–170.

Iglehart, H. (1982). The unnatural divorce of spirituality and politics. In C. Spretnak (Ed.), *The politics of women's spirituality* (pp. 404–414). Garden City, NY: Anchor Press.

Irvin, D. (1980). Archaeology supports women's ordination. *The Witness, 68* (2), 4–8.

Kleinplatz, P. J. (1997, August). *Spirituality and sex therapy: Celebrating erotic transcendence and spiritual embodiment.* Paper presented at the meeting of the American Psychological Association, Chicago.

Marshall-Green, M., & Hinson, E. G. (1990). Contribution of women to spirituality. In B. J. Leonard (Ed.), *Becoming Christian: Dimensions of spiritual formation* (pp. 116–130). Louisville, KY: Westminster/John Knox.

McCrae, R. B., & Costa, P. T., Jr. (1987). Validation of the five-factor model of personality across instruments and observers. *Journal of Personality and Social Psychology, 52,* 81–90.

Morgan, R. (1984). Introduction: Planetary feminism, theopolitics of the 21st century. In R. Morgan (Ed.), *Sisterhood is global* (pp. 1–37). Garden City, NY: Anchor Press.

Morris, J. (1973). *The lady was a bishop: The hidden history of women with clerical ordination and the jurisdiction of bishops*. New York: Macmillan.

Nelson, J. B. (1987, February). Reuniting sexuality and spirituality. *The Christian Century*, 187–190.

Northup, L. A. (1996, August). *Bitten from behind: Babies, big institutions, and backlash*. Paper presented at the meeting of the American Psychological Association, Toronto, Canada.

Ogden, G. (1997, August). *Beyond skin hunger: Mystical union in women's sexual relationships*. Paper presented at the meeting of the American Psychological Association, Chicago.

Ozorak, E. W. (1996, August). *The social construction of women's religious self*. Paper presented at the meeting of the American Psychological Association, Toronto.

Piedmont, R. L. (1995). Big five adjective marker scales for use with college students. *Psychological Reports, 77*, 160–162.

Piedmont, R. L. (1997, August). *Gender differences in the spiritual and personal correlates of leadership*. Paper presented at the meeting of the American Psychological Association, Chicago.

Piedmont, R. L. (in press). Does spirituality represent the sixth factor of personality? Spiritual transcendence and the five-factor model. *Journal of Personality*.

Piedmont, R. L. (1999). *Development of the Spiritual Transcendence Scale*. Paper presented at the Third Annual Roundtable on Religious Research, Loyola College Maryland, Columbia, MD.

Rayburn, C. A. (1981). Some reflections of a female seminarian: Woman, whither goest thou? *Journal of Pastoral Counseling, 16*, 61–65.

Rayburn, C. A. (1984a). Impact of nonsexist language and guidelines for women in religion. *Journal of Pastoral Counseling, 1*, 5–8.

Rayburn, C. A. (1984b, August). *Religious women and organizational structures: Joining, leading, following*. Paper presented at the meeting of the American Psychological Association, Toronto.

Rayburn, C. A. (1985). Promoting equality for women seminarians. *Counseling and Values, 29*, 164–169.

Rayburn, C. A. (1989). Power struggles, equality quests, and women in ecclesia. *Journal of Pastoral Counseling, 24*, 145–150.

Rayburn, C. A. (1993). Ritual as acceptance/empowerment and rejection/disenfranchisement. In L. A. Northup (Ed.), *Women and religious ritual* (pp. 87–101). Washington, DC: Pastoral Press.

Rayburn, C. A. (1995). The body in religious experience. In R. W. Hood, Jr. (Ed.), *Handbook of religious experience* (pp. 476–494). Birmingham, AL: Religious Education Press.

Rayburn, C. A. (1996, August). *Religion and spirituality: Can one exist independently of the other?* Paper presented at the meeting of the American Psychological Association, Toronto.

Rayburn, C. A. (1997). *Sports, Exercise, Leadership, Friendship (SELF)*. Washington DC: U.S. Copyright Office.

Rayburn, C. A., Natale, S., & Linzer, J. (1982). Feminism and religion: What price holding membership in both camps? *Counseling and Values, 26*, 154–164.

Rayburn, C. A., & Osman, S. (1998, August). *Relationship of women's leadership to spirituality, religiousness, body image, and sports.* Paper presented at the meeting of the American Psychological Association, San Francisco.

Rayburn, C. A., Osman, S., Young, E., Richmond, L. J., Davis, C., Francoeur, R., & Siderits, M. A. (1997, August). *Body and soul: Relationships between body image, intimacy, and spirituality.* Paper presented at the meeting of the American Psychological Association, Chicago.

Rayburn, C. A., & Richmond, L. J. (1998). "Theobiology:" Attempting to understand God and ourselves. *Journal of Religion and Health, 37,* 345–356.

Rayburn, C. A., & Richmond, L. J. (1996a). *Body Awareness and Sensitivity of Intimacy Comfort Scales (BASICS).* Washington, DC: U.S. Copyright Office.

Rayburn, C. A., & Richmond, L. J. (1996b). *Inventory on Spirituality (IS).* Washington, DC: U.S. Copyright Office.

Rayburn, C. A., & Richmond, L. J. (1999). *Inventory on the Supreme and Work (ISAW).* Washington DC: U.S. Copyright Office.

Rayburn, C. A., Goetz, D., Osman, S., Siderits, M. A., & Austria, A. M. (1998). *Relationship of women's leadership in spirituality, religiousness, body images, and sports.* Paper presented at the meeting of the American Psychological Association, San Francisco.

Rayburn, C. A., Hansen, L. S., Siderits, M. A., Burson, P., Richmond, L. J. (1999). *Life Choices Inventory.* Washington DC: U.S. Copyright Office.

Richmond, L. J. (1998, March). *Gender differences across age in religiousness and spirituality.* Paper presented at the meeting of the Association for Women Psychology, Baltimore.

Siderits, M. A. (1996, August). *Where is the voice of God? Women confront religious authority.* Paper presented at the meeting of the American Psychological Association, Toronto.

Spretnak, C. (1982). The politics of women's spirituality. In C. Spretnak (Ed.), *The politics of women's spirituality* (pp. 393–403) Garden City, NY: Anchor Press.

Swedlund, N. (1998, March). *Spirituality and sexual abuse. What are the connections?* Paper presented at the meeting of the Association for Women in Psychology, Baltimore.

Swidler, L. (1977, Spring/Summer). Beruriah: Her word became law. *Lilith,* 9–12.

Swidler, L. W. (1979). *Biblical affirmations of woman.* Philadelphia: Westminster Press.

Part III

Women's Health

Chapter 9

HIV among Elderly Women: Ignored and Overlooked by Health Care Providers and Public Policy Makers

Jennifer M. Hillman and Kristin J. Broderick

The oldest person to be diagnosed with the AIDS virus was an 88-year-old woman (Rosenzweig & Fillit, 1992). At the time of her diagnosis, this elderly woman had been a widow for more than seven years. She reported that she had never engaged in any high-risk behaviors; it was initially unclear how she could possibly have contracted the disease. It was later revealed by other sources, however, that her late husband was an IV drug user who contracted AIDS through the sharing of contaminated needles. Her treatment team then concluded that this elderly woman had contracted the AIDS virus through unprotected sex with her husband; she reported having no knowledge of his drug use. This pioneering case study, offered by Rosenzweig and Fillit (1992), provided the impetus for other researchers and clinicians to explore the possibility that infection with HIV is more prevalent among older adults than once believed. However, it remains unclear to what extent health care providers are aware of the risk factors for HIV (particularly those unique to women) among older adults. It is also notable that despite the fact that the oldest person with a documented case of AIDS is an elderly heterosexual woman, most educational and preventative efforts have been targeted at elderly gay men. It is as though elderly women, as a whole, have been ignored and overlooked as a risk group for HIV.

The purpose of this chapter is to dispel the myth that older women do not engage in high-risk behaviors or find themselves placed in situations that put them at risk for contracting HIV. The rapid growth of the elderly female population will be highlighted, with an emphasis placed upon the increasing numbers of older women who are likely to become infected with HIV. Overall risk factors for HIV will be presented, with emphasis upon the factors typically unique to women (e.g., caregiving for adult children with AIDS; surviving a sexual assault). Information suggests that older women may inadvertently be at higher risk for contracting HIV than younger women in some situations and that older women with AIDS are more likely to be misdiagnosed than their younger counterparts. Case studies will be used to illustrate situations in which mental health care providers ascribed to myths or stereotypes about elderly women and HIV and were negligent in making timely, appropriate diagnostic and treatment decisions. Because little data exists to evaluate the extent to which clinicians are aware of HIV among elderly women, we conducted an empirical pilot study in which health care providers were asked to evaluate a fictional patient with symptoms of AIDS; the patient was described as either middle-aged (35 years of age) or elderly (75 years of age). The results of the study will be presented, as will a review of current public policies and resources for elderly women coping with HIV related issues. The final portion of the chapter is intended to offer attainable goals for the future regarding public policy, funding options, and educational programs aimed at elderly women, health care providers, and the general public. With the increase in numbers of women in the older adult age group, political changes may also be forthcoming.

DEMOGRAPHIC INDICATORS

Diagnostic and public policy issues of older women and HIV will become even more important in the third millennium. The age cohort that is comprised of predominantly middle-aged adults (i.e., the Baby Boomers), which accounts for a large share of our nation's population, will enter old age within the next 20 to 30 years. Epidemiological data suggest that by the year 2000, approximately 16% of the American population will be comprised of adults over the age of 65; the proportion of adults over the age of 65 will rise to more than 23% by the year 2030 (U.S. Bureau of the Census, 1996). The numbers of elderly women currently exceed the numbers of elderly men, and they are projected to continue to do so.

The rapid rate of growth of the elderly population will be concentrated among adults over the age of 85. This subgroup of the elderly, known as the oldest-old, contains the largest proportion of women to men. By the mid-1980s, there were two and a half more women than men over the age of 85 (U.S. Bureau of the Census, 1988). It is also important to note that the vast majority of the women in the oldest-old category will be living on a fixed income without the instrumental or emotional support of a living spouse or partner. In other words, elderly women over the age of 85 will have limited disposable income, and these women will be largely dependent upon social security, government programs, community sponsored health and education programs, Medicaid and Medicare, and immediate family members for help and support. This feminization of poverty among the elderly has been predicted to take place well into the year 2020 (Coalition on Women and the Budget, 1983).

THE PREVALENCE OF HIV AMONG OLDER ADULTS

This expected increase among the sheer numbers of elderly women in our country will certainly impact the numbers of older women at risk for contracting the AIDS virus. Health care providers and public policy makers must expect that due to advances in treatment, middle-aged adults with HIV will live to become older adults with HIV (Linsk, 1994). Currently, 10% of all AIDS cases are among adults over the age of 50 (Linsk, 1994). According to the Centers for Disease Control and Prevention (CDC, 1998), adults aged 50 years and older who have been diagnosed can be categorized into a variety of risk groups. The majority of older adults living with AIDS are men; according to the CDC, 60 percent of all AIDS cases among adults over the age of 50 were contracted through homosexual, male to male contact. The second most prevalent risk factor for AIDS among men and women aged 50 and older is IV drug use. Approximately 15% of the AIDS cases in this age group have been attributed to the sharing of needles and other drug equipment with another infected individual. It also remains unclear to what extent men and women are distributed in this risk group; older women have traditionally been overlooked as potential recreational drug users. Perhaps most important for the impact of risk factors for women over the age of 50, the percentage of AIDS cases in this age group has risen to over 10% of men and women who contracted the HIV virus through heterosexual contact. Before 1985, virtually no cases of heterosexual transmission were documented in the over-50 age group.

This percentage increase in the number of AIDS cases attributed to heterosexual transmission is greater than that for any other age group (Stall & Catania, 1994). It also is likely that this increase in HIV infection via heterosexual contact will continue to increase among older adults. The next cohort (i.e., the Baby Boomers) to enter older adulthood have lived through the sexual revolution, are more likely to live in age-segregated communities in which there is greater availability of a partner, and are more likely to live longer than members of previous generations. Thus, heterosexual contact (e.g., vaginal, oral, or anal intercourse) represents a clear and formidable risk factor for middle-aged and elderly women.

Although AIDS cases among older adults represent less than 11% of all AIDS cases, the absolute numbers of older adults with this illness are quite compelling. In 1994, more adults over the age of 50, including women over the age of 50, died from AIDS and AIDS-related complications than the number of Americans who died during the Vietnam War (Stall & Catania, 1996). Certain regions of the U.S. are already reporting significant increases in the numbers of older adults contracting HIV. For example, large increases in HIV infected older adults have been reported in states with large elderly populations, including California and Florida. In Palm Beach, Florida, the numbers of adults over the age of 50 who contracted HIV doubled within a 10-year period to 15% (Speyer, 1994). The overall increase in the incidence of AIDS among older men and women can not be ignored or discounted.

RISK FACTORS FOR OLDER WOMEN

The misdiagnosis of HIV infection or AIDS among older adults, including the rapidly growing numbers of elderly women, is fraught with dire consequences (Aupperle, 1996; Linsk, 1994). Elderly patients who do not receive a timely diagnosis of HIV infection can not receive vital pharmacological treatment, which typically calls for a series of protease inhibitors. Due to general decreases in the immune system with advancing age, an older woman who is infected with HIV can expect to display symptoms of AIDS and to lose her life much sooner than a younger woman infected at the same time. In other words, compared to younger adults, a misdiagnosis and delay of medical treatment results in a lower overall quality of life and increased mortality for elderly women. A misdiagnosis of HIV among elderly women and men can also increase the likelihood that the disease is inadvertently passed on to others. Because elderly adults, particularly elderly women, are not typically suspected of carrying the AIDS virus, health care providers may not subscribe to universal precautions (i.e., means to prevent the exchange of bodily fluids between patient and care provider, such as wearing latex gloves and eye shields) when treating an elderly woman. Other elderly adults who are unknowingly infected with the disease may infect their sex partners.

Vaginal Changes

The CDC has identified a variety of risk factors for contracting AIDS among adults over the age of 50, but what they do not mention is that many of these risk factors pose unique issues for elderly women. For example, it is clear that elderly women may contract HIV through unprotected heterosexual contact. Although a smaller proportion of elderly women than women in general engage in sexual intercourse on a regular basis (e.g., Matthais, Lubben, Atchison, & Schweitzer, 1997; Starr & Weiner, 1981), elderly women who do engage in sexual intercourse are at much greater risk of contracting HIV per each sexual encounter. Following menopause, the related drop in estrogen results in a thinning of the vaginal walls, a reduction of length of the vaginal cavity, and a reduction in vaginal lubrication during periods of rest and sexual excitation. Elderly women who engage in sexual intercourse are more likely to experience microscopic tears in their vaginal lining and swelling and bleeding of the labia and vagina (Muram, Miller, & Cutler, 1992). These micro and macroscopic injuries allow easier access of HIV into the elderly woman's bloodstream. In addition, both younger and older women are at increased risk for contracting HIV through sexual contact than are men of either age group.

Limited Condom Use

Postmenopausal women are also significantly less likely to use condoms than their younger counterparts. The use of any contraceptive simply does not enter their minds because pregnancy is no longer a concern. For the vast majority of elderly women, condoms are regarded as protection from an unwanted pregnancy (Allers, 1990; Solomon, 1996), not as protection from sexually transmitted diseases (STDs). In addition, many women from this older age cohort were socialized when it was not acceptable to talk about sex with their husbands, their children, their mothers and sisters, their friends, or even their family physician. Elderly women have not been socialized to be assertive and to ask their partners to use condoms; the idea of carrying a supply themselves in case a sexual situation arises would be shocking to many. One elderly woman with whom one of us worked in therapy mentioned repeatedly that asking a male suitor to use a condom would be implying either that she was "easy" or that he was "dirty." She was afraid that if she even broached the subject with her partner, he would reject her as well as her request to use a condom. Women often remain silent because of financial dependency on men or fear of disrupting the relationship (Zablotsky, 1998). Speaking openly about sexual matters also appears to be quite novel for many elderly women. Although it is now virtually expected that young women are provided with some form of sex education about the risks associated with unprotected sex during their school years, women from this older age cohort have never been provided with public education regarding HIV and AIDS; some have not even received basic reproductive information.

Ignorance of Partners' High-Risk Behaviors

Because elderly women are generally assumed to be at very low risk for IV drug use, little or no information is given to this segment of the population about the dangers associated with sharing needles. Elderly women are also unlikely to recognize signs of drug abuse among their sexual partners, and thus they may expose themselves to high-risk behavior without being aware of it. Because there is so little discussion of sexual behavior among this age cohort, older women may simply assume that their partners are faithful to them, especially if they are married. Elderly men do have sexual affairs, do engage in sex with prostitutes, and do engage in IV drug use, and elderly women are less likely than young women to question the participation of their partners in high-risk behavior (Goldstein & Manlowe, 1997). An older woman who find herself involved in sexual relations with an older (or younger) man who engages in high-risk behavior inadvertently becomes a participant in high risk behavior for HIV herself.

Sexual Assault

Elderly women can also be exposed to HIV via non-consensual sexual contact or rape. Some criminals appear to target older women for sexual crimes because they appear to be, and often are, vulnerable to attack (Muram, Miller, & Cutler, 1992). Elderly women in institutional settings such as nursing homes may also be at greater risk. Some estimates suggest that up to 15% of elderly nursing home residents have been victims of either sexual or physical abuse (Polaneczky, 1995). As with younger women, rape against elderly women appears to be motivated by violence, anger (Cartwright & Moore, 1989), and a desire to humiliate rather than to fulfill the assailant's sexual needs or desires. An analysis of crime statistics also shows that elderly women are more likely to be sexually assaulted in their own homes by a stranger (71%), often in connection with burglary, than by someone with whom they are acquainted (Muram et al., 1992). In contrast, the majority of younger adult women who are sexually assaulted are attacked by an acquaintance in a location other than their own home (64%). Elderly women are also at significantly greater risk for vaginal injury following the rape for reasons discussed earlier (e.g., thinning of the vaginal wall). An important study by Muram et al. (1992) revealed that more than 25% of rape victims over the age of 65 in their sample required surgical intervention after the attack, whereas only 6% percent of younger rape victims required medical or surgical intervention. The elderly women who were sexually assaulted were more likely to suffer from bruising, contusions, hematomas, and lacerations. It also is notable that the elderly women were not more likely than the younger women in the study to have other physical injuries to other organ systems or parts of their bodies after the rape. The authors concluded that even when the force of the attack appears to be similar among older and younger women, post-menopausal women have a significantly greater chance of suffering vaginal injuries. It follows that, in relation to HIV, elderly women again find themselves at greater risk of entry of the virus into their blood stream during a sexual assault.

To compound the problem that elderly women are more likely to suffer physical injuries during a sexual assault, many elderly women appear hesitant to report the crime or to seek help from the police, medical doctors, psychologists, or crisis intervention centers (e.g., Muram et al., 1992). Poignant case studies of elderly rape victims suggest that these women may tend to blame themselves for the attack (e.g., Polaneczky, 1995). Some elderly rape victims with whom the first author has worked have discussed their beliefs and fears that "bad things only happen to bad girls" or that dressing in a certain way can be enough "to provoke a man and make him lose control." Even if an elderly woman seeks help through a rape crisis center or hot line, it is unlikely that the staff member helping her has had any training in supporting an elderly rape victim. Older women who decide to join a support group for rape survivors may also feel alienated or intimidated because the other members of the group are significantly younger (Polaneczky, 1995). Other elderly women have indicated that they simply would not know who to contact if they were raped. All of these barriers to treatment further inhibit health care providers' ability to help these women by making an accurate and appropriate HIV assessment.

Caregiving for Infected Children

Exposure to blood tainted with HIV also may occur when an older woman provides care to adult children who may be suffering from AIDS (Levine-Perkell, 1996). Allers (1990) revealed that more than one third of all adults who contract AIDS and require assistance with activities of daily living are cared for by their elderly parents. Caregiving for an individual who has AIDS may require a myriad of activities including bathing, feeding, changing bed linens, inserting and removing catheters, and changing the dressings on open wounds or sores. Because most caregivers from this generation tend to be women, elderly women find themselves at greater risk for exposure to HIV through their caregiving activities. Even though universal precautions are sufficient to prevent exposure to HIV though contact with bodily fluids, most elderly women are not even aware of the necessity of universal precautions. An elderly mother caring for a sick son or daughter may attribute her child's AIDS status as "an accident" or as a result of "bad sex" or drug use. Sadly, because AIDS may be viewed as victim specific, elderly women may not see themselves at risk in any way when they are exposed to their children's bodily fluids during caregiving.

Lack of Knowledge

An analysis of the National Health Interview Survey (NHIS; Zablotsky, 1998) found that nearly half (47%) of all women age 65 and older reported knowing "little or nothing" about AIDS. In contrast, only 14% of the women in the 18-to-49 age category reported that they knew "little or nothing" about AIDS. In addition, older women were more likely than younger women to answer "don't know" in response to factual questions about AIDS. Other discrepancies between women from different age groups is reflected in the frequency of HIV testing of older and younger women.

Only one in six women aged 50 to 54 had been tested for HIV. In comparison, nearly one in three women aged 18–24 had (Zablotsky, 1998). Zablotsky's analysis of this national data set indicates that older women maintain limited knowledge about their personal vulnerability to HIV and AIDS.

Misdiagnosis of HIV-Induced Dementia

Elderly women who contract HIV are also at greater risk of being misdiagnosed with Alzheimer's disease or other common forms of dementia. More than two thirds of all individuals with HIV are expected to develop some form of dementia (American Academy of Neurology AIDS Task Force, 1991), and many elderly adults infected with HIV are asymptomatic except for the cognitive changes associated with AIDS-related dementia (Aupperle, 1996). In other words, cognitive symptoms may be the first to emerge in an overall symptom presentation. Because Alzheimer's disease is the most common form of dementia among older adults, it is likely that family members, friends, and even health care professionals may elect to pursue a more familiar and stereotypical diagnosis of Alzheimer's disease rather than ruling out HIV associated dementia complex.

Fortunately, a number of clinical neuropsychologists and other researchers have identified some critical differences between these two disorders (e.g., Greenwood, 1991; Lipton & Gendelman, 1995; Mapau & Law, 1994). For example, Alzheimer's dementia often proceeds in a slow, steady course over many years. It often takes more than two to three years for the most severe symptoms to emerge. In contrast, HIV-induced dementia has an acute onset, and its symptoms increase to maximum severity within a six-month to one-year period. Patients with Alzheimer's disease also tend to display inappropriate affect. For example, an elderly person with Alzheimer's disease might laugh or giggle when told that her pet cat has died. In contrast, most people with HIV-induced dementia display appropriate affect; their emotional responses are consistent with the nature of the actual events that occur around them. Older adults with Alzheimer's dementia also have great difficulty with language. They may have difficulty speaking and understanding spoken and written words. In contrast, most people suffering from HIV-induced dementia maintain a command of language well into the course of the illness. Overall, the memory deficits associated with HIV-induced dementia appear to be related to short term memory and general lapses in attention, which lead to apathy and confusion. Many of these memory-related deficits are overlooked by others close to the patient, even well into the later stages of the disease. In comparison, the memory deficits typically observed among patients with Alzheimer's disease tend to be severe, related to both short term and long term memory, and often are immediately obvious to others who interact with the patient. This information should be able to provide health care providers with an enhanced ability to differentiate between Alzheimer's disease and HIV-induced dementia.

ILLUSTRATIVE CASE STUDIES

A number of case examples encountered in clinical practice and supervision by one of us will be presented here in order to illustrate the pervasive nature of ageism, sexism, and ignorance in the failure of many health care professionals to make an appropriate assessment of HIV among elderly women. (All identifying information about these patients has been changed, and the results of their HIV testing will not be disclosed in order to further protect the women's confidentiality.) One of the primary factors responsible for this lack of sensitivity may be the fact that both lay persons and health care professionals tend to believe that women simply do not engage in sexual activity or other high risk behaviors later in life.

Failure to Recognize a Partner's High-Risk Behavior

This first case study involves Ms. R, a 76-year-old woman who was brought to an outpatient mental health clinic by her daughter for a dementia assessment. Ms. R's daughter noted that her mother sometimes had trouble remembering what she did during the past few days. Ms. R confirmed that she often did not feel like eating, that she had lost 10 pounds in the last month or so, and that she sometimes had trouble remembering things. When asked if she engaged in any enjoyable activities, Ms. R replied that she spent most of her time with a man whom she had recently met at the local senior center. Ms. R's daughter added that she did not know this man very well, and she was concerned that they were spending so much time together. Ms. R snapped at her daughter, "Your father has been gone for a long time . . . Don't you think it's about time that I have some companionship?" At this point, the interviewer asked if they could continue the interview separately.

When alone, Ms. R admitted that she was quite taken with her new companion. She described him as fun loving and romantic. She also added that she felt very lucky to be his "special friend" because he was practically the only single man at the senior center. When asked about her companion's background, Ms. R said that he was a widower who had recently moved to the area from a neighboring state. When asked about other details, Ms. R was unable to provide much additional information about his family or medical history. At the conclusion of the interview, the intake worker determined that Ms. R was probably suffering from minor cognitive deficits related to an underlying depression. She then recommended that Ms. R enroll in a day hospital program as well as to continue to attend her activities at the senior center. The intake worker encouraged Ms. R to foster her relationship with her new companion if that "made her feel better." It is notable that this intake worker never inquired about Ms. R's interest in sex, much less her sexual activity with her new companion. In a discussion of the issue during a staff meeting, the intake worker replied, "Well, it never even occurred to me that this older woman would be having sex. I mean, when she said her boyfriend was romantic, I was thinking of them taking slow walks in the garden and holding hands."

Three weeks later, Ms. R returned to the clinic and reported being heartbroken because she was no longer seeing her boyfriend. (Ms. R referred to her companion as her "boyfriend.") Apparently, he decided to become friendly with another woman at the senior center. He also indicated that he would be moving to Florida at the end of the year. When asked directly about their sexual activities, Ms. R said that she and this gentleman had had sex on numerous occasions; "It made me feel good to be alive. And he was so gentle . . . I just thought I was the only one." When asked about condom use, Ms. R scoffed and replied, "I'm not a spring chicken anymore, you know. What would I use that for? It's not like I have to worry about having a baby." When Ms. R. was asked about whether she should have had protected sex with her boyfriend because she was unsure of his prior sexual activities and partners, she replied in a tone of voice that suggested disbelief, "He's a nice man. He's not dirty or anything like that." After an extended discussion with her mental health care provider, Ms. R agreed to have some testing for sexually transmitted diseases, including HIV. Although she initially stated that "this is just silly," Ms. R agreed to the testing because she did feel "a bit uncomfortable that this man just seems to skip from woman to woman. . . . It makes me feel so stupid, but who knows what else he has been doing."

Denial of Older Women's High-Risk Behavior

A second case study illustrates an additional stereotype that health care providers may have regarding elderly women. In this particular case, Mr. B was a 67-year-old, divorced man who was a patient in an outpatient treatment center for treatment of a generalized anxiety disorder. Mr. B liked to paint ceramics, and he soon became a fixture in the arts activity unit. While working on his crafts, he spoke with a social worker about his two-year relationship with his girlfriend, a 66-year-old divorcee. (Mr. B also identified his companion as his "girlfriend.") He described her as funny, flirtatious, and spirited. (Apparently he liked her so much that he had been signing over a significant part of his social security benefits to her each month.) Although Mr. B mentioned that his girlfriend would be upset if she knew that he had told anyone, he said that she often stayed over at his apartment during the weekends. He smiled and said, "It's nice to feel wanted again and to have someone around." Mr. B was most excited about going with her to the beach next month for a five-day vacation.

As the time for their vacation approached, Mr. B displayed increasing symptoms of anxiety. When the social worker asked him if something were bothering him, he replied that he was very concerned because his girlfriend was not answering her phone. Mr. B was not able to drive due to a serious heart condition, and he could not easily make the trip by himself to her home. He said that he was worried that she could be hurt, "just lying there on the floor or something," until the phone was finally answered . . . "by another man!" He added that when he finally got in touch with his girl-friend the following day, she seemed distant and defensive. Mr. B exclaimed, "She wouldn't tell me who answered the phone at her place at nine o'clock at night. I tell you, I don't think the Maytag repairman would be coming over at that time of night." Within a week's time, Mr. B's girlfriend told him that she was going to go on her beach vacation with "another friend." Mr. B said that he was very upset because his girlfriend would not answer him when he asked her "if she were going with a male friend or a female friend."

Mr. B became so upset with the rift in their relationship that he began to see the social worker for psychotherapy. He tried to involve his girlfriend in couple's therapy to discuss their relationship, but she refused. When Mr. B. began to complain of forgetting things and being "unsteady on [his] feet" a few weeks later, his social worker feared that in addition to his heightened anxiety about his relationship with his girlfriend, a more serious, underlying medical condition might be responsible for these symptoms. When these concerns were brought up at a treatment team meeting, the team conferred and agreed that Mr. B be referred to his primary care physician for a physical and to a neurologist to rule out a stroke or other vascular problem.

When one staff member broached the subject of Mr. B's relationship with his girlfriend, another staff member indicated that "their relationship has been over for a few weeks now, and I don't think that woman has any intentions of getting back together with Mr. B." However, when the psychologist on the treatment team mentioned that Mr. B's girlfriend appeared to be promiscuous (Mr. B said that he was no longer sure if he was the only man to be "romantically involved" with his girlfriend at one time), the majority of the staff members thought that this was either unlikely or unimportant because their relationship had been terminated. By the end of the meeting, however, the psychologist helped the other staff members to recognize that elderly women may be sexually promiscuous, whether or not that behavior is consistent with current stereotypes of older women. Subsequently, the treatment team agreed that Mr. B's social worker should discuss testing for HIV and other sexually transmitted diseases, as his symptoms also appeared consistent with HIV-induced dementia. Mr. B later agreed to the testing. It was quite unfortunate that Mr. B was unable to contact his ex-girlfriend to discuss his concerns about her potential risk factors for HIV. Neither Mr. B. nor his health care providers ever found out whether this elderly woman, who engaged in high-risk behaviors, received appropriate counseling and testing regarding her potential HIV status.

Difficulties in Dealing with Sexual Assault

Another case study illustrates the circumstances surrounding a sexual assault made against an elderly woman and the appropriate and inappropriate actions initially taken by health care professionals. Ms. C was an 81-year-old, single woman who resided in a nursing home. She suffered from bipolar disorder, and for most of her life she was cared for by others in institutions; she had no living, immediate family. As she aged, she became increasingly sensitive to most of the medications commonly prescribed for her manic depressive symptoms (e.g., lithium, valproic acid, depakote). Like many other older adults with bipolar disorder, Ms. C began to cycle rapidly between depressed and manic states, and she displayed psychotic symptoms on a consistent basis. To help manage her symptoms, Ms. C was active in group therapy at the nursing home, and she would participate in planned activities if she were told about them. Ms. C also needed assistance in ambulating with a walker; severe arthritis often made walking difficult and painful for her. She spent most of her time alone in her room or sitting in the lobby on her floor.

One morning Ms. C was extremely agitated during her group therapy session. She alternated between crying and yelling indiscriminately at other patients in the room. Ms. C even tried to get out of her chair and move away from the table; her behavior was extremely unusual due to the severity of her arthritis. When her therapist asked her what going on, Ms. C began to cackle and flap her arms. "I'm a bird, and I'm going to fly away, fly away, fly away into the blue sky, blue." For the rest of the session, Ms. C sat quietly and looked down at the floor. When the group was over, her therapist assisted Ms. C back to her favorite chair in the lobby. Ms. C looked up at her and began to sob, "Can't you stay with me, please, please, please?" Ms. C's therapist rearranged her schedule so that she could meet with her. At that time, Ms. C told her therapist that she was angry with another patient, Mr. K, who "kept touching me when I told him not to!"

With this revelation, Ms. C's therapist became increasingly concerned. Mr. K was recently moved from the independent living section of the community to the nursing home unit. He had been placed in the community by his family members who said that they could no longer care for him. He had been diagnosed with paranoid schizophrenia, and he was significantly younger than most of the other men and women in the nursing home. Aside from his mental illness, Mr. K appeared to be in good physical health. He often roamed the halls wearing headphones. He would stare inappropriately at others, and often he attempted to enter other patients' private rooms at inappropriate times without permission (e.g., when the door was clearly shut, after a nurse had entered to assist someone with bathing). Even though Mr. K had been assigned to a section of the nursing home where patients were asked to remain on their own floor unless they were accompanied by a staff member, he was seen at various locations throughout the facility. Staff described Mr. K as argumentative, inappropriate, and paranoid.

Further inquiry into Ms. C's complaint proved difficult. Ms. C said that she was afraid to talk about the matter further and that she would just rather "be a bird again and fly away. . . . Ok, we're done now." However, after more gentle but direct questioning, Ms. C said that Mr. K had come into her room the previous evening and "touched [her] where boys like to touch girls." When asked if they had sexual intercourse, Ms. C said, "Oh, no. God doesn't want me to do that. But he didn't listen." When asked who did not listen, Ms. C said, "He kept touching me with all kinds of things. It wasn't so bad, but I never done that before. Do you think I have been bad? I really didn't like it that much because it started to hurt me." At this point, Ms. C's therapist asked her patient if they could speak about this to the entire treatment team, including her personal physician.

The response of the treatment team was mixed. Some members of the team wanted to make sure that Ms. C was not imagining that this event took place. Other staff members believed that Ms. C may have been sexually assaulted, but they were unsure if she were competent to identify Mr. K as the perpetrator. Ms. C's therapist also stated her concern that her patient should see a gynecologist as soon as possible to ascertain whether she had been penetrated vaginally and to what extent she might have internal or external injuries. Mr. K was to be separated from other patients until a determination of his involvement could be made. It is also notable that it took two days for someone on the treatment team to suggest that Ms. C be encouraged to be tested for HIV and other sexually transmitted diseases. One staff member balked at the suggestion and said, "If this rape really happened, God forbid, why do we have to traumatize her again for an AIDS test? . . . I'm concerned that the additional stress would cause her to decompensate even more." In response, the staff psychologist asked, "If Ms. C were a 30 year old patient who just reported that she was assaulted by another patient, wouldn't that be the first thing we think of? Just because she's old and we are upset by this, we can't pretend that Ms. C will magically be spared. She does not have the luxury of us assuming that HIV 'just doesn't happen' to older people." The treatment team then concurred that HIV testing should be broached immediately with Ms. C.

AN EMPIRICALLY BASED PILOT STUDY

Although a variety of case studies and clinical anecdotes suggest that health care providers may lack the appropriate education to deal effectively with HIV among older women, empirical information regarding the extent to which health care providers have accurate knowledge of the risk factors associated with HIV and HIV-induced dementia among elderly women remains virtually unknown. The results of our empirical pilot study, conducted with 40 registered nurses, psychologists, and physician's assistants from a mental health facility, allow us to draw tentative conclusions about the level of knowledge among health care providers. (The study protocol was approved by the medical center's Institutional Review Board, and all participants gave their informed consent.) The 40 health care providers who volunteered as participants were asked to respond to a clinical vignette, a series of written questionnaires, and a brief interview regarding their experience with patients with HIV. Each participant in the study read a clinical vignette of a patient who presented with symptoms of HIV and HIV-induced dementia, including apathy, confusion, psychomotor slowing, poor gait, depression, poor recall of newly learned information, skin discoloration, an unusual form of pneumonia, persistent low grade fevers, night sweats, incontinence, diarrhea, a significant weight loss, fungal infections (i.e., thrush), and an increased susceptibility to colds and minor infections.

Participants were randomly assigned to evaluate a clinical vignette in which the patient was described as either 35 or 75 years of age (the sex of the patient was not disclosed). Thus, the health care providers were asked to generate possible diagnoses, treatment plans, and projected treatment outcomes for either a young adult or elderly patient who displayed the identical symptoms associated with HIV. Portions of the clinical vignette are provided below.

Ms. X, a 35 (or 75) year old patient, was interviewed by a mental health provider after being admitted to the hospital for pneumonia accompanied by a high fever. . . . Within the past year, Ms. X has been forced to leave her job at a local art store due to frequent illness. For example, she was admitted to the hospital twice in the past six months for pneumonia and diarrhea. Ms. X is no longer able to care for her own needs. She often is too weak and confused to go grocery shopping, to help clean the apartment, to prepare meals, or to get into the shower without assistance. . . . Ms. X also complains of night sweats, headaches, low grade fevers, and muscle weakness. She spends much of her time at home in front of the television set. If she gets up from her chair, she moves with a slow, unsteady gait. . . . A brief mental status examination revealed that Ms. X has significant problems with her attention, concentration, and short term memory. . . . [Ms. X's friend] has remarked that he often is afraid that Ms. X will leave the stove turned on by accident when he is not there to help care for her. . . . Ms. X and [her friend] agree that these memory problems have increased significantly and suddenly within the past year. . . . Ms. X appears weak and frail; she has lost more than 25 pounds in the past six months, and her skin has a number of visible splotches and lesions. . . . [Ms. X] no longer seems interested in any hobbies or friendships; she appears very apathetic and withdrawn. . . . Ms. X said that she used to enjoy reading, but that she has become bored with it now that she often can not remember what she has just read.

All participants were then asked to complete a short questionnaire regarding the risk factors associated with HIV among elderly women and to answer some open-ended questions about their exposure to HIV among elderly women in a brief, structured interview. The 30 female and 10 male health care providers who volunteered for the study ranged in age from 23 to 60, and had an average age of 43 (s.d. = 9.78).

It was hypothesized that the health care professionals would have rather limited knowledge about HIV base rates and its differential modes of transmission, particularly among older adult women. It also was expected that ageism would manifest itself in that the elderly patient would be regarded as more impaired and would be given a poorer prognosis than the younger patient with identical symptoms. Despite the fact that the majority of the health care professionals reported that they had had advanced training in sexuality (40%), HIV and AIDS (55%), geriatrics (68%), or neuropsychology (40%), and that they had experience working with patients infected with HIV (67%), the health care providers in this pilot study did not maintain accurate knowledge of HIV among older adults or make appropriate queries of possible HIV infection for the older adult patient. The health care providers also displayed ageism in their evaluation of the patient's symptoms, despite the fact that the majority (70%) of the participants indicated that their current patient load included older adults.

Regarding the patient in the clinical vignette, the clinicians' ratings on the overall functioning of Ms. X were compared according to her indicated age. The health care providers were asked to provide a global assessment of functioning (GAF) score from 0 to 100. This measure of functioning is a scale employed in the standard diagnostic procedures described in the *Diagnostic and Statistical Manual of Mental Disorders* (DSM-IV; American Psychiatric Association, 1994). Higher scores on the GAF indicate better modes of functioning and lower levels of social, psychological, and occupational impairment. An independent t-test revealed that the health care providers regarded Ms. X as displaying significantly more impaired functioning when she was described as an elderly, 75-year-old woman (X = 31.00, s.d. = 12.47) than when she was described as a younger, 35-year-old woman (X = 48.75, s.d. = 11.75), $t(39) = 2.03$, $p < .05$. Thus, even though Ms. X's symptoms were identical in the two clinical vignettes, an elderly label was enough to generate more negative diagnostic evaluations, even among a sample of health care professionals who worked with elderly patients.

A frequency analysis showed that 80% of the health care providers identified HIV or AIDS as a possible diagnosis for Ms. X when she was described as 35 years of age. In contrast, only 40% of the health care providers provided HIV or AIDS as a possible diagnosis for Ms. X when she was identified as an elderly, 75-year-old woman. A chi square confirmed that these clinicians were significantly more likely to identify HIV or AIDS as a possible etiology for Ms. X's symptoms when she was described as 35-years-old, $\chi^2 = 8.00$, $p < .01$. Thus, the participants in this study displayed a significant, ageist bias when making diagnostic decisions regarding an elderly female patient. It was as though the majority of them simply did not even consider the fact that an elderly woman could be at risk for contracting HIV.

When asked to consider the risks associated with contracting HIV in a situation in which a 35- and a 75-year-old woman were both exposed to the HIV virus via heterosexual contact by the same man, a significant number of the participants also failed to identify the older adult woman's higher risk for contracting HIV, $\chi^2 = 30.65$, $p < .01$. The overwhelming majority (72%) of the participants incorrectly believed that the women were at equal risk for contracting HIV. Only 25% knew that the 75-year-old women was at greater risk. When asked to estimate the numbers of older adults by risk group, four individuals, who represented 10% of the sample, incorrectly maintained that women over the age of 50 were not represented in these risk groups: IV drug users, women who have heterosexual contact with infected men, and mothers of adult children with AIDS. Thus, training in geriatrics, AIDS, sexuality, or neuropsychology was not associated with increased knowledge among the health care providers, p's $> .05$. Even more interesting is the fact that the female clinicians in the study did not display greater knowledge of risk group membership or individual risk factors than their male counterparts, p's $> .05$. Thus, even female health care providers appear to manifest an overall lack of knowledge regarding the presence of HIV among elderly women.

When the participants' responses to the open-ended interview questions were analyzed, our findings revealed that the vast majority (75%) reported that they had never considered the issue of AIDS among elderly women. More than 95% of the clinicians indicated that they never received any formal training regarding HIV among older adults. That is, more than 95% of the sample were never provided with critical information regarding AIDS among older adults in degree-related course work, sponsored clinical internships, on the job training, continuing education programs, or staff workshops. Despite their lack of exposure to this topic, 90% of the participants in the study stated that they would be "very interested" in receiving formal education regarding HIV among older adults.

LIMITATIONS IN RESOURCES AND FUNDING

Despite this demonstrated interest among health care providers in our present study to become educated about HIV among older adults, no specific public policies that target the growing problem of HIV infection for the elderly population are available to provide direction or assistance. No governmental policy exists that addresses ageism, misdiagnosis, preventive measures, and education for those over 65 years of age. It is also notable that the moneys that have been allotted to HIV treatment and prevention among elderly adults have been targeted almost exclusively at elderly gay men. In the following section we examine the current health policies and programs available to the elderly with HIV.

Medicare and Medicaid

Medicare, founded in 1965, was developed to cover the elderly who, as retirees, were no longer eligible for health insurance benefits. Those eligible for Medicare include people who are more than 65 years of age, individuals who are deemed disabled and eligible for Social Security cash benefits, and those who are suffering from end-stage renal disease (ESRD) or kidney failure" (Patel & Rushefsky, 1995). The Medicare program includes hospital insurance (i.e., inpatient hospital expenses) and supplementary medical insurance (i.e., physician and outpatient services). In addition, the Americans With Disabilities Act classifies AIDS as a disability. Thus, an AIDS patient who is physician-certified for 24 months is eligible for Medicare benefits (Cohan & Torgan, 1997). This requirement for physician certification highlights the need for accurate and timely diagnoses of HIV and AIDS by all health care professionals.

Medicaid is another, separate federal program designed to provide access to health care for the poor, including impoverished older adults. For individuals over the age of 65, Medicaid provides inpatient and outpatient hospital services, physician care, laboratory and X-ray services, home health services, skilled nursing care, early screening measures, and nursing home care (Cochran, Mayer, Carr, & Cayer, 1999). The federal Medicaid program works in conjunction with state governments in providing assistance for medical needs. At the federal level, program guidelines are developed and financial assistance is given through matching grants. State governments control how these guidelines are implemented and how moneys are dispensed; "state governments enjoy discretionary authority for establishing eligibility standards, the nature and scope of benefits provided, and mechanisms used to reimburse health care providers (Patel & Rushefsky, 1995, p. 53). Thus, the implementation of Medicaid can vary greatly from state to state.

Because Medicare does not cover long term care, such as nursing home care, many Medicare beneficiaries also receive Medicaid. Recent estimates suggest that more than 40% of Medicaid costs are related to intermediate and nursing home care (Cochran et al., 1999). However, there are tight restrictions on those who require such care. Many Medicare recipients must "spend down" their financial resources until they fall close enough to the poverty line to quality for Medicaid benefits (Cochran et al., 1999). For older women on a fixed income without the financial support of a partner or extended family, the financial losses alone are devastating.

Formidable Costs

To compound this problem of dwindling personal resources, the care for HIV infected elderly tends to be more intensive and to require greater staffing. The range of services required should consist of specialized IV therapy, rehabilitation, psychological services, nutrition counseling, behavior management, oncology support, pain management, hospice support, and counseling for decisions about advance directives (Cohan & Torgan, 1997). Further, elderly adults in the acute phases of AIDS often require nursing home care. All of these services are quite expensive. In fact, Fasciano, Cherlow, Turner, and Thornton (1998) estimated that Medicare costs for elderly AIDS patients are no less than $2,400 per month or $28,800 annually. Thus, the costs to Medicare for reimbursing elderly AIDS patients dramatically exceeds the expenditures for all other disabled beneficiaries, which average slightly less than $4,000 per year. The projected lower mortality rates of Medicare beneficiaries with AIDS also indicate an increase in the provision of medical care and the high costs often associated with it (Fasciano et al., 1998).

Existing governmental programs face a potential financial crisis as middle-aged HIV infected persons live longer and are eligible for health care benefits. Medical advances have extended the life span of the general population. As previously noted, the CDC estimates that over 11% of the HIV positive population is age 55 and older (Cohan & Torgan, 1997). A comprehensive policy must be developed in light of the CDC's report that AIDS cases are growing the fastest among heterosexuals older than 50 (CDC, 1998). In addition, approximately 25% of men and 17% of women who are infected with HIV are in their 40s (Linsk, 1994). With the general increase in life span, these cases, in addition to those not yet infected with HIV, point to a potential crisis for Medicare and Medicaid.

Quality of Care

Physicians, psychologists, and other mental health care professions who accept Medicaid must accept Medicaid's fee schedule as full payment

(Cochran et al., 1999). Many providers note that the governmental reimbursement rates are low compared to their own fee schedules, and they may decline to participate in the Medicaid program in order to garner higher fees from patients with private insurance. A primary limitation for both Medicare and Medicaid is structural in that both programs were created to pay merely a portion of health care bills; older women may not seek out treatment because they know that they will be unable to pay the balance of their bills. Thus, the quality and quantity of health care provided for elderly women who rely on Medicare and Medicaid becomes questionable.

Existing Outreach

Few public or privately sponsored programs have attempted to provide services to the elderly with HIV. Many outreach programs for elders are not formally instituted; rather, they fall under family service or mental health programs. The American Association of Retired Persons (AARP) has begun to circulate information about HIV through its various publications. In addition, they have made available an informational video on HIV to their members. Senior Action in a Gay Environment (SAGE), located in New York City, provides support services for HIV infected older persons. SAGE sends social workers to senior centers to conduct educational programs on HIV. The Brookfield Gerontology Center and the School of Social Work at Hunter College have both established a monthly forum for sharing information, planning, needs assessment, and conference sponsorship (Linsk, 1994). Although these organizations represent benchmark programming and novel methods of information sharing, none have targeted elderly women in particular.

GOALS FOR THE FUTURE

Calls for Funding

With the feminization of poverty looming into the twenty-first century, public policy makers should be encouraged to allot funding to this important cause. For example, the CDC should be asked to specify the numbers of older adults with HIV and AIDS who are between 65 and 84 years of age (i.e., the young-old) versus those more than 85 years of age (i.e., the oldest-old), instead of lumping all of these older women and men in the more simplistic, "over 50" age category. The information gained from this statistical analysis would be invaluable in tracking the rate of HIV infection among older women, particularly because so many more women are in the oldest-old age cohort. Although the National Institutes of Aging has offered some grant moneys toward behavioral issues in HIV among older adults, older women have not been targeted specifically for such funded research. Perhaps more importantly, it is vital that further funded research be related to all aspects of this growing problem—financial, medical, psychological, and social. The issues involved in HIV among elderly women are interdisciplinary, and funding will be required from all sectors. In addition to such epidemiological reporting and research, funds also can be used to benefit elderly women directly in the form of free or low cost, confidential, government subsidized HIV testing.

Education

Aside from the macro-level issues of health care coverage, health care at the micro-level (i.e., education) must be improved. Since the beginning of the epidemic, most educational programs have targeted a young audience. However, it is a necessity that the elderly population becomes informed due to the rapid increase in HIV infection among adults over the age of 50. Logically, much of this educational programming should be directed to elderly women, who make up a disproportionate number of those over age 65. The lack of understanding of the basic facts by elderly women reinforces the misperception that they are not at risk when engaging in certain behaviors. Basic information and education regarding transmission of HIV, symptoms of AIDS, and methods of prevention are critical in halting the spread of the disease.

Public service announcements also could be presented to inform older adults about the dangers associated with various high-risk behaviors, as well as the effective measures available to prevent or avert participation in such high-risk activities (e.g., use of condoms). Public service campaigns could be aimed at several subgroups of older women. For example, it is vital to target elderly survivors of sexual assault. It is extremely important that older women understand that that they are *in no way* to blame for an assault and that free, professional help is available for them if they have been raped. Older adults should also be provided with information about the warning signs for IV drug use and about available treatments and support groups. Older women who are caregivers of adult children with AIDS should be targeted for life saving information concerning easily applied universal precautions. One of the benefits of such public service campaigns would be to raise awareness among the general public as well as among older women.

As demonstrated in our pilot study, health care providers also need to be educated about the growing problem of HIV among elderly women. It appears that even though many clinicians receive training about AIDS, gerontology, sexuality, and neuropsychology, these programs typically do not include information about HIV infection among older adults in particular. Specific programs must be developed to address this need, and curricula must be expanded to incorporate critical women's issues. In addition to gathering basic medical and social information about HIV infection among older adults, however, health care professionals also must learn to cope with their own comfort issues in discussing HIV with their older female patients in order to employ what they have learned. Full sexual histories must be conducted and subsequent HIV testing must be encouraged for all at-risk older women.

Social Mores and Support

In addition to providing general information, cultural factors such as socialization must be addressed in order for older women to recognize the necessity of preventive measures. Goldstein and Manlowe (1997) argued that this is related to cultural definitions of femininity and popular conceptions of heterosexual romance. In addition to socialization, the imbalance of power between men and women in sexual decision making affects the likelihood of women demanding condom use (Leonardo & Chrisler, 1992). The use of pre-existing peer groups for older adults may provide inroads for altering misperceptions and stereotypes about women's roles in intimate relationships, family relationships, and society in general. For example, senior centers and church groups could be employed as contact points for launching educational programs and HIV specific support groups for elderly women. Although social mores may be among the most difficult to change, a supportive environment in which older women speak to other older women may be most effective.

Virtually Unexplored Areas

Last, because rural and minority elderly women represent often overlooked populations, a concerted effort should be made to include these women in all public service announcements, educational programs, and funding opportunities. For elderly women in rural settings, the use of the Internet may help women connect with one another to share information and viewpoints. Work with minority elderly women must include recognition and respect for various cultural and ethnic traditions and beliefs. For the oldest-old women, who are likely to encounter a variety of chronic illnesses as they age, information about HIV might be delivered most efficiently in conjunction with medical policies and programs.

OPPORTUNITIES FOR CHANGE

In sum, the purpose of this chapter was to challenge the traditional view that older adult women do not engage in behaviors that may put them at high risk for contracting HIV. Women, who account for the majority of persons over the age of 65, appear to be overlooked by health care providers and public policy makers regarding vital issues in HIV education, prevention, assessment, treatment, epidemiological tracking, and research funding. These barriers to care have been demonstrated consistently in both case studies and in empirical research. However, a variety of means are available to institute these changes. Educational programs aimed at health care providers, as well as elderly women themselves, will provide one of the first steps in addressing this critical medical, psychological, and societal problem. Addressing these issues offers feminists a unique opportunity to harness the resources that the growing numbers of elderly women can offer, including personal resources, wisdom, life experience, wisdom, and as well as a majority vote in political and public policy issues. Addressing these issues is also an important step in our goal to chart a new course for better physical health, mental health, and an improved quality of life for all women.

NOTE

Please address all correspondence to Jennifer Hillman at Penn State Berks, Department of Psychology, Tulpelhocken Road, Reading, PA 19610 or to Kristin Broderick at Kutztown University, Department of Political Science, Kutztown, PA 19530.

REFERENCES

Allers, C. T. (1990). AIDS and the older adult. *Gerontologist, 30*, 405–407.

American Academy of Neurology AIDS Task Force. (1991). Nomenclature and research case definitions for neurologic manifestations of human immunodeficiency virus-type 1 (HIV-1) infection. *Neurology, 41*, 778–785.

American Psychiatric Association. (1994). *Diagnostic and statistical manual of mental disorders* (4th ed.). Washington, DC: American Psychiatric Association.

Aupperle, P. (1996). Medical issues. In K. M. Nokes (Ed.), *HIV/AIDS and the older adult* (pp. 25–31). Washington, DC: Taylor & Francis.

Cartwright, P. S., & Moore, R. A. (1989). The elderly victim of rape. *Southern Medical Journal, 82*, 988–989.

Centers for Disease Control and Prevention. (1998). AIDS among persons aged 50 years—United States, 1991–1996. *Morbidity and Mortality Weekly Report, 47* (2), 21–27.

Coalition on Women and the Budget. (1983, March 16). *The inequality of sacrifice: The impact of the Reagan budget cuts on women.* Washington, DC: Author.

Cochran, C. E., Mayer, L. C., Carr, T. R., & Cayer, N. J. (1999). *American public policy.* New York: Worth.

Cohan, D., & Torgan, M. (1997). AIDS patients. *Nursing Homes, 46*, 38–40.

Fasciano, N. J., Cherlow, A. L., Turner, B. J., & Thornton, C. V. (1998). Profile of

Medicare beneficiaries: Application of an AIDS casefinding algorithm. *Health Care Finance Review, 19,* 19–38.

Goldstein, N., & Manlowe, J. L. (1997). *The gender politics of HIV/AIDS in women.* New York: New York University Press.

Greenwood, D. U. (1991). Neuropsychological aspects of AIDS dementia complex: What clinicians need to know. *Professional Psychology: Research and Practice, 22,* 407–409.

Leonardo, C., & Chrisler, J. C. (1992). Women and sexually transmitted diseases. *Women & Health, 18* (4), 1–15.

Levine-Perkell, J. (1996). Caregiving issues. In K. M. Nokes (Ed.), *HIV/AIDS and the older adult* (pp. 115–128). Washington, DC: Taylor & Francis.

Linsk, N. L. (1994). HIV and the elderly. *Families in Society, 75,* 362–373.

Lipton, S. A., & Gendelman, H. E. (1995). Dementia associated with the acquired immunodeficiency syndrome. *New England Journal of Medicine, 332,* 934–940.

Mapau, R. L., & Law, W. A. (1994). Neurobehavioral aspects of HIV disease and AIDS: An update. *Professional Psychology: Research and Practice, 25,* 132–141.

Matthias, R. E., Lubben, J. E., Atchison, K. A., & Schweitzer, S. O. (1997). Sexual activity and satisfaction among very old adults: Results from a community-dwelling Medicare population survey. *Gerontologist, 37,* 6–14.

Muram, D., Miller, K., & Cutler, A. (1992). Sexual assault of the elderly victim. *Journal of Interpersonal Violence, 7,* 70–76.

Patel, K., & Rushefsky, M. E. (1995). *Health care politics and policy in America.* Armonk, NY: M. E. Sharpe.

Polaneczky, R. (1995). The sex scandal America overlooks. *New Choices for Retirement Living, 35,* 42–46.

Rosenzweig, R., & Fillit, H. (1992). Probable heterosexual transmission of AIDS in an aged woman. *Journal of the American Geriatrics Society, 40,* 1261–1264.

Solomon, K. (1996). Psychosocial issues. In K. M. Nokes (Ed.), *HIV/AIDS and the older adult* (pp. 33–46). Washington, DC: Taylor & Francis.

Speyer, R. (1994, March 30). Sexy seniors flirt with AIDS. *New York Daily News,* p. 6.

Stall, R., & Catania, J. (1994). AIDS risk behaviors among late middle-aged and elderly Americans. *Archives of Internal Medicine, 154,* 57–63.

Stall, R., & Catania, J. (1996). Foreword. In K. M. Nokes (Ed.), *HIV/AIDS and the older adult* (pp. 33–46). Washington, DC: Taylor & Francis.

Starr, B. D., & Weiner, M. B. (1981). *The Starr-Weiner report on sex and sexuality in the mature years.* Briarcliff Manor, NY: Stein and Day.

U.S. Bureau of the Census. (1988). *United States population estimated by age, sex, and race, 1980 to 1987* (Current Population Reports, Series P-25, No. 1022). Washington, DC: U.S. Government Printing Office.

U.S. Bureau of the Census. (1996). *65 + in the United States* (Current Population Report, Special Studies, P23–190). Washington, DC: U.S. Government Printing Office.

Zablotsky, D. (1998). Overlooked, ignored, and forgotten: Older women at risk for HIV infection and AIDS. *Research on Aging, 20,* 760–775.

Chapter 10

Black Battered Women: New Directions for Research and Black Feminist Theory

Carolyn M. West

After more than two decades of research, it is clear that intimate partner violence transcends race, economic class, and religious background (Goodman, Koss, & Russo, 1993). It has also been discovered among lesbian couples (West, 1998a) and dating, engaged, married, and divorced heterosexual couples (Erez, 1986; Neff, Holamon, & Schluter, 1995). The pervasiveness of this social problem has led some researchers to take a "color blind" approach, which is the assumption that the rates of aggression and the dynamics found in violent relationships are similar across ethnic groups (Williams, 1993). Alternatively, other researchers have considered violence to be a problem that plagues people of color, particularly African Americans (Hawkins, 1987).

The reality is that violence in the lives of Black women is both very similar and at times vastly different from the violence experienced by their White counterparts (Collins, 1998; Crenshaw, 1994; Kanuha, 1996). The challenge for researchers is to articulate the racial similarities in intimate partner violence without negating the experiences of Black women. This should be done while simultaneously highlighting racial differences without perpetuating the stereotype that Black Americans are inherently more violent than other ethnic groups. Meeting this challenge requires researchers to chart a new course. In order to travel in a new direction, we must first understand where we have been. Accordingly, the first section of this chapter will review the research on racial differences and similarities in the rates and types of physical partner violence across the relationship continuum. In the second section, I will focus on new directions for research. More specifically, methodological problems may influence the research findings, and thus our understanding of racial differences in domestic violence. I will review these research limitations and offer suggestions for more appropriate research methods. The goal of the final section is to articulate a Black feminist theoretical perspective that better explains violence in the lives of Black women.

RACIAL SIMILARITIES AND DIFFERENCES IN PHYSICAL PARTNER VIOLENCE

The studies conducted to date present a complex, and at times a contradictory, picture of racial differences in the rates of physical partner violence (for reviews see Asbury, 1999; West, 1998b). Several investigators discovered that the rates were similar across ethnic groups. For instance, in a community sample, one-third of both Black and White women were physically abused (Lockhart, 1987, 1991). Likewise, similar rates of violence were found between Black and White women in shelter (O'Keefe, 1994), urban prenatal clinic (McFarlane, Parker, Soeken, Silva, & Reed, 1999), high school (Symons, Groer, Kepler-Youngblood, & Slater, 1994), and undergraduate samples (Rouse, 1988). These findings were discovered in nationally representative samples as well. According to the National Victim Survey, the three largest ethnic groups (Blacks, Whites, and Latino/as) reported similar rates of serious intimate partner violence (Bachman, 1994).

Although the rates of battering may be similar, the types and severity of violence may vary by ethnicity. For example, battered women who were recruited from family court and battered women's shelters reported comparable levels of physical, verbal, and sexual abuse. However, when compared to Latinas and White women, Black women were more likely to have had weapons used against them. They were also more likely to be hospitalized as a result of the injuries sustained during a violent episode (Gondolf, Fisher, & McFerron, 1991; Joseph, 1997). A similar pattern of racial differences in severity of violence was discovered between incarcerated Black and White battered women (Richie, 1996). This greater severity of violence may be one explanation for why homicide by intimate partners is the leading cause of death for African-American women between the ages of 15 and 24 (National Center for Health Statistics, 1997).

Other studies more clearly indicate that Black women, when compared to their White counterparts, are at particular risk for victimization at every point on the relationship continuum. For instance, during the premarital period they experienced more mild and severe dating violence (DeMaris, 1990). In addition, among couples who were engaged to be married, Black women were more likely to have been hit or slapped (Boye-Beaman, Leonard, & Senchak, 1993; McLaughlin, Leonard, & Senchak, 1992). For many couples, these violent interactions continued into the marital relationship. Several large national probability samples revealed higher rates of wife assault in African-American families. In the First National Family Violence

Survey, which consisted of more than 2,000 households, the overall rate of Black husband-to-wife abuse was four times higher than that of White husband-to-wife abuse (113 vs. 30 per 1,000) (Cazenave & Straus, 1979; Straus, Gelles, & Steinmetz, 1980). A similar pattern of racial differences emerged 10 years later when the researchers conducted a second national survey of more than 6,000 families. Although the rate of severe violence against Black women declined by 43%, they continued to be twice as likely as White women to have been battered (Hampton & Gelles, 1994).

Partner violence can also continue after the woman terminates the relationship, as in the case of divorced couples. The limited research on racial differences indicates that Black women were more likely than White or Mexican American women to be victimized by former spouses (Neff et al., 1995). Furthermore, this violence may continue over a long period of time. Despite having ended their abusive relationships, Sullivan and Rumptz (1994) found that one-third of the African-American women in their sample continued to be abused by the same partner 10 weeks after leaving a battered woman's shelter. A similar pattern emerged in a longitudinal study that followed a predominately Black sample over three years. The researchers concluded that "ending the relationship does not necessarily end the violence" (Campbell, Rose, Kub, & Nedd, 1998, p. 759).

The research also suggests that Black women are more likely to perpetrate partner violence. When compared to White women, they were approximately three times more likely to beat their husbands (Neff et al., 1995). Equally high rates of husband assaults were found in large probability samples. In the First National Family Violence Survey, Black wives were only slightly more likely to have slapped their husbands within the year prior to the survey. However, in comparison to White wives, they were almost twice as likely to have engaged in severe violence against their husbands (76 vs. 41 per 1,000) (Cazenave & Straus, 1979; Straus et al., 1980). A replication of the survey in 1985 revealed that the rate of wife-to-husband abuse committed by Black women rose to nearly three times greater than the rate for White women (108 vs. 39 per 1,000) (Hampton, Gelles, & Harrop, 1989).

In summary, some researchers found similar rates of partner violence across racial groups (Bachman, 1994; Lockhart, 1991). In contrast, other investigators discovered that Black women, when compared to their White counterparts, were significantly more likely to sustain and inflict aggression. Moreover, they were more likely to be victims of severe violence. This pattern was reported at every stage on the relationship continuum (Hampton et al., 1989; Neff et al., 1995).

NEW DIRECTIONS FOR RESEARCH

The growing body of research on racial differences in domestic violence appears to be contradictory. Methodological problems may partially account for these findings. Specifically, there are definitional and measurement limitations as well as problems with how data has been collected, analyzed, and interpreted. The purpose of the next section is to discuss these limitations and offer new directions for research.

Definitional and Measurement Problems

Many investigators have focused on defining and measuring physical aggression. In order to distinguish between levels of violence, researchers have categorized aggressive acts as "mild" or "less injurious" forms of violence, which includes slapping, pushing, and shoving. Beatings and assaults with weapons have been classified as "severe" violence (Straus, 1990). Limiting the investigation of abuse to physical assaults can promote ease of comparison across studies. However, feminists argue that this narrow definition does not capture the full range of violence against women (Smith, 1994; Smith, Smith, & Earp, 1999).

These research limitations can be addressed in several ways. First, researchers can broaden the definition of partner violence to include psychological, emotional, and verbal abuse. After an extensive review of the literature, partner violence has been defined as "acts of recurring criticism and/or verbal aggression toward a partner, and/or acts of isolation and domination of a partner. Generally, such actions cause the partner to be fearful of the other or lead the partner to have very low self-esteem" (O'Leary, 1999, p. 19). Although researchers have been rather slow to turn their attention to psychological abuse, it is pervasive enough to warrant attention. For example, more than one-half of a community sample of physically abused women reported a high frequency, defined as once a week or more, of three types of emotional abuse, including restriction of activities, jealousy, and ridicule (Follingstad, Rutledge, Berg, Hause, & Polek, 1990). Moreover, the emotional impact of psychological abuse can be equally as detrimental as the emotional impact of physical violence. It has been linked to low self-esteem, depression, and fear (Sackett & Saunders, 1999). Despite the challenges of operationalizing psychological abuse, researchers should continue to make efforts to measure this form of aggression.

Psychological abuse is prevalent across ethnic groups. More than two-thirds of Black and White shelter residents were victims of emotional and verbal abuse (Joseph, 1997). Similarly high rates of possessiveness and rejection were discovered among Black, White, and Latino/a undergraduates (Rouse, 1988). Black women, like women of other ethnic backgrounds, can experience serious emotional consequences as a result of psychological abuse, such as symptoms of posttraumatic stress disorder (Dutton, Goodman, & Bennett, 1999). In addition, psychological abuse is likely to precede physical abuse (O'Leary, 1999). Although this pattern of abuse can occur regardless of ethnicity, African Americans were more likely to move from verbal to physical aggression (Stets, 1990). Factors that are associated with this escalation of violence are worthy of additional investigation.

Sexual aggression should be incorporated into the definition of intimate violence as well. Researchers have defined rape as unwanted sexual penetration, perpetrated by force, threat of harm, or when intoxication or mental impairment make it impossible for the victim to consent to sexual contact (Warshaw, 1994). Although this definition is consistent with many legal statutes, it does not fully capture the range of date and marital rape in the lives of women. Therefore, researchers should move toward a more inclusive definition, such as "sex without consent, sexual assault, rape, sexual control of reproductive rights, and all forms of sexual manipulation carried out by the perpetrator with the intention or perceived intention to cause emotional, sexual, and physical degradation to another person" (Abraham, 1999, p. 592). Regardless of the definition, it is apparent that sexual abuse is an alarmingly common form of aggression. According to one of the most comprehensive studies conducted to date, 25% of women have been the victims of attempted or completed rape, and most of these rapes (57%) occurred in the context of a dating relationship (Warshaw, 1994). Substantial rates of marital rape have also been reported, with between 10% and 14% of ever-married or cohabiting women having been raped at least once by their partners (for a review see Mahoney & Williams, 1998). Given the negative mental health outcomes associated with sexual abuse, including anxiety, fear, sexual dysfunction, and depression, this form of aggression should be included in future studies (Neville & Heppner, 1999).

Like other forms of abuse, researchers have found comparable rates of date (Rouse, 1988) and marital rape (Russell, 1990) across ethnic groups. Based on the limited research, Black and White rape victims also exhibit similar physical, psychological, and sexual health problems (Wyatt, 1992). Despite these similarities, it is important to consider ethnic differences in the definition of sexual violence. Wyatt (1992) contends that "economic and legal factors have influenced cultural definitions of sexual assault for American women, and especially for women of African descent" (p. 78). This seems to be supported by the disturbing evidence that some African Americans, when compared to their White counterparts, endorse more rape myths, such as most rapes are committed by strangers and a man has a right to assume that a woman desires sexual intercourse if she allows a man to touch her in a sexual way (for reviews see Johnson, Kuck, & Schander, 1997; Lonsway, & Fitzgerald, 1995). Black women may not perceive themselves as victims if they believe these rape myths or adhere to a narrow definition of rape. As a result, their help-seeking efforts and post-rape recovery may be compromised (Neville & Pugh, 1997; Wyatt, 1992).

It is not enough to simply broaden the definition of partner violence to include psychological and sexual abuse. There are problems with how violence is measured. More specifically, researchers have often measured discrete acts of physical violence by asking participants if they had sustained or inflicted varying degrees of aggression. When violence is measured in this way it appears that women use violent tactics with the same frequency as their male counterparts. This is because researchers have merely counted the number of violent acts experienced by a couple without considering the context, motives, and outcome of these aggressive actions. When these factors are taken into consideration, it is apparent that intimate partner violence is not generally mutual, but rather it is frequently violence committed against women (for a feminist review of these definitional and measurement problems see Currie, 1998).

One solution is to improve the instruments used to measure aggression. These changes are starting to take place. For example, the Conflict Tactics Scales (CTS), one of the most widely used measures of partner violence, has been revised to include measures of psychological and sexual aggression (Straus, Hamby, Boney-McCoy, & Sugarman, 1996). However, the focus on counting discrete episodes of violent acts continues to be a problem. According to feminist researchers, the solution is to broaden "the conceptualization of battering to define it in the context of women's lives and to focus on battered women's experiences rather than on the discrete events of male behaviors" (Smith et al., 1999, p. 183). This can be accomplished by using a flexible combination of qualitative and quantitative research methodology. By listening to the voices of battered women, researchers can gain greater insight into the context, motives, and outcomes of woman abuse. In addition, this research methodology will help to emphasize the overlapping nature of physical battery and rape in women's lives.

Additional changes are necessary to shed light on the experiences of Black women. For example, there is the risk that standardized measures, although valid and reliable, may not adequately assess the experiences of diverse populations. These concerns appear to be legitimate. As evidence, a different factor structure emerged when the Index of Spouse Abuse (ISA), a scale designed to measure physical, sexual, and psychological abuse, was administered to a sample of Black women. This implies that they made different interpretations of many of the items than was found in the original instrument development (Campbell, Campbell, King, Parker, & Ryan, 1994). This finding also provides empirical support for the contention that "the consequences of excluding women of color from instrument development is that White European Americans and their experiences have been taken as the norm" (Sorenson, 1996, p. 137).

This problem can be solved by using diverse samples in instrument development. Greater cultural sensitivity can also be achieved by including scale items that reflect the types of violence experienced by Black women. For instance, abusers often use both racist and sexist slurs to demean and denigrate their victims. Evelyn Barbee (1992), an African-American nurse, was physically assaulted in public. Prior to the assault, the Black assailant screamed "You Black bitch!" Although this is an anecdotal account, this example illustrates the importance of considering how psychological aggression may take different forms in the lives of Black women.

Data Collection, Analyses, and Interpretation of Results

Some researchers have collected data in a way that neglects the experiences of a broad range of Black battered women. For example, Black women may be excluded from samples or surveyed in small numbers, which make it impossible to conduct meaningful racial comparisons (for a Black feminist perspective on this data collection problem see T. C. West, 1999). Alternatively, other researchers rely on samples that are drawn from services that are overwhelmingly used by African Americans and the poor, such as the criminal justice system (Dutton et al., 1999; Erez, 1986), shelters for battered women or the homeless (Joseph, 1997; Sullivan & Rumptz, 1994), and public hospitals (McFarlene et al., 1999). Certainly, individuals who utilize these services warrant attention because they are at increased risk for violence. Nevertheless, these samples are not representative of battered women or African Americans who have greater access to material resources.

Data collection is further limited by the focus on married heterosexual couples (Hampton & Gelles, 1994; Lockhart, 1987, 1991). As previously discussed, violence can occur across the relationship continuum. However poverty and social inequalities, such as the lack of marriageable men due to high rates of incarceration and unemployment, means that Black couples are disproportionately more likely to report lower rates of marriage and higher rates of divorce (Tucker & Mitchell-Kernan, 1995). Consequently, researchers who focus exclusively on legally married Black couples will overlook violence among dating, cohabitating, and divorced couples.

These problems with data collection can be addressed in several ways. First, meaningful racial comparisons can be made by including larger samples of Blacks. Researchers are beginning to take these steps. The First National Family Violence Survey included only 147 African Americans (Straus et al., 1980). Ten years later, the number of surveyed Blacks rose to 600 (Hampton et al., 1989). Second, researchers can investigate within-group differences. For instance, they could compare the rates of battering between working-class and middle-class Blacks. When researchers used this methodology, they discovered that the level and types of violence varied among Blacks based on social class and gender (Hampton & Gelles, 1994; Lockhart, 1987; Russo, Denious, Keita, & Koss, 1997). This knowledge will enable service providers to target their intervention efforts more appropriately. In addition, this methodology can help avoid the problems associated with inappropriate racial comparisons. Finally, researchers should investigate violence across the relationship continuum. Fortunately, more research is focusing on violence among Black couples who are dating (Clark, Beckett, Wells, & Dungee-Anderson, 1994; West & Rose, 2000) or who have terminated their relationship (Campbell et al., 1998; Moss, Pitula, Campbell, & Halstead, 1997; Neff et al., 1997). The next challenge is to investigate violence among Black lesbians, a population that is even more marginalized as a result of discrimination based on race, gender and sexual orientation (Kanuha, 1990; Mendez, 1996; Waldron, 1996).

After the data are collected, there can be problems with how it is analyzed. For example, researchers have often failed to control for indices of socioeconomic status when considering racial differences in battering. This is a significant problem because African Americans are overrepresented in socioeconomic and demographic categories that are at greater risk for violence. This includes individuals who are youthful, urban residents, and have lower educational, income, and occupational levels (Sorenson, Upchurch, & Shen, 1996). Consequently, what appears to be racial differences may in fact be socioeconomic differences between Blacks and Whites. As evidence, these racial differences disappear when income and husband's occupational and employment status are taken into consideration (Cazenave & Straus, 1979; Hampton & Gelles, 1994; Lockhart, 1987, 1991). Future researchers should control for these confounding variables.

During the final stages of the research process, biases in interpretations may become more apparent. More specifically, substantial rates of partner violence among some subgroups of Black Americans, coupled with the failure to consider socioeconomic status and other research limitations, such as inadequate sampling techniques, have in some cases contributed to inappropriate interpretations of the research findings. For instance, researchers compared 38 Black and 195 White students and concluded that: "The finding that Blacks were more involved in violence in courtship than other racial groups was expected. The violence that characterizes the Black subculture seems to enter also in courtship relations" (Plass & Gessner, 1983, p. 202). Not only is such an interpretation offensive, it precludes our understanding of battering in the African-American community. By focusing on violence as somehow innate or unique to the Black culture, investigators have fostered stereotypes, which can shape the direction of future research and public policy. If violence is perceived as inevitable, politicians and service providers may erroneously conclude that intervention efforts are futile (Hawkins, 1987). In response, community leaders and members may discourage research efforts for fear that the information will be used to further oppress them. Although their concerns are legitimate, the failure to document racial differences in partner violence limits the understanding of this problem and ultimately makes it difficult for Black battered women to receive assistance (Crenshaw, 1994).

Other researchers have attempted to highlight the racial similarities between battered Black and White women. For example, based on a small numbers of Black, Latina, and Asian women, Lenore Walker (1979) asserted that "Anglo and minority women alike told similar battering stories and experienced similar embarrassment, guilt and inability to halt their men's assaults" (p. 22). Her conclusions are not necessarily inappropriate. However, it becomes problematic when researchers interpret similarities to mean that racial differences are not worthy of attention or do not exist (Kanuha, 1996).

Feminist research that is culturally competent and sensitive can reduce some of these faulty research interpretations. This can be accomplished by involving participants in every step of the research process. When the research project is being conceptualized, investigators should invite community members and leaders to discuss how partner violence can best be defined and measured. Focus groups are an effective way to gather this information (Sorenson, 1996). African-American researchers and activists should also participate in the data collection. This will minimize participants' concerns about disclosing personal information or airing the community's "dirty laundry" to outsiders. Integrated research teams should be used to interpret the research findings (Fontes, 1997, 1998; Kanuha, 1996; Wyatt, 1994). Moss and colleagues (1997) explain the importance of this strategy by writing "Because the principal investigator and other authors of this article are upper-class White female feminists, we chose to collaborate with Black feminist women to aid us in understanding and interpreting the Black women's experiences with abuse" (p. 434). Finally, care should be taken in the dissemination of the findings. Participants may not have access to scholarly publications; therefore, the information should be made available through community leaders, religious institutions, ethnic events, and radio campaigns (Oliver, 2000; West, 1998b). A well-drafted, culturally sensitive statement concerning partner violence could also be published in Black oriented newspapers. This technique has been used to successfully raise the Black community's awareness concerning sexual harassment (Ransby, 1995) and rape (White, 1999).

To summarize, there can be problems at every stage of the research process from definitional and measurement limitations to how the data is collected, analyzed, and interpreted. In order to begin charting a new course, participants must be included at every stage of the research process from planning to implementing, interpreting, and disseminating the results.

THEORETICAL PERSPECTIVES

A broad range of theoretical perspectives have been used to explain domestic violence. Unfortunately, most partner violence theories are unidimensional, rather than interdisciplinary in nature. For example, microtheories seek to explain why some individuals commit more family violence than others. These theories encompass the social learning perspective, which argues that individuals learn aggression by witnessing or experiencing violence in their families of origin. Other researchers have linked partner violence to intrapersonal difficulties, such as alcohol abuse use/abuse, or couples' interpersonal problems, including marital discord and communication difficulties (for a review see Barnett, Miller-Perrin, & Perrin, 1997). There is a substantial body of literature to support these various microtheories. Although there has been less research on African Americans, domestic violence in this population has been linked to violence in the family of origin (DeMaris, 1990; Hampton & Gelles, 1994), alcohol use (Joseph, 1997; Neff et al., 1995), and marital discord (Lockhart, 1991; Lockhart & White, 1989). Microtheories are valuable because they highlight the similarities between ethnic groups. However, these theories have often been applied without the recognition of important ethnic group differences (Barnes, 1999; Bell & Mattis, 2000).

In contrast, macrotheories address important structural factors, including sexism, racism, and classism. These larger structural inequalities increase the likelihood of partner violence and must be addressed in the study of domestic violence among African Americans. Accordingly, the final section of this chapter will utilize a feminist perspective. Feminist scholars, regardless of their academic discipline, attribute partner violence to gender, power, and structural imbalance (for reviews see Bograd, 1988; Marin & Russo, 1999; Yllo, 1993). Although feminist theory has made important contributions to our understanding of domestic violence, it can be enhanced by including Black feminist thought, which will create a theoretical perspective that is more appropriate for understanding violence in the lives of African-American women. I will review the tenets of feminist theory and then offer a Black feminist analysis.

History of Patriarchy

Feminists contend that domestic violence is rooted in the history of patriarchy and male dominance. For example, based on English common law the "rule of thumb" legalized and regulated wife beating by granting a man the right to chastise his wife with a rod "not thicker than his thumb" (see Lentz, 1999 for a feminist history of wife abuse). This historical perspective is important; however, it fails to address Black women's history. As Christensen (1988) pointed out, "No other woman has suffered physical and mental abuse, degradation, and exploitation on North American shores comparable to that experienced by the Black female" (p. 191). This victimization took the form of rape, forced breeding, and slavery. In addition, Black women received less protection from abuse. Although they were victimized by both White and Black men without legal sanction, assaults against White women were more likely to be severely punished, particularly if the assailant was an African American (see Wriggins 1983 for a Black feminist historic perspective).

Black feminists would consider the historical trauma experienced by African-American women. Stories of rape and abuse are frequently shared across generations to warn Black girls and women of their vulnerability. As a result, contemporary Black women receive the message that their victimization is less significant and credible (Wyatt, 1992). These concerns are justified. Even today, forced sexual encounters that involve Black women are perceived as less serious and worthy of legal intervention (Foley, Evanic, Karnik, King, & Parks, 1995). Not surprisingly, this has contributed to a culture of silence, which ultimately discourages Black women's help-seeking efforts (Neville & Pugh, 1997; Wyatt, 1992).

The Intersection of Sexism, Racism, and Classism

Based on this brief historical overview, it is clear that a feminist theoretical perspective that focuses on patriarchy and sexism as the primary source of domestic violence can not fully explain violence in the lives of Black women. According to Black feminists, researchers and theorists must acknowledge the overlap and intersectionalities of various forms of oppression (Collins, 1998; Crenshaw, 1994; Richie, 1996). Bograd (1999) explains how this can be applied to domestic violence:

We exist in social contexts created by the intersections of systems of power (e.g., race, class, gender, and sexual orientation) and oppression (prejudice, class stratification, gender inequality, and heterosexist bias). . . . In this framework, domestic violence is not a monolithic phenomenon. Intersectionalities color the meaning and nature of domestic violence, how it is experienced by self and responded to by others, how personal and social consequences are represented, and how and whether escape and safety can be obtained. (p. 276)

Intersectionality explains how Black women can be both simultaneously advantaged and disadvantaged as victims. For example, when compared to poor women and lesbians, social class and heterosexual privilege can protect middle-class or heterosexual Black women from some types of aggression. At the same time, racism can make it difficult for Black women, regardless of their economic status and sexual orientation, to escape racially based forms of oppression and violence (Bograd, 1999; Collins, 1998; Crenshaw, 1994). The combination of sexism, racism, and classism not only influences domestic violence, but influences the range of violence experienced by victims, the imbalances in male-female gender roles, the structure of social institutions that support partner violence, and the victims' help-seeking behavior. A Black feminist analysis will be presented below.

The Range of Violence

Feminists argue that intimate partner violence is merely one example of violence in the lives of women. They advocate the use of a broader definition, which could encompass violent acts such as incest, sexual harassment in the workplace, forced prostitution, and female infanticide (Marin & Russo, 1999). Other researchers have documented the broad range of violence experienced by Black women (West, Williams, & Siegel, 2000; Wyatt, Axelrod, Chin, Carmona, & Loeb, 2000). However, Black feminists would also consider the influence of community violence. Black feminist theologian T. C. West (1999) argues that "For womanists, violence against women within the Black communities must never be separated from an understanding of violence against the community" (p. 120). Other researchers have supported her contention. Exposure to community violence has been linked to dating aggression among African-American adolescents (Malik, Sorenson, & Aneshensel, 1997). It has also been linked to rape. As a result of poverty, Black women are more likely to live in dangerous communities. Erratic work hours often force them to travel at night or to rely on public transportation, which leaves them vulnerable to assaults. Black rape victims are astute enough to make this association between their unsafe environment and their sexual assaults (Wyatt, 1992). Finally, Black feminists also suggest that researchers investigate the connection between intimate partner violence among African Americans and the societal violence that they experience, for example in the form of police presence in the Black community, and international violence against African people, including military action (Collins, 1998).

Imbalance of Gender Roles

Feminists believe that the patriarchal structure of society gives men more power and control in their families (Marin & Russo, 1999). Black feminists make similar assertions about Black family violence. However, Black feminists point out that African-American families have seldom conformed to "traditional" family configurations, with dominant men who function as primary income producers and women who are passive and responsible for household and child care duties (Collins, 1990). Historically, Black women have been compelled to adopt relatively androgynous roles; for example, they have been able to function as both wage earners and family caretakers. In contrast, a substantial percentage of Black men have not been able to function in the traditional role of providers for their families because they have been denied access to economic resources and jobs (Ucko, 1994).

Although it is not always economically possible, many African-American couples attempt to enact these traditional gender roles and family configurations. This may contribute to conflict and violence. For instance, middle-class Black men who endorse the belief that Black women have more opportunities were more accepting of violence (Cazenave, 1983), whereas Black women who endorsed such beliefs were more likely to be victimized. The young Black women surveyed by White (1997) perceived their working class boyfriends as dominant and aggressive. Although they did not enjoy the sexual abuse that accompanied these gender roles, they frequently acquiesced to the sexual demands of their partners. They believed that sexuality was one of the few arenas where their boyfriends could assert their fragile sense of masculinity. Characterizing themselves as supporters and caretakers required them to avoid the "emasculation" of their boyfriends by refusing sexual contact, even if it meant tolerating sexual aggression. Despite the aggression in their dating relationships, they had a strong desire to perform as traditional caretakers and for their boyfriends to behave as protectors, roles that have been linked to partner violence. Similar findings were discovered in community (Moss et al., 1997) and incarcerated samples (Richie, 1996) of battered Black women. Because of their perceived economic advantage, many of these women felt guilty about their accomplishments, while simultaneously feeling responsible for their partners' limited economic opportunities. According to Richie (1996), this set of belief patterns is an example of "gender entrapment," which can make it difficult for some battered Black women to extract themselves from abusive relationships.

According to Black feminists we should dispel the myth that Black women, when compared to their Black counterparts, are financially and socially more advantaged. This notion may be linked to a misinterpretation of history. Black women were able to obtain jobs, for example as domestic workers, when Black men were unemployed. Although it may appear that Black women are privileged, the reality is that race and gender discrimination frequently leaves them more impoverished than other race-gender groups (Sanchez-Hucles, 1997). Black feminists have also challenged the Black community to reconceptualize its notions of Black masculinity. Rather than attempting to adhere to traditional male roles, which emphasize dominance and aggression, African Americans should seek to create more egalitarian, cooperative, androgynous roles for both genders. Perhaps this may reduce some of the conflict, frustration, and potential violence that results from trying to enact unattainable gender roles (hooks, 1992).

Structure of Social Institutions

Feminists assert that major societal institutions, including the media, legal and health care systems, reflect patriarchal values and encourage and maintain violence against women. For example, the criminal justice system often fails to adequately protect battered women and prosecute their victimizers. Likewise, medical professionals may miss signs of partner violence or fail to detect the connection between battering and other physical and mental health problems (Marin & Russo, 1999). Social institutions may be unsupportive of Black battered women as well. They may endure an oppressive police force that is likely to arrest both the victim and her abusive partner (Moss et al., 1997), negative media images that give the impression that they deserve to be abused (Bell & Mattis, 2000; West, 2000), laws that make it difficult for them to extricate themselves from violent relationships (Kupenda, 1998), and a health care system that is unresponsive to their needs (Richie & Kanuha, 1993). All these factors converge to exacerbate the battered woman's feelings of helplessness. bell hooks (1989), a Black feminist scholar, makes this point eloquently when she writes, "I was hit by my companion at a time in life when a number of forces in the world outside our home had already 'hit' me, so to speak, made me painfully aware of my powerlessness, my marginality" (p. 85).

The obvious solution is to create more culturally appropriate services to meet the needs of both Black victims and perpetrators (Williams & Becker, 1994). Black feminist thought can make a significant contribution by keeping the focus on historical perspectives. During slavery and well into reconstruction, Black women witnessed their husbands, fathers, sons, and brothers being abducted by slave owners, police officers, and Klansman. For the contemporary Black woman, having her partner arrested may be reminiscent of these earlier historical traumas. Although she wants the violence to stop, she may be reluctant to thrust her batterer into a system that is discriminatory, hostile, and overcrowded with Black males. Batterers realize this and will often use this history to further manipulate their partners. Black feminists recommend that this history be acknowledged while simultaneously holding African-American men accountable for their abuse (White, 1994; Richie, 1985).

Help-Seeking Behavior

Despite the violence sustained by battered women, feminists believe that they are active help seekers (Bograd, 1988; West, Kaufman Kantor, Jasinski, 1998). Black feminists have also highlighted the survival and resistance strategies of Black abuse victims (T. C. West, 1999). However, they criticize traditional feminist theorists for failing to recognize the race based stereotypes that make the claims of Black battered women appear inauthentic. Alternatively stated, Black women have historically been depicted as angry, aggressive, domineering, masculine Sapphires (West, 2000). This image makes Black women seem contrary to the societal stereotype of victims who are more deserving of sympathy and intervention, most notably victims who are White, middle-class, passive, weak, and do not physically defend themselves (Harrison & Esqueda, 1999). Rather than refuting these stereotypes, in some cases feminists have developed theories that reinforce them, such as the battered woman's syndrome (Allard, 1991; Ammons, 1995; Moore, 1995).

This places Black battered women in a disadvantaged position when they claim victimization status. Some women internalize this image and consequently perceive physical retaliation as an appropriate response to abuse. One Black woman described her self-defense technique: "I started hitting him back, I got tired of hitting on me. And I popped him across the head with a skillet one day" (Moss et al., 1997, p. 447). Although this form of self-defense may be effective in the short term, it may contribute to an escalation of violence and possibly murder. As previously discussed, homicide by intimate partners is a leading cause of death for African-American women (National Center for Health Statistics, 1997). Another drawback is that the Sapphire image, coupled with Black women's propensity to fight back when physically (Moss et al., 1997) and sexually assaulted (Bart & O'Brien, 1985), makes them appear to be mutual combatants. As result, service providers may neglect the violence in Black relationships. In some cases, they may perceive the violence as normative or as an example of the bestial nature of African Americans. For instance, Officer Laurence Powell, who was convicted in federal court of violating the civil rights of Rodney King, referred to a domestic violence call at a Black family's home as something out of *Gorillas in the Mist* (Ammons, 1995).

Black feminists offer several solutions to combating these stereotypes. Service providers need to understand the broad range of stereotypes. In addition, to being perceived as angry Sapphires, Black women may be characterized as self-sacrificing Mammies who should keep the family together, even at the expense of their personal safety. They may also be viewed as Jezebels who invite rape because of their seductive mannerisms or attire. Service providers need to educate their colleagues and Black battered women about the damage done by these images (Ammons, 1995; Brice-Baker, 1994; West, 1998c).

CONCLUSION

The purpose of this chapter was to begin charting a new course in the research on domestic violence in the Black community. If we look toward the past, we find that the research has been contradictory. In some studies African-American women are equally as likely as their White counterparts to be victimization (Bachman, 1994; Lockhart, 1991), in other studies they sustain and inflict more partner aggression (Hampton et al., 1989; Neff et al., 1995). Methodological problems, including definitional and measurement limitations and problems with how the data is collected, analyzed, and interpreted, further add to the confusion about racial differences. The solution is to involve research participants at every stage of the research process from planning to implementing, interpreting, and disseminating the results (Fontes, 1997). Another solution is to develop a new framework for investigating violence in this population. Researchers have taken a "color blind" approach, which is the assumption that violence is similar across ethnic groups (Williams, 1993). Conversely, other researchers have considered violence to be a problem that plagues African Americans (Hawkins, 1987). Neither approach is appropriate. However, a Black feminist perspective can move scholars toward a deeper understanding of violence in the lives of African-American women. This approach should consider the Black women's history; the intersection of racism, sexism, and classism; the range of violence experienced by Black women; the imbalance of gender roles; the structure of social institutions; and help-seeking behaviors. A Black feminist model has already been shown to increase anti-rape advocacy in Black communities (White, Potgieter, Strube, Fisher, & Umana, 1997; White, Strube, Fisher, 1998). Perhaps by embracing this perspective, we can begin to chart a new course by reversing the tide of intimate partner violence.

REFERENCES

Abraham, M. (1999). Sexual abuse in South Asian immigrant marriages. *Violence Against Women, 5*, 591–618.

Allard, S. A. (1991). Rethinking battered woman syndrome: A Black feminist perspective. *UCLA Women's Law Journal, 1*, 191–207.

Ammons, L. L. (1995). Mules, madonnas, babies, bathwater, racial imagery, and stereotypes: The African-American woman and the battered woman syndrome. *Wisconsin Law Review, 5*, 1003–1080.

Asbury, J. (1999). What do we know now about spouse abuse and child sexual abuse in families of color in the United States? In R. L. Hampton, T. P Gullotta, G. R. Adams, E. H. Potter, & R. P. Weissberg (Eds.), *Family violence: Prevention and treatment* (pp. 148–167). Thousand Oaks, CA: Sage.

Bachman, R. (1994). *Violence against women: A national crime victimization survey report.* Washington, DC: U.S. Department of Justice.

Barbee, E. L. (1992). Ethnicity and woman abuse in the United States. In C. M. Sampselle (Ed.), *Violence against women: Nursing research, education, and practice issues* (pp. 153–166). New York: Hemisphere.

Barnes, S. Y. (1999). Theories of spouse abuse: Relevance to African Americans. *Issues in Mental Health Nursing, 20*, 357–371.

Barnett, O. W., Miller-Perrin, C. L., & Perrin, R. D. (1997). *Family violence across the lifespan.* Thousand Oaks, CA: Sage.

Bart, P. B., & O'Brien, P. H. (1985). *Stopping rape: Successful survival strategies.* New York: Pergamon Press.

Bell, C. C., & Mattis, J. (2000). The importance of cultural competence in ministering to African American victims of domestic violence. *Violence Against Women, 6*, 515–532.

Bograd, M. (1988). Feminist perspectives on wife abuse: An introduction. In K. Yllo & M. Bograd (Eds.), *Feminist perspectives on wife abuse*. Newbury Park, CA: Sage.

Bograd, M. (1999). Strengthening domestic violence theories: Intersections of race, class, sexual orientation, and gender. *Journal of Marital and Family Therapy, 25,* 275–289.

Boye-Beaman, J., Leonard, K. E., & Senchak, M. (1993). Male premarital aggression and gender identity among Black and White newlywed couples. *Journal of Marriage and the Family, 55,* 303–313.

Brice-Baker, J. R. (1994). Domestic violence in African American and African-Caribbean families. *Journal of Social Distress and the Homeless, 3,* 23–38.

Campbell, D. W., Campbell, J. C., King, C., Parker, B., & Ryan, J. (1994). The reliability and factor structure of the Index of Spouse Abuse with African American women. *Violence and Victims, 9,* 259–274.

Campbell, J. C., Rose, L., Kub, J., & Nedd, D. (1998). Voices of strength and resistance: A contextual and longitudinal analysis of women's responses to battering. *Journal of Interpersonal Violence, 13,* 743–762.

Cazenave, N. A., & Straus, M. A. (1979). Race, class, network embeddedness and family violence: A search for potent support systems. *Journal of Comparative Family Studies, 10,* 281–300.

Cazenave, N. A. (1983). Black male-Black female relationships: The perceptions of 155 middle-class Black men. *Family Relations, 32,* 341–350.

Christensen, C. P. (1988). Issues in sex therapy with ethnic and racial minority women. *Women & Therapy, 7,* 187–205.

Clark, M. L., Beckett, J., Wells, M., & Dungee-Anderson-D. (1994). Courtship violence among African American college students. *Journal of Black Psychology, 20,* 264–281.

Collins, P. H. (1990). *Black feminist thought: Knowledge, consciousness, and the politics of empowerment*. New York: Routledge.

Collins, P. H. (1998). The tie that binds: Race, gender and US violence. *Ethnic and Racial Studies, 21,* 917–938.

Crenshaw, K. W. (1994). Mapping the margins: Intersectionality, identity politics, and violence against women of color. In M. A. Fineman & R. Mykitiuk (Eds.), *The public nature of private violence: The discovery of domestic abuse* (pp. 93–118). New York: Routledge.

Currie, D. H. (1998). Violent men or violent women? Whose definition counts? In R. K. Bergen (Ed.), *Issues in intimate violence* (pp. 97–111). Thousand Oaks, CA: Sage.

DeMaris, A. (1990). The dynamics of generational transfer in courtship violence: A biracial exploration. *Journal of Marriage and the Family, 52,* 219–231.

Dutton, M. A., Goodman, L. A., & Bennett, L. (1999). Court-involved battered women's responses to violence: The role of psychological, physical, and sexual abuse. *Violence & Victims, 14,* 89–104.

Erez, D. (1986). Intimacy, violence, and the police. *Human Relations, 39,* 265–281.

Follingstad, D. R., Rutledge, L. L., Berg, B. J., Hause, E. S., & Polek, D. S. (1990). The roles of emotional abuse in physically abusive relationships. *Journal of Family Violence, 5,* 107–120.

Fontes, L. A. (1997). Conducting ethical cross-cultural research on family violence. In G. K. Kaufman & J. L. Jasinski (Eds.), *Out of the darkness: Contemporary research perspectives on family violence* (pp. 296–312). Thousand Oaks, CA: Sage.

Fontes, L. A. (1998). Ethics in family violence research: Cross-cultural issues. *Family Relations, 47,* 53–61.

Foley, L. A., Evanic, C., Karnik, K., King, J., & Parks, A. (1995). Date rape: Effects of race and assailant and victim and gender on subjects on perceptions. *Journal of Black Psychology, 21,* 6–18.

Gondolf, E. W., Fisher, E., & McFerron, J. R. (1991). Racial differences among shelter residents: A comparison of Anglo, Black, and Hispanic battered women. In R. L. Hampton (Ed.), *Black family violence: Current research and theory* (pp. 103–114). Lexington, MA: Lexington Books.

Goodman, L. A., Koss, M. P., & Russo, N. F. (1993). Violence against women: Physical and mental health effects: Part 1. Research findings. *Applied and Preventive Psychology, 2,* 79–89.

Hampton, R. L., & Gelles, R. J. (1994). Violence toward Black women in a nationally representative sample of Black families. *Journal of Comparative Family Studies, 25,* 105–119.

Hampton, R. L., Gelles, R. J., & Harrop, J. (1989). Is violence in Black families increasing? A comparison of 1975 and 1985 national survey rates. *Journal of Marriage and the Family, 51,* 969–980.

Harrison, L. A., & Esqueda, C. W. (1999). Myths and stereotypes of actors involved in domestic violence: Implications for domestic violence culpability attributions. *Aggression and Violent Behavior, 4,* 129–138.

Hawkins, D. F. (1987). Devalued lives and racial stereotypes: Ideological barriers to the prevention of family violence among Blacks. In R. L. Hampton (Ed.), *Violence in the Black family* (pp. 189–205). Lexington, MA: Lexington Books.

hooks, b. (1989). *Talking back: Thinking feminist, thinking Black.* Boston: South End Press.

hooks, b. (1992). *Black looks: Race and representation.* Boston: South End Press.

Johnson, B. E., Kuck, D. L., & Schander, P. R. (1997). Rape myth acceptance and sociodemographic characteristics: A multidimensional analysis. *Sex Roles, 36,* 693–707.

Joseph, J. (1997). Woman battering: A comparative analysis of Black and White women. In G. K. Kantor & J. L. Jasinski (Eds.), *Out of the darkness: Contemporary perspectives on family violence* (pp. 161–169). Thousand Oaks, CA: Sage.

Kanuha, V. (1990). Compounding the triple jeopardy: Battering in lesbian of color relationships. In L. S. Brown & M. Root (Eds.), *Diversity and complexity in feminist therapy* (pp. 169–184). New York: Harrington Park Press.

Kanuha, V. (1996). Domestic violence, racism, and the battered women's movement in the United States. In J. L. Edleson & Z. C. Eisikovits (Eds.), *Future interventions with battered women and their families* (pp. 34–50). Thousand Oaks, CA: Sage.

Kupenda, A. M. (1998). Law, life, and literature: A critical reflection of life and literature to illuminate how laws of domestic violence, race, and class bind

Black women based on Alice Walker's book *The Third Life of Grange Co-peland. Howard Law Journal, 42,* 1–26.

Lentz, S. A. (1999). Revisiting the rule of thumb: An overview of the history of wife abuse. *Women & Criminal Justice, 10,* 9–27.

Lockhart, L. L. (1987). A reexamination of the effects of race and social class on the incidence of marital violence: A search for reliable differences. *Journal of Marriage and the Family, 49,* 603–610.

Lockhart, L. L. (1991). Spousal violence: A cross-racial perspective. In R. L. Hampton (Ed.), *Black family violence: Current research and theory* (pp. 85–102). Lexington, MA: Lexington Books.

Lockhart, L., & White, B. W. (1989). Understanding marital violence in the Black community. *Journal of Interpersonal Violence, 4,* 421–436.

Lonsway, K. A., & Fitzgerald, L. F. (1995). Rape myths: In review. *Psychology of Women Quarterly, 18,* 133–164.

Mahoney, P. & Williams, L. M. (1998). Sexual assault in marriage: Prevalence, consequences, and treatment of wife rape. In J. L. Jasinski & L. M. Williams (Eds.), *Partner violence: A comprehensive review of 20 years of research* (pp. 113–162). Thousand Oaks, CA: Sage.

Malik, S., Sorenson, S. B., & Aneshensel, C. S. (1997). Community and dating violence among adolescents: Perpetration and victimization. *Journal of Adolescent Health, 21,* 291–302

Marin, A. J. & Russo, N. F. (1999). Feminist perspectives on male violence against women. In M. Harway & J. M. O'Neil (Eds.), *What causes men's violence against women?* Thousand Oaks, CA: Sage.

McFarlane, J., Parker, B., Soeken, K., Silva, C., & Reed, S. (1999). Severity of abuse before and during pregnancy for African American, Hispanic, and Anglo women. *Journal of Nurse Midwifery, 44,* 139–144.

McLaughlin, I. G., Leonard, K. E., & Senchak, M. (1992). Prevalence and distribution of premarital aggression among couples applying for a marriage license. *Journal of Family Violence, 7,* 309–319.

Mendez, J. M. (1996). Serving gays and lesbians of color who are survivors of domestic violence. In C. M. Renzetti & C. H. Miley (Eds.), *Violence in gay and lesbian domestic partnership* (pp. 53–60). Binghamton, NY: Haworth Press.

Moore, S. (1995). Battered women syndrome: Selling the shadow to support the substance. *Howard Law Journal, 38,* 297–352.

Moss, V. A., Pitula, C. R., Campbell, J. C., & Halstead, L. (1997). The experience of terminating an abusive relationship from an Anglo and African American perspective: A qualitative descriptive study. *Issues in Mental Health Nursing, 18,* 433–454.

National Center for Health Statistics (1997). *Vital statistics mortality data, underlying causes of death, 1979–1995.* Hyattsville, MD: Centers for Disease Control and Prevention, 1997.

Neff, J. A., Holamon, B., & Schluter, T. D. (1995). Spousal violence among Anglos, Blacks and Mexican Americans: The role of demographic variables, psychosocial predictors, and alcohol consumption. *Journal of Family Violence, 10,* 1–21.

Neville, H. A., & Heppner, M. J. (1999). Contextualizing rape: Reviewing sequelae and proposing a culturally inclusive ecological model of sexual assault recovery. *Applied & Preventive Psychology, 8,* 41–62.

Neville, H. A., & Pugh, A. O. (1997). General and culture-specific factors influencing African American women's reporting patterns and perceived social support following sexual assault. *Violence Against Women, 3,* 361–381.

O'Keefe, M. (1994). Racial/ethnic differences among battered women and their children. *Journal of Child and Family Studies, 3,* 283–305.

O'Leary, K. D. (1999). Psychological abuse: A variable deserving critical attention in domestic violence. *Violence and Victims, 14,* 3–23.

Oliver, W. (2000). Preventing domestic violence in the African American community: The rationale for popular culture interventions. *Violence and Victims, 6,* 533–549.

Plass, M. S., & Gessner, J. C. (1983). Violence in courtship relations: A Southern sample. *Free Inquiry in Creative Sociology, 11,* 198–202.

Ransby, B. (1995). A righteous rage and a grassroots mobilization. In G. Smithehrman (Ed.), *African American women speak out on Anita Hill–Clarence Thomas* (pp. 44–52). Detroit: Wayne State University Press.

Richie, B. E. (1985). Battered Black women: A challenge for the Black community. *The Black Scholar, 16,* 40–44.

Richie, B. E. (1996). *Compelled to crime: The gender entrapment of battered Black women.* New York: Routledge.

Richie, B. E., & Kanuha, V. (1993). Battered women of color in public health care systems: Racism, sexism and violence. In B. Blair & S. E. Cayleff (Eds.), *Wings of gauze: Women of color and the experience of health and illness* (pp. 288–299). Detroit: Wayne State University Press.

Rouse, L. P. (1988). Abuse in dating relationships: A comparison of Blacks, Whites, and Hispanics. *Journal of College Student Development, 29,* 312–319.

Russell, D. E. (1990). *Rape in marriage.* Bloomington: Indiana University Press.

Russo, N. F., Denious, J. E., Keita, G. P., & Koss, M. P. (1997). Intimate violence and Black women's health. *Women's Health: Research on Gender, Behavior, and Policy, 3,* 315–348.

Sackett, L. A., & Saunders, D. G. (1999). The impact of different forms of psychological abuse on battered women. *Violence and Victims, 14,* 105–117.

Sanchez-Hucles, J. V. (1997). Jeopardy not bonus status for African American women in the work force: Why does the myth of advantage persist? *American Journal of Community Psychology, 25,* 565–580.

Smith, M. D. (1994). Enhancing the quality of survey data on violence against women: A feminist approach. *Gender & Society, 8,* 109–127.

Smith, P. H., Smith, J. B., & Earp, J. L. (1999). Beyond the measurement trap: A reconstructed conceptualization and measurement of woman battering. *Psychology of Women Quarterly, 23,* 177–193.

Sorenson, S. B. (1996). Violence against women: Examining ethnic differences and commonalities. *Evaluation Review, 20,* 123–145.

Sorenson, S. B., Upchurch, D. M., & Shen, H. (1996). Violence and injury in marital arguments. Risk patterns and gender differences. *American Journal of Public Health, 86,* 35–40.

Stets, J. E. (1990). Verbal and physical aggression in marriage. *Journal of Marriage and the Family, 52,* 501–514.

Straus, M. A. (1990). The Conflict Tactics Scale and its critics: An evaluation and new data on validity and reliability. In M. A. Straus & R. J. Gelles (Eds.), *Physical violence in American families: Risk factors and adaptation in 8,145 families* (pp. 49–73). New Brunswick, NJ: Transaction Publishers.

Straus, M. A., Gelles, R. J., & Steinmetz, S. (1980). *Behind closed doors: Violence in the American family.* Garden City, NY: Anchor Books.

Straus, M. A., Hamby, S. L., Boney-McCoy, S., & Sugarman, D. B. (1996). The revised Conflict Tactics Scales (CTS2): Development and preliminary psychometric data. *Journal of Family Issues, 17,* 283–316.

Sullivan, C. M., & Rumptz, M. H. (1994). Adjustment and needs of African American women who utilized a domestic violence shelter. *Violence and Victims, 9,* 275–286.

Symons, P. Y., Groer, M. W., Kepler-Youngblood, P., & Slater, V. (1994). Prevalence and predictors of adolescent dating violence. *Journal of Child and Adolescent Psychiatric Nursing, 7,* 14–23.

Tucker, M. B., & Mitchell-Kernan, C. (1995). *The decline in marriage among African Americans: Causes, consequences, and policy implications.* New York: Russell Sage Foundation.

Ucko, L. G. (1994). Culture and violence: The interaction of African and America. *Sex Roles, 31,* 185–204.

Waldron, C. M. (1996). Lesbians of color and the domestic violence movement. In C. M. Renzetti & C. H. Miley (Eds.), *Violence in gay and lesbian domestic partnership* (pp. 43–53). Binghamton, NY: Haworth Press.

Walker, L. (1979). *The battered woman.* New York: Harper & Row.

Warshaw, R. (1994). *I never called it rape.* New York: Harper & Row.

West, C. M. (1998a). Leaving a second closet: Outing partner violence in same-sex couples. In J. L. Jasinski & L. M. Williams (Eds.), *Partner violence: A comprehensive review of 20 years of research* (pp. 163–183). Thousand Oaks, CA: Sage.

West, C. M. (1998b). Lifting the "political gag order": Breaking the silence around partner violence in ethnic minority families. In J. L. Jasinski & L. M. Williams (Eds.), *Partner violence: A comprehensive review of 20 years of research* (pp. 184–209). Thousand Oaks, CA: Sage.

West, C. M. (1998c). The connection between historical images of Black women and domestic violence. In *Assembling the pieces: Leadership in addressing domestic violence in the African American community.* Conference proceedings of the Institute on Domestic Violence in the African American Community. Washington, DC: U.S. Department of Health and Human Services.

West, C. M., Kantor, G. K., & Jasinski, J. L. (1998). Sociodemographic predictors and cultural barriers to help-seeking behavior by Latina and Anglo American battered women. *Violence & Victims, 13,* 361–375.

West, C. M. (2000). Developing an "oppositional gaze" toward the images of Black women. In J. C. Chrisler, C. Golden, & P. D. Rozee (Eds.), *Lectures on the psychology of women* (pp. 220–233). Boston: McGraw-Hill.

West, C. M., & Rose, S. M. (2000). Dating aggression among low income African American youth: An examination of gender differences and antagonistic beliefs. *Violence Against Women, 6,* 470–494.

West, C. M., Williams, L. M., & Siegel, J. A. (2000). Adult sexual revictimization among Black women sexually abused in childhood: A prospective examination of serious consequences of abuse. *Child Maltreatment, 5*, 49–57.

West, T. C. (1999). *Wounds of the spirit: Black women, violence, and resistance ethics.* New York: New York University Press.

White, A. M. (1999). Talking feminist, talking Black: Micromobilization processes in a collective protest against rape. *Gender & Society, 13*, 77–100.

White, A. M., Potgieter, C. A., Strube, M. J., Fisher, S., & Umana, E. (1997). An African-centered, Black feminist approach to understanding attitudes that counter social dominance. *Journal of Black Psychology, 23*, 398–420.

White, A. M., Strube, M. J., & Fisher, S. (1998). A Black feminist model of rape myth acceptance: Implications for research and antirape advocacy in Black communities. *Psychology of Women Quarterly, 22*, 157–175.

White, E. C. (1994). *Chain, chain, change: For Black women in abusive relationships.* Seattle, WA: Seal Press.

White, R. T. (1997). In the name of love and survival: Interpretations of sexual violence among young Black American women. In T. D. Sharpley-Whiting & R. T. White (Eds.), *Spoils of war: Women of color, culture, and revolutions* (pp. 27–45). Lanham, MD: Rowman & Littlefield.

Williams, O. J. (1993). Developing an African American perspective to reduce spouse abuse: Considerations for community action. *Black Caucus: Journal of the National Association of Black Social Workers, 1*, 1–8.

Williams, O. J., & Becker, R. L. (1994). Domestic partner abuse treatment programs and cultural competence: The results of a national survey. *Violence & Victims, 9*, 287–296.

Wriggins, J. (1983). Rape, racism, and the law. *Harvard Women's Law Journal, 6*, 103–142.

Wyatt, G. E. (1992). The sociocultural context of African American and White American women's rape. *Journal of Social Issues, 48*, 77–91.

Wyatt, G. E. (1994). Sociocultural and epidemiological issues in the assessment of domestic violence. *Journal of Social Distress and the Homeless, 3*, 7–21.

Wyatt, G. E., Axelrod, J., Chin, D., Carmona, J. V., & Loeb, T. B. (2000). Examining patterns of vulnerability to domestic violence among African American victims of domestic violence. *Violence Against Women, 6*, 495–514.

Yllo, K. (1993). Through a feminist lens: Gender, power and violence. In R. J. Gelles & D. R. Loseke (Eds.), *Current controversies on family violence* (pp. 47–62). Newbury Park, CA: Sage.

Chapter 11

Hormone Hostages: The Cultural Legacy of PMS as a Legal Defense

Joan C. Chrisler

Although the experience of negative effect prior to menstruation was first described in the medical literature in the 1930s (Frank, 1931), premenstrual syndrome (PMS) did not become well known among either the medical community or the general public until the 1980s. How did PMS go from a little-known, private experience to one so common and so public that most American women complain about it and jokes about it are ubiquitous? Media coverage of the murder trials of Sandie Smith and Christine English in London and the child abuse case of Shirley Santos in New York brought PMS and its principal proponent, the British endocrinologist Katharina Dalton, to worldwide attention as the "raging hormones" debate began anew.

THE TRIALS

In 1980 Sandie Craddock Smith was tried for the murder of a barmaid whom she had suddenly stabbed to death following an argument. Ms. Smith had a long record of previous convictions for impulsive acts of violence, had attempted suicide at least 25 times, and had had multiple commitments to psychiatric institutions (Boorse, 1987). Dr. Katharina Dalton was asked to examine her before the trial. She read the official court records and Smith's diaries, and concluded that Smith's violent acts occurred at intervals of approximately 29 days. Dalton thus diagnosed Ms. Smith as having severe premenstrual syndrome. She began treatment with massive doses of progesterone, after which Smith was reported to have become "calm and stable" (Boorse, 1987, p. 83). The prosecution accepted PMS as a cause of diminished responsibility and reduced the charge to manslaughter, for which Ms. Smith was given three years' probation.

In the summer of 1981, Smith sent a death threat to a police officer against whom she had a long-standing grudge. She was arrested when she appeared outside the police station with a knife. The jury rejected a plea of not guilty due to premenstrual syndrome, and convicted her of two counts of threatening a police officer and one count of carrying a weapon. However, the judge was affected by Dr. Dalton's testimony that she had recently reduced the dosage administered to Ms. Smith and the defense counsel's argument that with progesterone Smith was "sensible and benign" but without it the "hidden animal" in her escaped and turned to violence. Smith was once again sentenced to probation (" 'Woman's Period' Plea Rejected," 1981, p. 4).

In December 1980, Christine English killed her lover Barry Kitson following heavy drinking and a violent argument, which occurred while the couple was sitting in her car. He announced that he never wanted to see her again and that he was leaving to keep a date with another woman. Ms. English drove away, but then turned around in an attempt to find him and continue their conversation. She found Mr. Kitson, who made an obscene gesture at her. Ms. English aimed her car at him and accelerated. Kitson was crushed against a lamppost, and he died of his injuries two weeks later. Ms. English was arrested, and she began to menstruate while at the police station. Her attorney had read about Ms. Smith's case in *The Times of London*, and he called Dr. Dalton to come examine Ms. English. Although English had no previous record of violence nor any documented incidents of cyclic symptoms, Dalton diagnosed her with PMS and testified that it would make her irritable and aggressive and lead to a loss of control. The judge accepted a plea of diminished responsibility to the charge of manslaughter, and English's only sentence was a one-year ban on driving.

In December 1981 Shirley Santos, a 24-year-old single mother of six children, beat her four-year-old daughter badly enough that she needed to be hospitalized. Ms. Santos called the ambulance herself, and later she told authorities "I just don't remember what happened . . . I would never hurt my baby . . . I just got my period" (Boorse, 1987, p. 85). She was arrested and charged with assault. Her attorney had read about the British trials in the *New York Times*, and in a pretrial hearing she announced that she would enter a plea of not guilty due to PMS. Elizabeth Holtzman, who was the Brooklyn District Attorney at the time, argued that there was no credible scientific evidence to substantiate the plea and urged the court not to accept it. The Santos case never went to trial because the attorneys compromised on a guilty plea to a reduced charge of harassment, a misdemeanor. Ms. Santos received no sentence, fine, or probation in exchange for an agreement to enter counseling. She later lost custody of her daughter in a separate proceeding in the family court.

PMS has also been cited in an arson case in Great Britain (Berlins & Smith, 1981), a bankruptcy case in the United States (Benedek, 1988; Boorse, 1987), and two shoplifting cases in Canada (Gray, 1981). In her writings Dalton (1987) has mentioned other legal cases involving PMS, but she provided no documentation and few details, which makes it difficult to verify the information and impossible to comment on the cases. In his review of PMS and criminal responsibility, philosopher Christopher Boorse (1987) concluded that PMS is of little importance to criminal law. He predicted that it could, however, come to play a role in cases of employment discrimination, competency in contracts and wills, civil commitment, and child custody cases. So far, this does not seem to have happened.

Media Coverage of PMS

The cases of Smith, English, and Santos received considerable media coverage and excited much debate in legal, medical, and psychological circles, as well as among the general public. The coverage of one case affected the next; English's attorney read about Smith's trial in *The Times of London*, and Santos' attorney read about Smith and English in the *New York Times*. Between November 4, 1981 and April 28, 1982, *The Times of London* published five news articles, one feature story ("Should PMT Be a Woman's All-Purpose Excuse?", cowritten by the paper's legal and medical correspondents), one humorous column (about a male embezzler pleading not guilty due to a midlife crisis), one humorous news item (a psychiatrist suggested that hair dressers offer more effective treatment for PMS than do physicians), and six letters to the editor (from women for and against the courts' decisions and from three physicians, one of whom was Dalton's partner in her medical practice and each of whom admitted that little was known about PMS and called for more research).

Between December 29, 1981 and November 15, 1982, the *New York Times* published three news articles, two columns, one feature story (about a woman with PMS who started a self-help group), one editorial (reminding readers that despite PMS women actually commit few violent crimes), and one letter to the editor (from Stephanie Benson, attorney for Santos, to defend her legal strategy). In addition, *Newsweek* published two articles about the trials, and the Canadian newsmagazine *Macleans* also covered them. *People* magazine profiled Smith, English, and Dalton, and *Glamour* magazine ("This Is What You Thought About," 1983) polled its readers about their opinions of the use of PMS as a defense (24% for, 71% against, 5% unsure). Feminist analyses by psychologists Mary Parlee (1982) and Barbara Sommer (1984) later appeared in *Ms.* and *Psychology Today*, respectively.

The press coverage of the trials was the first that many had ever heard of PMS, and journalists rushed to "educate" the public about it. A review of the entries in the Reader's Guide to Periodical Literature that was conducted for this chapter clearly documented the explosion of interest in PMS. In the five years preceding the trials (1976–1980) North American magazines published 3 articles on PMS and 47 articles on other aspects of menstruation (e.g., menarche, dysmenorrhea, sports-related amenorrhea, myths about menstruation). In 1981 and 1982, the years the newspapers were covering the trials, magazines published 10 articles on PMS and 24 on other aspects of menstruation. In the five years after the trials (1983–1987) 45 articles on PMS and 41 on other aspects of menstruation were published. Media interest in PMS has remained strong. In the next five-year period (1988–1992) magazines published 30 articles on PMS and 33 on other aspects of menstruation.

In 1984, the first year that more articles were published on PMS than on all other aspects of menstruation combined, the *Reader's Guide to Periodical Literature* gave "premenstrual syndrome" its own category; it had previously been indexed under "menstruation-disorders." It is interesting to note that the 1980s *Index to The Times of London* contains the following notation: "menstruation—see women."

A STEREOTYPE EMERGES

The news coverage of the British trials focused on the issues of control and emotional stability. Dalton testified that PMS results in a loss of self-control, and Smith and English were repeatedly referred to as out-of-control when premenstrual. Smith's attorney described her as a "Jekyll and Hyde" (Nicholson-Lord, 1982, p. 2) and said that without progesterone injections the "hidden animal" in his client would emerge (" 'Woman's Period' Plea Rejected," 1981, p. 4). Journalists referred to both women as raging animals. No attention was paid to other possible causes of Smith's long psychiatric and criminal history or to the fact that English' lover was an alcoholic, abusive philanderer (Landers, 1988). A more likely defense for Ms. English today would be battered woman's syndrome (Boorse, 1987). American journalists had little to say about the quality of life of a 24-year-old single mother of six or the daily stresses and strains Ms. Santos must have had to endure.

Ms. Smith consented to an interview with *People* magazine (Fields, 1982), in which she said she was planning to write a book about her experiences, but Ms. English has apparently never spoken publicly about her encounter with the criminal justice system. Ms. Santos, in an interview on Phil Donahue's television talk show, later repudiated the PMS defense. She said, "My nerves are not that bad that I am just going to beat up on my kid because my period comes down" (Bird, 1982, p. 4).

A content analysis (Chrisler & Levy, 1990) of 78 articles published in North American magazines between 1980 and 1987 illustrates that the themes present in the coverage of the trials are also present in articles designed to "educate" the public about premenstrual syndrome. Journalists referred to the menstrual cycle as the "cycle of misery," a "hormonal roller coaster," "the monthly monster," the "menstrual monster," "the inner beast," the "battle between estrogen and progesterone," and the "war being waged by the body's hormones" (Chrisler & Levy, 1990, p. 98). The premenstrual and menstrual phases of the cycle are considered "weeks of hell" during which women are "hostages to their hormones," "crippled . . . handicapped." Premenstrual women are described as "raging beasts" and "raging animals" (Chrisler & Levy, 1990, p. 98). Titles of articles on PMS in the popular press include "Premenstrual Frenzy," "Dr. Jekyll and Ms. Hyde," "Coping with Eve's Curse," "PMS: The Return of the Raging Hormones," "Premenstrual Misery," "Once a Month I'm a Woman Possessed," "Can You Win the Hormone War?", "The Taming of the Shrew Inside of You" (Chrisler & Levy, 1990, p. 97), "Is PMS Ruining Our Marriage?", and "Hell Week." The references to Jekyll and Hyde and raging animals probably come directly from the "factual" accounts of the trials. The frequent military references (e.g., war, battle, hostages, hell week) may derive from the violence of the crimes with which Smith, English, and Santos were charged.

The content analysis (Chrisler & Levy, 1990) yielded 131 different "symptoms" of PMS reported in the articles; thus, almost every woman can find herself with something in common with PMS "victims." Rarely was a distinction made between typical cyclic variations in experience and a medical condition called premenstrual syndrome; most journalists seemed to take the position that any physiological or psychological change is pathological. Descriptions that reporters labeled "mild to moderate" PMS, menstrual cycle researchers would call "normal experience." Several writers even suggested that most women have PMS, although they may not realize it. Among the "symptoms" of PMS that were frequently mentioned in the articles were violence, anger, rage, hostility, out-of-control behavior, and suicidal ideation. Other neurological or psychiatric symptoms mentioned in the articles were child abuse, black outs, panic attacks, paranoia, mental breakdowns, hysteria, psychotic episodes, inability to cope, agoraphobia, epileptic seizures, and bouts of alcoholism.

The image of premenstrual women as enraged, violent, and out-of-control has moved beyond the print media to the general culture, and with it has come the implication that all menstruating women (not just those with a diagnosable disorder) are capable of behaving in an erratic, aggressive manner. Over the years I have collected many cultural artifacts that depict premenstrual women the same way the media depicted Smith and English. Among my collection are buttons (e.g., "It's not PMS, I'm psychotic," "It's not PMS, I'm always bitchy"), bumperstickers (e.g., "A woman with PMS and ESP is a bitch who knows everything"), an ad for PMS nail polish that changes its shade in order to warn others about the wearer's mood ("pouty pink," bloated blue"), a calendar of cartoons about a woman with a particularly bad case of PMS (e.g., "To take her mind off her premenstrual syndrome, Melinda decides to rearrange her furniture" by hacking it to pieces with an axe), and greeting cards that offer advice about such things as why women with PMS shouldn't cut their own birthday cakes or carve pumpkins on Halloween (premenstrual women should not handle knives because Sandie Smith stabbed her victim).

Several "humorous" books about PMS also share themes from the media coverage of the trials. *P.M.S. Attacks And Other Inconveniences of Life* (Phillips, 1988), *Hormones from Hell* (King, 1990), and *Raging Hormones: The Unofficial PMS Survival Guide* (Williamson & Sheets, 1989), the cover of which shows Joan Crawford as an axe murderer, all describe women as violent, unpredictable, "hormone hostages." Many comic strips that make fun of premenstrual women have appeared in newspapers and magazines, and the violence theme is common there too, as in, for example, the cartoon where a man decides he is safer in shark infested waters than on a small desert island with a premenstrual woman. References to premenstrual women's angry and erratic behavior have occurred frequently in movies and television shows in recent years; some readers may recall the episode of *Roseanne* where everyone was frightened because the main character's premenstrual phase coincided with Halloween. Conversational and cultural references to PMS seem to have come to outnumber references to any other aspect of the menstrual cycle (when was the last time you heard someone refer to menstrual cramps?). The stereotype of premenstrual women has merged with ancient images of women as dangerous, untrustworthy beings who lured men to their doom, but now a biological basis for women's hostility and duplicity is being claimed (Chrisler, 1996).

The idea that women can "go crazy" when they are premenstrual has been furthered by the American Psychiatric Association's decision to include Premenstrual Dysphoric Disorder (originally known as Late Luteal Phase Dysphoric Disorder) in their *Diagnostic and Statistical Manual of Mental Disorders* (DSM-IIIR, DSM-IV). The Association defended its decision, in part, by stating that the definition of a premenstrual mood disorder would benefit women by making a clear distinction between a serious psychiatric condition and the more common experience of mild to moderate cyclic variations in mood, physiology, and behavior. The psychiatrists' decision also received considerable media attention, and it was greeted with anger by feminists within and outside medical circles (Carey, 1986). The opportunity to stigmatize all menstruating women as potentially mentally ill may yet provide the means to bring PMS into the civil courts as Boorse (1987) predicted.

Is There Scientific Evidence to Support the Stereotype?

Although there are hundreds more research reports in the literature now than when Sandie Smith came to trial, we actually know little more about

PMS now than we did then. The letters to the editor of *The Times of London* by the physicians who summarized what was known and called for additional research could as well have been written in the late 1990s as in the early 1980s. Scientists still cannot agree on a definition of PMS and do not know what causes it or how to "cure" it. A few things are clear, however. Hormones don't rage; they cycle. Hormones do not cause emotions, although they may exacerbate those that are experienced—positive emotions as well as negative ones, despite the fact that we rarely consider the possibility that premenstrual women could feel good (Chrisler, 1996). Behavior is multiply determined. Simplistic suggestions such as the notion that hormone levels cause women to lose control of themselves are not defensible. Although a number of researchers have reported that women with psychiatric conditions may worsen when premenstrual, there appears to be no evidence that premenstrual hormone shifts induce psychiatric conditions.

The earliest suggestion that women are out-of-control when premenstrual came from Frank (1931), who expressed concern about women's tendency to engage in "foolish and ill considered actions" (p. 1054) during that particular phase of the menstrual cycle. Women commonly complain of feeling out-of-control because they are irritable, angry at someone, craving chocolate, or not inclined to work as hard as usual, and many describe this "lack of control" as the most disturbing aspect of being premenstrual. Landers (1988) suggested that PMS is a metaphor for the common inability of women to control their life situations. Martin (1988) hypothesized that women may be less willing, as opposed to less able, to discipline themselves when premenstrual. Mainstream American culture encourages us to believe that people can have more control over our lives than is actually possible (Brownell, 1991; McDaniel, 1988), and control has become so important to many that even the notion of being temporarily out-of-control frightens them. Researchers have not directly addressed the issue of controllability across the menstrual cycle, but the frequency of anger and impulsivity in men and their greater involvement in accidents, crime, and violent behavior suggests that the role of female hormones in being in or out of control is minimal.

Oddly, despite the interest in PMS and crime that followed the trials, little empirical work has been done in this area. The first suggestion that the menstrual cycle may affect women's tendency to commit crimes comes from a study by Dalton (1961) in which she examined the medical records of women prisoners and deduced that more crimes were committed when they were premenstrual than at other times in the cycle. This was a post hoc analysis based only on notations in the women's records about whether they were or were not menstruating at the time they were arrested and jailed; actual cycle phase could not be verified. The main problem with studies such as this is that stress can affect the menstrual cycle by altering its timing. If we assume that many (if not most) of the women were under stress when they committed their crimes and/or while they were questioned by the police and initially jailed, then it may be that stress brought on the start of menstruation earlier than expected. Therefore, a number of the women whose charts noted that they were menstruating may not have actually been in the premenstrual phase (with its specific biochemical markers) when their crimes were committed. Remember that Christine English began to menstruate in the police station while being questioned about the violent argument that ended with her running down Mr. Kitson with her car.

Dalton (1980) later published three short case histories of women who reportedly engaged in cyclic criminal activities. They all made suicidal gestures or attempts, engaged in "bizarre behavior" (e.g., shaving the head and eyebrows, self cutting, running away from home, extreme drunkenness), and seemed to commit primarily minor criminal acts (e.g., shop lifting, writing threatening letters, falsely reporting emergencies to police or fire stations, fire setting). Dalton diagnosed PMS, and she reported that she successfully treated all three young women with progesterone. Today they would probably be diagnosed with a personality or conduct disorder and a history of abuse suspected. Dalton (1966, 1975) has also written about her clinical impression that women are more likely to abuse their children when they are paramenstrual, although she has never reported any data to substantiate her beliefs. If Shirley Santos' case had proceeded to trial, Dalton's "impressions" might have formed the basis of her plea.

In an article published around the time of the British trials D'Orban and J. Dalton (1980) reported that their survey of 50 women's criminal records indicated that 44% of the crimes were committed *para*menstrually, (i.e., in the days *before and after* menstruation began). That means, of course, that most crimes were not committed *pre*menstrually, a fact that often gets lost in the translation from scientific to popular reports. In a study of physical and verbal attacks on others by women in a state prison Ellis and Austin (1971) found that 41% of the documented incidents (64% of which were verbal, not physical, aggression) occurred *para*menstrually. However, they did not collect data on who initiated the incidents, which makes it impossible to tell post hoc whether the paramenstrual women were "acting out" or defending themselves.

After a careful survey of the literature that does exist, Harry and Balcer (1987) wrote that it can not be concluded that crime is related to any phase of the menstrual cycle. They complained that the research they reviewed was seriously flawed in its definitions of menstrual cycle phases, lack of verification of which phase the women were actually in at the time they committed their crimes, lack of appropriate (or in some cases any) statistical analyses, and other methodological errors. Although the researchers' concerns have been primarily with the relationship of premenstrual syndrome to violent crimes, none of them made any attempt to determine whether the women in question actually suffered from premenstrual syndrome, nor did most of them limit their studies to violent crimes. The women in Dalton's (1961) study, for example, had been arrested for drunkenness, prostitution, and theft. Yet, the poor quality of the research has not prevented it from being repeatedly cited in both professional and popular literature. An article in *Science Digest* (Marsh, 1978), for example, proclaimed that "evidence now is mounting to indicate that premenstrual tension may be an underlying factor in all . . . types of [criminal] offenses" (p. 65). The author of the article thoughtfully included "a warning on driving" (p. 66) that encouraged women not to take any car trips during the eight days before and after the onset of menstruation, during which time they would be at increased risk of having an accident. It is unclear from the article whether women are to refrain from long drives for 8 or 16 days; either way, it is a significant reduction in women's freedom of movement, especially when there is no reliable evidence to support the advice. Note that the driving warning was issued prior to Ms. English's use of her car as a weapon and was probably based on another of study of Dalton's (1960) that has been frequently critiqued.

The results of studies of the moodiness of premenstrual women depend in large part on how moods are defined and measured. Women do tend to report increased negative effects (e.g., depression, irritability) premenstrually when they are questioned retrospectively. However, when women are asked to complete daily mood questionnaires, such changes are not reliably found. For example, Hood (1992, 1996) reported that participants in her research indicated retrospectively (i.e., at the conclusion of the study) that they had been more likely to "feel aggressive" when premenstrual than at other times. However, the daily self-reports they completed during the study did not reveal such a pattern; nor was there evidence of increased aggression during weekly behavioral observations. It may be that premenstrual mood shifts are so subtle that most psychological tests are not sensitive enough to measure them or that women have been so influenced by the stereotype of the premenstrual woman that they "remember" all of their negative emotions to have occurred at that time rather than randomly throughout the month (Golub, 1992). Some researchers (e.g., Rossi & Rossi, 1977) have even found that day of the week has a greater influence on women's mood than day of the month.

The study of menstrual cycle-related changes is further complicated by the fact that premenstrual experience is highly variable and personal. Some women experience symptoms that could be rated "strong" or "severe," and others are unaware of any changes. Not all women experience the same symptoms, and the experience of a given woman may vary from cycle to cycle. This is true of even the most common premenstrual changes, such as water retention. Yet stories in the media continue to suggest that all premenstrual women are irritable and moody and thus have the potential to spin out of control and become violent. Cartoons and other cultural products (e.g., buttons, greeting cards) have reinforced this message to the point where most people accept it as an accurate description of women's behavior even though the vast majority of violent incidents are perpetrated by men.

That the facts about PMS and premenstrual women in general do not support the stereotype should not be surprising. The stereotype was constructed by the reaction of journalists to legal and scientific information, which they have interpreted for the general public. Stories about PMS, like all stories, are shaped by their newsworthiness; negative or sensational information (e.g., "Once a Month I'm a Woman Possessed") is seen as more newsworthy (Parlee, 1987) than positive information. It is not news that most women cope well with premenstrual changes. It is news when a woman "cannot" restrain her aggressive impulses or claims that PMS is ruining her marriage.

THE AFTERMATH

The legal cases against Sandie Smith, Christine English, and Shirley Santos, and the media coverage of them, have had a major impact on our society and culture. With hindsight we can see how the development of interest in PMS coincided with the conservative political shift in the United States and the United Kingdom during the 1980s. We can also clearly see the use of the stereotype of the premenstrual woman in the backlash against feminism, which was delineated by Susan Faludi (1991). PMS can be considered a collection of negative "facts" about women's nature, a nature that "requires" medical management and the protection of men, who are stronger and "healthier" than menstruating women (Zita, 1988).

The trials led to a new stereotype of women, which in turn influenced many aspects of popular culture, including books, cartoons, television, movies, and stand-up comedy. The trials also led to a split among women as they debated the pros and cons of PMS as a legal defense. This disagreement later came to be seen as an argument between those who "believed" in the "existence" of PMS and those who didn't; both sides insisted that they had women's best interests at heart. Even today, 20 years later, it remains difficult to theorize about the social construction of PMS as a medicalization of normal experience without being accused of suggesting that premenstrual symptoms are "all on women's heads" and thus not "real." Similar arguments occurred among members of the legal community. Articles were written about the strategy of using PMS as a defense (see Allen, 1990; Benedek, 1988; Chait, 1986), and debates about it occurred at attorneys' conventions.

The trials had a major effect on the medical and scientific communities, and they contributed to a significant increase in the amount of research that was conducted on the menstrual cycle and its concomitant changes. Several international, interdisciplinary conferences were held to explore PMS and its ramifications. Hundreds of scholarly articles and dozens of books have been written about PMS since the early 1980s. Probably the most important effect of the trials and their surrounding publicity was the development of the psychiatric diagnosis Premenstrual Dysphoric Disorder.

What effect will the diagnosis have on women? Will it, in turn, influence the legal system by providing a means to suggest that women with PMS are unfit mothers, too irresponsible for certain employment categories, or not competent to enter into a contract or make a will? Only time will tell. However, what evidence exists (Nash & Chrisler, 1997) suggests that the diagnosis supports and enhances the stereotype.

Can the Stereotype Be Changed?

Stereotypes are not static; they are always in flux. We can see this clearly after tracing the emergence of the aggressive aspect of the stereotype of the premenstrual woman. R. T. Frank (1931), who described premenstrual women as tense, anxious, irritable, and likely to engage in foolish activities, would not recognize the axe or knife wielding, violent, out-of-control hormone hostages that are so prominently illustrated in today's culture. If stereotypes can change for the worse, they can also change for the better. Reversing the direction of the change is a challenge I would like to see feminist psychologists accept.

Social psychologists who study attitudes and persuasion have provided us with tools to use to effect the change. People need new information to integrate into their existing beliefs, and they need to hear this information in the form of strong, cogent arguments from credible sources. We need to increase the availability and salience of alternative images of premenstrual women through multiple messages from multiple sources. We must also show women that they should care about (rather than laugh about) cultural images of premenstrual women; these images are personally relevant to us all whether we have experienced severe premenstrual symptoms or not. After all, these negative images and stereotypes serve to restrict our personal freedom and professional opportunities; they are a form of social control.

We must begin with ourselves and vow to stop thinking of menstruation only as a negative experience. It has positive aspects, too. Its presence is a sign of good health, it is symbolic of our connection to other women, it represents biological maturity, it symbolizes our ability to bear children, and lets us know that we are not pregnant (Chrisler, 1996). We must stop using negative slang to describe the menses, and we should describe our premenstrual experiences as "changes" rather than as "symptoms." A change is a neutral thing; a symptom implies an illness (Chrisler, 1996).

Psychologists (whether scientists, therapists, professors, or all of the above) have the credibility and access to audiences and resources that are necessary to begin the serious work of challenging the stereotype. We must do the necessary research and publicize the results to our students and clients. We should volunteer to give talks to community groups and attempt to form partnerships with journalists in order to get the word out. It is not always easy to interest the media in ideas that fly against conventional wisdom (e.g., diets don't work; there are positive aspects to menstruation), but my experiences suggest that it is possible. I have even managed to get some media coverage of studies that are critical of the media; in both cases, newspaper reporters happily wrote stories about what we have found wrong with magazines. It will no doubt be more difficult to persuade reporters to write critically of their own media outlets. However, we don't have to wait for the journalists to come to us; psychologists can write "op ed" pieces and letters to the editor, and we can send reprints and story ideas to feminist-friendly writers that we think might be interested.

We must teach critical thinking skills to our students and clients. Ask, "How can you accept the stereotype of the premenstrual woman as accurate when you don't know anybody who behaves that way?" Ask, "Who benefits from the portrayal of women as unstable, inept, and potentially out-of-control for two weeks per month from menarche to menopause?" Ask, "Why women? Why now?" Use feminist humor to fight misogynist humor; encourage everyone you know to read Gloria Steinem's (1983) essay "If Men Could Menstruate." Model positive coping, and resolve never to make or enjoy another misogynist PMS joke.

CONCLUSION

Charting a new course for feminist psychology requires an examination and understanding of the past. After all, how can we know where we're going if we don't know where we've been? I found pulling out the microfiche and reading (or rereading) the media coverage of the trials to be a fascinating exercise. It was not difficult to see the emergence of the PMS and violence discourse and to observe its integration into the existing stereotype. I wonder how many other topics would lend themselves to a similar examination and thus help us to understand better how the psychology of women has been shaped by cultural influences.

Charting a new course for women also requires a return to feminist psychology's activist roots. It is not enough to conduct research as a purely intellectual exercise and then share our results only with each other. Studies that have the potential to improve women's condition must be our top priority, and we must take steps to share our findings with the wider public so that more women can know what we know and participate in deciding what the utility of the knowledge is. Let's use our professional and political skills to "subvert the dominant paradigm" of menstrual distress. If we work together, women can reject medical imperialism (Gannon, 1998) and misogynist humor and reclaim the full variety of our cyclic experience.

REFERENCES

Allen, H. (1990). At the mercy of her hormones: Premenstrual tension and the law. In P. Adams & E. Cowie (Eds.), *The woman in question* (pp. 200–229). Cambridge, MA: MIT Press.

Benedek, E. P. (1988). Premenstrual syndrome: A view from the bench. *Journal of Clinical Psychiatry, 49,* 498–502.

Berlins, M., & Smith, T. (1981, November 12). Should PMT be a woman's all-purpose excuse? *The Times of London,* p. 12.

Bird, D. (1982, November 4). Defense linked to menstruation dropped in case. *New York Times,* p. 4, sec. 2.

Boorse, C. (1987). Premenstrual syndrome and criminal responsibility. In B. E. Ginsburg & B. F. Carter (eds.), *Premenstrual syndrome: Ethical and legal implications in a biomedical perspective* (pp. 81–124). New York: Plenum.

Brownell, K. (1991). Personal responsibility and control over our bodies: When expectation exceeds reality. *Health Psychology, 10,* 303–310.

Carey, J. (1986, May 26). Is PMS mental illness? Debate grows. *U.S. News & World Report,* p. 60.

Chait, L. R. (1986). Premenstrual syndrome and our sisters in crime: A feminist dilemma. *Women's Rights Law Reporter, 9* (3/4), 267–293.

Chrisler, J. C. (1996). PMS as a culture-bound syndrome. In J. C. Chrisler, C. Golden, & P. D. Rozee (Eds.), *Lectures on the psychology of women* (pp. 106–121). New York: McGraw-Hill.

Chrisler, J. C., & Levy, K. B. (1990). The media construct a menstrual monster: A content analysis of PMS articles in the popular press. *Women & Health, 16,* 89–104.

Dalton, K. (1960). Menstruation and accidents. *British Medical Journal, 2,* 1425–1426.

Dalton, K. (1961). Menstruation and crime. *British Medical Journal, 2,* 1752.

Dalton, K. (1966). The influence of mother's menstruation on her child. *Proceedings of the Royal Society of Medicine, 57,* 262–264.

Dalton, K. (1975). Letter to the editor: Paramenstrual baby battering. *British Medical Journal, 16,* 279.

Dalton, K. (1980). Cyclic criminal acts in premenstrual syndrome. *Lancet, 2,* 1070–1071.

Dalton, K. (1987). Should premenstrual syndrome be a legal defense? In B. E. Ginsburg & B. F. Carter (Eds.), *Premenstrual syndrome: Ethical and legal implications in a biomedical perspective* (pp. 287–300). New York: Plenum.

D'Orban, P. T., & Dalton, J. (1980). Violent crime and the menstrual cycle. *Psychological Medicine, 10,* 353–359.

Ellis, D. P., & Austin, P. (1971). Menstruation and aggressive behavior in a correctional center for women. *Journal of Criminology, Criminal Law, and Police Science, 62,* 388–395.

Faludi, S. (1991). *Backlash: The undeclared war against American women.* New York: Crown.

Fields, S. (1982, April 5). In England, two killers go free on grounds that they were victims of premenstrual tension. *People,* pp. 94, 97.

Frank, R. T. (1931). The hormonal causes of premenstrual tension. *Archives of Neurology and Psychiatry, 26,* 1053–1057.

Gannon, L. (1998). The impact of medical and sexual politics on women's health. *Feminism & Psychology, 8,* 285–302.

Golub, S. (1992). *Periods: From menarche to menopause.* Newbury Park, CA: Sage.

Gray, C. (1981, June 15). Raging female hormones in the courts. *Maclean's,* pp. 16–18.

Harry, B., & Balcer, C. M. (1987). Menstruation and crime: A critical review of the literature from the clinical criminology perspective. *Behavioral Sciences and the Law, 5,* 307–321.

Hood, K. E. (1992). Contextual determinants of menstrual cycle effects in observations of social interactions. In A. J. Dan & L. L. Lewis (Eds.), *Menstrual health in women's lives* (pp. 83–97). Chicago: University of Illinois Press.

Hood, K. E. (1996). Intractable tangles of sex and gender in women's aggressive development: An optimistic view. In D. M. Stoff & R. B. Cairns (Eds.), *Aggression and violence: Genetic, neurobiological, and biosocial perspectives* (pp. 309–335). Mahwah, NJ: Erlbaum.

King, J. (1990). *Hormones from hell.* Chatsworth, CA: CCC Publications.

Landers, L. (1988). *Images of bleeding: Menstruation as ideology.* New York: Orlando Press.

Marsh, T. O. (1978, September). Women and violent behavior: Natural cycle suspected as link in crime. *Science Digest,* 65–67.

Martin, E. (1988). Premenstrual syndrome: Discipline, work, and anger in late industrial societies. In T. Buckley & A. Gottlieb (Eds.), *Blood magic: The anthropology of menstruation* (pp. 161–181). Berkeley: University of California Press.

McDaniel, S. H. (1988). The interpersonal politics of premenstrual syndrome. *Family Systems Medicine, 6,* 134–149.

Nash, H. C., & Chrisler, J. C. (1997). Is a little (psychiatric) knowledge a dangerous thing? The impact of premenstrual dysphoric disorder on perceptions of premenstrual women. *Psychology of Women Quarterly, 21,* 315–322.

Nicholson-Lord, D. (1982, April 28). Judges reject menstrual tension defense. *The Times of London,* p. 2.

Parlee, M. B. (1987). Media treatment of premenstrual syndrome. In B. E. Ginsburg & B. F. Carter (Eds.), *Premenstrual syndrome: Ethical and legal implications in a biomedical perspective* (pp. 189–205). New York: Plenum.

Parlee, M. B. (1982, September). New findings: Menstrual cycles and behavior. *Ms.,* 126–128.

Phillips, S. (1988). *P.M.S. attacks and other inconveniences of life.* Berkeley, CA: Ten Speed Press.

Rossi, A., & Rossi, E. (1977). Body time and social time: Mood patterns by menstrual cycle and day of the week. *Social Science Research, 6,* 273–308.

Sommer, B. (1984, August). PMS in the courts: Are all women on trial? *Psychology Today,* 36–38.

Steinem, G. (1983). *Outrageous acts and everyday rebellions.* New York: Putnam.

This is what you thought about . . . Premenstrual syndrome as a legal defense. (1983, January). *Glamour,* 15.

Williamson, M., & Sheets, R. (1989). *Raging hormones: The unofficial PMS survival guide.* New York: Doubleday.

"Woman's period" plea rejected. (1981, November 4). *The Times of London,* p. 4.

Zita, J. N. (1988). The premenstrual syndrome: "Dis-easing" the female cycle. *Hypatia, 3* (1), 77–99.

Part IV

Women's Mental Health
and Feminist Therapy

Chapter 12

Prevention of Eating Disorders: Problems, Pitfalls, and Feminist Possibilities

Lori M. Irving

Eating disorders affect women disproportionately (90% of those diagnosed with anorexia and bulimia are female; APA, 1994) and occur primarily in cultures that promote and profit from women's obsession with their weight and appearance (Nasser & Katzman, 1999). Understandably, eating disorders are important topics for consideration by feminist psychologists (Fallon, Katzman, & Wooley, 1994; Piran, 1999a, 1999b; Shisslak & Crago, 1994; Striegel-Moore & Steiner-Adair, 1998). Feminist psychology has brought to awareness the role that social and cultural factors play in the *development* of eating disorders in girls and women (Gilbert & Thompson, 1996). However, feminist psychology can also chart a new course in efforts to design and implement interventions to *prevent* eating disorders. Indeed, with its emphasis on empowerment rather than pathology, contextual rather than individual sources of distress, and a relational approach to development, feminist psychology redresses problems and pitfalls that have inhibited the success of previous efforts to prevent eating disorders (Piran, 1999a, 1999b; Striegel-Moore & Steiner-Adair, 1998). In this chapter, I review hopeful new courses and possibilities for eating disorders prevention, with a focus on the work of investigators who adopt a feminist approach (e.g., Friedman, 1999a; Piran, 1996, 1999b).

EATING DISORDERS: A PUBLIC HEALTH PROBLEM

Anorexia nervosa, bulimia nervosa, and binge eating disorder (DSM-IV, American Psychiatric Association [APA], 1994) are public health problems for girls and women in the United States. The incidence of "diagnosable" eating disorders is modest (.5 to 1% of adolescent girls meet the diagnostic criteria for anorexia nervosa, 1% to 3% of adolescent and young adult women meet the criteria for bulimia; APA, 1994), yet eating disorders are the third most common chronic condition observed in adolescent girls (Fisher et al., cited in Shisslak et al., 1998), and an estimated 10 to 15% of young women meet a subset of the criteria for an eating disorder (Drenowski, Yee, Kurth, & Krahn, 1994; Killen et al., 1986). Eating disorders are thought of as problems of adolescence and adulthood; however, studies indicate that weight preoccupation begins much earlier, in the primary grades (Flannery-Schroeder & Chrisler, 1996; Gustafson-Larson & Terry, 1992; Koff & Rierdan, 1991; Maloney, McGuire, Daniels, & Specker, 1989; Smolak & Levine, 1994; Thelen, Powell, Lawrence, & Kuhnert, 1992).

Eating disorders are accompanied by myriad psychological and medical problems; common co-existing psychological problems include low self-esteem, difficulty coping with stress, depression, anxiety, and substance (ab)use (Dykens & Gerrard, 1986; French, Story, Downes, Resnick, & Blum, 1995; Leon, Fulkerson, Perry & Cudeck, 1993). Serious medical complications include retarded growth, osteoporosis, and reproductive, gastrointestinal, and cardiovascular problems (Pike & Striegel-Moore, 1997). The health dangers of eating disorders are underscored by the finding that the mortality rate for anorexia is estimated to be 12 times higher than it is for young women in the general population (Sullivan, cited in Becker, Grinspoon, Klibanski, & Herzog, 1999).

Initial Efforts to Prevent Eating Disorders

Increased awareness and concern about eating disorders has led to the development of programs to prevent them. A number of initial eating disorders prevention programs produced disappointing results (see Franko & Orosan-Weine, 1998, for a review), which led some to conclude that prevention efforts are premature (Grilo, Devlin, Cachelin, & Yanovski, 1997), unlikely to succeed (Killen, 1996; Killen et al., 1993), and potentially harmful to participants (Carter, Stewart, Dunn, & Fairburn, 1997; Mann et al., 1997). Those writing from a feminist perspective argued that initial programs were unsuccessful because they: (a) focused on individuals' eating disordered attitudes and behaviors and neglected the context in which these attitudes and behaviors develop; (b) were highly structured and, therefore, not responsive to the unique needs of the target audience(s); and (c) adopted an "illness" rather than "wellness" approach by focusing on pathology rather than empowerment and resiliency (Irving, 1999; Piran, 1999b; Striegel-Moore & Steiner-Adair, 1998).

Although some prevention efforts have been unsuccessful (Carter et al., 1997; Killen et al., 1993; Mann et al., 1997), other programs designed to prevent weight and shape preoccupation and eating disorders have produced a variety of positive results, including improved eating habits (Neumark-Sztainer, Butler, & Palti, 1995), reduced disordered or restrictive eating behaviors (Piran, 1998, 1999a, 1999c; Stice, Mazotti, Wiebel, & Agras, 2000), reduced intentions to diet to lose weight (Moreno & Thelen, 1993; Phelps, Dempsey, Sapia, & Nelson, 1999), and increased skepticism about media that depict a thin ideal of beauty (Berel & Irving, 1998a, 1999; Irving, DuPen, & Berel, 1998: Huon, 1994; Kater, 1998; Koff & Bauman, 1997; Phelps et al., 1999; Piran, 1999a, 1999c; Posavac, Posavac, & Weigel, in press; Stice et al., 2000). These successful programs vary widely in content and structure; however, a number of them adhere to core feminist values (Brown, 1994; Enns, 1997) such as connecting personal experience to sociopolitical realities, emphasizing resiliency and empowerment rather than vulnerability, and using a relational or "connected learning" approach (Jordan, 1994; Sadker & Sadker, 1994).

Below, I discuss the future of eating disorders prevention by reviewing *problems* that have impeded progress in this field, *pitfalls* to avoid in constructing prevention programs, and *possibilities* for future prevention efforts. It is my hope that readers will gain a better understanding of what prevention is and how it might be applied successfully to eating disorders; in addition, I hope to show readers how and why feminist approaches are uniquely appropriate to preventing eating disorders and preoccupation with body weight and shape—problems that develop in a context where girls and women are defined and rewarded for how they appear to others rather than who they really are (Steiner-Adair & Vorenberg, 1999).

PROBLEMS

Problem #1: We Don't Know What Prevention Is

Before developing and implementing a program to prevent a specific health problem, it is important to identify the goals of such a program and, correspondingly, the form of prevention and types of prevention strategies that are appropriate to meet those stated goals (Durlak, 1997). Ignorance and misconceptions about prevention have slowed progress in developing programs to prevent mental health problems (Albee & Gullota, 1986). Psychologists are familiar with the "terminology" of prevention (e.g., primary, secondary, tertiary), however, few understand what these terms mean in practice, and fewer still receive training in how prevention tools can be used to prevent or minimize mental health problems. To clarify the meaning and potential applications of prevention, I will review prevention terminology and provide examples relevant to the prevention of eating disorders and weight and shape preoccupation.

Primary prevention strategies target unaffected persons—that is, individuals not yet showing signs of a disturbance (Albee & Gullota, 1986). The goal of primary prevention is to keep a disorder from occurring; therefore, it is likely that primary prevention programs will occur early, before the onset of a problem behavior. Rather than target a "high-risk" group, primary prevention strategies are likely to focus on the broader population from which high-risk individuals and problem behaviors emerge. An elementary school program that discourages weight-related teasing and promotes acceptance of diverse body shapes is an example of a program geared toward primary prevention of eating disorders (Irving, 1998; Pabst, 1996).

Secondary prevention strategies target individuals who demonstrate early signs of a problem; alternately, secondary prevention might target individuals who exist in a context that actively promotes or cultivates problem behaviors (e.g., a women's gymnastics team). The goal of secondary prevention is to keep the initial signs of a problem (e.g., restrictive dieting) from developing into a more serious problem (e.g., dietary restraint followed by bingeing and purging). A program that targets elite athletes or dancers who demonstrate early signs of an eating disorder (e.g., restrictive dieting, self-evaluation heavily dependent on weight and shape) is an example of secondary prevention. In some cases, secondary prevention may take the appearance of "therapy." For example, dancers at risk may complete a structured psychoeducational group that provides education about sound nutritional practices and cognitive-behavioral strategies for challenging negative self-statements about weight and shape. A feminist-informed approach to secondary prevention might also encourage dancers to analyze critically those aspects of ballet culture that promote unhealthy appearance norms and empower dancers to challenge those norms by refusing to practice unhealthy (e.g., fasting, cigarette smoking) or self-destructive (e.g., purging) behavior, or by removing oneself completely and permanently from ballet culture (Piran, 1999a).

Most psychologists are engaged in *tertiary prevention*; that is, interventions designed to minimize the impact of an existing behavior problem. Often, tertiary prevention is referred to as *treatment* or *rehabilitation*. The goal of tertiary prevention is to help the individual regain and maintain the highest level of functioning possible. Individual, family, and group therapy for individuals with an existing eating problem would be considered tertiary prevention. In some settings (e.g., university, ballet school, hospital), it may be possible or advisable to develop a comprehensive program that includes primary, secondary, and tertiary prevention components (Hotelling, 1999; Piran, 1999a; Powers & Johnson, 1999; Weiner, 1999).

Problem #2: We Don't Know What to Prevent

Some in the field of eating disorders argue that prevention efforts are premature because we lack knowledge of *specific* risk factors for eating disorders (Grilo et al., 1997). Some eating disorders experts disagree, and argue that there is considerable agreement about certain specific and general risk factors (Striegel-Moore & Steiner-Adair, 1998). Prevention specialists, however, challenge the premise—based on a "medical model" perspective—that prevention is *impossible* without knowledge of specific causes (Albee & Gullota, 1986). Durlak (1997) argues that the prevention approach differs from the medical model that demands a specific pathogen for every identifiable "disease":

In prevention, it is assumed that most outcomes are multiply determined. We will probably never discover a missing link or single causal agent for most problems or negative outcomes. Therefore, it is important to develop programs that can modify some short- and long-term effects. Careful inspection of the outcome data will determine whether research and practice are on the right path. (p. 9)

One of Durlak's assumptions is that prevention studies can *inform* the search for causal factors; if a preventive intervention reduces the frequency of a problem behavior, then specific targets of the intervention are likely to have been at least partly responsible for the behavior. For example, if installing bright lights in the parking lot of a busy shopping mall is associated with reduced instances of sexual assault and theft, we have evidence that poor lighting conditions contributed to the observed criminal activity. If a new policy that requires ballet instructors to evaluate students on the basis of strength and stamina rather than body weight is associated with reductions in the number of students diagnosed with eating disorders, we have evidence that evaluating students on the basis of body weight contributed to disordered eating practices (Piran, 1999a).

Problem #3: We Lack Knowledge of Prevention Techniques

Clinical psychologists are familiar with tools that make therapy work—empathy, genuineness, assertiveness training, exposure, and cognitive restructuring are part of the psychotherapy lexicon. Clinical psychologists are not familiar with how prevention works; however, prevention *does* have a set of tools. These tools include (Albee & Gullotta, 1986, pp. 209–210) *education*, (e.g., activities to build specific skills), *competency promotion* (e.g., activities to improve self-esteem), *systems intervention* (e.g., activities to change/reform inequities, policies), and *natural caregiving* (e.g., activities to promote self-help and healthy interconnections between citizens). These tools resonate with feminist psychologists; prevention tools have their feminist analogues in *empowerment* through self-awareness and political activism (similar to "competency promotion"); a *contextualized approach* to understanding and intervening with problems (similar to "systems intervention"), and *interpersonal relationships* as an agent of healing and, if desired, behavior change ("natural caregiving") (Brown, 1994).

Most tools of traditional psychotherapy are targeted to the level of the individual; however, prevention tools often are implemented on multiple levels. For example, campaigns to reduce smoking have involved "macro-level" policy changes (e.g., non-smoking flights, restaurants, hotels; restrictions on advertising), "meso-level" peer awareness campaigns (e.g., teaching teens to resist pressure to smoke), and "micro-level" education about the health consequences of smoking. As with smoking, it is generally understood that eating disorders are multiply determined—in part the result of sociocultural influences (Stice, 1994). Given this, prevention programs are well-advised to address meso-level influences (e.g., social pressures to be thin, reinforcement of weight loss, anti-fat attitudes, and weight-related teasing) and macro-level factors (e.g., cultural appearance norms, such as "women should be thin") as well as the more traditionally targeted micro-level factors (e.g., negative cognitions, preoccupation with weight and shape) that are believed to contribute to eating disorders and to weight and shape preoccupation (Berel & Irving, 1998b; Irving, 1999; Piran, 1999b).

Problem #4: Eating Disorders Prevention as a Subversive Act

Perhaps the biggest obstacle to preventing eating disorders is the political nature of this work. Eating disorders prevention involves swimming upstream against a cultural current that glorifies thinness and stigmatizes fatness;[1] even feminists acknowledge their personal struggle to abandon the pursuit of the thin ideal (Brown, 1989; Rothblum, 1994). Preventing eating disorders means challenging the foundation upon which the thin ideal is based; namely, that in our competitive, achievement-oriented society "the extent to which one successfully creates an ideal body is an important index of achievement" (Steiner-Adair & Vorenberg, 1999, p. 106). Furthermore, we must strive to understand why "women's" problems such as eating disorders emerge during "periods of change in socially prescribed gender roles, when the increased importance placed on achievements in traditionally masculine pursuits produces conflicts among nontraditional women" (Silverstein & Perlick, 1995, p. 8). This analysis leads inevitably to the (subversive) conclusion that the cultural beliefs that underlie eating disorders (e.g., glorification of thinness and fear of fatness) are social justice issues, not "women's issues," that are part of a culture that categorizes and rewards (or fails to reward) people based on how closely they resemble the "ideal" as defined by members of the dominant culture (e.g., slender, light-skinned) (Steiner-Adair & Vorenberg, 1999). Eating disorders prevention involves questioning how different groups come to be marginalized (e.g., women, persons of color, fat people) and what can and must be done to change this system of values.

In committing ourselves to eating disorders prevention, we must meet sociocultural and political obstacles head-on by acknowledging our role in participating in and perpetuating a cultural context that is unhealthy for women (Friedman, 1999a; Irving, 1999; Levine, 1994; Piran, 1999b). This commitment not only involves challenging personal and cultural beliefs about food and weight, but proactively challenging actions taken on the basis of these beliefs. For example, we can confront friends or family members who tell "fat" jokes, approach a colleague who is discriminatory in how they treat students or clients who are fat, or question the consistent or exclusive funding of research that supports cultural appearance norms (e.g., weight loss treatment) (Striegel-Moore & Steiner-Adair, 1998).

PITFALLS

As stated previously, before developing and implementing a specific prevention program, one must identify program goals and, correspondingly, the type of prevention techniques that are appropriate to those goals (Durlak, 1997). Failure to identify goals and strategies clearly can be hazardous and unwittingly lead to a number of the "pitfalls" described below.

Pitfall #1: Lack of Clarity Regarding Prevention Goals and Strategies

Lack of consideration for program goals is illustrated by Mann et al.'s (1997) evaluation of a Stanford University eating disorders prevention program that had been in existence for eight years before it was evaluated (Mann & Burgard, 1998). The 90-minute program, led by two undergraduate women with personal histories of an eating disorder, provided information about eating disorders including symptoms, prevalence, treatment, and referral for symptomatic individuals. Presenters also shared how their eating problems began, the course of their disorders, when they realized they had a problem, how they sought help, what their treatment was like, how they got better, and their ongoing process of coping with body image concerns. According to the authors, the program was designed to achieve two goals: (1) to prevent eating disorders in unaffected individuals through education about clinical eating disorders and their consequences (i.e., primary prevention), and (2) to encourage individuals with existing eating problems to seek help through reducing the stigma attached to eating disorders (i.e., secondary prevention). Unfortunately, the creators of the program failed to see how these goals might be incompatible; "normalizing" eating disordered behaviors (i.e., secondary prevention) might undermine attempts to heighten awareness of the "dangers" of eating disorders (i.e., primary prevention), and conversely, speaking about the dangers of eating disorders might frighten symptomatic individuals and discourage them from seeking treatment.

The Stanford prevention program failed at its intended goals. Four weeks after the program, participants reported engaging in *more* eating disordered behaviors than did control group members (the effect was small, $d = .34$; three months after the program, there were no group differences in symptomatic behavior). This result underscores the importance of designing preventive interventions carefully, with a specific purpose in mind, and with thoughtful consideration of the potential consequences (intended or unintended!) of the program (Mann et al., 1997; Mann & Burgard, 1998).

Pitfall #2: Teaching "Eating Disorders 101"

Results of the Mann et al. study (1997) and other initial studies of eating disorders prevention (Carter et al., 1997; Killen et al., 1993; Smolak, Levine, & Schermer, 1998) led to concerns that eating disorders prevention programs might inadvertently "do more harm than good" (Carter et al., 1997) by increasing knowledge about program-specific content (e.g., purging techniques) without altering unhealthy attitudes (e.g., body dissatisfaction, drive for thinness) that motivate women to engage in disordered eating practices (Berel & Irving, 1998b; Cohn & Maine, 1998). One can imagine the consequences of such a program; a young woman who learns about dieting, bingeing and purging "skills," yet remains dissatisfied with her body shape and driven to be thin may choose to binge and purge as a means to achieve an "ideal" body.

In addition to providing participants with disordered eating strategies, prevention programs might inadvertently encourage disordered eating by utilizing persons in recovery who model the positive consequences of eating disordered behaviors. For example, the panelists who led the Stanford prevention program (one of whom continued to engage in bulimic behaviors) were described as "poised, self-assured, attractive, and personable. Both panelists were effective speakers and held other high profile positions on campus" (Mann et al., 1997, p. 217). The description of the panelists raises the question of whether these young women taught participants about the dangers of eating disorders or about how to be successfully eating disordered (Cohn & Maine, 1998). Prevention programs must avoid presenting eating disorders in a socially desirable light, either by instructing participants about eating disordered behaviors or relying on presenters or facilitators who may not be healthy role models.

Pitfall #3: Decontextualizing Eating Disorders and Related Problems

Most prevention programs include a discrete sociocultural "component" that emphasizes the roles of peers, family, and media in promoting preoccupation with weight and shape. Education about sociocultural influences often is one among a number of discrete lessons that focus on multiple, seemingly orthogonal contributors to eating disorders, including biological factors (e.g., genetic basis of body weight, set-point theory, pubertal development), attitudinal factors (e.g., body dissatisfaction, self-esteem), and behaviors (e.g., restrictive dieting, bingeing). By presenting contributing factors as discrete, prevention programs decontextualize eating disorders—and conceptualize them as the result of disconnected "parts" of people and the system in which they live, rather than as an interconnected "whole." In turn, a decontextualized view of eating disorders may contribute to programs that fall prey to pitfalls #1 and #2; individuals will take away lessons about eating disorder symptoms and how to use them to succeed in a context where beauty and thinness are valued for women.

From a feminist perspective, a decontextualized, individual-level approach is simplistic and inauthentic, and results in attributing eating disorders to deviance within the person, rather than the disordered cultural context in which that person exists (Bordo, 1993; Piran, 1999b). From a feminist perspective, women's issues with food and weight are grounded in cultural notions of beauty that are, in turn, founded in a patriarchal system wherein women derive power from their ability to attract and maintain connections to men (Bordo, 1993; Brumberg, 1997; Chernin, 1981; Fallon, Katzman, & Wooley, 1994; Faludi, 1991; Freedman, 1986; Schoenfielder & Wieser, 1983; Wolfe, 1991). Some feminists argue that eating disorders can be conceptualized as understandable, creative (albeit self-injurious) adjustments to unrealistic and unhealthy cultural norms and values (Bordo, 1993). Conceptualized in this manner, prevention might involve channeling energy into subverting cultural norms by finding new ways for girls and women to acquire and exercise power, control, and creativity (Piran, 1999a, 1999b). By interweaving personal, interpersonal, and sociocultural factors, we legitimize the individual's power and suggest that the self-destructive energy involved in the eating disorder can be translated into solutions that emphasize taking constructive action to combat unhealthy influences that exist outside of the individual.

Pitfall #4: Failure to Evaluate Outcomes

Most published eating disorders prevention studies have come from the academic community. However, many creative efforts to prevent eating disorders have come from outside of academe, from nonprofit organizations and other grassroots efforts (Striegel-Moore & Steiner-Adair, 1998). For the most part, these non-academic groups lack the expertise, time, and financial resources to conduct outcome research. For this reason, many, if not most prevention efforts that originate at the level of the community go without evaluation (Irving, 1997). Including an outcome evaluation—even a simple tool—is crucial for a number of reasons; we must find out if what we are doing *works* and which approaches work better than others; more importantly, we must make sure that programs do no harm (Irving, 1997). It is important that we learn from and not repeat the problems and pitfalls described by those who have contributed to the dialogue on prevention thus far (Mann & Burgard, 1998).

FEMINIST POSSIBILITIES

In the remainder of this chapter, I review promising efforts to prevent eating disorders and body weight and shape preoccupation, with an emphasis on programs that have avoided problems and pitfalls by adhering to feminist principles. Below, I review programs that attempt to prevent eating disorders and related problems by promoting acceptance of diverse body shapes (Irving, 1998), teaching young women how to challenge unhealthy media messages (Berel & Irving, 1998a, 1999; Irving, DuPen, & Berel, 1998; Levine et al., 1999; Posavac et al., in press; Stice et al., 2000; Stormer & Thompson, 1995), and adopting a "relational" approach to promoting healthy body image (Friedman, 1999a; Piran, 1999a, 1999b, 1999c).

Promoting Size Acceptance: The EDAP Puppet Program for Elementary School Children

Those who study prejudice agree that the seeds of bigotry are sown early and that efforts to prevent prejudice should target children before negative attitudes about members of stigmatized groups are firmly established (Carter & Rice, 1997; Rooney-Rebeck & Jason, 1986). Stereotypes about body shape are observed in children as young as six and become better defined with age (Brylinsky & Moore, 1994; Caskey & Felker, 1971; Staffieri, 1967). Anti-fat attitudes are similar—structurally and politically—to other forms of prejudice such as racism, sexism, and homophobia, and weightism remains one of the few "acceptable" prejudices (Brown, 1989; Steiner-Adair & Vorenberg, 1999). Anti-fat attitudes are accompanied by increased fear of becoming fat; studies indicate that girls' concern with their own weight emerges between the ages of 9 and 11 (Flannery-Schroeder & Chrisler, 1996; Koff & Rierdan, 1991; Shapiro, Newcomb, & Loeb, 1997). Efforts to *prevent* anti-fat attitudes and body dissatisfaction (i.e., rather than *change existing* prejudicial or self-derogatory attitudes) should take place *before* such attitudes are established (Smolak, 1999); before girls develop a well-articulated "thinness schema," or belief that thinness is necessary for attractiveness and personal success (Smolak, Levine, & Schermer, 1998; White, Mauro, & Spindler, 1985).

Because children spend a significant portion of their day in school and because classrooms provide children with the opportunity to interact and develop relationships with dissimilar others (including those from stigmatized groups), the school environment is an opportune venue in which to introduce programs to prevent prejudicial attitudes. School-based programs have been used successfully to promote cross-race friendships (Carter & Rice, 1997) and reduce gender-related stereotypes (Gash & Morgan, 1993). Writers who adopt a feminist perspective argue that similar programs might be used to prevent stereotypes and discrimination on the basis of body size (Irving, 1998; Steiner-Adair & Vorenberg, 1999).

During the 1998–1999 school year, my students and I implemented an educational program to reduce prejudice about body shape and weight in elementary school children. The program, developed by Eating Disorders Awareness and Prevention (EDAP, Inc.),[2] uses life-sized, multiethnic puppets to target children grades K–5, before anti-fat attitudes and body dissatisfaction are firmly entrenched. Although the puppet program has been in existence for several years, its impact had not been evaluated formally.

The puppet program addresses attitudes associated with the development of eating disorders; specifically, the three goals of the puppet program are to promote in children: (1) a healthy self-concept, (2) healthy attitudes about food and eating, and (3) acceptance of their own bodies and diverse body shapes generally. The puppets (created by Next Door Neighbors, an organization that develops puppet programs to help children cope with familial and social pressures) speak about issues of body acceptance, dieting, and emotional distress in developmentally appropriate language that children can understand (Pabst, 1996).

The program includes three shows or "scripts" (two for grades 4–5, one for grades K–3) and features four puppet characters: *Josh*, a European-American boy who is teased by his peers for being fat; *Tamika*, an African-American girl who is Josh's best friend and source of support; *Heidi*, a European-American girl who is preoccupied with her weight and what she eats; and *Ms. Helen*, an African-American teacher who helps the children cope with being teased and teaches them what to do when they feel sad, lonely, or bad about themselves. The scripts teach children that, under normal conditions, human body shapes are diverse, that families and peers should not exert unreasonable pressures concerning weight and shape, and that teasing of, discrimination against, and dislike of overweight people are forms of prejudice that can have devastating effects. The performance of one script lasts 15 to 20 minutes and is followed by 10 to 20 minutes of questions (fielded by the puppets) on messages presented in the script. Teachers are provided with educational information for themselves and fun follow-up class activities for the children that are designed to provide further reinforcement of the messages presented in the scripts (Pabst, 1996).

From January to May of 1999, my undergraduate students[3] performed the puppet program at 12 schools in the southwest region of Washington state. Elementary school audiences ranged in size from 30 to 250 students; the program reached approximately 2,400 children. We are in the process of developing tools to evaluate the puppet program and its impact. Currently, evaluation tools include a program evaluation completed by students after the puppet performance and a body figure rating scale administered either before the performance (i.e., as a pre-test) or after the performance (i.e., as a post-test).

The program evaluation is administered in the classroom by teachers; my students collect these evaluations approximately one week after the performance. On this evaluation, children indicate what they liked about the puppet show, which puppet they liked best and why, and what they thought the puppet show was trying to teach them. Children also are asked to "draw a picture of the puppet show." To-date, student evaluations have been completed by 152 children; of these children, 126 (83%) responded to the question "Which puppet do you like best?" Of these respondents, 36% reported liking "Josh" (i.e., the boy who is teased for being fat) best, 36% reported liking Tamika (Josh's friend), 14% reported liking Heidi, and another 14% reported liking Ms. Helen best. Students reported that they like Josh best because (among other things) "he was fat and strong," "he shared his feelings and acted good," "he was a cool friend to other people," and "he looked like me." We were pleased that a considerable proportion of children reported having greatest affection for Josh, a child who was stigmatized by peers because of his size, and we hope that this and similar programs might discourage teasing by increasing empathy for persons who are ridiculed for being "different."

The figure rating scale (Brylinsky & Moore, 1994) is administered to children in the classroom by my students. This scale consists of drawings of a large (endomorph), medium (mesomorph), and thin (ectomorph) figure; each figure is evaluated on six bipolar adjective pairs (e.g., "cute/ugly," "teased/not teased," "friends/no friends," "lazy/works hard," "not stupid/stupid," and "happy/sad"). Positive and negative adjectives are presented on the extreme ends of the scale, and, to avoid response bias, positive and negative adjectives appear on both the right and the left side of the scale. The order of drawings is counterbalanced to control for order effects. Students are instructed to rate each body shape on the six adjective pairs on a five-point scale. Specific instructions were as follows: "Look at the little girl, do you think she is teased, not teased, or somewhere in between?" until the six adjective pairs were completed.

The figure rating scale has been completed by 44 fifth grade girls from two classes. The scale was administered as a pre-test in one class ($n = 20$) and as a post-test in a second class ($n = 24$). Mean comparisons of large, medium, and thin body shapes were conducted at pre-test (i.e., with respondents who completed the scale as a pre-test) and at post-test (i.e., with respondents who completed the scale as a post-test); in addition, pre-post differences were calculated on the six adjective pairs for each body shape. At pre-test, the large body shape was evaluated less favorably than the medium body shape on all six adjective pairs; the thin body shape was evaluated less favorably than the medium body shape on four of six adjective pairs. At post-test, the large body and thin body shapes were evaluated less favorably than the medium body shape on only three of the six adjective pairs (cute/ugly, teased/not teased, and happy/not happy). Pre-post test comparisons revealed that, compared to children who completed the figure rating scale as a pre-test, students who completed it as a post-test rated the large figure as *cuter*, as *having more friends*, and as *more hard working*. Fifth grade girls evaluated medium body shapes more favorably; however, participation in a puppet program that encourages acceptance of diverse body shapes was associated with more favorable attitudes toward large body shapes.

Obviously, a "one-shot" intervention is unlikely to prevent the development of anti-fat attitudes; however, the puppet program offers a promising approach to preventing weightist attitudes in children before they develop highly resistant prejudicial attitudes and firmly entrenched attitudes about their own body shape and weight.

Knowledge = Power: Media Education as Prevention

Feminist writers were among the first to identify the media as a contributor to women's unhappiness and subordinate status (Faludi, 1991; Freedman, 1986; Kilbourne, 1977, 1994; Wolfe, 1991); it is not surprising, therefore, that feminists also have been the first to promote media literacy and media activism as tools to improve the lives of girls and women (Berel & Irving, 1998b; Irving, 1999; Levine & Smolak, 1998). Proponents of media literacy as a strategy to prevent eating disorders argue that critical viewing skills may reduce the degree to which women internalize social beauty standards and, consequently, prevent the development of body dissatisfaction and disordered eating (Berel & Irving, 1998b; Levine et al., 1999). There is a precedent for using media education to modify unhealthy attitudes and behavior; in children, media literacy programs have been used successfully to reduce intentions to use alcohol (Austin & Johnson, 1997) and to increase critical attitudes toward violent media (Voojis & van der Voort, 1993).

There is growing empirical evidence that images of thinness in the media contribute to body weight and shape preoccupation and disordered eating practices (Levine & Smolak, 1996; Stice & Shaw, 1994; Stice, Schupak-Neuberg, Shaw, & Stein, 1994). However, it is only recently that researchers have studied the impact of interventions designed to use media literacy and media activism to promote critical thinking about and resistance to media messages. Below, I review (brief and long-term) programs that use media education as a tool to prevent eating disorders and body weight and shape preoccupation.

Brief Interventions. Irving, DuPen, and Berel (1998) compared the impact of a 50-minute media literacy program to no-intervention among 10th grade girls enrolled in English classes. One class (*n* = 24) was assigned to the media literacy program; students in a second class (*n* = 17) served as the control group. The program was based on the premise that teaching girls to become more active, critical consumers of appearance-related media may help to prevent the internalization of societal beauty standards, the development of body dissatisfaction, and ultimately, the development of disturbed eating practices (Berel & Irving, 1998b; Stice, 1994). The program, led by an 11th grade girl, consisted of watching and discussing an excerpt from Jean Kilbourne's 1995 film "Slim hopes: Advertising and the obsession with thinness," after which participants were taught skills for challenging media internally—by questioning derogatory self-thoughts in response to the media, and externally—by asking critical questions about the media and engaging in media activism. Measures of body satisfaction and critical thinking about the media were administered immediately after the program. Compared to the control group, students who participated in the media literacy program reported less internalization of the thin beauty standard and lower perceived realism of media images; however, the groups did not differ on measures of body satisfaction. In a replication of this program with a larger sample and additional follow-up assessments, increased critical thinking skills were found to decrease over the course of the school year (Irving, DuPen, Green, & Cody, 1998).

Berel and Irving (1998a, 1999) compared the impact of three forms of this same media literacy intervention (versus a no intervention control) on media skepticism and body image in a sample of 110 college women. Led by a graduate student, the program consisted of watching and discussing an excerpt from Jean Kilbourne's film "Slim hopes: Advertising and the obsession with thinness," after which participants either: (a) learned skills for questioning derogatory self-thoughts in response to the media (cognitive-behavioral condition), (b) learned skills for asking critical questions about the media and engaging in media activism (media activism condition), or (c) engaged in an unstructured discussion (minimal intervention condition). A control group completed measures but did not participate in the intervention. Measures of body satisfaction and critical thinking about the media were administered immediately after the program. The two interventions were similar to the minimal treatment control condition in decreasing two aspects of media skepticism—perceived *realism* and perceived *similarity* of media images.

In a similar program, Stormer and Thompson (1995) assigned 112 college women to either: (a) a 30-minute psychoeducational program and discussion concerning how the media manipulate women's bodies in order to present "perfect" images, and how to challenge the negative impact of the media by reminding oneself of their deceptive methods; (b) a 30-minute control condition that provided information on nutrition, exercise, stress management, and dental hygiene, or (c) no intervention. Participants completed surveys immediately before and after the program. Compared to no program or the control condition, women in the psychoeducational media education program reported decreases in appearance- and weight-related anxiety and reduced internalization of the sociocultural ideal of beauty after the 30-minute intervention.

Heidi Posavac and colleagues (in press) examined the ability of a brief media education program to buffer college women "at risk" from the potential negative impact of the media. Female undergraduates with moderate to high body dissatisfaction were randomly assigned to one of four psychoeducational interventions: (a) "Artificial Beauty," (b) "Genetic Realities," (c) Combined (Artificial Beauty + Genetic Realities), or (d) "Parenting Skills." The first three interventions were intended to promote greater body acceptance and critical thinking about media. After completing the intervention, participants viewed slides of fashion models or automobiles. Participants completed pre- and post-test measures; post-test measures included body esteem and a list of thoughts that they had while watching the slides. Participants exposed to fashion models reported greater body dissatisfaction than those exposed to automobiles; however, the negative impact of exposure to the models was lessened by participation in a media education intervention.

Longer-term Programs. Stice and colleagues (in press) invited 30 undergraduate women (10 intervention, 20 delayed intervention) to participate in a three session program to improve body image. During the three sessions, participants were invited to help develop an ostensive "body acceptance program" for high school girls. Guided by a psychologist and an undergraduate student, participants discussed ways that teens can avoid internalizing the thin ideal; topics addressed included the origins of the thin ideal, how it is perpetuated, the impact of the ideal, and who benefits from the thin ideal. As part of their involvement, participants engaged in a counter-attitudinal role-play and completed a counter-attitudinal essay in which they provided reasons for challenging the thin ideal. Measures were completed at baseline, post-intervention, and one-month post-intervention. At post-test, the intervention group reported reduced thin-ideal internalization, body dissatisfaction, and dieting; these changes remained at the one-month follow-up.

Perhaps the most extensive effort to teach young women to be critical, active consumers of appearance-related media is the GO GIRLS!™ (Give Our Girls Inspiration and Resources for Lasting Self-esteem) program, a media education program developed by EDAP ("GO GIRLS!™ Program Provides Inspiration," 1998). The program provides high school girls with adult women mentors who teach them to promote responsible advertising and to advocate for more positive, diverse images of youth in the media

(Levine, et al., 1999). The program is unique in its emphasis on "social marketing" (i.e., how to use the media in a "prosocial" manner to bring about healthier attitudes and behavior). The program educates participants about marketing strategies; at the same time, it is highly personal, and participants keep journals in which they apply program material to their personal lives. The goals of the GO GIRLS!™ program are to provide young women with the tools they need to: (a) become more accepting of diverse body weight and shapes, including their own, (b) become more critical viewers of the media, and (c) voice their opinions to the companies they frequently support.

The 15-week format requires that 8–10 interested students meet once a week with an adult woman mentor. After a core curriculum that addresses the link between the media and body image/eating disorders and principles and strategies of social marketing, each group designs a "project" that they will execute during the remainder of the 15-week program. Projects may involve interviewing representatives of the advertising industry, writing business letters, developing marketing concepts, and making presentations to advertisers to propose a change in their marketing strategies (e.g., a group in Seattle met with clothing merchandisers from several large department stores and proposed that they use mannequins of diverse shapes and sizes). Results from the first phase of pilot testing revealed that young women were satisfied with the program, believed that the program improved their critical thinking abilities, provided tools for reacting to the media, and increased participants' confidence in expressing their opinions (Levine et al., 1999). The program was not successful, however, in boosting confidence and reducing weight and shape preoccupation. The GO GIRLS!™ curriculum and outcome evaluation tools have been modified to address empowerment and weight and shape preoccupation better. Currently, additional data are being collected at sites across the country.

Feminist Relational Approaches

The most comprehensive work in the area of eating disorders prevention has been completed in Canada by clinical psychologist Niva Piran (1996, 1999a, 1999c) and counselor and public health educator Sandra Susan Friedman (1994, 1999a, 1999b). Both Piran and Friedman have adopted a feminist, relational approach: Piran is best known for her prevention work in an elite ballet school in Toronto, Ontario; Friedman is the author of "Girls in the '90s" (recently renamed "Just for Girls" in time for the new millennium), a widely-used program that utilizes an education and support group format to "help girls safely navigate the rocky road through adolescence and avoid pitfalls such as eating disorders and preoccupation with weight" (Friedman, 1999a, cover page). The work of each of these women is highlighted below.

Transforming culture in a high-risk setting: Niva Piran. Since 1989, Dr. Niva Piran, Director of the Counseling Program at the University of Toronto, has been engaged in a systemic prevention program delivered at an elite residential ballet school for students aged 10–18. Piran's work in this setting illustrates the importance of responding to the unique needs of a community when developing a prevention intervention. Prior to implementing any intervention, Piran spent a great deal of time meeting with and observing students, faculty, and staff in an effort to understand the school's values, norms, and expectations (Piran, 1996, 1999a). By the time Piran began her preventive intervention, she understood the culture from the perspective of all of its members (especially students); in addition, she had developed strong, trusting relationships with faculty, staff, and students.

The preventive intervention, delivered by Piran, consisted of ongoing interventions with school administrators, staff, and meetings with age- and grade-cohesive groups of students. Based on feminist and self-in-relation theories, the program attempted to "create a school environment where students felt comfortable with the processes of puberty and growth and believed in their right to feel both safe and positive in their diverse bodies" (Piran, 1996, p. 8). Piran's intervention included changing policies about how students were evaluated by teachers, how teachers instructed their classes, and how peers spoke with each other about body weight and shape (e.g., a student "monitor" delivered violations to students "caught" teasing other students about their weight). These policy changes ensured that the intervention would affect all components of the cultural system.

Three evaluations of all 7th–9th grade and 10th–12th grade students were conducted across the 10-year implementation period (in 1987, 1991, and 1997). Outcome data included self-report measures of disturbed eating practices (Piran, 1999a, 1999c). Across the three evaluations, an impressive linear decline was observed in the rate of disturbed eating practices in successive cohorts of 7th–8th and 11th–12th grade students, which suggests that, over the course of the ongoing intervention, the school's "culture" shifted in a healthier direction (Piran, 1999a, 1999c). In addition to reporting quantitative data, Piran has described the impact of the intervention through qualitative data, from notes taken during her meetings with students (Piran, 1996). Below, I provide an example of the empowering impact that the program had on student participants.

A group of girls victoriously described how they dealt with a negative comment from their dance teacher. The teacher told a girl in the group that she was getting "chunky," actually violating rules about teachers' behaviors that were agreed upon in staff meetings as part of the prevention program. The particular rules that this teacher violated were that teachers were not allowed to make any comments about their students' body shapes, and that they were not allowed to treat students' bodies disrespectfully. Indignantly, the girl responded by telling the teacher that she was in a growth spurt and that restricting her nutritional intake at this time could threaten both her health and her growth. Failing to get the message, her teacher continued to insist that she do something about her weight. Risking altercation with the teacher, her peers formed a strong and united supportive network around her and insisted that the teacher retract this dangerous perspective. Following the class they approached another staff person requesting that the incident in the class be explored. With administrative support, the system was able to effect a change in attitude. The teacher has not repeated these comments. (Piran, 1999a, p. 152)

Piran's work suggests that, in order for prevention to be effective, there must be honest and consistent communication between different members of the social system in which girls live. Indeed, this work provides insight into why interventions that focus on one component of the "system" may fail to produce favorable outcomes. A program that promotes body acceptance and critical analysis of the media could easily be nullified if other sociocultural pressures (e.g., from peers and family) that encourage girls and women to dislike their bodies remain unchanged.

Decoding the "Language of Fat": Sandra Friedman. "Just for Girls" (formerly "Girls in the '90s," Friedman, 1994, 1999a) is a 12-week support group program for 6th and 7th grade girls that is designed to prevent weight and shape preoccupation, eating disorders, and other problems observed in middle school girls. Friedman developed the program in response to the observation that, during adolescence, girls move into a culture that is populated by "perfect" girls and women (i.e., White, attractive, and thin; women who are fat, old, handicapped, wear glasses, are pregnant or represent ethnic minorities rarely appear). The program helps girls decipher messages in the media and the community/society at large, and provides girls with a wider range of options for developing a unique identity. Over 100 individuals and agencies in Canada and the United States have adopted this program (Friedman, personal communication, June 11, 1998); however, its impact has not been evaluated.

"Just for Girls" is a "prevention" program because its primary goal is to challenge early signs of preoccupation with food or weight before they become entrenched ways for girls to interpret and respond to their experiences. The program's objectives include: (a) to help girls become aware when they are using punitive language (e.g., "I'm fat") that makes them feel bad about themselves; (b) to encourage girls to become aware of and talk about experiences that underlie their derogatory language; (c) to validate girls' experiences and the way these experiences make them feel; (d) to provide girls with an understanding of their thoughts, feelings, and behaviors in the context of healthy female development and female socialization in this culture; and (e) to provide girls with an understanding of how support groups and networks function so that they can continue to develop systems of support as they mature (Friedman, 1994, 1999a).

Groups meet after school weekly for 12 weeks; sessions are 90-minutes long. The optimal group size is six to eight girls in sixth or seventh grade. "Just for Girls" was founded in a relational understanding of female development (Jordan, 1994) that assumes that girls' sense of self evolves in connection with others. Therefore, groups rely on relational strategies (e.g., story telling, role-playing) to understand issues such as weight and shape preoccupation in order to cope with being a female/relational person in a male/separation-oriented world (Friedman, 1994, 1999a). The group operates in a drop-in format in order to keep the group from feeling like a formal "class" and to prevent girls from assuming that, if they miss one week, they cannot return to the group. The relationship between group leaders and participants is non-hierarchical, and group leaders are expected to be open to sharing some of their own experiences. At group sessions, girls are asked to remember a time in the previous week where they were "hit by a grungie" (i.e., derogatory thoughts or feelings) and to investigate what they were feeling at the time that they had these negative thoughts. Group leaders validate the experiences of girls and guide them through the process of identifying experiences that lead participants to engage in self-derogatory thinking. When possible, activities are included that allow the girls to move around or have a different experience of their bodies (e.g., yoga, relaxation, role-plays). At the end of each session, each girl is encouraged to say something positive about herself, about her abilities, or about what makes her interesting as a person.

Topics covered during the 12 weeks of the group concern the interconnected systems that make up girls' lives: (a) self, (b) feelings, (c) body, (d) family, (e) relationships, (f) school, (g) community, and (h) society (Friedman, 1994, 1999a). The group provides participants the opportunity to develop a stronger sense of *self* by reflecting on and articulating who they are, where they have come from (e.g., ethnicity, family history), what they like to do and are good at, what they need and value, and what they would like to create for themselves in the future. *Feelings* are addressed by having girls expand their feeling "vocabulary" so that they become better aware of the emotions that may underlie the use of "the language of fat" and other destructive behavior. The group addresses body weight and shape preoccupation by educating group members about their *bodies*—how they work, how they grow and change during puberty, the role of proper nutrition in healthy development, and what happens to the body when it is deprived of adequate nutrition, particularly during this important time of development. *Family* is addressed by validating girls' experiences and by trying to help girls find ways to express their feelings and opinions to their parents in a manner that will encourage their parents to be responsive and supportive. *Relationships* are addressed by getting group participants to recognize and articulate their own responses to others, as well as validating those skills that they use to support and empower each other. *School-*

related issues are addressed by validating and naming girls' experience in the school setting, including experiences with sexual harassment.

The "Just for Girls" program, although less systemic and comprehensive than Piran's work, provides an alternative for those who work outside of a school "system," yet want to provide some options for prevention. One hopes that the future will bring opportunities to evaluate the impact that this popular and widespread program has had.

SUMMARY AND CONCLUSION

Feminist psychology is charting a new course in eating disorders prevention by offering innovative perspectives and corresponding strategies and redressing problems that have slowed progress in this field. Feminist psychology has brought to awareness the role that sociocultural factors play in the development of eating disorders (Gilbert & Thompson, 1996), and this understanding is informing primary, secondary, and tertiary prevention efforts. Indeed, the influence of feminist psychology is seen currently in programs that seek to prevent eating disorders by promoting acceptance of diverse body shapes (Irving, 1998), teaching young women how to challenge and subvert unhealthy media messages (Berel & Irving, 1998a, 1999; Irving, DuPen, & Berel, 1998; Levine et al., 1999; Posavac et al., in press; Stice et al., 2000; Stormer & Thompson, 1995), and using relational approaches to promote the development of healthy body image (Friedman, 1999a, Piran, 1999a, 1999b, 1999c).

While feminist psychology offers promising new directions for eating disorders prevention, we must avoid the pitfalls outlined earlier (e.g., lack of clarity regarding program goals and strategies) and remain mindful of the potential pitfalls of feminist-informed interventions. As feminists, we must remain aware of our personal investment in a culture that rewards thinness and stigmatizes fatness (Rothblum, 1994) and ever vigilant regarding the impact that this may have on our work. We must consider and outline constructive ways to respond to feelings of guilt (e.g., for "buying into" cultural norms) and powerlessness (e.g., at being asked to challenge cultural norms) that might result from feminist-informed interventions that emphasize sociocultural influences and empowering oneself to challenge such influences.

Equipped with an awareness of personal, political, and methodological resources for and obstacles to the goal of preventing eating disorders, feminist psychology is charting a new course in efforts to create a cultural context where girls and women are acknowledged and appreciated for who they are rather than what they look like.

NOTES

The elementary school puppet program and the high school media literacy project (Irving, DuPen, & Berel, 1998) were supported in part by grants from the Southwest Washington Forward Thurst (SWIFT), the Washington Institute for Mental Illness Research and Training (WIMIRT), and the Washington State University Department of Psychology and College of Liberal Arts (the Meyer Fund Faculty Project Award).

1. Consistent with the position of the National Association to Advance Fat Acceptance, the term "fat" is used in this chapter because it is descriptive and does not imply a medical condition (e.g., "obese") or deviation from a cultural ideal (e.g., "overweight").

2. Eating Disorders Awareness and Prevention, Inc. (EDAP) is a national, nonprofit organization located in Seattle, Washington. For more information about EDAP and its mission, or to learn more about the puppet program or the Go-Girls!™ curriculum, contact EDAP at (206) 382-3587.

3. Student performers included Amy E, Brodhead, Deanna Green, Stephen Jarman, Georgianna Jones-Williams, Katherine Ritter, and Suzanne Ryan, all undergraduate students in the psychology program at Washington State University in Vancouver, WA. Kris Bluett, a professional with *Tears of Joy Puppet Theatre*, trained student puppeteers.

REFERENCES

Albee, G. W., & Gullotta, T. P. (1986). Facts and fallacies about primary prevention. *Journal of Primary Prevention, 6*, 207–218.

American Psychiatric Association (1994). *Diagnostic and statistical manual of mental disorders* (4th ed.). Washington, DC: Author.

Austin, E. W., & Johnson, K. K. (1997). Effects of general and alcohol-specific media literacy training on children's decision making about alcohol. *Journal of Health Communication, 2*, 17–42.

Becker, A. E., Grinspoon, S. K., Klibanski, A., & Herzog, D. B. (1999). Eating disorders. *New England Journal of Medicine, 340*, 1092–1098.

Berel, S., & Irving, L. M. (1999, March). *In their own voice: College women's subjective experience of a program to prevent weight and shape preoccupation*. Paper presented at the 24th Annual Conference of the Association for Women in Psychology, Providence, RI.

Berel, S. R., & Irving, L. M. (1998a, March). A media literacy approach to the prevention of preoccupation with weight and shape. In L. M. Irving (Chair), *Feminist approaches to the prevention of preoccupation with weight and shape*. Symposium presented at the meeting of the Association for Women in Psychology, Baltimore.

Berel, S., & Irving, L. M. (1998b). Media and disturbed eating: An analysis of media influence and implications for prevention. *Journal of Primary Prevention, 18*, 415–430.

Bordo, S. (1993). *Unbearable weight: Feminism, western culture, and the body*. Berkeley, CA: University of California Press.

Brown, L. S. (1989). Fat oppressive attitudes and the feminist therapist: Directions for change. *Women & Therapy, 8* (3), 19–30.

Brown, L. S. (1994). *Subversive dialogues: Theory in feminist therapy*. New York: Basic Books.

Brumberg, J. J. (1997). *The body project: An intimate history of American girls*. New York: Random House.

Brylinsky, J. A., & Moore, J. C. (1994). The identification of body build stereotypes in young children. *Journal of Research in Personality, 28,* 170–181.

Carter, C., & Rice, C. L. (1997). Acquisition and manifestation of prejudice in children. *Journal of Multicultural Counseling and Development, 25,* 185–194.

Carter, J. C., Stewart, D. A., Dunn, V. J., & Fairburn, C. G. (1997). Primary prevention of eating disorders: Might it do more harm than good? *International Journal of Eating Disorders, 22,* 167–172.

Caskey, S. R., & Felker, D. W. (1971). Social stereotyping of female body image by elementary school age girls. *Research Quarterly, 42,* 251–255.

Chernin, K. (1981). *The obsession: Reflections on the tyranny of slenderness.* New York: Harper & Row.

Cohn, L., & Maine, M. (1998). More harm than good. *Eating Disorders: The Journal of Treatment and Prevention, 6,* 93–95.

Drenowski, A., Yee, D. K., Kurth, C. L., & Krahn, D. D. (1994). Eating pathology and DSM-III-R bulimia nervosa: A continuum of behavior. *American Journal of Psychiatry, 151,* 1217–1219.

Durlak, J. A. (1997). *Successful prevention programs for children and adolescents.* New York: Plenum.

Dykens, E. M., & Gerrard, M. (1986). Psychological profiles of purging bulimics, repeat dieters, and controls. *Journal of Consulting and Clinical Psychology, 54,* 283–288.

Enns, C. Z. (1997). Basic principles of feminist therapy. In C. Z. Enns (Ed.), *Feminist theories and feminist psychotherapies: Origins, themes, and variations* (pp. 1–34). Binghamton, NY: Harrington Park Press.

Fallon, P. A., Katzman, M. A., & Wooley, S. C. (Eds.). (1994). *Feminist perspectives on eating disorders.* New York: Guilford Press.

Faludi, S. (1991). *Backlash: The undeclared war against American women.* New York: Anchor Books.

Flannery-Schroeder, E. C., & Chrisler, J. C. (1996). Body esteem, eating attitudes, and gender-role orientation in three age groups of children. *Current Psychology: Developmental, Learning, Personality, 15,* 235–248.

Franko, D. L., & Orosan-Weine, P. (1998). The prevention of eating disorders: Empirical, methodological, and conceptual considerations. *Clinical Psychology: Science and Practice, 5,* 459–477.

Freedman, R. (1986). *Beauty bound.* Lexington, MA: Lexington Books.

French, S. A., Story, M., Downes, B., Resnick, M. D., & Blum, R. W. (1995). Frequent dieting among adolescents: Psychosocial and health behavior correlates. *American Journal of Public Health, 85,* 695–701.

Friedman, S. S. (1999a). *Just for girls: Facilitators manual.* Vancouver, BC: Salal Books.

Friedman, S. S. (1999b). Discussion groups for girls: Decoding the language of fat. In N. Piran, M. P. Levine, & C. Steiner-Adair (Eds.), *Preventing eating disorders: A handbook of interventions and special challenges* (pp. 122–133). Philadelphia: Brunner/Mazel.

Friedman, S. S. (1994). *Girls in the '90s: Facilitators manual.* Vancouver, BC: Salal Books.

Gash, H., & Morgan, M. (1993). School-based modification of children's gender-related beliefs. *Journal of Applied Developmental Psychology, 14*, 277–287.

Gilbert, S., & Thompson, J. K. (1996) Feminist explanations of the development of eating disorders: Common themes, research findings, and methodological issues. *Clinical Psychology: Science and Practice, 3*, 183–202.

GO-GIRLS!™ program provides inspiration (1998, Winter). *EDAP Matters: Newsletter of Eating Disorders and Prevention, Inc.*, 1, 8.

Grilo, C. M., Devlin, M. J., Cachelin, F. M., & Yanovski, S. Z. (1997). Workshop report: Report on the National Institutes of Health (NIH) workshop on the development of research priorities in eating disorders. *Psychopharmacology Bulletin, 33*, 321–333.

Gustafson-Larson, A. M., & Terry, R. D. (1992). Weight-related behaviors and concerns of fourth-grade children. *Journal of the American Dietetic Association, 92*, 818–822.

Hotelling, K. (1999). An integrated prevention/intervention program for the university setting. In N. Piran, M. P. Levine, & C. Steiner-Adair (Eds.), *Preventing eating disorders: A handbook of interventions and special challenges* (pp. 208–221). Philadelphia: Brunner/Mazel.

Huon, G. F. (1994). Towards the prevention of dieting-induced disorders: Modifying negative food- and body-related attitudes. *International Journal of Eating Disorders, 16*, 395–399.

Irving, L. (1997, Winter). Research: A tool to prove that EDAP makes a difference. *EDAP Matters: Newsletter of Eating Disorders and Prevention, Inc.*, 1, 4–5.

Irving, L. M. (1998, March). Promoting size-acceptance in children: The EDAP puppet prevention project. In L. M. Irving (Chair), *Feminist approaches to the prevention of preoccupation with body weight and shape*. Symposium presented at the meeting of the Association for Women in Psychology, Baltimore.

Irving, L. M. (1999). A bolder model of prevention: Science, practice, and activism. In N. Piran, M. P. Levine, & C. Steiner-Adair (Eds.), *Preventing eating disorders: A handbook of interventions and special challenges* (pp. 63–83). Philadelphia: Brunner/Mazel.

Irving, L. M., DuPen, J., & Berel, S. (1998). A media literacy program for high school females. *Eating Disorders: The Journal of Treatment and Prevention, 6*, 119–131.

Irving, L. M., DuPen, J., Green, D., & Cody, C. (1998, August). *A media literacy program for high school females*. Poster presented at the meeting of the American Psychological Association, San Francisco.

Jordan, J. V. (1994). A relational perspective for understanding women's development. In J. V. Jordan (Ed.), *Women's growth in diversity: More writings from the Stone Center* (pp. 9–24). New York: Guilford Press.

Kater, K. J. (1998). *Healthy body image: Teaching kids to eat and love their bodies too!* Seattle: Eating Disorders Awareness and Prevention, Inc.

Kilbourne, J. (1994). Still killing us softly: Advertising and the obsession with thinness. In P. A. Fallon, M. A. Katzman, & S. C. Wooley (Eds.), *Feminist perspectives on eating disorders* (pp. 395–418). New York: Guilford Press.

Kilbourne, J. (1977). Images of women in TV commercials. In J. Fireman (Ed.), *TV book* (pp. 293–296). New York: Workman.

Killen, J. D. (1996). Development and evaluation of a school-based eating disorder symptoms prevention program. In L. Smolak, M. P. Levine, & R. H. Striegel-Moore (Eds.), *The developmental psychopathology of eating disorders: Implications for research, prevention, and treatment* (pp. 313–339). Mahwah, NJ: Lawrence Erlbaum.

Killen, J. D., Taylor, C. B., Hammer, L. D., Litt, I., Wilson, D. M., Rich, T., Hayward, C., Simmonds, B., Kraemer, H., & Varady, A. (1993). An attempt to modify unhealthful eating attitudes and weight regulation practices of young adolescent girls. *International Journal of Eating Disorders, 13,* 369–384.

Killen, J. D., Taylor, C. B., Telch, M. J., Saylor, K. E., Maron, D. J., & Robinson, T. N. (1986). Self-induced vomiting and laxative and diuretic use among teenagers: Precursors of the binge-purge syndrome? *Journal of the American Medical Association, 255,* 1447–1449.

Koff, E., & Bauman, C. L. (1997). Effects of wellness, fitness, and sport skills programs on body image and lifestyle behaviors. *Perceptual and Motor Skills, 84,* 555–562.

Koff, E., & Rierdan, J. (1991). Perceptions of weight and attitudes toward eating in early adolescent girls. *Journal of Adolescent Health, 12,* 307–312.

Leon, G. R., Fulkerson, J. A., Perry, C. L., & Cudeck, R. (1993). Personality and behavioral vulnerabilities associated with risk status for eating disorders in adolescent girls. *Journal of Abnormal Psychology, 102,* 438–444.

Levine, M. P. (1994). Beauty myth and the beast: What men can do and be to help prevent eating disorders. *Eating Disorders: The Journal of Treatment and Prevention, 2,* 101–113.

Levine, M. P., Piran, N., & Stoddard, C. (1999). Mission more probable: Media literacy, activism, and advocacy as primary prevention. In N. Piran, M. P. Levine, & C. Steiner-Adair (Eds.), *Preventing eating disorders: A handbook of interventions and special challenges* (pp. 3–25). Philadelphia: Brunner/ Mazel.

Levine, M. P., & Smolak, L. (1998). The mass media and disordered eating: Implications for prevention. In W. Vandereycken & G. Noordenbos (Eds.), *The prevention of eating disorders* (pp. 23–56). New York: New York University Press.

Levine, M. P., & Smolak, L. (1996). Media as a context for the development of disordered eating. In L. Smolak, M. P. Levine, & R. H. Striegel-Moore (Eds.), *The developmental psychopathology of eating disorders: Implications for research, prevention, and treatment* (pp. 235–237). Mahwah, NJ: Lawrence Erlbaum.

Maloney, M. J., McGuire, J., Daniels, S. R., & Specker, B. (1989). Dieting behavior and eating attitudes among children. *Pediatrics, 84,* 482–489.

Mann, T., & Burgard, D. (1998). Eating disorders prevention programs: What we don't know *can* hurt us. *Eating Disorders: The Journal of Treatment and Prevention, 6,* 101–103.

Mann, T., Nolen-Hoeksema, S., Huang, K., Burgard, D., Wright, A., & Hanson, K. (1997). Are two interventions worse than none? Joint primary and secondary prevention of eating disorders in college females. *Health Psychology, 16,* 215–225.

Moreno, A. B., & Thelen, M. H. (1993). A preliminary prevention program for eating disorders in a junior high school population. *Journal of Youth and Adolescence, 22,* 109–124.

Nasser, M., & Katzman, M. (1999). Eating disorders: Transcultural perspectives inform prevention. In N. Piran, M. P. Levine, & C. Steiner-Adair (Eds.), *Preventing eating disorders: A handbook of interventions and special challenges* (pp. 26–43). Philadelphia: Brunner/Mazel.

Neumark-Sztainer, D., Butler, R., & Palti, H. (1995). Eating disturbances among adolescent girls: Evaluation of a school-based primary prevention program. *Society for Nutrition Education, 27,* 24–31.

Pabst, M. (1996, Spring/Summer). EDAP Prevention Puppet Project. *EDAP Matters: Newsletter of Eating Disorders and Prevention, Inc., 1,* 5.

Phelps, L., Dempsey, M., Sapia, J., & Nelson, L. (1999). The efficacy of an eating disorder school-based prevention program: Building physical self-esteem and personal competence. In N. Piran, M. P. Levine, & C. Steiner-Adair (Eds.), *Preventing eating disorders: A handbook of interventions and special challenges* (pp. 163–174). Philadelphia: Brunner/Mazel.

Pike, K. M., & Striegel-Moore, R. H. (1997). Disordered eating and eating disorders. In S. J. Gallant, G. P. Keita, & R. Royak-Schaler (Eds.), *Health care for women: Psychological, social, and behavioral influence* (pp. 97–114). Washington, DC: American Psychological Association.

Piran, N. (1996). The reduction of preoccupation with body weight and shape in schools: A feminist approach. *Eating Disorders: The Journal of Treatment and Prevention, 4,* 323–333.

Piran, N. (1998). A participatory approach to the prevention of eating disorders in a school. In W. Vandereycken & G. Noordenbos (Eds.), *The prevention of eating disorders* (pp. 173–186). New York: New York University Press.

Piran, N. (1999a). On the move from tertiary to secondary and primary prevention: Working with an elite dance school. In N. Piran, M. P. Levine, & C. Steiner-Adair (Eds.), *Preventing eating disorders: A handbook of interventions and special challenges* (pp. 256–269). Philadelphia: Brunner/Mazel.

Piran, N. (1999b). The reduction of preoccupation with body weight and shape in schools: A feminist approach. In N. Piran, M. P. Levine, & C. Steiner-Adair (Eds.), *Preventing eating disorders: A handbook of interventions and special challenges* (pp. 148–159). Philadelphia: Brunner/Mazel.

Piran, N. (1999c). Eating disorders: A trial of prevention in a high-risk school setting. *Journal of Primary Prevention, 20,* 75–90.

Posavac, H. D., Posavac, S. S., & Weigel, R. G. (in press). Reducing the impact of media images on women at risk for body image disturbance: Three targeted interventions. *Journal of Social and Clinical Psychology.*

Powers, P. S., & Johnson, C. L. (1999). Small victories: Prevention of eating disorders among elite athletes. In N. Piran, M. P. Levine, & C. Steiner-Adair (Eds.), *Preventing eating disorders: A handbook of interventions and special challenges* (pp. 241–255). Philadelphia: Brunner/Mazel.

Rooney-Rebeck, P., & Jason, L. (1986). Prevention of prejudice in elementary school students. *Journal of Primary Prevention, 7,* 63–73.

Rothblum, E. D. (1994). "I'll die for the revolution but don't ask me not to diet": Feminism and the continuing stigmatization of obesity. In P. Fallon, M. A. Katzman, & S. C. Wooley (Eds.), *Feminist perspectives on eating disorders* (pp. 53–76). New York: Guilford Press.

Sadker, J. M., & Sadker, D. (1994). *Failing at fairness: How America's schools cheat girls*. New York: Guilford Press.

Schoenfielder, L., & Wieser, B. (Eds.). (1983). *Shadow on a tightrope: Writings by women on fat oppression*. San Francisco: Aunt Lute Books.

Shapiro, S., Newcomb, M., & Loeb, T. B. (1997). Fear of fat, disregulated eating, and body esteem: Prevalence and gender differences among eight- to ten-year old children. *Journal of Clinical Child Psychology, 26,* 358–365.

Shisslak, C. M., & Crago, M. (1994). Toward a new model for the prevention of eating disorders. In P. A. Fallon, M. A. Katzman, & S. C. Wooley (Eds.), *Feminist perspectives on eating disorders* (pp. 419–437). New York: Guilford Press.

Shisslak, C. M., Crago, M., Gray, N., Estes, L. S., McKnight, K., Parnaby, O. G., Sharpe, T., Bryson, S., Killen, J., & Taylor, C. B. (1998). The McKnight Foundation prospective study of risk factors for the development of eating disorders. In W. Vandereycken & G. Noordenbos (Eds.), *The prevention of eating disorders* (pp. 57–74). New York: New York University Press.

Silverstein, B., & Perlick, D. (1995). *The cost of competence: Why inequality causes depression, eating disorders, and illness in women*. New York: Oxford University Press.

Smolak, L. (1999). Elementary school curricula for the primary prevention of eating problems. In N. Piran, M. P. Levine, & C. Steiner-Adair (Eds.), *Preventing eating disorders: A handbook of interventions and special challenges* (pp. 87–104). Philadelphia: Brunner/Mazel.

Smolak, L., & Levine, M. P. (1994). Critical issues in the developmental psychopathology of eating disorders. In L. Alexander & D. B. Lumsden (Eds.), *Understanding eating disorders* (pp. 37–60). Washington, DC: Taylor & Francis.

Smolak, L., Levine, M. P., & Schermer, F. (1998). Lessons from lessons: An evaluation of an elementary school prevention program. In W. Vandereycken & G. Noordenbos (Eds.), *The prevention of eating disorders* (pp. 137–172). New York: New York University Press.

Staffieri, J. R. (1967). A study of social stereotypes of body image in young children. *Journal of Personality and Social Psychology, 7,* 101–104.

Steiner-Adair, C., & Vorenberg, A. P. (1999). Resisting weightism: Media literacy for elementary school children. In N. Piran, M. P. Levine, & C. Steiner-Adair (Eds.), *Preventing eating disorders: A handbook of interventions and special challenges* (pp. 105–121). Philadelphia: Brunner/Mazel.

Stice, E. (1994). Review of the evidence for a sociocultural model of bulimia nervosa and an exploration of the mechanisms of action. *Clinical Psychology Review, 14,* 633–661.

Stice, E., Mazotti, L., Wiebel, D., & Agras, S. (2000). Dissonance prevention program decreases thin-ideal internalization, body dissatisfaction, dieting, negative affect, and bulimic symptoms: A preliminary experiment. *International Journal of Eating Disorders, 27,* 206–217.

Stice, E., Schupak-Neuberg, E., Shaw, H. E., & Stein, R. I. (1994). Relation of media exposure to eating disorder symptomatology: An examination of mediating mechanisms. *Journal of Abnormal Psychology, 103,* 836–840.

Stice, E., & Shaw, H. E. (1994). Adverse effects of the media portrayed thin-ideal on women and linkages to bulimic symptomatology. *Journal of Social and Clinical Psychology, 13,* 288–308.

Stormer, S. M., & Thompson, J. K. (1995, November). *The effect of media images and sociocultural beauty ideals on college-age women: A proposed psychoeducational program.* Paper presented at the meeting of the Association for the Advancement of Behavior Therapy, Washington, DC.

Striegel-Moore, R. H., & Steiner-Adair, C. (1998). Primary prevention of eating disorders: Further considerations from a feminist perspective. In W. Vandereycken & G. Noordenbos (Eds.), *The prevention of eating disorders* (pp. 1–22). New York: New York University Press.

Thelen, M. H., Powell, A. L., Lawrence, C., & Kuhnert, M. E. (1992). Eating and body image concerns among children. *Journal of Child Clinical Psychology, 21,* 41–46.

Voojis, M. W., & van der Voort, T.H.A. (1993). Learning about television violence: The impact of a critical viewing curriculum on children's attitudinal judgments of crime series. *Journal of Research and Development in Education, 26,* 133–142.

Weiner, R. (1999). Working with physicians toward the goal of primary and secondary prevention. In N. Piran, M. P. Levine, & C. Steiner-Adair (Eds.), *Preventing eating disorders: A handbook of interventions and special challenges* (pp. 285–303). Philadelphia: Brunner/Mazel.

White, D. R., Mauro, K., & Spindler, J. (1985). Development of body-type salience: Implications for early childhood educators. *International Review of Applied Psychology, 34,* 433–442.

Wolfe, N. (1991). *The beauty myth.* New York: Anchor Books.

Chapter 13

Body Image Disturbance and Disordered Eating in African-American and Latina Women

Eleanor F. Gil-Kashiwabara

A drive for thinness has been previously described as a necessary factor in the etiology of disordered eating behaviors (Polivy & Herman, 1993; Striegel-Moore, Schreiber, Pike, Wilfley, & Rodin, 1995). The construct of drive for thinness involves aspiring to a thin body ideal, placing excessive importance on thinness, and experiencing excessive fear of becoming fat. Although eating disorders such as anorexia nervosa and bulimia nervosa[1] have been largely conceptualized as drive for thinness and fear of fat, this perspective is not the only possible etiology. One alternate etiology overlaps with feminist theory and is used to understand disordered eating behaviors in women of color. This latter perspective is a major aspect of the current chapter.

Although this chapter focuses on body image disturbance[2] and disordered eating in African-American and Latina women, it begins by briefly addressing the theories of etiology from which eating disorders are traditionally conceptualized. Following this brief background, the literature on eating disorders in ethnic minority women is then introduced, reviewed, and discussed. In order to illustrate the discussion, excerpts from interviews I conducted with adolescent girls have been included. Because the chapter involves a feminist perspective, it will close with an emphasis on charting a new course toward understanding women's feelings about their bodies.

THEORETICAL OVERVIEW OF ETIOLOGY

In order to understand body image disturbance and disordered eating in women of color, it is useful to know some of the theoretical background related to their general etiology. Eating disorders, particularly anorexia nervosa and bulimia nervosa, and body image disturbance have been addressed from a variety of theoretical perspectives including psychodynamic, developmental, cognitive-behavioral, family systems, biological, and feminist theories, to name a few (Attie, Brooks-Gunn, & Petersen, 1990; Heinberg, 1996). Risk factors that have been identified include, but are not limited to, gender (mostly female), age (mostly teens and 20s), location (Westernized societies value thinness), individual personality development, certain family contexts, biogenetic predispositions, and sociocultural influences (Andersen, 1999; Attie et al., 1990). An extensive background of each eating disorder theory is beyond the scope of this chapter, however, major points from some of the better known theories will be provided as background for understanding the material in the current chapter.

Developmental Theories

A developmental perspective for understanding eating disorders and body image disturbance concerns the emergence of these difficulties in the context of childhood and adolescent developmental challenges (Attie et al., 1990; Heinberg, 1996). This perspective includes consideration of the major events faced by individuals during the life phase of adolescence. For example, developmental theories have noted the importance of puberty and maturational timing with regard to body image development. Overall empirical findings suggest that girls who mature later than their peers (i.e., menstrual cycle begins after age 14) have a more positive body image than those who reach menarche early (prior to age 11) or on time (between the ages of 11 and 14). Various explanations have been offered to interpret these findings, including the relationship between late maturation and lower levels of body fat and weight (J. K. Thompson, 1992). More recently, teasing has emerged as a developmental factor that plays an important role in body image formation (Fabian & Thompson, 1989).

Other research suggests greater evidence for a model that emphasizes synchronous stressful events occurring during puberty (e.g., synchronous onset of menstruation, dating, and academic demand) rather than a model that focuses on the timing of puberty in relation to body image disturbance (Heinberg, 1996; Levine, Smolak, Moodey, Shuman, & Hessen, 1994). Childhood sexual abuse history is another developmental stressor that has been addressed in relationship to body image and eating disturbance (Hastings & Kern, 1994; Palmer, 1995; Wooley, 1994). What is important to keep in mind with regard to developmental theories is that the emphasis is placed on understanding eating problems and body image disturbance from the context of childhood and adolescent developmental events, traumas (i.e., sexual abuse), and challenges.

Psychodynamic Theories

Several psychodynamic perspectives address the personality development of the child vulnerable to eating disorders. These perspectives include object relations, ego psychology, and self psychology (Bruch, 1973, 1978; Geist, 1985; Sugarman, Quinlan, & Devenis, 1981). Attie, Brooks-Gunn, and Petersen (1990) noted that these theories are basically developmental in nature because etiological relevance is attributed to developmental blocks occurring in early infancy and childhood. Bruch's (1973, 1978) classic writings provided a major impetus for the modern psychodynamic theorizing on anorexia nervosa. Bruch suggested that a disturbance in body image was one of the three central features of anorexia nervosa and that this disturbance reflected the female patient's equation of thinness with her sense of identity and of ownership of her body (Attie et al., 1990). Bruch also described the anorexic patient as having ego deficiencies that stem from a disturbed mother-daughter relationship and result in an adolescent with an underdeveloped sense of self and little autonomous control. An eating disorder, then, develops as a way for the adolescent to experience being effective and in control in at least one area of life (Bruch, 1984).

Psychoanalytic writings have also portrayed anorexia nervosa as a major form of narcissistic or self pathology that results from lack of parental empathic response and subsequently interferes with the child's development of a sense of wholeness and secure self-esteem (Attie et al., 1990; Bruch, 1984; Geist, 1985). In general, psychoanalytic perspectives view body image disturbance and disordered eating as reflecting underlying disturbances in personality development, with deficits related to sense of self, autonomy, and identity (Bruch, 1984).

Biological Theories

Biological perspectives have addressed genetics, neurochemistry, medical complications, medications, and other factors in relation to the onset and development of body image disturbance and disordered eating (Attie et al., 1990; Goldbloom & Kennedy, 1995; Heinberg, 1996; Kaye, 1995; Mitchell, 1995; Weiner, 1999). Genetic studies suggest that a predisposition to disordered eating may be familial in origin, however, the nature of this vulnerability and the related environmental influences remain unclear (Attie et al., 1990). Biological perspectives have questioned the relationship between affective illness (e.g., depression) and eating disorders, as well as the physiological consequences of eating disorders (e.g., effects of self-starvation physiologically reinforce the eating disorder and body image disturbance) (Attie et al., 1990; Irwin, 1993). Overall, it seems that biological perspectives offer important theoretical and empirical contributions, however, a lack of clarity exists when they are considered without integration of psychological, social, and other factors.

Sociocultural Theories

Sociocultural perspectives examine the influences of culture-wide social ideals, expectations, and experiences on the etiology and maintenance of body image disturbance and eating disorders. There is strong empirical evidence to suggest that sociocultural factors play a role in the development of body image disturbance and disordered eating in Western societies (Heinberg, 1996; Wilfley & Rodin, 1995). This perspective emphasizes that whereas familial, psychological, and other factors place certain individuals at greater risk, it is actually the cultural meanings placed on thinness and eating associated with Westernized orientations that encourage the development of body image disturbance and eating disorders such as anorexia nervosa and bulimia nervosa (Wilfley & Rodin, 1995). According to Heinberg (1996), the current (Westernized) societal standard for thinness in women is pervasive and unrealistic for the average woman. Furthermore, societal reinforcement of body image and eating problems seems to be exacerbated by the stigmatization of obesity (Heinberg, 1996; Rand & Kuldau, 1990).

In keeping with sociocultural perspectives, feminist theory[3] asserts that the Westernized culture of thinness imposes a link between self-esteem and physical attractiveness, and this relationship is reinforced by society's view that unattractiveness involves greater social negative consequences for women than men (Thompson et al., 1999). Some authors have suggested that the culture of thinness emerged as a way for patriarchal society to subjugate women effectively (Wooley, 1995). Historical analyses demonstrate that as women in North America and Europe became more liberated, and therefore more threatening to patriarchal society, an angular and more restricted body preference emerged (Thompson et al., 1999). Feminist theorists assert that the shift to a culture of thinness, which has persisted since the 1960s, served as society's means to de-emphasize the Women's Movement and re-focus women's energies into unrealistic appearance goals, which has resulted in obsessive weight control and lowered self-esteem (Thompson et al., 1999; Wolf, 1994). According to feminist theories, then, cultural constructions of gender are central to understanding and treating body image disturbance and disordered eating (Thompson et al., 1999; Wooley, 1995).

Sociocultural and feminist theories view the mass media as the primary communicator and reinforcer of the thin standard of beauty (Heinberg, 1996; Thompson et al., 1999). Because of its enormous role in maintaining the culture of thinness, it is important for mass media to be emphasized beyond the heading of "sociological risk factors" and into the realm of mechanisms of influence (Levine & Smolak, 1996). According to Levine and Smolak (1996), mass media promote and reflect images (e.g., body shapes) that embody complex themes of gender, race, class, beauty, identity, desire, success, and self-control in post-industrialized societies. Furthermore, the mass media extend into the sociocultural network (e.g., families, peers, schools), which, when combined with other factors (e.g., low self-esteem) further promotes body image and eating problems in women (Levine & Smolak, 1996). The mass media's current portrayal of the ideal woman places a high value on Whiteness and extreme thinness (Levine & Smolak, 1996; Nichter & Nichter, 1991; Thompson et al., 1999). As discussed above, such media emphasis has potentially devastating effects on the average woman who can not meet the unrealistically thin ideal. Imagine the additional complexity involved for women of color who are reminded daily via the mass media of the value placed on Whiteness in our society.

Other Theories

Body image disturbance and eating disorders have also been addressed from various other theoretical positions including family systems, cognitive-behavioral, and biopsychosocial perspectives. However, as mentioned previously, an extensive review of each theory related to body image and eating problems is beyond the scope of this chapter. Readers should be aware that there are numerous theoretical positions (in addition to those covered in this introduction) from which body image disturbance and eating disorders have been conceptualized. The background provided above is intended as a basic theoretical foundation for readers who are new to the eating disorder literature. At this point, however, the discussion will shift to address body image disturbance and disordered eating in African-American and Latina women.

WHAT ABOUT AFRICAN-AMERICAN AND LATINA WOMEN?

What happens to some of the theories described above when trying to understand body image and eating problems in women of color? In many cases, it has been assumed that traditional theories of eating disorders addressed these concerns almost exclusively in relation to European-American women. The emphasis placed on a slender body shape and low weight has long been described as a Western, culture-bound syndrome. The slim ideal is not a widespread value in non-Western traditional cultures, contributing to the general belief that disordered eating behaviors are uncommon among racial and ethnic minorities in the West (Mumford, 1993).

Much of the literature on body image disturbance and eating disorders among women of color in the United States suggests a lower incidence of eating disorders due to a different cultural standard of beauty (Altabe, 1996; Neff, Sargent, McKeown, Jackson, & Valois, 1997; Rucker & Cash, 1992; Stevens, Kumanyika, & Keil, 1994; Thompson, 1996). This different standard of beauty has been noted to involve a larger body size, greater body-esteem, and less concern about dieting, fatness, and weight fluctuations (Allan, Mayo, & Michel, 1993; Osvold & Sodowsky, 1993; Rucker & Cash, 1992; Stevens et al., 1994). However, there is a growing body of research that indicates that there have been increases in body image and eating problems among African-American and Latina women in the United States (Hsu, 1987; Pate, Pumariega, Hester, & Garner, 1992; Root, 1990; Silber, 1986; Smith & Kreji, 1991; Snow & Harris, 1989). For example, Striegel-Moore, Schreiber, Pike, Wilfley, and Rodin (1995) found the drive for thinness to be greater in African-American preadolescent girls than their European-American counterparts. There are also a few studies that have noted no differences in body image disturbance between European-American and other ethnic groups (Altabe, 1996), which suggests a greater prevalence of body image disturbance than previously reported in racial and ethnic minority women. Furthermore, Dolan (1991) noted that the prevalence of anorexia nervosa and bulimia nervosa in women of color is estimated to range from 1% to 4%, depending on the individual's age, ethnicity, and location. In addition, clinicians' beliefs that prevalence is lower among women of color may result in significant underestimation of the prevalence rate in this population (Dolan, 1991).

Themes Identified in the Body Image/Eating Disorder Literature Pertaining to Women of Color

In reviewing the research reports of the existence of and increases in disordered eating attitudes and behaviors among women of color, I identified two prominent themes that emerged as explanations. The first theme addresses the relationship between acculturation levels and disordered eating attitudes and behaviors. Stated differently, this theme identifies a relationship between the increased rate of disordered eating and body image disturbance in women of color and a greater pressure to acculturate to White, middle-class standards of beauty (Abrams, Allen, & Gray, 1993; Pumariega, 1986; Rodin, Silberstein, & Striegel-Moore, 1985).

The second theme, which I will refer to as "combined oppression," addresses multiple oppressions in relation to body image and eating problems in women of color, including the oppression of racism and how it brings another level of complexity to these issues. This latter theme derives from a more recent emergence of literature whose authors propose a feminist/transcultural interpretation. This interpretation suggests that by construing anorexia nervosa as a body image disorder or Western culture-bound syndrome, extant models miss broader contexts and varied meanings of food refusal (Katzman & Lee, 1997). The feminist/transcultural perspective suggests that eating problems may begin as strategies for coping with various traumas including sexual abuse, racism, classism, poverty, and other difficulties (B. W. Thompson, 1992). For women of color, then, eating disorders may represent internalized means of oppression (Harris & Kuba, 1997).

Incorporating a Qualitative Perspective

In this chapter I will examine disordered eating attitudes and behaviors in women of color from the perspective of the two themes identified above. As I address first the established cultural body ideals in the European-American, Latina, and African-American populations, and then the relationship between acculturation level and eating problems, I will include interview data to allow their voices to be heard directly. The interview excerpts are based on a qualitative study I conducted with a small sample of European-American, African-American, and Latina adolescent girls who did not have a history of eating disorders. The interviews were geared toward understanding the cultural themes involved in their assessment of attractiveness. The excerpts lend a rich angle to the discussion of acculturation level in relation to body image, however, as the interviews focused on assessment of attractiveness, they are less applicable to the theme of combined oppression as it relates to the development of an eating disorder. Therefore, excerpts from the interviews will only be used to discuss established cultural body ideals and the relationship between acculturation level and disordered eating attitudes and behaviors in women of color.

Participants and Procedure

Semi-structured clinical interviews were conducted with a small sample of African-American (n = 3), Latina (n = 3), and European-American (n = 3) adolescent girls from an ethnically diverse high school in a large East Coast city. The sample represented a range of class backgrounds and ranged in age from 15 to 17 years old. All participants were born in this country and, as mentioned above, none of the participants had a history of disordered eating. Written parental and participant consent was obtained prior to the interview date. A brief demographic questionnaire was administered before beginning the interview session.

The interviews began with two inquiries: "What attributes do you believe are positive and attractive in others?" and "What attributes do you believe are positive in yourself and cause others to be attracted to you?" Due to the flexible structure of the interviews, further questioning from the investigator was guided by interviewee responses. The objective was to understand the cultural themes involved in assessment of attractiveness. The questions do not directly ask about physical attractiveness and were designed this way in order to see if physical attractiveness emerged as an important area of self assessment and assessment of others.

CULTURAL BODY IDEALS IN WOMEN OF COLOR AND EUROPEAN-AMERICAN WOMEN

European-American Cultural Body Ideals

It has been well documented that the definition of physical attractiveness for women in the United States especially includes thinness (Garner, Garfinkel, Schwartz, & Thompson, 1980; Gilbert & Thompson, 1996; Silverstein, Peterson, & Perdue, 1986; Smith & Cogswell, 1994; Wiseman, Gray, Mosimann, & Ahrens, 1992). However, despite the various ethnic minority groups represented in the United States, the pursuit for extreme thinness has been previously described as a White female phenomenon, which derives from the desire to attain a White, Western-European ideal of beauty (Root, 1990). It is a frequent practice for girls who are not overweight to engage in excessive dieting and other detrimental behaviors in an attempt to achieve this Western cultural standard of beauty (Graber, Brooks-Gunn, Paikoff, & Warren, 1994). The term "normative discontent" refers to the widespread dissatisfaction experienced by women regarding their appearance. This "normative discontent" is said to be one factor that places White women at a greater risk for eating disorders (Rodin, Silberstein, & Striegel-Moore, 1985). A 16-year-old, European-American girl named Alexa[4] shared the following about her experience with her body:

I have always been at a normal weight. It's funny because even though I know I'm not fat, I always watch what I eat. I don't necessarily diet but I am aware of what I eat because everyone around me is watching their weight or on some diet . . . like it's the "in" thing to do.

Alexa's reflection emphasizes the concept of normative discontent in that she knows she is not overweight, yet she feels compelled to watch her dietary intake. She describes herself as a "normal weight" individual, yet her tendency to watch what she eats implies dissatisfaction with her body and vulnerability to sociocultural influences ("everyone around me is watching their weight").

Body image dissatisfaction is a salient symptom of disordered eating behaviors and related definitions of body image disturbance are included among the DSM-IV (American Psychiatric Association, 1994) diagnostic criterion for anorexia nervosa and bulimia nervosa (Thompson et al.,

1999). One aspect of body image is one's perception of current body size. Dominant White values associated with desired body size and beauty ideals in women may influence women's perception of their own weight and choice of weight management approaches (Allan, Mayo, & Michel, 1993). Focus on the thin ideal as beautiful and healthy has been linked to inaccurate perception of body size in women (Allan et al., 1993; Hayes & Ross, 1987). In one study, Rucker and Cash (1992) assessed White and African-American women's perceptions of the thinness-fatness of female bodies; they found that White women's fatness perceptions related positively to weight anxiety and preoccupation, striving for thinness, and investment in appearance. Jenny, a 16 year old, European American girl provides a good example of inaccurate body size perception as she discusses a same age, European-American peer: "This friend of mine-she obsesses and is always worried about how her body looks, but she shouldn't be . . . she just doesn't need to be. She says she's fat-but she's not."

Jenny's friend is not alone in her body size misperception. Thompson, Heinberg, Altabe, and Tantleff-Dunn (1999) describe a continuum model of body image, with levels of disturbance that range from none to extreme, with most people falling close to the middle of this range and experiencing mild to moderate concern, distress, or dissatisfaction with their bodies. Previous findings suggest that the White standard of beauty influences body image disturbance to a greater extent in White women than in women of color (Rand & Kaldau, 1990; Rucker & Cash, 1992). In the next section I will elaborate on the cultural body ideals for women of color. However, I would like to close this section with another statement made by Jenny, who expressed the following about her interactions with others:

I would never think a person's body size would make them ugly, but I notice their body size . . . I wouldn't say "I can't be friends with them because they're fat" but I notice if someone is overweight when I meet them or just see someone on the street. It's just something I notice.

Jenny's statement captures the emphasis placed on thinness in our society. The White, Western-European body ideals are so pervasive in our society that even a girl like Jenny, who reported a positive body image in herself, automatically notices body size as she encounters people in her everyday life.

African-American and Latina Cultural Body Ideals

It has been reported that Black women adopt a larger ideal body size, are more satisfied with their body image, are more accepting of overweight body sizes, experience less social pressure about weight, and are therefore less likely than White women to pursue thinness and to diet (Striegel-Moore et al., 1995). In an early study, Gray, Ford, and Kelly (1987) compared a group of African-American female college students to a group of White female college students and found that fewer African-American women met the criteria for bulimia, used extensive purging methods, and exhibited negative affect associated with food and weight. Their study also supported the view that African-American women, despite weighing more on average than White women, have a more positive attitude toward their weight and body size. In a later study, Powell and Kahn (1995) found that White women reported significantly greater pressure to be thin and greater concern with dieting and weight than did Black women. Based on these results, it was suggested that adherence to African-American cultural body ideals might protect Black women from the unhealthy body image dissatisfaction associated with eating disorders (Powell & Kahn, 1995).

Allan, Mayo, and Michel (1993) reported a difference in the way that African-American and White women described attractive body size; they noted that White women emphasized a lean and athletic look, including an absence of "flab." In contrast, the African-American women described attractiveness in terms of shapeliness, the fit of clothing, some hips, and femininity (Allan et al., 1993). The following excerpt from an African-American adolescent girl named Marcy captures this acceptance of a shapelier figure and larger body size: "I weigh 150 pounds and have an average height—about 5'4, maybe 5'5. Some of my White friends seem to think I am too heavy but me and most of my Black friends have big behinds and small waists—we have been blessed with curves." Marcy's description moves beyond acceptance of a larger cultural body ideal by embracing this shapelier image ("we have been *blessed* with curves").

Rucker and Cash (1992) found, in comparing Black and White college women, that Black women were more positive in assessing their overall appearance, had fewer negative thoughts about their body, and were less concerned about dieting, fatness, and weight fluctuations. A comment made by an African-American adolescent named Angela seems to reflect less concern about body related issues: "I am not so concentrated on my body. I could spare to lose a few pounds, but there is nothing wrong with me . . . I think I look pretty." Angela's statement implies an awareness of her body ("I could spare to lose a few pounds"), however, this awareness does not seem to interfere with having a positive feeling about herself. Angela's body awareness, in other words, is not the focus of her physical self-evaluation ("there is nothing wrong with me . . . I think I look pretty").

Although fewer data have been collected on these issues from Latinas living in the United States, it has been documented that large, full-bodied women are considered healthy and of high status in many Latin American traditional cultures (Cassidy, 1991; Messer, 1989). Furthermore, Allan and colleagues (1993) described Massara's unpublished work in which she studied 99 Puerto Rican women of lower social status. She found that their perceptions of what was normal weight went beyond biomedical standards; they associated large body size with sexual desirability, health, and economic and marital success. An example of possible body ideals among Latinas can be seen in the following quote from Lucy, a 16-year-old Puerto Rican girl:

Some White girls think I have a good body but I think I'm too skinny—I'm about 5'7 and weigh around 120 to 123 pounds. My family and my Black and Hispanic friends say the opposite of what my White friends say . . . that I'm too skinny. I feel good about my body, but sometimes I get self-conscious that I might be too skinny. The guys around my way—most of them are Puerto Rican, they want girls with more meat on their bones.

Despite an awareness of the European-American standards ("some White girls think I have a good body"), Lucy's emphasis on feeling too skinny seems strongly influenced by the Puerto Rican cultural body ideal ("The guys around my way . . . , they want girls with more meat on their bones").

Based on the discussion so far, the body ideal for women of color seems to embrace a larger body as an attractive trait. Lucy further emphasizes the attractiveness of a larger body size in the following reflection:

I'm not afraid to admit if someone is pretty because you know, I don't mind. If they're fat it doesn't matter because that's not really part of it. . . . Say I was fat, I wouldn't look right cause of my face, my bones—you know, how I'm built. But someone else who was chubbier, it might look right on them. They might look really pretty and without the extra weight they would look bad. It depends on the person.

From Lucy's perspective, a larger body could add to a woman's beauty rather than take away from it. This is very different from the European-American standard that would automatically consider a larger body size to be a flaw in appearance.

Other Factors That Influence Body Image in Women of Color

One might question what other factors are valued by women of color to assess beauty if thinness is less emphasized. Neal and Wilson (1989) provided a historical account of the role skin color, facial features, and hair type have played in Black America. Their work suggested that for many Black Americans, central feelings related to intelligence, success, perceived self-worth, and attractiveness are determined by such factors as the lightness of their skin, the broadness of their nose, the thickness of their lips, and the kinkiness of their hair. Bond and Cash (1992) studied skin color and body images among African-American college women and found that although skin color did not predict various facets of body image satisfaction, it was positively related to satisfaction with overall appearance and with the face. This finding supports the implication that skin color plays a role in assessing beauty in the Black community. The following reflection shared by Angela demonstrates an emphasis on physical characteristics excluding body size in her assessment of attractiveness:

My mother said something that is rather interesting before. Most of my female friends are attractive or can be considered pretty. Most of them look very different. One of them is Egyptian and she has very dark eyes but light skin and dark hair. So, I guess I look more for people who are striking or who have odd colored eyes like turquoise rather than the standard blond hair and blue eyes type.

In the above statement, Angela has made note of skin tone, hair, and eyes as factors she looks at when determining attractiveness in her female friends. At a later point in the interview, Angela elaborated on the importance placed on hair in her family as follows:

My mother didn't really want me to put braids in my hair. And we had a big argument about it for like a year cause she said it wasn't feminine looking. And she didn't want me to cut my hair either because it used to be really long and she said I wouldn't look good with short hair—but I cut it anyway. Most of the women in my family tend to have the long hair look . . . I think she's a little disappointed that I have braids now.

In both quotes Angela made reference to her mother's observation of attractiveness, which implies a historical component in Angela's own learning about the African-American beauty ideals. Both quotes provided by Angela seem to support the perspective that appearance-related factors aside from body size might influence a woman of color with regard to her overall body image.

Another factor that should be considered with regard to women of color is the high rates of obesity among African-American and Latina women (Flynn, 1995). Whereas only 32% of White women are obese, 48% of all African-American women are obese. Latina women demonstrate comparable obesity rates to those of African-American women; 47% of Mexican-American women meet criteria for obesity (Flynn, 1995). Researchers have suggested that the cultural ideals for heavy body size may be related to the high incidence of obesity among African-American women (Flynn, 1995; Stevens, Kumanyika, & Keil, 1994). It is possible that there may be a similar relationship between body image ideals and rates of obesity among Latinas in the United States.

The above literature and interview excerpts have described a body ideal for African-American and Latina women that has been considered a possible protection against developing an eating disorder (Powell & Kahn,

1995). However, as mentioned previously, body image disturbance and eating disorders are not unheard of among women of color, and these problems are increasing in ethnic minority populations. Because body standards for women of color are not drawn from the European-American culture, the traditional European-American standards of attractiveness and beauty may be experienced as oppressive for African-American and Latina women (Harris & Kuba, 1997; Root, 1990). In the following sections I will address some of the reasons why women of color, in some cases, are vulnerable to the European-American cultural body ideal. The role of oppression is included in this discussion.

THE RELATIONSHIP BETWEEN ACCULTURATION LEVEL AND DISORDERED EATING ATTITUDES AND BEHAVIORS IN WOMEN OF COLOR

Acculturation level is one factor that may contribute to body image and eating related concerns in African-American and Latina women. Acculturation refers to the process an ethnic group goes through in adopting the social patterns and cultural traits of another people (Negy & Woods, 1992). Evidence suggests that the increased rate of disordered eating in women of color especially affects those girls who experience more pressure to acculturate to White, middle-class standards of beauty (Pumariega, 1986; Rodin, Silberstein, & Striegel-Moore, 1985). The essence of this concept is that protective factors (e.g., different cultural body ideal) may not hold in cases where ethnic minority individuals are subject to the standards of the dominant society. The devaluation of non-Western European originated groups has resulted in an ethnic identity development stage that tends to involve a rejection of the culture-of-origin during adolescence in order to gain acceptance from mainstream society. This stage leaves an individual with a lost sense of identity and without a feeling of specialness. These difficulties, combined with the corresponding timing of both the ethnic identity stage and the developmental vulnerability to eating disorders suggests that "protective factors" in women of color are limited in their explanatory value when trying to understand these issues in African-American and Latina women (Root, 1990).

Other factors that influence women of color to acculturate into the White American mainstream include an increase in the social, vocational, and economic opportunities available to this group. These opportunities are the source of many pressures for women of color, including a feeling of responsibility to correct negative images and stereotypes of their ethnic groups (Abrams, Allen, & Gray, 1993). Subsequently, the pressure to act and look like the mainstream cultural images may increase among women of color in an attempt to gain acceptance from the dominant society (Root, 1990). Physical appearance, especially smaller body size, may become an essential ingredient in gaining acceptance and feeling accepted. In addition, the devaluation of racial features, foods, rituals, and manners by the dominant group may lead some African-American and Latina women to react against stereotypes by adopting European-American standards. Some women of color adopt the White standards of beauty because attributes that are equated with success are based to a large extent on women's appearance, almost exclusively appearance characteristics that epitomize the White, Western-European ideal of beauty. An eating disorder may develop as a way to gain acceptance and cope with issues of identity (Root, 1990).

Various researchers have documented a relationship between acculturation levels and disordered eating attitudes and behaviors. In a study of 16- to 18-year-old White and Latina girls in this country, Pumariega (1986) found a significant correlation between eating attitudes as measured by the Eating Attitudes Test (EAT) scores and level of acculturation. Silber (1986) conducted a study that nicely demonstrates the role of acculturation in this area. He studied seven minority adolescents with anorexia nervosa (five Latina; two African-American), most of whom were children of professional, upper-middle-class parents who were achievement oriented. The Black adolescents were essentially the only Black adolescents in their peer group, and they were enrolled in highly competitive, predominantly White, exclusive private schools. They expressed disappointment regarding their "big" (athletic) bodies and felt an obligation to "correct the image of Blacks." The Latina girls had a similar background, with the added stress of having recently arrived in the United States. Therefore they experienced a sense of loss in relation to a peer group, extended family, familiar culture, and homeland. Silber noted that the process of acculturation played a key role in the development of anorexia nervosa in these individuals because their low self-esteem and overwhelming desire to be accepted caused them to seek assimilation into the mainstream by adopting extreme measures to attain the thin standard of beauty in the United States.

In a sample of middle to upper-middle class White and Black female college students, Abrams, Allen, and Gray (1993) found that weight loss efforts and body dissatisfaction were significantly associated with actual weight among Black but not White students and were more frequent in Blacks who rejected Black identity and idealized White identity. In my research, I interviewed an African-American adolescent named Tanya who grew up and went to school in a White community throughout her childhood and early adolescence before moving to an area where she could attend a school with a more integrated racial and ethnic student population. The following statement from Tanya depicts a possibly acculturated view on how she feels about her body:

I never had a problem with my body because I have always been thin, and I knew that was the way you should be. . . . But now that I'm in this school, I see a difference. This is the most integrated school I have ever been in, and I notice that the Black guys like curvier girls and the Black girls want to have hips. . . . they want to be fuller. My other schools were all White. . . . I was the only Black student in honors classes . . . I know I could get away with being bigger in this school but I still want to be relatively thin.

Growing up in a White community may have exacerbated the pressure Tanya may have experienced to acculturate to mainstream standards of beauty. Her desire to stay "relatively thin" is different from the earlier perspective shared by Marcy who described the African-American women in her community as being "blessed with curves." These two views are a good illustration of the way in which acculturation might influence one's body image. Tanya, who expressed concern with maintaining her thinness, did experience more pressure to adopt mainstream standards of beauty. Tanya's experience is in contrast to Marcy's, who grew up in a neighborhood that was mostly comprised of African Americans.

Tanya also experienced some familial pressure to be thin. During her interview, she relayed the following regarding the messages she received about body size from the women in her family:

All of the women in my family were very thin when they were younger. My mom is heavier now—well she's had four children. She says she is going to lose the weight so she can fit into all of her old clothes. . . . I think the women in my family talk about it a lot—especially with each other—they'll say "oh you are heavier now than you were before." I think they probably do put a lot of emphasis on it (thinness).

Both quotes from Tanya's interviews imply that she has probably experienced a pressure to adhere to the mainstream ideal from her school/community environment and her family. Tanya's body size happened to correspond with the thin ideal, which may have influenced her self-report of a positive body image in herself ("I never had a problem with my body because I have always been thin"). However, her awareness of thinness as something that is valued is evident (". . . . and I knew that [thin] was the way you should be"). It is possible that if Tanya had a larger body size, paired with the same pressure to adhere to the thin standard of beauty, she may have been at risk of responding similarly to the participants in Silber's (1986) study described previously.

The personal definition of beauty and resulting self-image is initially guided by a woman's culture of origin. It may become problematic when her cultural concept of beauty is in conflict with the definition put forward by another culture (Harris & Kuba, 1997). According to the acculturation perspective, a woman's level of acculturation may have a great influence on how this conflict is dealt with and resolved.

COMBINED OPPRESSION

A Description of Combined Oppression

What happens when women develop body image concerns and eating problems despite being raised in families and communities in which thinness is not considered a criterion for beauty? This question supports the exploration of alternate meanings related to the development of eating problems. B. W. Thompson (1992) proposed that body image and eating concerns might arise as logical solutions to problems rather than as problems themselves. The women she interviewed developed eating problems as they tried to cope with a variety of traumas. B. W. Thompson found links between eating problems and a number of oppressions including sexual abuse, classism, sexism, heterosexism, and poverty. This finding shifts the focus away from portraying body image and eating disturbances as issues of appearance to seeing them as ways that women cope with trauma. To propose that women, regardless of ethnic background, might respond to trauma in this way helps to alleviate the possibility that stereotyping (i.e., African Americans and Latinas = larger body preference) will occur in the study of eating disorders in ethnic minority women. Trauma, in other words, makes all women vulnerable, and the stressors that induce disordered eating behaviors in White women might also cause these behaviors in women of color. However, women of color have the additional oppression of racism, which increases the complexity of body image and eating disturbance in ethnic minority women.

The perspective just described, which I refer to as "combined oppression," is rooted in feminist and transcultural theories and emphasizes the point that little effort is made to deconstruct the local meaning of food refusal, let alone the nature of gender roles within a society. Rather than examining cultural forces other than drive for thinness, attention is often sidetracked to debates about whether or not the criteria for culture-bound syndrome are met in Western and non-Western countries (Katzman & Lee, 1997). Stated differently, conceptualizations that depend on the body size and fat phobia of the individual may lose the message embodied in the struggle between eating and not eating. An overreliance on weight preoccupation as an etiologic variable in anorexia nervosa risks being inappropriately ethnocentric and overlooks the universal power of food refusal as an attempt to free oneself from the control of others.

Validating Multiple Oppressions: Looking Beyond the Oppression of Sexism

Katzman and Lee (1997) asserted that it is difficult to separate the meaning of self-starvation from gender because anorexia nervosa's categorization of being an illness of women and girls may not simply reflect a disorder that results from the internalization of popular media messages, but rather a fairly universal difference for males and females in the task of establishing self-definition and self-control. Therefore, anorexia nervosa may be a disorder that is linked more to power imbalances than gender (Katzman & Lee, 1997). Sexism itself involves a power differential, however, there are other power differentials such as the oppression of racism that may play a role in the development of an eating disorder. The combined oppression perspective posits that each power differential be considered in relation to an individual's development of eating problems. An overemphasis on gender and sexism, or any other singular variable, in relation to disordered eating excludes other aspects of the individual's experience, and therefore supports an incomplete and biased framework from which to understand the individual's eating struggles. It may be helpful to think of each power differential as a level of oppression in which the individual may be struggling to assert personal control.

Racism as a Level of Oppression

The power imbalance that is conveyed to women of color through their experiences with racism adds another level of complexity to the consideration of issues of eating disturbance. The traditional European-American standards of attractiveness and beauty, as mentioned previously, may be experienced as oppressive for many women, but particularly for women of color whose own body standards are not drawn from the European-American culture (Harris & Kuba, 1997; Root, 1990). One aspect of racial oppression for women of color may involve internalization of European-American norms, which results in devaluation of culture-of-origin norms of attractiveness and subsequently devaluation of self. A woman of color might unconsciously think that the only way to achieve mainstream standards is through changing her body because other aspects of her physical being (e.g., skin color, ethnic features) can not be changed. Espin (1997) described how this aspect of oppression affects the experience of ethnic minority women: "Women, regardless of ethnic group, are taught to derive their primary validation from their looks and physical attractiveness. The inability of most non-white women to achieve prescribed standards of beauty may be devastating for self-esteem" (Espin, 1997, p. 87).

The oppression of racism, as well as other levels of oppression, in relation to disordered eating in women of color may very well look like an attempt to be accepted into the mainstream via appearance oriented goals. Although it is important to attend to the symptoms of disordered eating that may emerge for women of color as they cope with this aspect of oppression (racism), it is especially important for clinicians and researchers to understand the often varied meanings of these symptoms. This understanding includes an awareness that the meanings attached to eating disorder symptoms likely extend beyond the realm of struggles with appearance and into the realm of internal conflict based on the oppressive experience of racism.

According to Harris and Kuba (1997), "An eating disorder can be understood as a metaphor for a young woman's self-destructiveness related to a rejection of her ethnoculture" (p. 342). In this situation, the woman of color may go back and forth between adopting the view of the oppressor (when she is dieting severely) and opposing this view (during binges). Her heavy body may be a metaphor for her wish to be recognized and acknowledged by a rejecting culture that happens to define beauty as thinness. Women of color, therefore, may exhibit the typical symptoms of an eating disorder, but the symptoms may involve meanings that reflect the actual conflict that is presented and experienced through the oppression of racism.

A Flexible Conceptualization of Eating Dysfunction

Whether disordered eating attitudes and behaviors manifest themselves in the form of food refusal or bulimic-like symptoms, it is suggested that a more flexible approach be considered in understanding the etiology of these symptoms. Katzman and Lee (1997) proposed a shift to thinking about eating disorders as "problems of disconnection, transition, and oppression, rather than dieting, weight, and fat phobia" (p. 392). So, for example, eating problems may be utilized in order to cope with the disconnection felt from leaving one's homeland and therefore losing a reference group or community with whom to identify. Any change in gender, country, or social class boundaries as well as other personal life changes can trigger this sense of disconnectedness. Eating dysfunction can also be used to cope with the transition of moving between two worlds and the oppression encountered in this process, which includes prejudices and a sense of isolation. Indeed, a negative acculturative experience may qualify as a traumatic experience in itself! Abandoning the narrowly defined etiology that emphasizes fear of fatness in favor of new meanings that allow for the experiences of oppression, transition, and disconnectedness will enable a broader recognition of personal experience and may introduce a new vocabulary for prevention as well as recovery.

WHAT NEXT? CONCLUSIONS AND SUGGESTIONS FOR CHARTING A NEW COURSE TOWARD UNDERSTANDING WOMEN'S FEELINGS ABOUT THEIR BODIES

In this chapter I identified and presented two major themes in the literature that relate to the incidence of and increase in body image disturbance and disordered eating in African-American and Latina women. The first theme addressed the relationship between level of acculturation and disordered eating attitudes and behaviors in women of color. The literature on acculturation level has emphasized a number of interesting conclusions, including the perspective that the increased rate of disordered eating in women of color especially affects girls who experience more pressure to acculturate to White, Western-European standards of beauty. In addition, an increase in social, vocational, and economic opportunities for women of color has been noted to influence the pressure to adhere to mainstream standards. The relationship between acculturation level and disordered eating attitudes and behaviors, as can be seen in this chapter, has been widely documented.

The second theme I identified shifted in focus to address eating problems in all women as ways women coped with trauma rather than emphasizing issues of appearance. This perspective is rooted in feminist and transcultural theories, examines the multiple oppressions experienced by women, and suggests that the oppression of racism adds another level of complexity to eating disturbances in women of color. Therefore, what may look like a typical eating disorder for women of color may actually symbolize the conflict they have experienced through the oppression of racism.

By addressing both acculturation and combined oppression in this chapter, I hope to underscore the importance of the balance between understanding the themes that may be specific to women of color in the development of body image and eating problems and being flexible regarding the conceptualization of causal factors. This means that clinicians and researchers should have an understanding of the traditional body ideals held by the culture of origin and also understand the process of acculturation and its possible effects on the ways in which women of color might perceive their bodies. In addition, researchers and clinicians must be open to the possibility that eating problems might arise from a variety of traumas, which include the experience of oppression and discrimination. Furthermore, certain acculturation levels may be more about themes of oppression, disconnectedness, and transition than simply an expression of fat phobia stemming from a desire to fit in.

This chapter has addressed some of the major issues to consider regarding women of color with body image and eating disturbance, however, there is still a scarcity of empirical data available from which to draw firm conclusions that might assist those who treat African-American and Latina women with these difficulties. When do we know to consider the issue of acculturation level as a strong factor? How do we identify issues related to the complexity of racism in the oppressive experience of an ethnic minority woman with body image and eating disturbance? These and other questions will need to be addressed and clarified.

Feminist psychologists have already made some important contributions toward charting a new course in understanding body image and eating disturbance in women of color. These contributions have especially been addressed in the discussion of combined oppression. There are several ways in which feminist psychologists might continue this course of exploration. One suggestion is in the spirit of the narrative approach to thinking and involves attending to stories of women who experience body image and eating disturbance. According to Mair (1988):

We live in and through our stories. They conjure worlds . . . Stories inform life . . . We are *lived* by the stories of our race and place. It is this enveloping and constituting function of stories that is especially important to sense more fully. We are, each of us, locations where the stories of our place and time become partially tellable. (p. 127)

Stories lend a personal perspective, and therefore have the potential for getting at other meanings behind eating disturbance. In terms of research, this may require an incorporation of qualitative techniques to our studies. A renewed interest in qualitative analytic tools has been noted (Katzman & Lee, 1997), which I hope will help to shift the frame from which issues of body image and eating disturbance in women of color are currently studied. This modification involves moving away from instruments that make inquiries about fat phobia, therefore allowing less restricted answers to emerge. As a result, psychologists will be able to obtain data based on personal stories that women tell to define themselves.

Altabe (1998) has provided a strong example of how mixed quantitative and qualitative analysis might tap other levels of complexity behind eating disturbance and body image problems in women of color and European-American women. The qualitative instrument, entitled the Physical Appearance Discrepancy Questionnaire (PADQ; Altabe, 1998), asks participants to define their culture and to list traits associated with their actual physical appearance, their ideal, and their perception of what their culture idealizes. Although this instrument does focus on culture and issues of appearance, it leaves room for the participants' own words and definitions. Altabe (1998) found issues of skin color to be relevant, and furthermore found that the differences among ethnic groups in preference for lighter skin called for expanded exploration of these issues beyond just African Americans. This particular finding might not have been tapped with an instrument that focused on fear of fatness, which demonstrates how a qualitative instrument might allow for other meanings behind eating problems to emerge.

In terms of clinical interventions, individuals might be assisted in constructing narratives or stories that help them to express their personal trauma and to empower them to become the authority of their own care (Katzman & Lee, 1997). Lee (1997) has described a feminist narrative metaphor that involves helping women to "re-author" their lives. From this perspective, a re-authoring can occur when women create alternative meanings associated with new self-narratives. The flexibility involved in this approach permits the emergence of issues related to power and control, as well as other issues that are especially relevant to the experiences of African-American and Latina women, such as marginalization, racism, and exclusion. Such flexibility with regard to both clinical and research approaches is called for in addressing these issues. In this way, mental health professionals will be more adept at both treating all populations struggling with body image concerns and disordered eating behaviors and preventing the occurrence of these problems in a diverse world, thus helping women to chart a new course toward accepting and valuing their bodies.

NOTES

1. This chapter focuses on anorexia nervosa (AN) and bulimia nervosa (BN). Unless otherwise indicated, I use the term "eating disorders" to refer to AN and BN rather than the entire spectrum of disordered eating (i.e., binge eating disorder).

2. The term "body image" has become widely accepted as one's internal representation of their own outer appearance (Thompson, Heinberg, Altabe, & Tantleff-Dunn, 1999). The term "body image disturbance," as suggested by Thompson et al., (1999), will be used as an umbrella term that includes all appearance-based subcomponents of body image. Therefore, the term "body image disturbance" refers to the complex construct of body image that may involve affective, cognitive, behavioral, or perceptual features. Examples of body image disturbance include, but are not limited to size perception accuracy, body satisfaction, and body esteem (Thompson et al., 1999).

3. Because this section of the chapter is meant to provide a brief overview of eating disorder etiology, the reader should be aware that there is a vast feminist literature proposing multiple (eating disorder) hypothesis across writers (Gilbert & Thompson, 1996). The information regarding feminist theory in this section is meant to provide the reader with a basic sense of some of the feminist theoretical underpinnings. The reader who wishes to do more extensive reading about the feminist theoretical background of eating disorders is directed to the work of Gilbert and Thompson (1996) and Fallon, Katzman, and Wooley (1994).

4. All names of participants have been changed.

REFERENCES

Abrams, K. K., Allen, L. R., & Gray, J. J. (1993). Disordered eating attitudes and behaviors, psychological adjustment, and ethnic identity: A comparison of Black and White female college students. *International Journal of Eating Disorders, 14,* 49–57.

Allan, J. D., Mayo, K., & Michel, Y. (1993). Body size values of White and Black women. *Research in Nursing and Health, 16,* 323–333.

Altabe, M. N. (1996). Issues in the assessment and treatment of body image disturbance in culturally diverse populations. In J. K. Thompson (Ed.), *Body* image, eating disorders, and obesity: An integrative guide for assessment and treatment* (pp. 129–147). Washington, DC: American Psychological Association.

Altabe, M. N. (1998). Ethnicity and body image: Quantitative and qualitative analysis. *International Journal of Eating Disorders, 23,* 153–159.

American Psychiatric Association. (1994). *Diagnostic and statistical manual of mental disorders* (4th ed.). Washington, DC: Author.

Andersen, A. E. (1999). The diagnosis and treatment of eating disorders in primary care medicine. In P. S. Mehler & A. E. Andersen (Eds.), *Eating disorders: A guide to medical care and complications* (pp. 1–26). Baltimore: Johns Hopkins University Press.

Attie, I., Brooks-Gunn, J., & Petersen, A. C. (1990). A developmental perspective on eating disorders and eating problems. In M. Lewis & S. Miller (Eds.), *Handbook of developmental psychopathology* (pp. 409–420). New York: Plenum.

Bond, S., & Cash, T. F. (1992). Black beauty: Skin color and body images among African-American college women. *Journal of Applied Social Psychology, 22,* 874–888.

Bruch, H. (1973). *Eating disorders.* New York: Basic Books.

Bruch, H. (1978). *The golden cage.* Cambridge, MA: Harvard University Press.

Bruch, H. (1984). Four decades of eating disorders. In D. M. Garner & P. E. Garfinkel (Eds.), *Handbook of psychotherapy for anorexia nervosa and bulimia* (pp. 7–18). New York: Guilford Press.

Cassidy, C. (1991). The good body: When big is better. *Medical Anthropology, 13,* 181–214.

Dolan, B. (1991). Cross-cultural aspects of anorexia nervosa and bulimia: A review. *International Journal of Eating Disorders, 10,* 67–79.

Espin, O. M. (1997). *Latina realities: Essays on healing, migration, and sexuality.* Boulder, CO: Westview Press.

Fabian, L. J., & Thompson, J. K. (1989). Body image and eating disturbance in young females. *International Journal of Eating Disorders, 8,* 63–74.

Fallon, P., Katzman, M. A., & Wooley, S. C. (Eds.). (1994). *Feminist perspectives on eating disorders.* New York: Guilford Press.

Flynn, K. (1995, August). *Body image ideals of African American and Hispanic females.* Poster presented at the annual convention of the American Psychological Association, New York.

Garner, D. M., Garfinkel, P. E., Schwartz, D., & Thompson, M. (1980). Cultural expectations of thinness in women. *Psychological Reports, 47,* 483–491.

Geist, R. A. (1985). Therapeutic dilemmas in the treatment of anorexia nervosa: A self-psychological perspective. In S. W. Emmett (Ed.), *Theory and treatment of anorexia nervosa and bulimia* (pp. 268–288). New York: Brunner/Mazel.

Gilbert, S., & Thompson, J. K. (1996). Feminist explanations of the development of eating disorders: Common themes, research findings, and methodological issues. *Clinical Psychology: Science and Practice, 3,* 183–202.

Goldbloom, D. S., & Kennedy, S. H. (1995). Medical complications of anorexia nervosa. In K. D. Brownell & C. G. Fairburn (Eds.), *Eating disorders and obesity: A comprehensive handbook* (pp. 266–270). New York: Guilford Press.

Graber, J. A., Brooks-Gunn, J., Paikoff, R. L., & Warren, M. P. (1994). Prediction of eating problems: An 8-year study of adolescent girls. *Developmental Psychology, 30,* 823–834.

Gray, J. J., Ford, K., & Kelly, L. M. (1987). The prevalence of bulimia in a Black college population. *International Journal of Eating Disorders, 6,* 733–740.

Harris, D. J., & Kuba, S. A. (1997). Ethnocultural identity and eating disorders in women of color. *Professional Psychology: Research and Practice, 28,* 341–347.

Hastings, T., & Kern, J. M. (1994). Relationships between bulimia, childhood sexual abuse, and family environment. *International Journal of Eating Disorders, 15,* 103–111.

Hayes, D., & Ross, C. (1987). Concerns with appearance, health beliefs, and eating habits. *Journal of Health and Social Behavior, 28,* 120–130.

Heinberg, L. J. (1996). Theories of body image disturbance: Perceptual, developmental, and sociocultural factors. In J. K. Thompson (Ed.), *Body image, eating disorders, and obesity: An integrative guide for assessment and treatment* (pp. 27–47). Washington, DC: American Psychological Association.

Hsu, L.K.G. (1987). Are the eating disorders becoming more common in Blacks? *International Journal of Eating Disorders, 6,* 113–124.

Irwin, E. G. (1993). A focused overview of anorexia nervosa and bulimia: Part I—etiological issues. *Archives of Psychiatric Nursing, 7,* 342–346.

Katzman, M. A., & Lee, S. (1997). Beyond body image: The integration of feminist and transcultural theories in the understanding of self starvation. *International Journal of Eating Disorders, 22,* 385–394.

Kaye, W. H. (1995). Neurotransmitters and anorexia nervosa. In K. D. Brownell & C. G. Fairburn (Eds.), *Eating disorders and obesity: A comprehensive handbook* (pp. 255–260). New York: Guilford Press.

Lee, J. (1997). Women re-authoring their lives through feminist narrative therapy. *Women & Therapy, 20* (3), 1–22.

Levine, M. P., & Smolak, L. (1996). Media as a context for the development of disordered eating. In L. Smolak & M. P. Levine (Eds.), *The developmental psychopathology of eating disorders: Implications for research, prevention, and treatment* (pp. 235–257). Mahwah, NJ: Erlbaum.

Levine, M. P., Smolak, L., Moodey, A. F., Shuman, M. D., & Hessen, L. D. (1994). Normative developmental challenges and dieting and eating disturbances in middle-school girls. *International Journal of eating Disorders, 15,* 11–20.

Mair, M. (1988). Psychology as storytelling. *International Journal of Personal Construct Psychology, 1,* 125–138.

Messer, E. (1989). Small but healthy? Some cultural considerations. *Human Organization, 48,* 39–52.

Mitchell, J. E. (1995). Medical complications of bulimia nervosa. In K. D. Brownell & C. G. Fairburn (Eds.), *Eating disorders and obesity: A comprehensive handbook* (pp. 271–275). New York: Guilford Press.

Mumford, D. B. (1993). Eating disorders in different cultures. *International Review of Psychiatry, 5,* 109–114.

Neal, A. M., & Wilson, M. L. (1989). The role of skin color and features in the Black community: Implications for Black women and therapy. *Clinical Psychology Review, 9,* 323–333.

Neff, L. A., Sargent, R. G., McKeown, R. E., Jackson, K. L., & Valois, R. F. (1997). Black-White differences in body size perceptions and weight management practices among adolescent females. *Journal of Adolescent Health, 20,* 459–465.

Negy, C., & Woods, D. J. (1992). The importance of acculturation in understanding research with Hispanic Americans. *Hispanic Journal of Behavioral Sciences, 14,* 224–247.

Nichter, M., & Nichter, M. (1991). Hype and weight. *Medical Anthropology, 13,* 249–284.

Osvold, L. L., & Sodowsky, G. R. (1993). Eating disorders of White American, racial and ethnic minority American, and international women. *Journal of Multicultural Counseling and Development, 21,* 143–154.

Palmer, R. L. (1995). Sexual abuse and eating disorders. In K. D. Brownell & C. G. Fairburn (Eds.), *Eating disorders and obesity: A comprehensive handbook* (pp. 230–233). New York: Guilford Press.

Pate, J. E., Pumariega, A. J., Hester, C., & Garner, D. M. (1992). Cross-cultural patterns in eating disorders: A review. *Journal of the American Academy of Child and Adolescent Psychiatry, 31,* 802–809.

Polivy, J., & Herman, C. P. (1993). Etiology of binge eating: Psychological mechanisms. In C. G. Fairburn, & G. T. Wilson (Eds.), *Binge eating: Nature, assessment, and treatment* (pp. 173–205). New York: Guilford Press.

Powell, A. D., & Kahn, A. S. (1995). Racial differences in women's desires to be thin. *International Journal of Eating Disorders, 17,* 191–195.

Pumariega, A. J. (1986). Acculturation and eating attitudes in adolescent girls: A comparative and correlational study. *Journal of the American Academy of Child and Adolescent Psychiatry, 25,* 276–279.

Rand, C.S.W., & Kuldau, J. M. (1990). The epidemiology of obesity and self-defined weight problem in the general population: Gender, race, age, and social class. *International Journal of Eating Disorders, 9,* 329–343.

Rodin, J., Silberstein, L., & Striegel-Moore, R. (1985). Women and weight: A normative discontent. In T. B. Sonderegger (Ed.), *Psychology and gender. Nebraska symposium of motivation 1984* (pp. 267–307). Lincoln: University of Nebraska Press.

Root, M.P.P. (1990). Disordered eating in women of color. *Sex Roles, 22,* 525–536.

Rucker, C. E., & Cash, T. F. (1992). Body images, body-size perceptions, and eating behaviors among African American and White college women. *International Journal of Eating Disorders, 12,* 291–299.

Silber, T. J. (1986). Anorexia nervosa in Blacks and Hispanics. *International Journal of Eating Disorders, 5,* 121–128.

Silverstein, B., Peterson, B., & Perdue, L. (1986). Some correlates of the thin standard of bodily attractiveness for women. *International Journal of Eating Disorders, 5,* 895–905.

Smith, D. E., & Cogswell, C. (1994). A cross-cultural perspective on adolescent girls' body perception. *Perceptual and Motor Skills, 78,* 744–746.

Smith, J. E., & Krejci, J. (1991). Minorities join the majority: Eating disturbances among Hispanic and Native American youth. *International Journal of Eating Disorders, 10,* 179–186.

Snow, J. T., & Harris, M. B. (1989). Brief report: Disordered eating in Southwestern Pueblo Indians and Hispanics. *Journal of Adolescence, 12*, 329–336.

Stevens, J., Kumanyika, S. K., & Keil, J. E. (1994). Attitudes toward body size and dieting: Differences between elderly Black and White women. *American Journal of Public Health, 84*, 1322–1325.

Striegel-Moore, R. H., Schreiber, G. B., Pike, K. M., Wilfley, D. E., & Rodin, J. (1995). Drive for thinness in Black and White preadolescent girls. *International Journal of Eating Disorders, 18*, 59–69.

Sugarman, A., Quinlan, D., & Devenis, L. (1981). Anorexia nervosa as a defense against anaclitic depression. *International Journal of Eating Disorders, 1*, 44–61.

Thompson, B. W. (1992). A way outa no way: Eating problems among African-American, Latina, and White women. *Gender and Society, 6*, 546–561.

Thompson, J. K. (1992). Body image: Extent of disturbance, associated features, theoretical models, assessment methodologies, intervention strategies, and a proposal for a new DSM-IV diagnostic criteria-body image disorder. In M. Hersen, R. M. Eisler, and P. M. Miller (Eds.), *Progress in behavior modification* (pp. 3–54). Sycamore, IL: Sycamore.

Thompson, J. K. (1996). Body image, eating disorders, and obesity: An emerging synthesis. In J. K. Thompson (Ed.), *Body image, eating disorders, and obesity: An integrative guide for assessment and treatment* (pp. 1–20). Washington, DC: American Psychological Association.

Thompson, J. K., Heinberg, L. J., Altabe, M., & Tantleff-Dunn, S. (1999). *Exacting beauty: Theory, assessment, and treatment of body image disturbance.* Washington, DC: American Psychological Association.

Weiner, K. L. (1999). Multidisciplinary team treatment: Working together. In P. S. Mehler & A. E. Andersen (Eds.), *Eating disorders: A guide to medical care and complications* (pp. 27–43). Baltimore: Johns Hopkins University Press.

Wilfley, D. E., & Rodin, J. (1995). Cultural influences on eating disorders. In K. D. Brownell & C. G. Fairburn (Eds.), *Eating disorders and obesity: A comprehensive handbook* (pp. 78–82). New York: Guilford Press.

Wiseman, C. V., Gray, J. J., Mosimann, J. E., & Ahrens, A. H. (1992). Cultural expectations of thinness in women: An update. *International Journal of Eating Disorders, 11*, 85–89.

Wolf, N. (1994). Hunger. In P. Fallon, M. A. Katzman, & S. C. Wooley (Eds.), *Feminist perspectives on eating disorders* (pp. 94–111). New York: Guilford Press.

Wooley, S. C. (1994). Sexual abuse and eating disorders: The concealed debate. In P. Fallon, M. A. Katzman, & S. C. Wooley (Eds.), *Feminist perspectives on eating disorders* (pp. 171–211). New York: Guilford Press.

Wooley, S. C. (1995). Feminist influences on the treatment of eating disorders. In K. D. Brownell & C. G. Fairburn (Eds.), *Eating disorders and obesity: A comprehensive handbook* (pp. 294–298). New York: Guilford Press.

Chapter 14

Stories of Violence: Use of Testimony in a Support Group for Latin American Battered Women

Marja Booker

In recent years there has been an increasing interest in providing counseling services for culturally diverse groups of clients. Yet, very little has been written about the problems of Latin American battered women and the treatment techniques that might be helpful in addressing their experience of abuse. The existing professional literature on gender-specific violence focuses more on the traumas produced by civil wars and state sponsored terrorism (i.e., Aron, Corne, Fursland, & Zelwer, 1991; Becker, Lira, Castillo, Gómez, & Kovalskys, 1990; Bowen, Carscadden, Beighle, & Fleming, 1992; Bunster, 1993; Hollander, 1996; Lira, Weinstein, Dominguez, Kovalskys, Maggi, Morales, & Pollarolo, 1983; Lykes & Liem, 1990; Lykes, Brabeck, Ferns, & Radan, 1993; Suárez-Orozco, 1990) than by partner abuse. A beginning effort to approach this problem from the international perspective occurred in January 1999 when a whole issue of the *American Psychologist* was devoted to psychology and domestic violence around the world, although clinical treatment of battered women still received relatively little attention. Because of the scarcity of publications, I found it important to initiate a dialogue with other psychologists in order to examine the multiple levels of trauma that Latin American abuse survivors have often experienced. I will also discuss how victims can begin their healing process in women's support groups by presenting their testimonies or life stories in front of other women and I will illustrate the benefits of this technique with selected case examples.

One of the more comprehensive studies about violence, trauma, and survival has been written by Judith Herman. In *Trauma and Recovery* (1997) she looked at the intersections of state-sponsored terror and domestic abuse. She pointed out that "certain violations of the social compact are too terrible to utter aloud" (p. 1) and become unspeakable experiences of trauma. This is especially true of the atrocities committed in wartime situations by regimes that sanction state terrorism. Although men have always been viewed as the most common victims of politically motivated violence such as beating, choking, electric shock, smothering with a hood, submersion in water, and mock executions, women have not been spared these experiences. Ximena Bunster (1993) explained that in Central America women have often been injured or killed "in contexts of generalized violence" (p. 98) during massacres, attacks on churches, and burning of villages. Although she contrasted the systematic torture of women in, for instance, Pinochet's Chile with the more arbitrary war-related violence toward Central American women, there is evidence that in countries such as El Salvador women were also systematically identified and tortured by the military machine to force confessions, to obtain information, and to silence their critical voices (Amnesty International, 1991).

In Central America the most recent armed conflicts have been about distribution of land, economic resources, and political power. El Salvador, for instance, is a poor country with more than half of its population living off the land. In 1991 America's Watch reported that 70% of the rural population lived in poverty. The GNP was estimated at $900 per capita, and 20% of the people received 66% of the national income. In the countryside, 85% of the houses lacked electricity, running water, and sanitary facilities. Half of all Salvadoran children were malnourished, and only 37% of the population had access to medical care (America's Watch, 1991). The extreme poverty and the unequal distribution of resources were among the factors that led to popular demands for reform and civil unrest, which the government forces were determined to crush. With all the avenues closed to a peaceful resolution, the conflict developed into a civil war (1979–1992) that resulted in the death and disappearance of large numbers of civilians. Already by the year 1985, 750,000 people had become refugees in other countries, and another 500,000 had been displaced from their homes (Brown, 1985).

Although acts of violence committed by terrorist states have attracted the attention of human rights groups worldwide, partner abuse has remained a more hidden problem, in spite of the fact that it affects large numbers of people in all cultural, socioeconomic, and racial groups. It was not until 1994 that the Violence Against Women legislation in the United States defined domestic violence as a human rights violation (Walker, 1999). In recent years many other countries have started a more systematic study of the problem in an effort to make legislative changes and to create services for both the victims and the offenders of mate-related abuse.

In Latin America the level of family violence is quite high. There are reports that in some countries of that region roughly half of the women have been abused by men. Statistics (see Heise, Pitanguy, & Germain,

1994) show that, for instance, in Ecuador 60% of the women in a low income neighborhood of Quito were abused. In rural Mexico and Guatemala, these figures were respectively 44.2% and 49% (Heise, Pitanguy, & Germain, 1994). In a small study (Ellsberg, Caldera, Herrera, Winkvist, & Kullgren, 1999) conducted in Nicaragua, 52% of the married women revealed that they had experienced some physical violence. The study also showed that women who complained of emotional distress were six times more likely than others to report lifetime spousal violence. In El Salvador, Góngora (1997) found that over 57% of the women have been physically assaulted by their partners at some point in their lives.

Because the Central American countries have been plagued by long-lasting civil wars that have had a profound impact on family life and structure, immigrants from that area are likely to suffer from symptoms of post-traumatic stress. Aron et al. (1991) emphasized that people who live in countries where they have no protection against the violent acts of the armed forces perceive their whole environment as hostile, dangerous, and without possibilities for relief. Because there are no avenues of support for the victims of military violence, people tend to live under conditions of pervasive terror. These circumstances often promote development of significant psychological symptoms. For instance, Deborah Bowen and her colleagues (1992) reported that many women in the refugee camps of El Salvador suffer from PTSD. Their relatively small study documented that more than 50% of the respondents they interviewed in a camp near the capital had such symptoms as intrusive thoughts, dreams about the violent events, difficulty sleeping, feeling as if the past events were recurring, and avoidance of stimuli related to the abuse.

We know that war alone has a profound psychological impact on its victims, and it is easy to understand that those women who have also suffered domestic violence can be traumatized on multiple levels. At the same time, as Brinton Lykes and her research group (1993) advised, it is important to acknowledge the social dimensions of the trauma in addition to its intrapsychic impact because "the psychological effects of private and structural acts of violence and abuse are seen in individuals, families, and communities" (p. 527). This level of violence has far-reaching consequences for whole groups of people, and it is not enough to treat individual victims alone; it is equally important to denounce the social structures that support the violence. According to Comas-Diaz, Lykes, and Alarcón (1998), psychologists who ignore the meaning of ethnicity and culture or who only look for similarities in the different groups of trauma survivors are more likely to identify individual effects of trauma than are those psychologists who consider trauma in its sociohistoric and cultural context. Historicity is one of the key concepts of liberation psychology. As pointed out by its pioneers Ignacio Martín-Baró (1994) and Paulo Freire (1999), liberation can happen only when the oppression is exposed and people gain control over their own existence. Therefore, the role of the psychologist is not simply to free the client of her inner "persecutors" but to work towards changing the oppressive sociopolitical conditions that enslave her.

Testimony is a treatment technique that incorporates both the private and public aspects of trauma, as it addresses the need for inner healing and the need to denounce the wrong. In its simplest form, it is "a story that needs to be told because of the struggles it represents" (Stephen, 1994, p. 224). The telling, therefore, becomes a major curative element and a catalyst for social change, which makes testimony a useful therapeutic method for victims of violence and victims of state imposed repression. In many countries of Latin America women have bravely come forward to demand social justice and punishment for the perpetrators of human rights violations. By expecting truth and answers from those in power they as a group "carry the banners of memory and justice" (Agosín, 1993, p. 28) and often establish for themselves a new social identity that had previously been alienated by the repression (Aron, 1992).

With this background in mind, I will present two stories in this chapter: one about previously published accounts of human rights violations against women in Central America, and the other about my personal experience of family violence with Central American refugees here in the United States. To narrow the scope I will use El Salvador's political situation during the civil war and testimonies of Salvadoran women as an example of how the state-sponsored violence and domestic abuse are rooted in the patriarchal structures that support male *machismo* and subordination of women. Although not all refugees have been direct targets of state terrorism, many have witnessed its horrors. Therefore, understanding the political situation of their countries of origin sheds light on these women's inner experiences and, in many cases, their profound conviction that government structures are not to be trusted.

The stories of violence are also stories of courage and survival. Although they focus on the multiple traumas that many Central American victims of abuse have experienced, they also show that it is possible to live through even most horrendous acts of terror. In that sense, they may serve as an inspiration and promote understanding of the complex phenomenon of trauma in Latin American woman.

THE HUMAN RIGHTS STORY

The terrorist state often tries to silence the critical voice of women through different forms of abuse. Nancy Hollander (1996) explained this in her landmark article about the gendering of human rights in Latin America. "When women have spoken against extreme economic and social inequities, their protests have often been met with the wrath of the torturer's weapons as the terrorist state ruthlessly implemented an ideological cleansing of the body politic. Often women have been targets of misogynist military and paramilitary forces that abduct, murder and torture at will" (p. 42). Many experts in the field have pointed out that rape has been one of the main forms of torture used against women (Aron et al., 1991; Bunster, 1993; Hollander, 1996; Lykes et al., 1993). A telling example of this was the El Mozote massacre in 1981 when the Salvadoran security forces separated the young women and the older girls from the men and raped them repeatedly before killing them (Binford, 1996). Historically, other forms of torture against women have included use of electric shock on their vaginal and nipple areas, slicing their breasts, and inserting animals and objects in their vaginas (Hollander, 1996).

Maria Teresa Tula, a human rights activist from El Salvador, explained in her testimony how the military state inflicted pain on her and other women to get them to talk and to serve as informants for the government.

This [the questioning] went on for three days and three nights. After they administer all these psychological tortures, you get to a difficult point. They tell you, they are going to kill your whole family. They told me that they had my sister and my children and they were going to kill them all. When they tell you that, you prefer that they kill you instead of your whole family because you have already been living through torture. These are the kind of moments you don't wish on anybody, not even your worst enemy. It's terrible to endure the methods of torture they use on men, women and children, too. They even rape people. They raped me. That's how they get information. (Stephen, 1994, p. 134)

The torture of women frequently involves gender-specific strategies to weaken them psychologically. In addition to rape, it includes threats against the victim's family or doing harm to her developing fetus. This is a calculated method of terror that causes psychological trauma. Hollander (1996) described the agony of "pregnant women whose tortured bodies cannot shield the infant growing inside them and of women who go through labor surrounded by taunting and cursing soldiers" (p. 69). She also pointed out that these strategies of abuse are a brutal representation of the intersection between psychological and political processes and an extreme example of male domination of women.

For the Latin American woman whose traditional role is that of mother, the death and torture of her children becomes an unbearably painful experience. When the military state threatens the victim with the loss of her children, it hopes to exhaust her and to break her down. This process is described by a survivor in the following words:

I was tortured for four days. They put me in a room where they said I was no better than a dog. They insisted I was in charge of things I had nothing to do with. On the fourth day of being blindfolded, they took me out to the National Police. For twenty-four hours I had to sit without moving. When one group of the interrogators was tired they would send another group and question me again. They threatened to rape me, to attack my children. (Golden, 1991, p. 124)

Some victims have lost everything they had due to military violence. The grief of a mother who was able to escape from El Mozote after capture and who witnessed the murders of her family and other villagers was described by the human rights organization Tutela Legal in the following way. "In a story that has been told many times and in many places and has assumed mythic dimensions in Northern Morazán, Amaya crawled across the road and a barbed-wire fence in the blackness of the night and hid herself in a patch of maguey: there she carved a little hole in the ground and stuck her face into it so that she could mourn for her murdered family" (cited in Binford, 1996, p. 23).

A lot of families died during military attacks or as a result of torture, and the wartime conditions of poverty and flight themselves created life-threatening circumstances for others, especially the young and the sick. Many women who had to flee the military forces through the hills, experienced the same loss as Amaya.

During the forced flight I was struck by how many children died. The bodies of the children would swell from malnutrition during the month-long marches. Mothers would not even stop to bury their children except to push them aside under the brush and leave them there. (Golden, 1991, p. 48)

Some women experienced an unbelievable amount of death and terror in their personal lives, so much that it is hard to imagine how they could psychologically survive it. One of these women was Lupe.

In the past fifteen years, during the death purges, Lupe has seen her brother, a delegate of the word, murdered; her husband and her brothers fled through the hills where they slept for five years; her sister was captured; her home was surrounded by soldiers; she was interrogated by a member of the ORDEN; her daughter's godmother was assassinated; her husband's cousin was killed with machetes—chopping off parts of her body, starting with her nose. (Golden, 1991, p. 84)

As these examples show, even those Salvadoran women who were not direct victims of the military machine were often witnesses to the torture and death of others. Becker et al. (1990) have pointed out that in conditions of state sponsored violence (e.g., Chile), people had to get accustomed to such things as torture, disappearances, rape, and dead bodies lying on the road. This brought about a situation in which "the limits between reality and fantasy were disturbed as reality continually exceeded even the most pervasive fantasies. This sense of the *uncanny* (my emphasis) provided the basis for the development of chronic fear" (p. 137).

The idea of the uncanny can be applied to the Central American conditions as well. Having to live through persecution and unimaginable acts of abuse gives rise to fantasies and fears of even greater violence (Lira et al., 1983). Therefore, many victims believe that they would be killed if they were returned to their countries of origin. This type of preoccupation with violence is typical of survivors of civil wars and can be observed, for instance, in the TAT responses of Central American youth whose stories have a strong torture-assassination focus (Suarez-Orozco, 1990).

TESTIMONY AND LATIN AMERICAN BATTERED WOMEN: RECOVERING LOST VOICES

Testimony has typically been used to denounce injustices suffered by a marginalized group of people. In the United States it has its roots in the oral heritage of the Native American culture, African-American slave narratives, and orally transmitted family histories. In Latin America testimony started in revolutionary movements (Stephen, 1994). The written form of testimony, such as the testimonial novel of Miguel Barnet and the diaries of José Martí and Che Guevara, is at the other end of the continuum. According to Barnet the mission of the writer of testimonies consists of uncovering histories that have been repressed by the dominant culture and collaborating in the expression of the collective memory (cited in Yúdice, 1992).

Testimony was developed as a treatment method by Chilean psychologists Elizabeth Lira and Eugenia Weinstein to help victims of political repression. Because of the dangerous political situation in their country they wrote under the pseudonyms Cienfuegos and Monelli. Their idea was to create a record of the persons' traumatic experiences, which were later turned into formal documents about their lives and suffering. The goal was to enable the repetition of the facts so that they would serve as a trip to the past, "a trip that allows the individual to transform past experience and personal identity, creating a new present and enhancing the future" (Cienfuegos & Monelli, 1983, p. 46). The professional literature on trauma emphasizes the idea that elaboration of the past is necessary to make a new future possible because "it opens up the possibility for grief and mourning and facilitates the development of a more coherent self-image" (Becker et al., 1990, p. 142).

Agger and Jensen (1996) explained that all healing work with victims of political repression has three fundamental principles: denunciation, investigation, and treatment. According to them, testimony is a method that unifies these principles by denouncing the human rights violations, supplying new information about the repression, and having a healing effect on the witnesses. Similarly, Lykes and Liem (1990) asserted that traditional psychotherapy tends to privatize social trauma, whereas testimony provides a means for victims to regain their status as social actors and enable therapeutic catharsis.

Summarizing findings of other authors, Herman (1997) wrote about the restorative power of truth telling and the fact that testimony serves as a ritual healing, a story telling through which victims regain the world they have lost. Being able to put one's pain in words is an important part of working with survivors of trauma because the experience of pain tends to shatter the victim's language and contribute to the disintegration of her world and self (Scarry, 1985). Therefore, healing can happen when the victim is able to reclaim her language and integrate her world, her self, and her voice again.

Survivor groups have been a popular treatment modality in the United States. Yet there is no published literature about their helpfulness with foreign-born populations, such as Latin American battered women, nor about the use of testimony in them. The Latin American progenitors of the clinical technique of testimony developed it primarily for individual work, although it has been utilized in the public arena by women's groups as they have demanded political changes or tried to keep alive the collective memory of atrocities committed by repressive military governments. There is, however, literature on incest survivor groups. Some of these studies document that "telling one's story" promotes resolution of isolation and shame and enhances working through of the incest trauma (Gold-Steinberg & Buttenheim, 1993). In these groups the "telling" is usually done in a session either at the beginning or at the mid-point of the treatment. Although this technique is not necessarily used to denounce the crime of incest, its impact on the victim can resemble that of a more formal testimony.

It is my personal belief that much of the therapeutic work with Latin American spouse abuse survivors can be accomplished in support groups, which are a good forum for clients to present their testimonies. By telling her story again and again, the victim gains mastery over the traumatic experience. The group members validate her feelings of suffering and help her gain an understanding of the social, political, and psychological forces that contribute to her victimization. The commonality of the experience creates solidarity among group members and decreases the isolation that is produced by holding in secrets. In essence, testimony "promotes a new, accurate understanding of objective conditions that derives from personal experience, yet exceeds the boundaries of the individual psyche" (Aron, 1992, p. 176). In a group setting, the listeners also gain a benefit from each testimony because it helps them reflect on their own victimization. The fact that the "witness" speaks to others who have experienced similar traumas creates an atmosphere that resembles that of a public declaration of injustice. Also, although most spouse abuse victims do not have the opportunity to become politically active, many of them have gone to court and felt "publicly" validated when they were able to present their case to a judge, a representative of the social order, who provided them with protection. The stories of these court hearings are told and retold in groups frequently and form the core for the empowerment of each individual member. In addition, as clients succeed with the court procedures, they gain a sense that they can make a difference in their own lives and bring justice to situations in which they had no power before. Aron (1992) also wrote that testimony affirms "critical, ego-sustaining principles that have been compromised as a result of the traumatic experiences" (p. 178). This reinforces the victim's reality testing, her personal and social identity, and her sense of self worth.

The Latina support groups that I have been involved in both as a supervisor and as a therapist meet once a week and accept nearly anybody who wants to participate, as long as she is a victim of partner abuse. Because the groups are open, the number of members varies a lot, from one or two to 12. The women's educational level tends to be low, and they have limited economic resources. The sessions are facilitated by two female therapists. Because of the nature of the group, testimonies are often given spontaneously during introductions when new clients first come in. Therefore, each survivor's life story is repeated again and again, which makes it possible to work through the trauma gradually. The women also name their countries of origin during the introductions to establish their ethnic identities early on. In the course of the treatment, the therapists often emphasize that the group is a forum of and for its members and that the healing happens when they mobilize their individual and collective powers as women.

STORIES OF VIOLENCE: CENTRAL AMERICAN WOMEN SPEAK

The survivor testimonies usually reveal how much suffering each abuse victim has undergone at the hands of her mate. The women whose case histories are presented here have been members of my support group and have given me a permission to write about their lives. For their protection, all the names have been changed to pseudonyms and no identifying information is provided. Also, the examples are selected in a way that they describe the central dynamics or concerns of many other Latina survivors of violence. Even though they refer to specific women they are also composites of other life stories: over the years I have listened to the testimonies of many Marias, Vivianas, and Sabinas.

Although less spoken about, the trauma of these women has often been exacerbated by the political situation in their countries, and many do not wish to return to their homelands because of the conviction that without the North American system of legal protection they could be killed by their abusers. Regardless of the danger, there are women who are no longer willing to remain silent. Many of them have been in the support group for a long time and are well on their way to recovery from the painful past.

Maria came to the program after a shooting incident involving her husband. She was still hurting from the bullet wounds and traumatized by the severity of the violent episode. Although she was glad to be alive, she was anxious about the possibility that the offender would come back to "finish the job" and felt too afraid to stay in the area. She had done everything "right"; she had separated from her abuser and obtained a protection order; yet he found her and tried to kill her. Her sense of danger was heightened by the fact that he had been trained in his country's military and had served in the war a number of years. "The worst of all," she whispered, "people say that before he had been a *guerrillero* and that is really bad."

Maria stayed in the group only long enough to work through the acute trauma. Although initially reluctant to talk, she quickly opened up and received support from other members. She went through episodes of increased depression but remained hopeful that there would be an end to her suffering. She started to view the group as her "life line," the place where she could speak and be heard. By revealing the full details of her husband's violence and her anxiety about his military training, she was able to receive validation from other women and confirmation of his potential dangerousness. This helped her take maximum safety precautions and plan for a very different future than she had first envisioned. In this case, she herself had been protected from the violence of the war in her country of origin although a family member had been murdered there. Her abuser, however, was trained "to kill" in the military. This and his possible connection to the *guerrilleros* were enough to convince her that he was capable of killing her as well. This knowledge added to her trauma but made it possible for her to understand how this man who had appeared loving in the early part of the marriage now had no regard for her life: due to her commitment to separation she had literally become the target of his anger, "the enemy" whom he was trying to eliminate.

Viviana was a long-term group member who still lived with her husband because he had finished a counseling program and had not been physically violent since. According to her testimony, her problems started after her father's death when she was a young child. Her mother married again and left her with adult siblings who yelled at her, made her baby sit their children, and if anything went wrong, grabbed her by the hair or hit her with a belt. Later Viviana moved back with her mother whose spouse drank a lot and made sexual comments about her. She got involved with her present husband to get out of her home. He himself had been traumatized by abandonment, abuse, and the war in his country, and he became violent soon after the marriage.

Although Viviana had been an on-going group member, she had been absent for lengthy periods of time because her husband did not want her to be involved with women "who might put things in her head." She had been vacillating between a decision about whether to stay in the marriage or leave. Through her participation in the group she was able to become more assertive and ask for new privileges, for instance, permission to write checks. She started to set limits on her husband, and she explained to him that she should not be treated like a household object. Through her own and other members' testimonies she gained an understanding of her own and her husband's childhood traumatization. She became firm in her decision to leave, should the violence reoccur.

Sabina was referred to the group after her husband had abused her and their baby. She was an extremely nonverbal woman with no formal education. She was not able to tell much about her family. She was severely beaten and sexually abused in her childhood. The few memories she had involved images of dead bodies on the road and rapes by the soldiers who came through her village.

Sabina attended the group for quite a number of months but rarely talked. She was withdrawn and showed her understanding of the group discussion only by an occasional smile. When she talked, her responses were limited to "yes" or "no." In spite of the risk of her becoming a group scapegoat because of her inability to engage with the other women and her seeming lack of participation, I allowed her to stay because she appeared to listen intently to the other women's testimonies and slowly to make changes in her life. In her individual sessions she became more animated and showed more understanding of her own victimization. Sabina had been severely traumatized in her family of origin and by the rapes and killings around her village. The group provided for her a frame of reference through which she could examine her own situation. This task could not have been accomplished in individual sessions alone due to her difficulty in verbalizing what had happened to her. In her case, the testimonies of other victims became a critical part of her treatment.

CONCLUSION

In spite of the fact that the human rights violations in Central America have decreased significantly in the 1990s, the impact of state terrorism has been profound on many men, women, and children. For instance, battered women who seek counseling services have often suffered from multiple traumas in their families of origin, in their marriages, and in their home countries as targets and witnesses of violence and torture. It is important to remember, however, that there are circumstantial and cultural differences among Central American women and that it is necessary to evaluate each case in its own specific context. For instance, Ellsberg et al. (1999) emphasized that due to the support of women's advocacy groups, Nicaraguan women were better able to recover from the negative effects of having been raped and robbed of their children, whereas Salvadoran women who did not have such support and who suffered from a high incidence of domestic abuse became hopeless and unable to resist the violence (see Walker, 1999). Therefore, in their treatment it is important to create an atmosphere of support and to open up avenues of self-expression that have not been available before for women of underprivileged groups. Sadly enough, they often continue to be an oppressed group in the host country due to their status as poor minority women who do not speak the language of the dominant culture.

It appears that the use of testimony is beneficial because it is a technique that considers both the need for intrapsychic healing and the social denouncement of the wrong. In a group setting, the survivors are able to declare the social injustices they have suffered, receive validation, and work through the traumas of their past so that a new future is possible. This is especially important with women who have experienced domestic violence, wars, and state-sanctioned terrorism in their countries of origin and who have not been able to talk about their abuse before. For them, testimony in a group may become the vehicle that enables them to reveal the secrets behind their traumatization and begin to "speak the unspeakable" (Agosín, 1993, p. 28).

Although the use of testimony can facilitate successful working through of the trauma, produce significant symptom relief, and reinforce the victim's sense of self and social identity, it does not address her other life problems. Therefore, additional treatment strategies are often needed. For some clients, listening to the life stories of others can be depressing, and they tend to leave the group too soon. For the most traumatized clients the group can be overly stimulating or disintegrating, and it is important to provide them simultaneously with individual sessions. I have also found that the idea of the group often has to be "sold" to the clients because many Latin American victims do not initially feel comfortable with it. Therefore, it is important to educate them about how group work can promote their personal growth and how each life story is connected to the larger problem of women's subordination. Without the consciousness-raising element the group can easily lose some of its therapeutic focus.

Although testimony is not a new technique, it promotes social and political change because it returns feminist psychology to its activist roots. Its application in support groups with refugees and victims of violence charts a new course for all psychology because it brings the clinical practice where liberation is mostly needed—at the heart of poverty, oppression, and suffering. Work with refugees broadens our horizons beyond North America and helps us create solidarity between people of different races and cultures.

Latin American women have taught us that healing begins when a victim makes a meaningful connection between her individual self and the collective trauma of her community (Agosín, 1993). Therefore, it is important for feminist psychology to take an active role in helping us to understand and to safeguard the memory of this trauma in order to create a new and different future for all survivors of violence.

REFERENCES

Agger, I., & Jensen, S. B. (1996). *Trauma and healing under state terrorism.* London: Zed Books.

Agosín, M. (Ed.). (1993). *Surviving beyond fear: Women, children and human rights in Latin America.* Fredonia, NY: White Pine Press.

Americas Watch. (1991). *El Salvador's decade of terror: Human rights since the assassination of Archbishop Romero.* New Haven, CT: Yale University Press.

Amnesty International. (1991). *Women in the front line: Human rights violations against women.* New York: Amnesty International Publications.

Aron, A. (1992). Testimonio: A bridge between psychotherapy and sociotherapy. In E. Cole, O. Espin, & E. D. Rothblum (Eds.), *Refugee women and their mental health: Shattered societies, shattered lives* (pp. 173–189). New York: Haworth Press.

Aron, A., Corne, S., Fursland, A., & Zelwer, B. (1991). The gender-specific terror of El Salvador and Guatemala: Post-traumatic stress disorder in Central American refugee women. *Women's Studies International Forum, 14,* 37–47.

Becker, D., Lira, E., Castillo, M. I., Gómez, E., & Kovalskys, J. (1990). Therapy with victims of political repression in Chile: The challenge of social reparation. *Journal of Social Issues, 46,* 133–149.

Binford, L. (1996). *The El Mozote massacre: Anthropology and human rights.* Tucson: University of Arizona Press.

Bowen, D., Carscadden, L., Beighle, K., & Fleming, I. (1992). Post-traumatic stress disorder among Salvadoran women: Empirical evidence and description of treatment. In E. Cole, O. Espin, & E. D. Rothblum (Eds.), *Refugee women and their mental health: Shattered societies, shattered lives* (pp. 267–280). New York: Haworth Press.

Brown, C. (Ed.). (1985). *With friends like these: The Americas Watch report on human rights and U.S. policy in Latin America.* New York: Pantheon Books.

Bunster, X. (1993). Surviving beyond fear: Women and torture in Latin America. In M. Agosin (Ed.), *Surviving beyond fear: Women, children and human rights in Latin America* (pp. 98–125). Fredonia, NY: White Pine Press.

Cienfuegos, A. J., & Monelli, C. (1983). The testimony of political repression as a therapeutic instrument. *American Journal of Orthopsychiatry 53,* 43–51.

Comas-Diaz, L., Lykes, M. B., & Alarcón, R. D. (1998). Ethnic conflict and the psychology of liberation in Guatemala, Peru, and Puerto Rico. *American Psychologist 53,* 778–792.

Ellsberg, M., Caldera, T., Herrera, A., Winkwist, A., & Kullgren, G. (1999). Domestic violence and emotional distress among Nicaraguan women. *American Psychologist, 54*, 30–36.

Freire, P. (1999). *Pedagogy of the oppressed.* New York: Continuum.

Golden, R. (1991). *The hour of the poor, the hour of women: Salvadoran women speak.* New York: Crossroad.

Gold-Steinberg, S., & Buttenheim, M. C. (1993). "Telling one's story" in an incest survivors group. *International Journal of Group Psychotherapy, 43*, 173–189.

Góngora, A. F. (1997, April). *La verdadera y acertada revolución de las mujeres salvadoreñas.* Paper presented at the 20th Congress of the Latin American Studies Association, Guadalajara, Mexico.

Heise, L., Pitanguy, J., & Germain, A. (1994). *Violence against women: The hidden health burden.* (World Bank Discussion Papers No. 255). Washington, DC: The World Bank.

Herman, J. (1997). *Trauma and recovery: The aftermath of violence—from domestic abuse to political terror.* New York: Basic Books.

Hollander, N. (1996). The gendering of human rights: Women and the Latin American terrorist state. *Feminist Studies, 22*, 41–80.

Lira, E., Weinstein, E., Dominguez, R., Kovalskys, J., Maggi, A., Morales, E., & Pollarolo, F. (1983). *Psicoterapía y represión política.* Mexico: Siglo Veinteuno Editores.

Lykes, B. M., & Liem, R. (1990). Human rights and mental health in the United States: Lessons from Latin America. *Journal of Social Issues, 46*, 151–165.

Lykes, B. M., Brabeck, M. M., Ferns, T., & Radan, A. (1993). Human rights and mental health among Latin American women in situations of state sponsored violence. *Psychology of Women Quarterly, 17*, 525–544.

Martín-Baró, I. (1994). *Writings for a liberation psychology.* Cambridge, MA: Harvard University Press.

Scarry, E. (1985). *Body in pain: The making and unmaking of the world.* New York: Oxford University Press.

Stephen, L. (Ed.). (1994). *Hear my testimony: Maria Teresa Tula, human rights activist of El Salvador.* Boston: South End Press.

Suárez-Orozco, M. M. (1990). Speaking the unspeakable: Toward a psychosocial understanding of responses to terror. *Ethos, 18*, 353–383.

U.S. Department of State. (1986). *Country reports on human rights violations for 1985.* Washington, DC: Government Publication Office.

Walker, L. (1999). Psychology and violence around the world. *American Psychologist, 54*, 21–29.

Yúdice, G. (1992). Testimonio y concientización. *Revista de Crítica Literaria Latinoamericana, 36*, 207–227.

Part V

Feminist Activism in the Public Interest

Chapter 15

"We All Need Different Kinds of Help": Poor Women's Perspectives on Welfare Reform

Ingrid Johnston-Robledo and Renee N. Saris

For the past six decades, Aid to Families with Dependent Children (AFDC) has been our nation's primary program to assist poor families by offering income support, food stamps, and Medicaid benefits to parents and their children. Contrary to popular stereotypes, the average family on AFDC, also known as welfare, "aid," and "state," is comprised of a mother and her two children (Withorn, 1996). Approximately 50% of AFDC mothers have at least a high school diploma, most were employed before they went on the welfare rolls, and most are on welfare for two years or less (Withorn, 1996). In 1996, there were approximately 12 million individuals, primarily women and children, on AFDC (Department of Health and Human Services, 1999).

In 1996 President Clinton signed into law the Personal Responsibility and Work Opportunity Reconciliation Act, which drastically changed the welfare system. This legislation replaced the federal program of AFDC with state block grants known as Temporary Assistance to Needy Families (TANF). The bill authorized temporary, time-limited benefits, a mandatory work requirement after two years of welfare receipt, a five-year lifetime limit per family, and major reductions in Food Stamp provisions. The primary purposes of this welfare reform legislation were to reduce and discourage welfare receipt, promote job preparation and permanent involvement in the work force, and encourage heterosexual marriage. Since this legislation was passed the number of welfare recipients has dropped approximately 40% from 12 million to 7 million (Department of Health and Human Services, 1999).

As social psychologists interested in issues related to women and poverty, we are concerned about the impact of this legislation on women, their families, and their lives. In order to learn more about women's reactions to the legislation and their experiences with the transition from welfare to work we conducted a focus group with a small group of experts—four poor women, all former AFDC recipients. In the state of Connecticut where the women reside, former AFDC recipients are required to participate in Jobs First, a job placement program. They are also granted Temporary Family Assistance (TFA) for a limited time of 21 months. If the income from their jobs does not bring them above the federal poverty level, they may be eligible for supplementation of income from the state. In this chapter we will share what we learned from these women about their experiences with welfare and their perspectives on its reform (referred to generally as "the 21 month program"). We do not intend to make generalizations to all poor women from our participants' experiences; we present our focus group data in order to supplement the social science literature and to provide first hand accounts of how this legislation is impacting poor women's lives and futures. Finally, we will propose ways that feminist psychologists can become more involved in charting a new course for welfare reform.

ASSUMPTIONS ABOUT WELFARE RECIPIENTS

Social scientists have investigated the many assumptions made about the demographics, personal characteristics, and lifestyles of women on welfare (e.g., Seccombe, James, & Walters, 1998; Sparks, 1998; Task Force on Women, Poverty, and Public Assistance, 1998). Women on welfare are generally assumed to be young, African-American, and to have large families. They are said to spend their welfare checks on nonessentials such as addictive drugs and expensive clothing. People even assume that women on welfare have more children in order to increase the amounts of their monthly payments. The myth of welfare dependency holds that women on welfare remain "dependent" on the system for long periods of time and are bad role models for their children. Their defective values are said to be transmitted to their children who are then likely to become welfare recipients themselves. It is further assumed that women on welfare have never worked, do not value work, and are generally lazy.

Aside from the demographic characteristics described earlier, what do we already know about women on welfare, and how is this information different from popular assumptions? The two assumptions that have been challenged most by empirical data are that (1) most women on welfare are long-term recipients and "dependent" on the system; and (2) this dependency is a function of their personal shortcomings, such as lack of motivation and personal responsibility. Because these two assumptions may influence the treatment of women on welfare as well as the design of welfare reform programs (Salomon, 1996), it is important to review the literature that debunks these myths and thus provide accurate information about welfare recipients' lives and experiences.

Women on Welfare Are "Dependent" on the System

A popular assumption about welfare mothers is that most are long-term recipients of aid and that their "dependency" extends across generations. This "dependency" is typically attributed to personal factors such as unproductive values and behaviors as opposed to structural factors such as unemployment and inadequate wages. These values and behaviors are then assumed to be transmitted from poor women to their children.

Through the use of large longitudinal data bases, researchers have concluded that women raised in households supported by AFDC are more likely than others to become recipients as adults (Santiago, 1995) and to remain on the welfare rolls longer than those whose parents were not recipients (Pepper, 1995). However, one cannot assume that most women who were raised in AFDC households will receive welfare in adulthood. Santiago (1995) found that 75% of the women raised in AFDC households were not welfare recipients as adults, and Salomon, Bassuk, and Brooks (1996) found that two thirds of their sample of poor, homeless, and housed women on AFDC were not raised in AFDC households.

Patterns of need for assistance, like poor women's lives, are varied, dynamic, and complicated. Researchers have identified a number of psychosocial, personal, and structural variables that predict the need for public assistance. Santiago (1995) found that women who relied on AFDC for more than 50% of their individual income most likely: (a) were African-American; (b) were raised in an AFDC household; (c) experienced the disruption of a marriage; (d) resided in an area with high rates of unemployment; (e) had few years of work experience; and (f) had disabilities. These predictors were more important than other variables such as attitudes toward work. Most of the women wanted to work and were willing to work at low-wage jobs, but these jobs were either unavailable or the pay was insufficient to bring their incomes above the poverty level. Contrary to assumptions about dependency, researchers (Brooks & Buckner, 1996; Salomon, Bassuk, & Brooks, 1996; Sonenstein & Wolf, 1991) have reported that as many as two-thirds of the AFDC recipients in their samples have work histories, however the types of positions the women have held are primarily service sector, low-wage positions.

Salomon, Bassuk, and Brooks (1996) examined psychosocial and demographic variables related to patterns of public assistance among homeless and housed poor women. Most of these women had been on welfare less than five years. On average, the homeless women were on for two years and the housed women for three years. They also reported that a third of their sample had been on AFDC more than once, approximately 1.5 times, on average. Long-term recipients, those who were receiving welfare for five or more years, were more likely than short-term recipients to be the victims of physical and sexual abuse, to have problems with substance abuse, and to report limitations in normal physical functioning. Physical violence from a male partner was especially prevalent among the long-term recipients who were homeless. Factors such as recent work history, race, ages of the women when their first children were born, and being raised with a mother on AFDC did not predict length of stay on AFDC.

Kunz and Born (1996) examined patterns of first-time welfare use of women between 1987 and 1991. They found that 45% of their sample left the welfare system within one year, and 62% left within two years. The researchers attempted to predict the length of welfare assistance with two sets of variables: cultural (e.g., having acquaintances or family members who are/were AFDC recipients) and economic (e.g., education, work experience, barriers to employment). Economic variables were far more important in predicting length of welfare need than were cultural variables.

In an earlier study, Popkin (1990) examined differences between short- and long-term recipients and interviewed samples of both in order to learn about the primary concerns of welfare mothers. Participants who had been long-term recipients of AFDC were more likely than short-term users to view it as a barrier to self-sufficiency. One common concern of both groups of women was the negative impact that public assistance had had on their families. They discussed feelings of depression and humiliation, as well as the difficulties of providing for their families with such limited resources. They were also concerned that they were setting a bad example for their children.

Women on Welfare Are Lazy and Irresponsible

Findings from studies on low-income women's attitudes toward and experiences with work challenge assumptions that women on welfare are lazy and do not have experience in the workforce. These women work very hard to fulfill their child care and other domestic responsibilities and they must spend lots of time and energy managing their limited resources to provide for their families. Withorn (1996) stated that welfare benefits, on average, provide women and their families with only 60% of what they would need to live above the poverty level. Thus, these poor women need to engage in a variety of activities or survival strategies just to make ends meet each month.

Edin and Lein (1997) conducted an extensive survey of over 350 poor women who were either welfare recipients or low-wage workers. Women on welfare received an average of $565 (1991 dollars) each month. This figure included cash income and food stamps. Almost all the women reported that this money did not cover their basic needs. As a result, 77% relied on network-based strategies (e.g., contributions from family, friends, and the men in their lives). Another 50% of the women supplemented their welfare checks with some form of work. Understandably, only 5% reported these jobs to the welfare agency.

Kemp, Jenkins, and Biehl (1996) conducted focus groups with women who were either current or former recipients of AFDC to learn more about their work experiences, which were identified as domestic work, economic work, and eligibility work. When discussing domestic work the women mentioned that it was difficult to provide for their families when they were limited to food stamps to purchase groceries and to public transportation to get to the store. Women were engaged in a variety of legal and illegal economic work to make ends meet, and they were worried about the possibility of losing their welfare benefits if discovered. Eligibility work was defined as the work involved in maintaining public assistance, such as record keeping, fielding questions from social workers, and participating in work programs. The women also discussed barriers to social service office visits, such as child care arrangements and transportation. The authors concluded that low-income women's lives are busy with a variety of types of work and that they must acquire important survival skills.

The common assumption that poor women are lazy and irresponsible implies that women on welfare do not have goals for themselves and their children. In order to learn about poor women's goals and aspirations, Dill (1998) interviewed a sample of low-income, single, African-American mothers who were living in the rural south. Most participants were either current or former AFDC recipients. She found that the poor women in her sample, particularly those who had graduated from high school, viewed education as an important goal for themselves and their children. Education was regarded as a source of pride as well as the ticket to job opportunities. However, participants named multiple barriers to education including their jobs, lack of access to reliable transportation, and their responsibilities as mothers. Furthermore, even if they did complete a certificate program and were working full-time, their wages were low and they were unable to survive without supplementation from their families or some form of government assistance.

What do welfare recipients themselves think of other women on welfare? How do welfare mothers explain their own use of AFDC? In an attempt to answer these important questions, Seccombe, James, and Walters (1998) interviewed 47 European-American and African-American women who were on the welfare rolls in Florida. Participants were aware of the negative stigma attached to welfare use. They reported having heard, in a variety of settings including the grocery store and the welfare office, negative comments about welfare recipients, such as the belief that they are lazy. What was especially interesting and alarming was that the recipients themselves subscribed to negative stereotypes about welfare mothers. They tended to attribute other women's use of the system to individualistic variables such as drug use, laziness, and irresponsible behavior. However, the women used structural attributions (e.g., lack of jobs with suitable wages, lack of transportation, and broader social issues such as racism and sexism) as well as fatalistic attributions (e.g., bad luck with relationships, unintended pregnancies, and health problems) for their own welfare use.

These two assumptions, that women on welfare are dependent on AFDC and that they are lazy and irresponsible, persist despite the fact that there is little empirical evidence to support them. This is particularly disturbing because, as noted often by social scientists, reform proposals themselves may be based on these assumptions, namely that personal defects of women on welfare, rather than structural problems with the national economy, are to blame for the increasing numbers of poor families (Aaronson & Hartmann, 1996; Axinn & Hirsch, 1993; Epstein, 1997; Sidel, 1996; Task Force on Women, Poverty, and Public Assistance, 1998; Withorn, 1996). Even the language used by politicians and within the text of the legislation reflects some of these widely shared beliefs (Watts, 1997). As Mills (1996) pointed out, whereas unwed fathers who are uninvolved with their children are referred to as "absent" and the stigma attached to them is typically associated with the lack of paying child support, unwed mothers on welfare are deemed "promiscuous," "dependent" on and "addicted" to welfare, and their children are "illegitimate." In his deconstruction of the language used to describe welfare recipients and their children, Mills (1996) exposed how such language is used as a political tool to demonize poor women and to make regressive welfare reform more palatable to the public.

FROM WELFARE TO WORK

Since August of 1996 when the welfare reform legislation was passed, many women have attempted to secure full-time employment and have been removed from the welfare rolls. Much of the social science literature published since the welfare reform legislation either focuses on barriers to work and self-sufficiency or evaluation of existing workfare programs. It does not adequately address women's lived experiences with this difficult transition, which was the primary purpose of our focus group discussion. Before we present our focus group data, we review literature related to barriers to work and evaluation of programs designed to assist women with the transition from welfare to work.

Barriers

Efforts to reform welfare must take into account the barriers that many poor women face as they attempt to secure and maintain employment that will allow them to be self-sufficient. These barriers include both unique, individual factors such as education, job skills, and health status, and common, structural factors such as child care, transportation, and characteristics of the secondary labor market.

Kates (1996) identified education as key to lifting women out of poverty. Single mothers who have acquired education and job skills are more likely to obtain permanent employment than those who have not (Harris, 1993). Brooks and Buckner (1996) found that compared to poor women who had never worked, poor women who were working were more likely to have obtained a high school education or GED. Puerto Rican women were less likely to be working than European-American and African-American women, especially if they had difficulty speaking and understanding English.

Another important personal barrier is health status. Johnson (1998) reviewed studies that indicated that approximately 30% of welfare recipients have documented work disabilities, and Salomon, Bassuk, and Brooks (1996) reported that 45% of their sample of poor housed and homeless women had one or more chronic medical conditions. Mental health may also be a barrier to employment and may worsen as a result of the new legislation. Based on the responses of 118 mental health clinic patients to a survey about the impact of the welfare reform legislation on mental health, Cohen (1997) concluded that poor persons being seen for psychiatric problems were at risk for symptom exacerbation.

Health issues are especially critical for women on welfare who are seeking employment, as the loss of health insurance benefits is a significant structural barrier to women's transitions from welfare to work (Kerlin, 1993; Piotrkowski & Kessler-Sklar, 1996). Another structural barrier is transportation. Ong (1996) found that only 25% of a large sample of women on welfare in California had a reliable car. Compared to women who did not own a reliable car, those who did were more likely to have worked in the past month, worked more hours on average in the past month, and had higher average monthly earnings.

Arguably the most crucial of the structural barriers are those that involve the labor market. These include sex and race discrimination (e.g., wage gaps), a substandard national minimum wage, and a secondary labor market that does not provide adequate benefits to families (Piotrkowski & Kessler-Sklar, 1996). Brooks and Buckner (1996) found that among the poor women they studied who were working or had been employed for three months within the last five years nearly 40% worked as cashiers or in food service. Other common forms of employment included clerical work and factory work. On average, the women worked 30 hours per week and made $6.00 per hour. The mean annual income of these women was less than $8,500.

An important structural barrier to securing and maintaining employment that poor mothers themselves cite is the lack of affordable and accessible child care (Bowen & Neenan, 1993; Brooks & Buckner, 1996; Holloway, Fuller, Rambaud, & Eggers-Pierola, 1997). This issue is even more complicated for poor women who are both single and unlikely to be employed in traditional "9 to 5" jobs. Researchers who have studied AFDC recipients' use of and satisfaction with different child care arrangements prior to welfare reform legislation have found that most women relied on relatives for child care while they worked or looked for employment (Bowen & Neenan, 1993; Sonenstein & Wolf, 1991). Cost and trust in the care provider were cited as reasons for using the main provider chosen (Bowen & Neenan, 1993). Regardless of the child care setting or the ages of their children, women rated convenient hours and adequate adult supervision as important qualities of a satisfactory arrangement (Sonenstein & Wolf, 1991).

As part of the Family Support Act of 1988, women were required to participate in the Job Opportunities and Basic Skills Training (JOBS) program and subsidized child care was an important component in this legislation. Hagen and Davis (1996) studied JOBS participants' views on their child care arrangements. They found that most women relied on formal child care settings with which they were extremely satisfied. Participants believed that their children's academic and social skills had been enhanced within their child care settings, and the mothers named this as one of the most important benefits of their involvement with the JOBS program. This is important because concerns about children's well-being and dissatisfaction with current child care arrangements may have negative effects on women's well-being and their attitudes toward working (Jackson & Huang, 1998).

The current welfare reform legislation includes federal block grant funding for child care that the States will receive on an annual basis. However, experts have raised concerns about the adequacy of State funding (Hagen & Davis, 1996) and the quality of care (Scarr, 1998). As Brooks and Buckner (1996) pointed out, although welfare recipients have had more opportunity in the 1990s to secure government funded child care subsidies, the demand is much larger than the supply, which has resulted in long waiting lists to access the benefit.

Welfare Reform and Service Programming

The Personal Responsibility and Work Opportunity Reconciliation Act of 1996 has shifted federal money for welfare-related services to the States in the form of block grants, in order to give State governments the power to determine the type of programming they will implement. Prior to this, the Family Support Act of 1988 provided wide-scale federal funding and guidelines that required the States to implement some form of the JOBS program mentioned earlier.

One program that was implemented prior to the nationwide JOBS program was California's Greater Avenue for Independence (GAIN) program, which then became the largest State run program operating under JOBS. According to Albert and King (1999), GAIN was a political compromise between people who favored the approach of providing training and education and those who favored the approach of immediate job searches and unpaid work experience (commonly referred to as workfare). Participants in the program took math and literacy exams, were interviewed by a service provider, and were then tracked to receive either basic education or to focus on a job search and quick entry into the job market. After three full years of implementation, GAIN was "associated with a modest increase in state-wide welfare terminations" (Albert & King, 1999, p. 144).

Programs such as these vary greatly in how effectively they decrease the number of welfare cases and increase former recipients' income. For example, Albert and King (1999) concluded that the Massachusetts' Employment and Training Choices (ET) program only initially decreased AFDC caseloads and that the reduction was small; however, Ohio's workfare program was largely successful in terms of exits from welfare. After reviewing various programs implemented throughout the country, Tenenbaum (1997) identified several variables related to exits from welfare and gains in income. Among the key components of successful programs were: addressing and removing barriers that limited program participants' ability to complete the program training and secure a job (e.g., child care, transportation); matching job skills training to the needs of the local labor market (e.g., increasing marketability); and collaborating with other organizations. Successful programs are flexible, treat clients as individuals, foster trusting relationships between service providers and clients, and are community-focused (Task Force on Women, Poverty, and Public Assistance, 1998).

What is missing from most evaluations of programs is attention to outcome variables other than caseload terminations and income increases. For example, Edwards, Rachal, and Dixon (1999) argued that programs should be assessed according to criteria such as whether they meet personal needs concerning physical and mental health issues (e.g., addiction). Also important to consider as an outcome variable are the types of benefits associated with the jobs former welfare recipients are likely to obtain. Although some programs claim "success" because welfare recipients make an initial transition from welfare to work, many of those women end up in low-paying, marginalized positions with little room for upward mobility (Kerlin, 1993; McCrate & Smith, 1998; Riemer, 1997). Piotrkowski and Kessler-Sklar (1996) argued that welfare reform should be accompanied by a reform of the secondary labor market so that former welfare recipients are able to secure jobs with adequate health insurance and other family benefits such as child care and paid family leave. It seems unlikely that women can maintain employment that allows them to be self-sufficient without addressing these broader needs. Missing from the literature are empirical studies in which women on welfare were asked to evaluate the services they receive, and very few evaluations of programs have examined women's psychological outcomes. With this in mind, we were interested in talking directly to women about their perceptions of the current welfare reform.

FOCUS GROUP

Purpose

What were women's lived experiences with this difficult transition from welfare to work? This was the over arching question that guided the discussion in our focus group. More specifically, we wanted to learn about women's experiences with the welfare system, their reactions to and perspectives on welfare reform legislation, and their concerns as they make the transition from welfare to work. We also asked them what services were available to facilitate their transition and whether the services were comprehensive and sensitive to the diverse needs of women on welfare. In the next section we will describe the focus group and summarize our participants' conversations about their experiences with welfare and the transition from welfare to work. We will then discuss the parallels between our findings and those we reviewed earlier.

Method

We invited a small number of women who were either current TANF or former AFDC recipients to participate in a focus group. Contact was first made with a current TANF recipient who invited these acquaintances so that a total of four women participated in the group. The discussion was held in the home of one of the women in the housing project where all members resided. The women varied in their demographic characteristics, in the amount of time they had been on the welfare rolls, in their life circumstances, health status, and attitudes toward and approaches to work.

Two of the participants were Puerto Rican, and two were African-American. They ranged in age from 29 to 50 years; none were currently married. One woman had four children for whom she was primarily responsible and three of the women had two children. Three of the women had a GED or high school diploma, and one had completed some college courses. Carmen (all participants' names have been changed) and Maria, the Puerto Rican women, had chronic health problems, were long-term recipients of AFDC (10 years or more), and were raised in households supported by AFDC. Louise and Regina, the two African-American women, had been on AFDC between two and four years, and they had had more experience in the work force than the other two women. Three of the women were current TANF recipients, and one had recently been removed from the rolls.

The first author, a European-American middle class woman, was the facilitator of the group. The focus group discussion occurred after a meal had been served by the facilitator. It was informal, lasted approximately two hours, and was audio taped. The women were asked to respond to questions related to three major topics: (a) experiences with AFDC; (b) affective and behavioral reactions to the welfare reform legislation; and (c) issues related to the transition from welfare to the work force. Participants also initiated conversation on topics that were important to them, such as their experiences with social workers, the need to hold the fathers of their children accountable, and their fears and concerns about working.

FOCUS GROUP DISCUSSION

Experiences with Welfare

Reasons and justifications. The women reported a variety of reasons for being on welfare. These included life events such as geographic relocation, childbirth, and divorce, as well as barriers such as lack of education and problems with child care. The women also expressed attitudes toward the system. Maria said, "Some people, they don't understand. They look at it (AFDC) as a crutch or that people really want to be in and abuse the system but that's not how it is for everybody. It's like a stepping stone to a better life." This viewpoint was shared by Carmen, who believed that welfare had helped her to be a good mother and allowed her to raise her children to be "good people in society." Contrary to popular assumptions, all of the participants reported having worked prior to receiving welfare. Louise and Carmen expressed a desire to work instead of being on welfare. Louise remarked, "I always liked to work. I don't like to depend on nobody. I like to have money in the bank . . . and they don't want you to save." Carmen believed that a welfare check was like getting "something for nothing" and would rather have worked outside the home to earn the welfare check. She went on to say, "I kind of wanted to work, ya' know, because everybody works, and I like getting out of the house." Regina, who had worked since she was 14 years old, felt entitled to receive welfare; "I'm not embarrassed or nothing because . . . I feel that I paid for it . . . I'm just getting my own money back."

Hardships. When they were asked, "What kinds of things made it hard to live each month?", the women reported feelings of frustration about not having enough money to live comfortably. This is reflected in Regina's comment, "It sucks. It's not like they really giving you anything . . . it's enough just to get by. It's a help but you cannot survive." She then went on to say that she is not in "a hardship situation" because the father of her children "helps" by sending money to her when she requests it. All of the women agreed that they are never able to pay all of their monthly bills and frequently experience termination of their telephone, cable television, and utilities. Carmen, who was once a primary caregiver to eight children, said that affording food for everyone was her biggest problem. She recalled a time when she could not afford milk for her children because she had purchased popsicles for them earlier in the day. Louise and Regina both seemed surprised by this and quickly asserted that their situations were quite different, primarily because they had fewer children for whom they were responsible.

As they discussed their daily hardships, they frequently mentioned other people's judgments about their needs and standards of living. Carmen said, "The point is really a lot of people think that you getting a lot of money or you doing good on welfare." They mentioned that people believe that women on welfare should not have cable television, telephones, cars, or sneakers. They also discussed the tendencies of other welfare recipients to misuse their welfare checks to purchase expensive sneakers and clothing instead of buying food or paying their bills. They were concerned that these few who "go overboard" taint people's perceptions of everyone. One important issue that was discussed in the context of the question about hardship was the difficulty of "keeping up with the Joneses." The women were particularly concerned about not being able to afford quality clothing and shoes for their children. They discussed the difficulty of affording name brand sneakers as well as more essential items such as winter coats. They felt guilty when their children were ridiculed by their peers at school for wearing inexpensive clothing. Carmen said, "The kids with the Nikes, they walked so cool. And my kids hide because they're embarrassed."

Survival. Given the difficulties of living month to month on a welfare check, participants were asked what kinds of things they did to make it easier to get through each month. Survival strategies mentioned were: selling drugs; living with a boyfriend who sells drugs; working under the table or accepting a job without notifying social services; and baby-sitting. Some of these strategies were employed by the participants themselves and others were mentioned as strategies other women have used. Louise talked about how difficult it was to survive on a welfare check alone and stated that, "If you don't have somebody else helping you out or if you don't have a job, you really can't do too much." They also discussed small strategies that they used on a daily basis such as buying fewer toys and encouraging their children to share them; selling food such as "icies" (homemade popsicles) and "Rice Krispie treats;" making large batches of affordable food and disguising it each night as something different.

Stigma. Only one participant (Carmen) believed her children were embarrassed because she was "on state." However, she reframed this in the next sentence by saying that, as a result of her struggles, all of her children are "savers." She said this as if she regarded herself to be a good model for them. She told her children that their struggles as a poor family would help each of them "become a harder, wiser person." Regina mentioned her own embarrassment when going to the bank with her welfare check. She stated that she never went to the bank on the first day she received her check, and that when she did go, the tellers looked at her "funny" because she is a welfare recipient with money in the bank.

Later, when the women discussed their experiences with work programs, Regina raised the issue of the stigma attached to being a welfare recipient applying for jobs. "You have to take a piece of paper to the boss for them to sign. That automatically lets them know you getting state. What if you didn't want people to know? You gotta take this damn paper and have them sign it so you can take it back to your social worker to verify that you found a job. People don't want to go through that. That's really totally embarrassing." Maria added that, "some people are actually scared of people on state. It's true. They're actually scared." The other women agreed and said that when employers and co-workers know you are a welfare recipient they might assume that you "sell drugs" or "are a criminal."

Women's Reactions to Welfare Reform Legislation

When asked about their initial reactions to the welfare reform programs in their state, they reported feeling angry, humiliated, pressured, and scared. Carmen's anger toward and criticism of the new system is illustrated in her statement, "We were angry, like, nobody gives a damn and if you really give a damn, there's a different way to do it." They reported having learned about the reform through their social workers, who were also the primary targets of their anger, as participants did not feel respected or understood by their caseworkers. For example, the women said that many caseworkers seemed to ignore the realities of women's job options and abilities to raise families. This is illustrated by Carmen's recollection of a conversation with her caseworker when she was told about the 21-month program: "The worker said simply, 'Get a job. I don't care what job you get. I don't care what they pay. [Regina interrupts: See? That's what I'm saying. That's how they treat you.] It doesn't matter what you make. Four or five dollars. Get a job.'" She said that this treatment made her "feel more like a piece of junk." Regina reported similar treatment, "She told me I was young and there was no reason I couldn't find a job." Her explanation for this treatment is illustrated in her statement, "The social worker acts as if that money is coming out of their pocket like when they get they paycheck, you're going to be taking their dollars."

As the women talked about their reactions to the new legislation, it was evident that some women were better informed than others about the details of the act. For example, when one participant asked the others whether a welfare recipient could apply for an extension of the benefits or return to welfare again, another quickly responded, "you can get a six month extension if you can't get a job. As long as you do what they say, follow the rules." When the women were asked what steps they took after learning about the new legislation, their responses seemed to be related to their previous work experience and their levels of confidence that they could secure and manage full-time employment. For example, Regina and Louise, the two women with the most work experience, looked for employment right away. As illustrated in the following quote, Louise emphasized her pride in getting herself out of the welfare system while acknowledging the possibility that she may need to turn back to the system. "I got a job right away. I'm so glad to get rid of them people [state workers] but if I need them I go right back up there [welfare office]." Whereas Carmen and Maria, long time recipients of welfare who also had health-related problems, did not take similar steps. In response to the question about steps taken, Carmen noted, "I slept more." Later in the conversation, it was apparent that she had experienced depression. "When you get sick, things become hard. The dishes, everything, becomes giant. And everything, little things like sweeping and cooking, little things you do automatically from the house becomes a terror. And then you don't live in the same place no more. You're not the same person 'cause you can't get up and do anything. You hate yourself, you can't deal with it and everything keeps going. When you're living a hard life, everything, just the whole picture, is just like rotten, isn't it?"

Barriers to Work and Self-Sufficiency

Low wages. The women's attitudes toward work led to a discussion of the lack of employment opportunities that would guarantee self-sufficiency. The women commented on the types of jobs that welfare recipients with a high school diploma were likely to get. As Carmen commented, "More than half of the people here, almost everyone around this project, all have housekeeping jobs." Clearly, full-time employment in jobs such as these does not keep a family above the poverty line. Maria and Regina noted how people who did find jobs quickly could not support their families on their earnings. This led the women to vocalize their concerns about the logic behind the 21-month program as a means to help families become self-sufficient. When Maria noted that, "this welfare reform is not really the solution," the group collectively agreed.

Health concerns. Health-related issues were central to the discussions about work. Maria, who had experienced bouts of intense pain while working, shared her experience. "You see, I tried working. I tried it and had a hard time. I have a condition in my feet from being abused by my kids' father. So, I used to go home with a swollen foot and everything and in pain. But I still worked even though I was going through pain, and after that I said I can't do this no more, you know, but I know that every situation is different." Carmen expressed her fear of becoming sick while working, "You gotta see unforeseen circumstances. What if the mother, if she's head of the household, if she comes down sick and she can't work, you know what I'm saying? Then what happens? Who's gonna support that family?"

The possible loss of their health benefits when they did find employment was of great concern to the women. Maria raised this concern when she discussed her reaction to the 21-month program, "I got a formal thing telling me about the 21 months, to look for a job. 'I don't care if it's five dollars per hour, just go out and get it.' But what happens then? They give you medical after you go off state, but a couple of years after that, what happens after that? And me being asthmatic and stuff, and getting seen the way I do, what am I gonna do? I'm worried about that." Carmen, the other woman with health concerns, noted that the extended two-year health benefit was "not long" considering that most of the jobs the women could get would not provide medical coverage. Regina also emphasized the difficulty of securing the type of employment that would guarantee medical coverage for her and her children. Based upon her experience of seeking employment she concluded, "They're not hiring anybody full time. You work part time. You cannot go get another job with benefits. So everybody's giving you part time just so they don't have to pay for medical."

Child care. The concern about the safety and care of their children was a core aspect of the women's discussions about work. The women noted the high cost of quality day care and the lack of child care options. As Louise noted, "Who's gonna watch the kids? You can't trust anybody. You don't know your neighbor next door by saying 'hi' and 'bye.'" Carmen echoed this concern, "I decided I couldn't go to work. I just know when I went to work once, my son wasn't very well taken care of." Louise also noted that although programs are in place to help finance child care, it is difficult to get the paperwork processed and payments sent right away. She recalled trying to help her sister get subsidized child care, "My sister didn't get a check for three months. I must have filled out 1,000 papers. They don't have not one, so they say. I called them like 50 times in one day. She finally got that check. I had to threaten them." Regina also discussed the difficulty of securing child care, "I told them, 'without a baby-sitter, I cannot work' and nobody can come watch your child because they talking about 'your check is coming, your check is coming' they not gonna keep watching your child. They don't want to do that. They wanna get paid. They want their money." Maria raised the issue of families with special needs children; "Kids that need special care. Who's gonna pay for that? Or does the system just have one set of money, 'this is what we pay'?"

In discussing the issue of child care, it became clear that the women are to some degree caught between the role of a low paid worker and the role of a mother as they struggle to decide which is more important to them. Carmen, the woman with the greatest number of children, talked about her role as a mother with great enthusiasm, saying her children are "so beautiful" and that she "loved them to death." She expressed great pride in her children and their accomplishments, and she took credit for her role in their development. She reminded the group that although she is not employed outside of the home, she does indeed work. In her words, "I work, I put my time into watching my kids, teaching my kids, showing my kids, whatever I have to do, you know?" She noted that other people often devalue the work that she does as a mother, to which she responds, "I do work. I would like to change shoes with yours. I'll go out to work, and you stay home and take care of my kids."

Multiple roles. The two women who were working outside the home at the time of the interview talked about the difficulty of juggling the demands of work and family as single parents. Regina noted, with a bit of laughter, that although she feels good about having a job, she's "tired of working." On a more serious note, she questioned whether or not she was spending enough time with her children. In the conversation, Regina's thoughts about this seemed to vacillate: "It's not like I don't spend time with them or whatever. But I'm always working to get them the best of things. So, it's like I spend weekends with them, but sometimes I'm required to work weekends. So then it gets hard because I'm working third shift so I'm sleeping in the morning. Then, by the time they come home, I'm still tired. Then you gotta feed them and everything, and try to lay down to go to work at 11:00 [P.M.], help 'em with their homework. So I try to lay down by 7:00 [P.M.]. So, I'm missing quite a lot of time spending with my kids." Louise unabashedly told the group that she can't wait to be 62 years old so she can stop working. "I'm serious. Every morning I do not feel like going to work. It's cold. I got to get up at 6:00 [A.M.], make sure I cook breakfast, make sure my kids are up, dressed, before I leave the house. I'm just tired. I go to work even when I don't feel good because I know I have to go to work. I have to go to bring that paycheck home." Louise emphasized her busy schedule; "On my days off I either got to cook, clean, wash or grocery shopping." She noted that she tries to make time for herself so she doesn't "lose her mind."

Fear of failure. Another point of interest in the discussions of work involved the fear of failure. Carmen seemed especially fearful of not being able to work outside the home and become self-sufficient. She looked up to Louise for getting off of welfare; however, she questioned whether she too could succeed in securing and maintaining employment. At one point in the dialogue, she stated, "I'm gonna do the best I can to move up but I can't move up as fast like Louise moved up. Louise went up there and she just moved ahead real quick. I wanna be like that, but it does seem scary. You know what I'm saying? It's scary because I don't wanna fail." This disclosure elicited supportive comments from the other women (e.g., "when you fail, just get back up, brush your butt off, and try it again!"). When asked about her current work experience in a temporary job at a retail shop (during the Christmas season), Carmen described the experience by saying that she felt like "a failure." She stated, "Everyone is nice to me because I'm older. And nobody tells me what to do, so I'm just standing there like a statue. She [an employee] said, 'you gonna be working in the back room.' Then things went crazy, so fast and she couldn't be there to tell me to do it. So, what I did was clean the damn toilet. I wasn't gonna get paid for nothing. I had to do something. I felt more stupid doing nothing but then they want you to learn like five things in one minute. I want to do good but it's so difficult." She was frustrated by the technical language used by the person who trained her and was embarrassed to ask for clarification. The group encouraged Carmen by telling her that she needs to get more hands on experience and more training. In response she stated, "I didn't get more training and now when I'm standing and everyone's going around like crazy, you feel about useless. And that bothered me more than taking welfare." Carmen hoped people would understand her conflicted feelings about work; "It isn't that we don't wanna work. But, you know, when you go to a job and you don't learn something you don't pick it up and you might forget [steps] number 1 or 2. Then you look stupid. They go, like, 'we'll do it again' [sarcastic]."

Evaluation of Social Service Programs

When asked to evaluate the services available to help women with the transition from welfare to work (and at other times during the focus group discussion) the women expressed frustration with some of the service providers with whom they were in contact. In Regina's opinion, "They don't even try to help you get a job. They don't care whether you have a babysitter. They don't care whether you have a car to go back and forth." Maria also expressed her frustration with what she described as "prejudiced" service providers. She recalled one incident that took place in a class that she elected to take, not one that was mandated by the state.

I was working on math and stuff like that just to prepare myself to try and help my children better. And I had a woman the minute I stepped in there, that was prejudiced against people on state. And she said, "Oh, you're here because of the welfare reform." . . . I'm trying to go into an educational environment to try and get, you know, to better myself.

The women agreed that a lack of education was a significant barrier to obtaining and maintaining a good job. In describing women she knew who were long time recipients of welfare Maria noted, "I know people who are illiterate. I know people who can't read and write." Regina felt very strongly about the importance of educating women on welfare; "I think they should make a law saying that it's mandatory for them to learn. Send them to school so they can learn. That's the only way." Regina had taken a Certified Nursing Assistant course, which she paid for herself, that allowed her to work on a regular basis.

Although the women identified education and job training as essential for making the transition to work, they did not believe that qualified people were available to help them in this manner at the classes that they were required to attend. In describing the class, Regina stated, "The first couple of days, you do a computer test . . . they want to see how well you do at math and stuff like that, to try and catch a feel of where you need to be. They do the computer to see what kind of field you would like to go in. Like human resources and stuff and then they supposed to try and whatever your strongest category is, they try to help you find a job in that category. But that doesn't always work out because people, regardless of what the computer says, some people don't want that category at all." Carmen seemed frustrated with this approach as well; "If I found out I needed more help in my math or whatever and they found my weakness, I think they should work with me there, and they should have shown me what I forgot or what I didn't know. . . . They should of helped us with [each] type of education and help us with more like the reading or whatever to give us more confidence." The women agreed that other requirements of the class, such as looking through newspapers and writing down jobs, were fairly useless and, as Louise noted, "something you can stay at home and do." The women also reported that they needed tangible assistance from service providers, not the empty encouragement that they often received. As Carmen explained, "you gotta take them by the hand, you really do. . . . You can't get up and say 'blah, blah, blah' and then do it." Regina further elaborated on this idea; "I think for people who never had a job, it's hard. If you never had nothing, you never did anything, you don't have experience except taking care of your kids or whatever, so how the hell you gonna send 'em out there and say 'you can do this' or 'you can do that.' " The women collectively agreed with Carmen as she offered this advice for improving services: "what we need, to me, is for them to say, 'oh, I'm gonna go with you.' And 'you're gonna do this type of testing, you can work on it, and you can get prepared for you to make sure you feel confident,' so you know, that you don't feel like a failure. I think that's what they should do."

The women believed that one helpful aspect of the class was that someone was available to transport them to job interviews. In addition to the lack of affordable, quality child care, lack of reliable transportation was a key barrier in the women's job searches. The women provided an example of a local community employer that had taken these barriers into consideration. As Regina described, "Foxwoods [Casino] is the only place that has a bus that comes . . . they're taking the welfare mothers, and they're taking the kids to daycare. They train you there, on the job, and ride back to pick up your kids and ride back home." The women agreed that this was what was needed. Carmen concluded that, "If they complain about we being on state, hey, all of us that's on state get up every morning like every working person. You get up, pick the kids up, and the parents up, bus them to some place they need, you know, a service and drop us back."

One interesting issue that was raised spontaneously in the dialogue was the role of fathers, as the women discussed the lack of programs or services directed toward men. The women's attitudes toward their ex-partners were mixed with frustration and disappointment, as well as real caring and compassion. Maria initiated this conversation with her statement, "I don't feel the, um, system really goes after the real problem, which is some of the fathers. Back in the day they said, 'we'll [the fathers] take care of you.' " Carmen, whose partner had been in and out of prison, summed it up best when she explained the problem this way: "sometimes as much as you hate them or [are] disappointed in them, but it still hurts that once you did love them or he's part of the kids. Or, and the point is, they don't really do corrections. Don't really correct him to help you or them. They just throw 'em and kick 'em and hit 'em . . . and now they're bums and criminals and you don't want to see one of your loved ones or part of your kids ridiculed all because of one thing when the only thing they have to do is train them. You know what I'm saying? Help them in a way." This statement drew agreement from the other women. Maria added, "I'm not talking per se, go after the fathers and beat them upside the head. I'm saying if he does have a job or him leaving his responsibility and now he's living in a mansion while you living in the projects. Hey, go and demand some of that to be put toward the kids so you don't put so much pressure on the mother, you know? Maybe there's a way they can counsel the fathers."

As demonstrated throughout the focus group discussion, the women varied in their job experience, confidence, health, and education and were frustrated by the "cookie cutter" approach that was applied to them. They wanted service providers to understand that they each had unique and individual experiences, that they were on welfare for a number of different reasons, and that they needed services that were sensitive to their varying needs and circumstances. As Carmen deftly noted, "there's the four of us, and we all need different kinds of help."

Conclusion

Our data, albeit from a small, limited sample, contribute to the social science literature by refuting stereotypes and providing suggestions for future research. Consistent with other literature, the women in our focus group wanted to work (Santiago, 1995), engaged in a variety of types of work (Edin & Lein, 1997; Kemp, Jenkins, & Biehl, 1996), and valued and pursued education (Dill, 1998). They varied in their demographic characteristics (Salomon, Bassuk, & Brooks, 1996; Santiago, 1995), work histories (Brooks & Buckner, 1996; Sonenstein & Wolf, 1991), reasons for needing public assistance, and support networks. They were aware of the negative stigma associated with welfare recipients and made negative statements about other women on welfare (Seccombe, James, & Walters, 1998).

Consistent with previous research, the two women who were long-term recipients of welfare, Carmen and Maria, had been raised in AFDC households themselves (Pepper, 1995). These two women appeared to have the least confidence in their ability to make the transition off of welfare. This lack of confidence may have been due to: (a) the length of time they were on welfare (Popkin, 1990); (b) the fact that they had less education and fewer job skills than Louise and Regina (Harris, 1993), (c) their chronic medical conditions (Salomon, Bassuk, & Brooks, 1996); and (d) their language barriers (Brooks & Buckner, 1996). In addition to these personal barriers, our participants identified a variety of structural barriers to self-sufficiency that were addressed in the literature. These included the low-wage labor market (Brooks & Buckner, 1996), the likelihood of securing jobs without adequate medical coverage (Piotrkowski & Kessler-Sklar, 1996), the lack of suitable child care options (Bowen & Neenan, 1993; Holloway, Fuller, Rambaud, & Eggers-Pierola, 1997), and transportation (Ong, 1996).

Finally, the women in our focus group were quite articulate in their critiques of the services available to assist them in their transition. Their primary criticism was the need for more individual treatment by professional staff in social service programs. It is especially interesting that the factors they identified as those that would facilitate their own success (e.g., being treated as individuals; having respectful, trusting relationships between service providers and clients; and assistance in overcoming barriers to work such as transportation) were those mentioned by professionals as key components of successful programs (Task Force on Women, Poverty, and Public Assistance, 1998; Tenenbaum, 1997). Clearly, researchers who conduct evaluations of welfare reform programs should expand the scope of outcome variables to include poor women's perspectives on their needs and whether these are being met by the services provided.

CHARTING NEW COURSES

The work described in this chapter represents a relatively new direction for feminist psychology. First, it focuses on and prioritizes low-income women's lived experiences as important, fruitful ground for research and theory. Poor women, despite calls for an inclusive feminist psychology, are marginalized in both mainstream and feminist psychological research and theory (Reid, 1993; Saris & Johnston-Robledo, in press). Social class should be an especially important status variable for feminist psychologists because it transcends other personal categories, such as ethnicity and age, and has a major impact on women's life circumstances, the stressors to which they are exposed, and the types of oppression they experience. Feminist psychologists can explore these issues empirically as well as enhance our knowledge base about a variety of general psychological constructs such as stress and coping, resilience, and self-efficacy. It is crucial that women's experiences with poverty be included in the psychology of women because women are more likely than men to live below the poverty level and are more likely to be heads of households that subsist below the poverty level.

Mainstream psychologists have been slow to contribute to research and theory related to poverty and welfare. When psychologists do examine socioeconomic status they are more likely to study middle class people's attitudes toward social services and attributions for poverty (Littrell & Diwan, 1998) than the concerns and needs of low-income women themselves. The social science research that does focus specifically on low-income women typically consists of studies that utilize large data bases to answer questions about issues such as intergenerational welfare receipt (Pepper, 1995; Santiago, 1995). Our recent analysis of PsycLit abstracts that contained the key words "women," "welfare," and/or "AFDC" revealed that only one third of those that reported empirical research involved qualitative methods. Clearly, low-income women are rarely invited by social scientists to speak in their own words about their everyday lives and experiences.

A second way we believe that our work contributes to feminist psychology is through our methodological approach. Although feminists have urged the incorporation of diverse methods of study (e.g., Crawford & Kimmel, 1999; Fine, 1992; Fonow & Cook, 1991; Harding, 1987; Peplau & Conrad, 1989; Reinharz, 1992), psychological researchers continue to rely primarily on quantitative approaches. Traditional psychological methods are valuable, but psychologists would be remiss to neglect the value of the qualitative methods that are frequently used in other disciplines. For example, in a recent article on the focus group method, Wilkinson (1999) noted that "few feminists (and even fewer feminist psychologists) use the method" (p. 222). We chose the focus group method as our means of investigation because it reflects the core feminist values of reducing the power imbalance between researcher and participants, prioritizes women's own voices and experiences, and accommodates the interactive and contextual nature of discourse. With this method, minimal constraints were put on the dialogue about welfare reform, and the women themselves determined the direction of the conversation, its tone, and the topics covered. By relating to us in this conversational manner, as opposed to being surveyed, the women were actively involved in the production of knowledge, which, too often, has been a privilege of White, middle-class, formally educated women (hooks, 1992).

Finally, we hope to encourage feminist psychologists to return to their activist roots and take a central role in transforming the critical and current political debate on welfare into a discussion of poverty. A solution to the problem of poverty would have tremendous implications for women, their families, and society. Our knowledge, theoretical perspectives, training, and values can contribute substantially to the development of programs and policies that are based on women's lived experiences and strengths rather than assumptions and myths about poor women. Feminist psychologists must join with other social scientists, policy makers, service providers, and poor women to chart a new course for welfare reform and the fight against poverty.

NOTE

The authors gratefully acknowledge the assistance of Christina Clark for her careful transcription of the focus group data.

REFERENCES

Aaronson, S., & Hartmann, H. (1996). Reform, not rhetoric: A critique of welfare policy and charting of new directions. *American Journal of Orthopsychiatry, 66*, 583–598.

Albert, V. N., & King, W. C. (1999). The impact of a mandatory employment program on welfare terminations: Implications for welfare reform. *Journal of Social Service Research, 25*, 125–150.

Axinn, J. M., & Hirsch, A. E. (1993). Welfare and the reform of women. *Families in Society, 74*, 563–572.

Bowen, G. L., & Neenan, P. A. (1993). Child day care and the employment of AFDC recipients with preschool children. *Journal of Family and Economic Issues, 14*, 49–68.

Brooks, M. G., & Buckner, J. C. (1996). Work and welfare: Job histories, barriers to employment, and predictors of work among low-income single mothers. *Journal of Orthopsychiatry, 66,* 526–537.

Cohen, C. I. (1997). The impact of welfare reform as perceived by users of mental health services in New York City. *Psychiatric Services, 48,* 1589–1591.

Crawford, M. C., & Kimmel, E. B. (Eds.). (1999). Innovations in feminist research [Special Issue]. *Psychology of Women Quarterly, 23* (2/3).

Department of Health and Human Services (1999). *US welfare case loads information.* http://www.acf.dhhs.gov/news/tables.htm.

Dill, B. T. (1998). A better life for me and my children: Low-income single mothers' struggle for self-sufficiency in the rural south. *Journal of Comparative Family Studies, 29,* 419–428.

Edin, K., & Lein, L. (1997). *Making ends meet: How single mothers survive welfare and low-wage work.* New York: Russell Sage Foundation.

Edwards, S. A., Rachal, K. C., & Dixon, D. N. (1999). Counseling psychology and welfare reform: Implications and opportunities. *Counseling Psychologist, 27,* 263–284.

Epstein, W. M. (1997). *Welfare in America: How social science fails the poor.* Madison: University of Wisconsin Press.

Fine, M. (1992). *Disruptive voices: The possibilities of feminist research.* Ann Arbor: University of Michigan Press.

Fonow, M. M., & Cook, J. A. (Eds.). (1991). *Beyond methodology: Feminist scholarship as lived research.* Bloomington: Indiana University Press.

Hagen, J. L., & Davis, L. V. (1996). Mothers' views on child care under the JOBS program and implications for welfare reform. *Social Work Research, 20,* 263–273.

Harding, S. (1987). *Feminism and methodology.* Bloomington, IN: Indiana University Press.

Harris, K. M. (1993). Work and welfare among single mothers in poverty. *American Journal of Sociology, 99,* 317–352.

Holloway, S. D., Fuller, B., Rambaud, M. F., & Eggers-Pierola, C. (1997). *Through my own eyes: Single mothers and the cultures of poverty.* Cambridge, MA: Harvard University Press.

hooks, b. (1992, July/August). Out of the academy and into the streets. *Ms.,* 80–82.

Jackson, A. P., & Huang, C. C. (1998). Concerns about children's development: Implications for single, employed Black mothers' well-being. *Social Work Research, 22,* 233–240.

Johnson, J. L. (1998). Welfare reform: Impact on former AFDC recipients with disabilities. *Journal of Vocational Rehabilitation, 11,* 137–149.

Kates, E. (1996). Educational pathways out of poverty: Responding to the realities of women's lives. *American Journal of Orthopsychiatry, 66,* 548–556.

Kerlin, A. E. (1993). From welfare to work: Does it make sense? *Journal of Sociology & Social Welfare, 20,* 71–85.

Kemp, A. A., Jenkins, P., & Biehl, M. (1996). Reconceptualizing women's work: A focus on the domestic and eligibility work of women on welfare. *Journal of Sociological and Social Welfare, 23,* 69–89.

Kunz, J. P., & Born, C. E. (1996). The relative importance of economic and cultural factors in determining length of AFDC receipt. *Social Work Research, 20,* 196–202.

Littrell, J., & Diwan, S. (1998). Social workers' attitudes toward welfare reform: Comparing Aid to Families with Dependent Children to work programs. *Journal of Applied Social Sciences, 22,* 137–149.

McCrate, E., & Smith, J. (1998). When work doesn't work: The failure of current welfare reform. *Gender & Society, 12,* 61–80.

Mills, F. B. (1996). The ideology of welfare reform: Deconstructing stigma. *Social Work, 41,* 391–395.

Ong, P. M. (1996). Work and automobile ownership among welfare recipients. *Social Work Research, 20,* 255–262.

Peplau, L. A., & Conrad, E. (1989). Beyond nonsexist research: The perils of feminist methods in psychology. *Psychology of Women Quarterly, 13,* 379–400.

Pepper, J. V. (1995). Dynamics of the intergenerational transmission of welfare receipt in the United States. *Journal of Family & Economic Issues, 16,* 265–279.

Piotrkowski, C. S., & Kessler-Sklar, S. (1996). Welfare reform and access to family-supportive benefits in the workplace. *American Journal of Orthopsychiatry, 66,* 538–547.

Popkin, S. J. (1990). Welfare: Views from the bottom. *Social Problems, 37,* 64–79.

Reid, P. T. (1993). Poor women in psychological research: Shut up and shut out. *Psychology of Women Quarterly, 17,* 133–150.

Reinharz, S. (1992). *Feminist methods in social research.* New York: Oxford University Press.

Riemer, F. J. (1997). Quick attachments to the work force: An ethnographic analysis of a transition from welfare to low-wage jobs. *Social Work Research, 21,* 225–232.

Salomon, A. (1996). Welfare reform and the real lives of poor women: Introduction. *American Journal of Orthopsychiatry, 66,* 486–489.

Salomon, A., Bassuk, S. S., & Brooks, M. G. (1996). Patterns of welfare use among poor and homeless women. *American Journal of Orthopsychiatry, 66,* 510–525.

Santiago, A. M. (1995). Intergenerational and program-induced effects of welfare dependency: Evidence from the National Longitudinal Survey of Youth. *Journal of Family & Economic Issues, 16,* 281–306.

Saris, R. N., & Johnston-Robledo, I. (in press). Poor women are still shut out of mainstream psychology. *Psychology of Women Quarterly.*

Scarr, S. (1998). American child care today. *American Psychologist, 53,* 95–108.

Seccombe, K., James, D., & Walters, K. B. (1998). "They think you ain't much of nothing": The social construction of the welfare mother. *Journal of Marriage and the Family, 60,* 849–865.

Sidel, R. (1996). The enemy within: A commentary on the demonization of difference. *American Journal of Orthopsychiatry, 66,* 490–495.

Sonenstein, F. L., & Wolf, D. A. (1991). Satisfaction with child care: Perspectives of welfare mothers. *Journal of Social Issues, 47* (2), 15–31.

Sparks, E. (1998). Against all odds: Resistance and resilience in African American welfare mothers. In C. G. Coll, J. L. Surrey, & K. Weingarten (Eds.), *Moth-*

ering against the odds: Diverse voices of contemporary mothers. (pp. 215–237). New York: Guilford Press.

Task Force on Women, Poverty, and Public Assistance (Division 35). (1998). *Making "welfare to work" really work.* Washington, DC: American Psychological Association.

Tenenbaum, E. (Ed.). (1997). *Westat casebook on promising welfare-to-work program practices.* Washington, DC: U.S. Department of Labor, Employment, and Training Administration.

Watts, J. (1997). The end of work and the end of welfare. *Contemporary Sociology, 26,* 409–412.

Wilkinson, S. (1999). Focus groups: A feminist methodology. *Psychology of Women Quarterly, 23,* 221–244.

Withorn, A. (1996). "Why do they hate me so much?" A history of welfare and its abandonment in the United States. *American Journal of Orthopsychiatry, 66,* 496–509.

Chapter 16

Women, Federal Policy, and Social Change: Bringing a Feminist Presence to Capitol Hill

Jeanine C. Cogan and Camille Preston

Federal policies have immediate and direct consequences for women's political and economic power, opportunities, and quality of life, which underscores the importance of women's involvement in the policy arena (Faludi, 1991; Nelson & Kahn, 1982; Russo & Denmark, 1984; Taylor & Rupp, 1993). As a way of charting a new course for the advancement of a feminist agenda, women can facilitate social change through working directly with federal policy makers to influence policies that directly challenge the roots of disempowerment and negative social conditions (Dauphinais, Barkan, & Cohn, 1992). Policies to address the needs of persons who are disadvantaged and the object of discrimination, including women, children, the aged, racial and ethnic minorities, people living in poverty, people with disabilities, lesbians and gay men, and other individuals with little social power, need to be advanced (Nelson & Kahn, 1982; Russo & Denmark, 1984; Taylor & Rupp, 1993). Women's involvement in policy development is central for correcting inaccurate assumptions that many policy makers hold of women (Russo & Denmark, 1984). Thus, the goal of attaining political power in the policy arena is a necessary priority for feminist activists.

With the hard-won victory of the suffragists in 1920, women began to participate in the electoral process as a way to gain social, economic, and political power (Nelson & Kahn, 1982; Russo & Denmark, 1984). The successful influx of women in the public sphere challenged men's exclusive power in that domain, which provoked a retaliation, or "backlash," against women's political gains (Faludi, 1991; Nelson & Kahn, 1982; Taylor & Rupp, 1993). The notable gains of the feminist movement began to be targeted through what some scholars call an antifeminist counterassault

(Faludi, 1991). This backlash was reflected in many policies of the 1980s (Faludi, 1991; Nelson & Kahn, 1982; Taylor & Rupp, 1993). A few examples include the defeat of the Equal Rights Amendment (Matthews & DeHart, 1990), budget cuts that pushed nearly seven million women and their children into poverty (Faludi, 1991; Minkler & Stone, 1985), the cutting of the budget to investigate claims of sexual harassment at a time when complaints rose sharply (Faludi, 1991), and a full scale assault on reproductive freedom (Luker, 1984). The backlash of the 1980s created a climate that sets the tone for the twenty-first century. As Katrina Shields (1994), a long time activist for peace and social justice, described it:

Whether we acknowledge it or not, we are collectively, in the tiger's mouth in a way which transcends all national boundaries. We are at risk of being overwhelmed by our wastes, of undermining our life support systems, and being damaged by our own technology—not to mention creating staggering inequalities between peoples of the world. (p. xiii)

Given these circumstances, it is imperative not only for the health and survival of women, but for our children and the world, that we be significant players in the policy arena. Yet federal policy is commonly portrayed as a closed arena open only to a few select stakeholders, as too complex to maneuver through, and/or too big for an individual to have an impact. Our goal is to replace these commonly held misperceptions with information and tools for how to influence federal policy successfully. The remainder of this chapter is organized into the following four sections: (1) Who are the players in federal policy development?; (2) Understanding the life on Capitol Hill; (3) How to influence policy; and (4) Strategies for integrating policy awareness into our careers.

WHO ARE THE PLAYERS IN FEDERAL POLICY DEVELOPMENT?

There are at least five central groups or stakeholders involved in influencing the federal legislative process: constituents, organizations or interest groups, coalitions, Members of Congress, and Congressional staffers. The role that each plays in the federal policy making process is briefly described below.

Constituents

Anyone eligible to vote is a constituent. Constituents' primary mechanism for influencing the federal legislative process is through their Members of Congress: Senators and Representatives. According to the American Psychological Association (1995), some Members of Congress view their constituents as having the most influence on their voting decisions, more than lobbying groups, their colleagues, and party pressures. Members of Congress are motivated to attend to constituent concerns because the people in their districts vote them into office. Indeed, constituent service is one of the most important aspects of Congressional life (Wells, 1996). Constituents articulate their views and concerns to their representatives through visits, letters, and/or phone calls. In addition, grass roots activism, such as rallies and/or protests, is effective to mobilize constituents within a community and to focus Congressional attention on specific issues. Constituents may also be a member of or become involved in organizations that work to influence policy.

Advocacy Organizations

There are many types of organizations or interest groups that advocate for specific federal policies; they cover a range of issues, including business and industry, science and technology, professional interests, labor, civil rights, public interest, and governmental interests (Lorion & Iscoe, 1996; Truman, 1987). Organizations often have a person or office responsible for advocating on behalf of their members' interests and concerns. Advocating on behalf of a large number of people across the nation can add more political weight to a message than simply advocating on behalf of one's own interests as a constituent (Ceaser, Bessette, O'Toole, & Thurow, 1995).

Congressional staff often work closely with advocacy groups (Nickels, 1994). For example, in order to move a bill forward, staffers may work with advocacy groups to identify key representatives in specific congressional districts that need to be contacted directly by their local constituents. Such grassroots support for a bill may help it gain active congressional consideration and increase its priority as an issue on the legislative agenda (Nickels, 1994).

A few examples of national organizations that focus on issues of the public interest and are involved in influencing national policy include: the American Psychological Association, the National Organization for Women, the Feminist Majority, the Human Rights Campaign, the National Association for the Advancement of Colored People, the National Gay and Lesbian Task Force, and the Anti-Defamation League. To be able to exert more significant influence, many of these advocacy groups coordinate efforts and work together through coalitions.

Coalitions

Coalitions typically are composed of clustered advocacy organizations that come together because of common interests or political positions with the aim of developing strength in numbers in order to influence policy. A coalition is designed to bring diverse organizations together to lobby on national policies, promote grassroots activism, and educate the public (Key, 1987). Members of a coalition try to establish personal relationships with Congressional staff and Members of Congress, which can be an important contributing factor to the success of a bill or other policy initiative (Nickels, 1994). Coalitions vary significantly in their membership, structure, and missions. Their constituencies and agendas may shift and adapt according to the changing policy environment and legislative focus. Membership within a coalition typically is on a group rather than individual basis. Coalition activities usually include regular meetings, federal and local outreach efforts, the sharing of knowledge and resources, and strategizing about how to influence federal policy optimally.

To illustrate the process and power of working in a coalition, we offer an example from our own policy experience in representing the American Psychological Association as part of the Leadership Conference on Civil Rights (LCCR) coalition to preserve federal affirmative action programs. LCCR is an umbrella civil rights organization that unites diverse interest groups with the aim of impacting national and state policies related to civil rights. LCCR oversees numerous coalitions on the following topics: affirmative action, hate crimes, census 2000, and others (Leadership Conference on Civil Rights, 1998).

In May of 1998, Representative Frank Riggs (R–CA) introduced an amendment on the House floor that would have prohibited universities and colleges from making admission decisions regarding any person or group on the basis of race, sex, color, or national origin. The amendment was offered to the Higher Education Act (H.R. 3330), which was being reauthorized. The Riggs' amendment was modeled after the California ballot Proposition 209, which passed in 1996 and resulted in a deep plunge of admissions of minority students to colleges and universities in that state. Admission of African-American students at three University of California law schools dropped by 71% in 1996–1997, and college admissions of African-American, Latino/a, and American Indian students for Fall 1998 semester dropped by more than 50% (Public Policy Office, 1998). Maintaining affirmative action programs helps redress gender, racial, and ethnic discrimination—practices that characterized university admissions for decades in the past (see Skedsvold & Mann, 1996).

A coordinated action of a broad-based coalition of organizations under the direction of the LCCR allowed a quick and influential response to this anti-affirmative action initiative. After the introduction of the Riggs Amendment, the coalition called on their members to contact their congressional representatives to urge them to oppose the initiative. Phone calls flooded congressional offices, and consequently this anti-affirmative action policy failed. Clearly, working in coalitions allows people to express their opinions on an issue in large numbers quickly, and it maximizes the like-lihood of influencing the legislative process successfully.

Members of Congress

Certainly, the 535 members of Congress are an important influence in creating federal policy (American Psychological Association, 1995). Many factors contribute to the decisions legislators make (American Psychological Association, 1995; Wells, 1996). Based on our experiences, the three pri-mary motivations that factor into legislators' political decisions are: (1) to satisfy constituents, (2) to enhance their personal reputations within Wash-ington, DC politics, and (3) to create good federal policy (Wells, 1996; Vincent, 1990). All three of these are most likely to be accomplished if Members of Congress have the skill to work successfully with and influence one another (Drew, 1987; Vincent, 1990). Members influence each other one-on-one through direct interaction, legislation, briefings, hearings, speeches, and the press (Rundquist, Schneider, & Pauls, 1992). The well-known "Dear Colleague" letter, in which Members of Congress explain legislation to their colleagues and urge them either to sign on as co-sponsors or to vote along similar lines, is a primary strategy for influencing other Members.

Members also influence each other greatly through party affiliation and loyalty. Party politics play a significant role in policy decisions (American Psychological Association, 1995). Members of Congress are informed by their party leadership how they ought to vote on specific legislation. Par-tisan politics are most apparent in party "whipping." Whipping is when a party strongly encourages their members to vote along party lines with the implied assumption that doing so will result in rewards. For example, Members of Congress may be "rewarded" for voting along party lines by being appointed to positions on more powerful committees, which in turn, gives them more power and clout with colleagues. This influence with col-leagues may translate into a greater likelihood of successfully addressing constituent concerns, and thus improves re-election possibilities.

Congressional Staff

Until the 1950s, Congress was largely a part-time institution that worked for nine of the 24 months of a Congressional term (Wells, 1996). Contrast this with the current 18 months worked by Members per 24-month term. The congressional workload has doubled in the last 30 years (Wells, 1996). The increased work load has resulted from a series of legislative enactments that enlarged congressional staff assistance beginning in 1946 with the Leg-islative Reorganization Act (Rundquist, Schneider, & Pauls, 1992). As a result, the 4,000 House personal staff in 1967 had doubled to 8,000 by

1990 (Rundquist et al., 1992). Some scholars have argued that the increase of staff has resulted in expanded staff autonomy (Rundquist et al., 1992); as the staff has increased, Members of Congress are able to take on more issues and to expand their workload. This in turn has led to the Members' need to rely more on their staff and to delegate increased independent authority to them (Redman, 1987; Rundquist et al., 1992).

Consequently, the congressional staff play a critical role in determining federal policy (American Psychological Association, 1995; Rundquist et al., 1992; Vincent, 1990; Wells, 1996). Members of Congress rely on their staff to track specific issues, to write their speeches, to educate them on a range of topics, to advise them on legislation and policy decisions, and to write legislation (Smith, 1988). The autonomy and influence of a staffer depends on a range of factors including their individual personalities, the structure of the office, and the Member's style (Redman, 1987; Rundquist et al., 1992).

UNDERSTANDING THE LIFE ON CAPITOL HILL

"To best understand the way in which federal policy is formulated, it helps to think of Capitol Hill as a community, or culture, with its own inhabitants, rules, norms, and social processes." (Vincent, 1990, p. 61).

Only by understanding the culture of Capitol Hill can scientists, lobbyists, activists, or anyone else who hopes to influence the federal process be effective in shaping policy (Bevan, 1996; Nissim-Sabat, 1997; Wells, 1996). Four central characteristics of congressional offices are the rapid pace, the large workload, the valuing of direct experience over baseline data, and the need to compromise (Rundquist et al., 1992; Vincent, 1990; Wells, 1996). Life on Capitol Hill is typically a lifestyle of rapid, unanticipated, urgent deadlines (Rundquist et al., 1992; Smith, 1988). Given the tight time-lines when urgent issues arise, it is not uncommon for staffers to become "experts" on a specific topic in a few hours or few days. Therefore, as they are searching for facts on a topic, staffers must rely on easily accessible and digestible resources—typically the Internet or talking points provided by interested advocates. The outcome of such "research" is often a blend of substantive and political information. The expanded congressional workload has staffers stretched so thin that reading one-page summaries may be all they have time to do. Extensive reports are often useless unless there is a one- or two-page summary known as "talking points" or a "briefing memo."

Although some policy makers appreciate the importance and usefulness of considering scientific data in their decision making process (Morrell, 1996), they tend to place greater value on precedent and anecdotal evidence or case examples. It is not unusual for legislation to lay stagnant until an event occurs to galvanize Members of Congress. For example, in 1998 the

Hate Crimes Prevention Act received attention and hearings took place in both the House and Senate only after an African-American man was brutally murdered in Jasper, Texas. Similarly, critical gun control legislation that had been introduced each session of Congress for a number of years was not seriously considered until after the Columbine High School shooting in Littleton, Colorado in 1999. The palpable role of real life stories in legislators' policy decisions may in part be due to the fact that they are primarily motivated to address the needs of their constituents and do so after hearing of their concerns and hardships (Vincent, 1990). In addition, research on persuasion shows that, depending on the audience, appealing to emotions, especially with fear-arousing messages, can be a powerful method of communication (e.g., Wilson, Purdon & Wallston, 1988). This lesson has not gone unnoticed on Capitol Hill.

Given the nature of the dichotomous two-party system of Congress, Members must work with individuals who may have very different opinions and perspectives on an issue. As a consequence, in order to move a policy initiative forward, one must have enough support, which often requires negotiation and compromise (Wells, 1996). The tendency to compromise may often collide with the desires and expectations of constituents and advocacy groups.

Understanding the unique culture of Capitol Hill allows the interested advocate to be more effective in influencing federal policy (Nissim-Sabat, 1997; Smith, 1988; Vincent, 1990). Given the rapid pace and heavy workloads in Congress, advocates can increase their effectiveness in working with Congressional offices by interacting with staff in a way that shows a respect for staffers' time and efforts. In addition, when working with staff, it is useful for advocates to offer personal stories of individuals who have been impacted by certain policies as well as empirical data. Advocates may be most successful in working with staff when they have an understanding of the limitations of the Members of Congress due to the institutional tendency for compromise.

HOW TO INFLUENCE SOCIAL POLICY

The advocate can utilize at least two avenues for influencing federal policy: (a) influencing legislators on already existing issues and (b) creating congressional support for an as yet unknown/invisible issue.

Influencing Legislators on Already Existing Issues

As discussed earlier, voting constituents are greatly valued in congressional offices. A constituent who communicates concerns to a Member of Congress can and does play an influential role in the legislative process. The most common way in which individuals view their role in influencing policy is to register opinions on already existing bills. Interested constituents communicate with Members of Congress or work in coalitions to promote or prevent the passage of particular legislation.

The first step in effective communication with Congress is to determine the right person to contact. Usually, contacting your own legislator, the person who represents your congressional district, is most effective. As your elected official, this is the person who represents you and who therefore must be sensitive to your views and concerns. Occasionally, however, in order to achieve a certain goal it will be more appropriate to contact other Members of Congress (American Psychological Association, 1995). For example, a person who is recognized as a leader on an issue in which a constituent has expertise may be the most appropriate Member to contact.

Constituents can contact Members of Congress through phone calls, letters, email, or a personal visit. The purpose of the communication often determines which mode of communication to use.

When an immediate impact is the goal. If a bill is currently being debated, is controversial, and/or there are other time pressures, constituents may be most successful in communicating their views to Members via phone calls. Members of Congress ask their staff what views their constituents are expressing and then consider these views when making policy decisions. Constituents who are interested in calling legislators should call the U.S. Capitol Switchboard at (202) 224-3121 and ask for their Representative and/or Senator's office.

When education or receiving a response is the goal. If a constituent wants to receive a response to an inquiry, or wants to offer information about an issue, then writing a letter is preferable. The most effective letters are those that are concise and focused on one issue (see Figure 1). To write an effective letter constituents should follow the following three steps:

1. *State the purpose.* The first paragraph should include who the constituent is and why s/he is writing this particular Member of Congress, for example, "I am writing you as a constituent in your district." This is followed by the purpose of the letter. Bill names and/or numbers should be used if possible and applicable, for example, "I am writing to urge you to vote for the Hate Crimes Prevention Act."

2. *State the evidence/argument.* The purpose is followed by a brief reason why the Member of Congress should do as advised. For example, "Given that so many states currently do not have laws that allow crimes to be investigated as hate crimes, the passage of this bill is necessary." Personal experiences of the constituent that support the stated position can be concisely summarized here. If the constituent would like to make a research-based argument, then a short summary of the research or the presentation of some data is effective.

3. *Ask for a response.* In order to optimize the impact of a correspondence, the letter writer should conclude by specifically asking the reader to

Figure 1
Example of Constituent Letter

The Honorable John Smith
U.S. House of Representatives
Washington, DC 20515

Dear Representative Smith:

I am a constituent and social scientist, and I am writing to ask you to oppose the proposed amendment by Congressman Todd Tiahrt (R–KN) to the D.C. appropriations bill that would prevent unmarried couples from adopting children in Washington, DC. This current bill is ill conceived and based on a number of inaccurate beliefs about lesbians and gay men as parents.

As a lesbian mother, I live in constant fear of losing custody of my child even though I am a nurturing, committed parent. I participate actively in the school board and related activities. My ability to be a caring and effective parent has nothing to do with my sexual orientation. This current amendment further threatens my daily existence as a parent.

Research shows that lesbians and gay men are fit parents. Contrary to the belief that gay parents may have a negative influence on their children, when compared to children of heterosexual parents children of gay men or lesbians show no marked difference in their intelligence, psychological adjustment, social adjustment, popularity with friends, development of gender role identity, or development of sexual orientation. Overall, the belief that children of gay and lesbian parents suffer deficits in personal development has no empirical foundation.

In sum, the characterization of homosexual parents as being a threat to children is inaccurate, therefore calling into question policy decisions based on this belief. I urge you to oppose this amendment. I look forward to hearing your perspective.

Respectfully,
Jane Doe, Ph.D.

Note: For the purposes of this chapter, the authors wrote this as an example of a good
    constituent letter. The Tiahrt amendment was indeed introduced to the D.C. appropriations bill in 1997, and a similar amendment has been introduced every year since then.

reply. Responding to constituent mail is a vital role of congressional offices. The last paragraph should reiterate the constituent's concern and ask for a response.

For more information on how to write an effective letter, see the APA's information brochure entitled *Psychology in the Public Interest: A Psychologist's Guide to Participation in Federal Policy Making* (American Psychological Association, 1995).

When writing a letter to your Member of Congress use the following addresses:

(Your Congressperson) The Honorable First, Last Name

U.S. House of Representatives

Washington, D.C. 20515

(Your Senator) The Honorable First, Last Name

U.S. Senate

Washington, D.C. 20510

Effective Advocacy

When interacting with policy makers, advocates may err on the side of being overly critical (Wells, 1996) without offering specific suggestions or alternatives. This mistake greatly limits the effectiveness of those advocates (Wells, 1996). Most legislators and their staff want to write the best bills possible and to implement effective policies. For this reason, a staffer should be viewed as a friend not a foe. Many staffers will be open to an advocate's expertise and ideas (though they may not always implement them). Therefore, if possible, it is useful to offer particular strategies for implementing the goals or ideas the advocate is promoting.

For example, if advocates are supportive of the overall purpose of a bill but think it has flaws, they may benefit from preparing talking points that (a) outline the concerns and (b) offer alternatives. To draw from our experiences as an illustration, the first author wrote a bill, the Patient Freedom from Restrain Act, for Congresswoman DeGette on prohibiting the use of inappropriate physical, mechanical, and chemical restraints in facilities for troubled youth, and people with psychiatric disabilities or developmental disabilities. This bill was based on the Nursing Home Reform Act of 1987, which defined when restraints were to be used. The reason for this legislation was to protect these vulnerable populations from death and serious injury that can result from inappropriate restraint use. After the bill was introduced, many provider groups met with us to critique the bill on a number of points. Whereas most groups raised legitimate concerns, the advocates who were most effective were those who offered alternative language. Due to work overload, even if staff agree with an advocate's perspective, they may not have the time or expertise to find a solution for the outlined concern. Therefore, advocates can play a unique role in the legislative process by offering specific solutions and assistance to the congressional staff.

Creating Congressional Support for an Unknown Issue

Advocates and stakeholders are not only successful at influencing important policy decisions about existing legislation and visible issues, but they can also help set the legislative agenda. For example, hate crimes legislation grew out of a national, coordinated movement that decided that hate crimes was an important policy priority. Individuals and organizations met with Members of Congress to urge them to recognize and address this growing problem.

Finding the right member to support and promote an issue. Members of Congress become known for their leadership in particular areas. Advocates should do research to find out which Members are likely to support and promote their issues. Information about Members' policy priorities and accomplishments is available on their website home pages. The address for home pages for the House of Representatives is http://www.house.gov and for the Senate http://www.senate.gov. Members' biographies are available by accessing the website on biographical directories of Members of Congress at http://bioguide.congress.gov/. An excellent book that provides descriptions of Members of Congress is published every session by the *Congressional Quarterly*. The most recent book is titled *Politics in America: 1998, the 105th Congress*. Another useful avenue for learning about the legislative priorities of Members is to see what bills they introduced or co-sponsored; this can be done easily by accessing the Thomas website at *http://thomas.loc.gov*. This site provides information about the bills Members have introduced, text of legislation, congressional records, committee information, and bill status and summaries.

Establishing relationships with congressional staff. Congressional staff play critical roles in policy development, and their influence can be substantial (Vincent, 1990; Wells, 1996). The staff serves as gatekeepers to Members of Congress, and they decide who will receive entrée into the offices. If a staffer advises the Member of Congress to meet with a particular advocacy group, chances are the Member will do so. Given this influence, advocates interested in making contact with their representatives should establish rapport with the legislative staff. To this end advocates may set up an appointment by calling the legislative assistant who is currently working on the issue of interest. In order to increase the chances of getting an appointment with a legislative assistant, the advocate should offer an explanation for choosing this particular Member and state the purpose of the proposed meeting. For example, "I am calling you because your boss is a leader on women's health issues. I know she led the fight against breast cancer and is concerned about good quality health care for all women. I would like to schedule an appointment with you to discuss another serious women's health threat: the proliferation of eating disorders."

Educating staff. The primary goal of working with Members of Congress is to increase their knowledge and understanding of a particular topic that can lead to congressional interest and action. As advocates have more detailed knowledge on specific topics than staffers, they typically welcome assistance. (Wells, 1996). Due to the workload constraints of staff discussed earlier, advocates should present concise summaries and clearly outlined

Figure 2
How to Write an Effective Briefing Memo or Talking Points

---

1. *First identify the goal and state it clearly.* Why is the advocate lobbying the Member of Congress? What is the reason for meeting with the staffer?
2. *Summarize the research and main arguments using bullet points.*
3. *Stay focused on one topic.* If an advocate wishes to discuss more than one topic with the staffer, separate briefing memos should be prepared (i.e., one per topic).
4. *Be concise.* Keep briefing memos to one page whenever possible. If the message cannot be conveyed in a page or two, the advocate may lose the opportunity to influence the staff.
5. *Make the briefing memo easy to read and visually appealing.*

---

points and goals. To do so, advocates may prepare talking points or briefing memos, which summarize the topic and can be distributed as handouts during meetings with congressional staff (see Figures 2 and 3).

An Example of Successfully Influencing the Policy Agenda

A primary policy concern of the first author is the public health threat posed by the large number of girls and women who engage in risky weight loss strategies and develop eating disorders (see Cogan, 1999; Cogan & Ernsberger, 1999). Through her initial policy efforts as the James Marshal Public Policy Scholar with the Society for the Psychological Study of Social Issues, it was evident that this issue was foreign and unfamiliar to policy makers, activists, and other stakeholders and therefore was not receiving policy attention. This brief summary of her activities illustrates a process of successful influencing of the policy agenda.

Educating Congress. The first author researched the leaders on women's health issues, scheduled meetings with their staffers, and presented them with information on the health threat posed by eating disorders. After a few meetings she found a Member of Congress, Rep. Louise Slaughter (D–NY) and her staffer who were also concerned about the problem and expressed an interest in creating a federal policy response. Together they organized a congressional briefing on eating disorders entitled the *Prevention of Eating Disorders and the Role of Federal Policy* sponsored by the staffer's boss, Representative Louise Slaughter (D–NY), and Representative Nita Lowey (D–NY).

A Congressional briefing is a forum for experts in certain areas to educate congressional staff about particular issues of concern and to offer possible policy strategies (Specter, 1996). Congressional briefings can also help shape the national agenda by drawing attention to specific policy issues

Figure 3
Example of Briefing Memo

Goal: We urge your boss to support the Hate Crimes Prevention Act (HCPA)

Why We Need the HCPA

- According to community surveys, violence against individuals on the basis of their real or perceived race, ethnicity, religion, sexual orientation, gender, disability and other social groupings is a fact of life in the United States.

- Civil rights statute, Section 245 of Title 18 U.S.C., gives federal prosecutors the authority to investigate allegations of hate violence based on race, religion, and national origin. This avenue for federal involvement is necessary in order to address cases where state and local authorities fail to properly respond to victims' allegations. Currently such federal investigations are minimal, with typically less than 10 prosecutions annually.

- This statute is critical for responding to the problem of hate violence, yet it does not include a broad definition of hate crimes in line with more recent legislation. In 1994 Congress passed the Hate Crimes Sentencing Enhancement Act as part of the *Violent Crime Control and Law Enforcement Act of 1994.* In this law, hate crimes were defined broadly as a crime committed against the person:

    "because of the actual or perceived race, color, religion, national origin, ethnicity, gender, disability, or sexual orientation of that person."

Purpose of the HCPA

- The main purpose of the HCPA is to bring Section 245 of Title U.S.C. in line with this recent hate crimes definition so that federal officials can investigate and prosecute crimes motivated by hate based on the victim's real or perceived gender, disability, and sexual orientation.

- The Department of Justice (DOJ) receives inquiries from families of gay victims asking for their involvement when local authorities have failed to respond. Unfortunately, the DOJ does not have the authority to investigate such cases. The DOJ considers this bill an important measure in assisting them to properly respond to victims' concerns.

Note: We wrote this example of a briefing memo specifically for the purposes of this chapter. The material is based on the advocacy of the first author while working in the Public Policy Office at the American Psychological Association.

(Specter, 1996). By conducting a Congressional briefing on the prevention of eating disorders, for example, Members of Congress learned why this is an important issue worthy of their attention. Although empirical measurements of the impact of this briefing were not possible, two notable outcomes are worth mentioning. First, after the briefing there was increased congressional support for the *Eating Disorders Information and Education Act (H.R. 2006)* that Representatives Slaughter and Lowey introduced months earlier. Second, the briefing continued to bridge the gap between scientists and policy makers as new collaborations emerged. For example, following this briefing, Senator Reid (D–NV) asked for assistance in organizing a public educational forum in his district.

Offering expertise to congressional offices. In the Spring of 1997, Representative Slaughter with her colleague Representative Lowey introduced the *Eating Disorders Information and Education Act (H.R. 2006, 1997)*, which would have established a public education and information campaign on the prevention and treatment of eating disorders and a 24-hour hot line. As a result of the established working relationship between the congressional staffer and the first author, Cogan was asked to write the findings for the bill and offer suggestions for appropriations report language. Report language accompanies each bill passed and assists the judicial and executive branch to understand congressional intent on how public laws are to be implemented (Nickels, 1994). Some committee reports include specific directives to and priorities for particular federal agencies (Nickels, 1994). Although report language is non-binding, federal agencies play close attention to the queries and recommendations of Congress because the Congress provides them with funding each year.

As a scientist and advocate, the first author's role in this process was to provide Members and their staff with research summaries about the prevalence of unhealthy eating habits among adolescents and how problematic eating and restrictive dieting serve as risk factors for the development of eating disorders (e.g., Griffiths & Farnill, 1996; Patton, 1992). With these important findings as a backdrop she assisted in drafting report language, which Congress incorporated into the language of the Health and Human Services funding bill as follows:

The [House Appropriations] Committee encourages the Secretary [of Health and Human Services] to develop a national media campaign targeting but not limited to adolescent girls and women to educate them about healthy eating behaviors. The program should educate the public about the risks of restrictive dieting and the prevention of eating disorders. The Secretary may consult with other agencies as appropriate, including the Center for Disease Control and Prevention and other public health agencies. Such programs may include development of a toll-free number and information clearinghouse on eating disorders. (H.R. Rep. 105–205, 105th Cong., 1st Sess., 133, 1997)

In response to this language the Office of Women's Health at Health and Human Services actively responded with a new "Eating Disorders Initiative." Experts in the area of eating disorders were convened to discuss research-based strategies for addressing the problem of eating disorders. The efforts of this office have resulted in the following outcomes: (a) the development of a website on eating disorders; (b) the development of a module on eating disorders to be included in information provided through the National Women's Health Information Center (which includes a 24-hour hot line on women's health issues); and (c) the development and eventual dissemination of information packets for teachers, coaches, nurses, and others who have contact with the middle school population.

STRATEGIES FOR INTEGRATING POLICY AWARENESS INTO YOUR CAREER

Many academics, therapists, and researchers are activists for women's rights within their communities. Examples of such activities include teaching women's studies courses, conducting feminist research, mentoring female students, and creating women's groups and similar resources (Stake, Roades, Rose, Ellis & West, 1994; Stake & Rose, 1994; Worrell & Etaugh, 1994). In addition to this activism many women may also want to increase their participation in the policy arena. In this section, we discuss strategies for political activism and various roles feminist academics, therapists, researchers, and students can play.

Strategies for Daily Acts of Political Awareness

It can be difficult to carve out the time necessary within already busy lives to stay abreast of policy issues relevant to women's lives. Beyond the traditional newspapers and weekly newsmagazines, new technologies and special interest groups can ease this burden. Many organizations operate free listservs that email legislative updates as issues arise. A second avenue for accessing policy information is through websites of organizations, government agencies, Members of Congress, and the White House. These websites often provide current legislative highlights and links to other relevant sites for more information. Two useful websites are the following:

http://thomas.loc.gov/. This site provides information about legislation, congressional record, committee information, and bill status and summary.

http://www.vcilp.org/Fed-Agency/. The Federal Web Locator offers information and links to the executive and judicial branches and federal agencies.

Influencing Policy through the Academy

One of the most important strategies for people within college and university settings to impact policy is to disseminate research findings and professional expertise beyond their immediate discipline in an easily accessible manner (DeLeon, 1996). Perhaps the single most effective avenue for doing so is to post research or a literature summary, preferably in the form of talking points, on the Internet. As described earlier, staffers often find their information on a particular issue through an internet search. Without credible scientific information, policies may be ill informed.

Scientists and other academics may also influence policy through the research they conduct (Caplan, & Nelson, 1996). Research questions and project designs can be framed and conceptualized to inform and evaluate policies. For example, with changes in welfare policies leading to the widely praised "welfare to work" programs, a researcher could design a study to evaluate the outcomes of the programs, and answer a number of related questions. Perhaps the policy is having unintended consequences, such as harming children or placing lower level workers out of jobs. Without research to answer important questions, Congressional supported programs and specific policies remain in place without appropriate evaluation.

Career in the Policy World

There are many professional opportunities for women interested in public policy, such as working within federal agencies, in Congress, in think tanks, and in non-profit or political organizations. Young women currently in or recently out of college may apply for internships or positions as legislative staffers with congressional offices. Individuals interested in doing so should call congressional offices and inquire directly. There are also positions with scientific organizations that offer fellowships for professionals who want to learn how to influence policy. For example, the American Psychological Association offers annual congressional science fellowships for both early and mid level career psychologists to work with a Member of Congress or committee staff. Similar fellowships are available for other scientific disciplines, which are coordinated by the American Association for the Advancement of Sciences. In addition, fellowship opportunities are available through institutes such as the Guggenheim and Rockefeller Foundations.

In Summary

Everyday thousands of people are actively lobbying Members of Congress in an effort to influence policy. From writing letters to establishing more enduring relationships with congressional staffers, women with social justice goals can be significant agents of change in the federal policy arena. We must be active participants in the legislative process thus charting a new course for improving the lives of disenfranchised individuals through influencing federal policy.

REFERENCES

American Psychological Association. (1995). *Advancing psychology in the public interest: A psychologist's guide to participation in federal policy making.* Washington, DC: American Psychological Association.

Bevan, W. (1996). On getting in bed with a lion. In R. P. Lorion, I. Iscoe, P. H. DeLeon, & G. R. VandenBos (Eds.), *Psychology and public policy* (pp. 145–163). Washington, DC: American Psychological Association.

Caplan, N., & Nelson, S. D. (1996). On being useful: The nature and consequences of psychological research on social problems. In R. P. Lorion, I. Iscoe, P. H. DeLeon, & G. R. VandenBos (Eds.), *Psychology and public policy* (pp. 123–144). Washington, DC: American Psychological Association.

Ceaser, J. W., Bessette, J. M., O'Toole, L. J., & Thurow, G. (1995). *American government: origins, institutions, and public policy* (4th ed.). Dubuque, IA: Kendall/Hunt.

Cogan, J. C. (1999). A new national health agenda: Providing the public with accurate information. *Journal of Social Issues, 55,* 383–400.

Cogan, J. C., & Ernsberger, P. (1999). Dieting, weight, and health: Reconceptualizing research and policy. *Journal of Social Issues, 55,* 187–206.

Dauphinais, P. D., Barkan, S. E., & Cohn, S. F. (1992). Predictors of rank-and-file feminist activism: Evidence from the 1983 General Social Survey. *Social Problems, 39,* 332–344.

Departments of Labor, Health and Human Services, and Education, and Related Agencies Appropriation Bill, H. R. Rep. 105–205, Union Calendar No. 126, 105th Cong., 1st Sess., 1997.

DeLeon, P. H. (1996). Public policy and public service: Our professional duty. In R. P. Lorion, I. Iscoe, P. H. DeLeon, & G. R. VandenBos (Eds.), *Psychology and public policy* (pp. 41–55). Washington, DC: American Psychological Association.

Drew, E. (1987). A day in the life of a United States Senator. In P. Woll (Ed.), *American government: Readings and cases* (pp. 487–497). Boston: Little, Brown.

Faludi, S. (1991). *Backlash: The undeclared war against American women.* New York: Crown.

Griffiths, A., & Farnill, D. (1996). Primary prevention of dieting disorders: An update. *Journal of Family Studies, 2,* 179–191.

Key, V. O. (1987). The nature and functions of interest groups: Pressure groups. In P. Woll (Ed.), *American government: Readings and cases* (pp. 266–273). Boston: Little, Brown.

Leadership Conference on Civil Rights. (1998). *Civil rights in the 21st century: Half-way home and a long way to go.* Washington, DC: LCCR.

Lorion, R. P., & Iscoe, I. (1996). Reshaping our views of our field. In R. P. Lorion, I. Iscoe, P. H. DeLeon, & G. R. VandenBos (Eds.), *Psychology and public policy* (pp. 1–19). Washington, DC: American Psychological Association.

Luker, K. (1984). *Abortion and the politics of motherhood.* Berkeley: University of California Press.

Matthews, D. G., & DeHart, J. S. (1990). *Sex, gender, and the politics of ERA: A state and the nation.* New York: Oxford University Press.

Minkler, M., & Stone, R. (1985). The feminization of poverty and older women. *Gerontologist, 25,* 351–357.

Morell, V. (1996). Using science to help shape the nation's policies. *Science, 271,* 1439.

Nelson, K., & Kahn, A. (1982). Conservative policies and women's power. *Journal of Sociology & Social Welfare, 9,* 435–449.

Nickels, I. B. (1994). Guiding a bill through the legislative process. *Congressional research service report for Congress, 94–322 GOV.* Washington, DC: Library of Congress.

Nissim-Sabat, D. (1997). Psychologists, Congress, and public policy. *Professional Psychology: Research and Practice, 28,* 275–280.

Patton, G. C. (1992). Eating disorders: Antecedents, evolution and course. *Annals of Medicine, 24,* 281–285.

Public Policy Office. (1998, May 1). *Urgent action alert: Amendments threaten access to education.* Washington, DC: American Psychological Association.

Redman, E. (1987). Congressional staff: The surrogates of power. In P. Woll (Ed.), *American government: Readings and cases* (pp. 452–461). Boston: Little, Brown.

Rundquist, P. S., Schneider, J., & Pauls, F. H. (1992). Congressional staff: An analysis of their roles, functions, and impacts. *Congressional research service report for Congress, 92–90S.* Washington, DC: Library of Congress.

Russo, N. F., & Denmark, F. L. (1984). Women, psychology, and public policy. *American Psychologist, 39,* 1161–1165.

Shields, K. (1994). *In the tiger's mouth: An empowerment guide for social action.* Philadelphia: New Society.

Skedsvold, P. R., & Mann, T. L. (Eds.). (1996). The affirmative action debate: What's fair in policy and programs. *Journal of Social Issues, 52* (4).

Smith, H. (1988). *The power game: How Washington works.* New York: Random House.

Specter, A. (1996). Congressional briefings and public policy: A letter to SPSSI. *Journal of Social Issues, 52* (4), 1.

Stake, J. E., Roades, L., Rose, S., Ellis, L., & West, C. (1994). The women's studies experience: Impetus for feminist action. *Psychology of Women Quarterly, 18,* 17–24.

Stake, J. E., & Rose, S. (1994). The long-term impact of women's studies on students' personal lives and political activism. *Psychology of Women Quarterly, 18,* 403–412.

Taylor, V., & Rupp, L. J. (1993). Women's culture and lesbian feminist activism: A reconsideration of cultural feminism. *Signs, 19,* 32–61.

Truman, D. B. (1987). The nature and functions of interest groups: The governmental process. In P. Woll (Ed.), *American government: Readings and cases* (pp. 255–262). Boston: Little, Brown.

Vincent, T. A. (1990). A view from the hill: The human element in policy making on Capitol Hill. *American Psychologist, 45,* 61–64.

Wells, W. G. (1996). *Working with Congress: A practical guide for scientists and engineers*. Washington, DC: American Association for the Advancement of Science.

Wilson, D. K., Purdon, S. E., & Wallston, J. (1988). Compliance to health recommendations: A theoretical overview of message framing. *Health Education Research, 3*, 161–171.

Worrell, J., & Etaugh, C. (1994). Transforming theory and research with women. *Psychology of Women Quarterly, 18*, 443–450.

Index

About the Contributors

MARJA BOOKER was trained as a clinical psychologist at Helsinki University, Finland. She is also completing a graduate degree in Latin American Literature at the University of Maryland. She has worked as a therapist and a supervisor in the field of domestic violence for more than 20 years. She has specialized in the problems and coping of child witnesses of domestic abuse. She has worked extensively with Hispanic battered women and has developed programming, given conference presentations, and advocated for women, both in the broader social services delivery and the judicial systems. Her academic interests include research and writing about the multiple problems that Latin American spouse abuse survivors experience in the United States, Latin American feminism, and development of treatment techniques that utilize Latin American literary works to empower victims of violence.

KRISTIN J. BRODERICK is Assistant Professor of Political Science at Kutztown University in Kutztown, Pennsylvania. Dr. Broderick's research focuses upon women's rights in regard to public policy in the United States, and in new democracies in Central and Eastern Europe. Her new text, *The Economy and Political Culture in New Democracies*, explores factors related to democratic consolidation.

JOAN C. CHRISLER is Professor of Psychology at Connecticut College. She is a Fellow of the American Psychological Association (Divisions 2, 9, 35, 38, and 52) and the American Psychological Society. Her areas of expertise are the psychology of women and health psychology, and she has published dozens of articles and chapters on various aspects of women's health. She is best known for her work on menstruation, menopause, weight, body image, and living with chronic illness. Dr. Chrisler is editor of four previous books: *New Directions in Feminist Psychology* (1992), *Variations on a Theme: Diversity and the Psychology of Women* (1995), *Career Strategies for Women in Academe: Arming Athena* (1998), and *Lectures on the Psychology of Women* (1996/2000), which won the 1997 Distinguished Publication Award from the Association for Women in Psychology. She has been politically active for more than 30 years, and has worked for women's rights in both civic and professional arenas.

JEANINE C. COGAN is currently an independent consultant, with the Harvard Eating Disorders Center as her main client. Dr. Cogan consults with Congress, government institutions, and non-profit organizations to ensure that policies promote the health and welfare of women and girls and other vulnerable populations. In 1996, she was awarded the James Marshall Public Policy Fellowship from the Society for the Psychological Study of Social Issues (SPSSI). In 1998 she received a highly competitive policy award from the American Psychological Association for her work as the Baily Science Congressional Fellow for a member of Congress. In 2000 she was awarded American Psychological Association Fellow status for her outstanding contributions to psychology and public policy.

LYNN H. COLLINS is Associate Professor of Psychology at La Salle University. She is on the Board of Directors of the Eastern Psychological Association, President-Elect of the Philadelphia Society of Clinical Psychology, and liaison for the Society for the Psychology of Women (American Psychological Association, Division 35) and the Association for Women in Psychology. She also serves as National Consultant and Regional Steering Committee Member for Psi Chi Psychology Honor Society. Dr. Collins is Chair of the American Psychological Association, Division 52's International Committee for Women and Co-Chair of the Gender Research Interest Group of the International Council of Psychologists. She publishes and presents in the areas of clinical psychology, psychology of gender, pedagogy, and international psychology. She is a Consulting Editor for the *Psychology of Women Quarterly* and *Psychological Assessment* and Contributing Editor for the *Journal of Genetic Psychology* and *Genetic, Social, and General Psychology Monographs*. Dr. Collins is co-editor of *Career Strategies for Women in Academe: Arming Athena* (1998).

LISA COSGROVE is a clinical psychologist with a background in theoretical and philosophical psychology. She teaches graduate-level courses in the Department of Counseling and School Psychology at the University of Massachusetts at Boston. She also has a private practice in Natick, Massachusetts. Her scholarship spans the areas of feminist research methods, the implications of postmodern theory for feminist research and practice, community psychology, feminist therapy, and treating children and families with PTSD. She has published articles and chapters in these areas. She recently received a grant to help fund her current research on women and homelessness.

MICHELLE R. DUNLAP is Associate Professor in the Human Development Department at Connecticut College. Dr. Dunlap is a social psychologist who specializes in social and personality development. Her research focuses on gender and race within intergroup relations, service learning, and multicultural child rearing. She is the author of many journal articles and the book *Reaching Out to Children and Families: Students Model Effective Community Service* (2000).

RUTH E. FASSINGER is Associate Professor of Psychology in the Counseling Program at the University of Maryland. She is also an affiliate faculty member in Women's Studies. Her areas of scholarly expertise in the psychology of women and gender include work and career development, mental health and counseling, lesbian issues, sexual violence, and women in the history of psychology. She is a Consulting Editor for *Psychology of Women Quarterly* and maintains a private therapy and consultation practice specializing in gender-related issues.

SUSAN H. FRANZBLAU is Professor of Psychology at Fayetteville State University in Fayetteville, North Carolina. Dr. Franzblau is a Marxist feminist and social constructionist. She has been active at grass roots and academic levels, fighting sexism, heterosexism, racism, and social class exploitation for many years. Dr. Franzblau's interests include challenging essentialist theories of motherhood and reductionistic clinical diagnoses, placing them in historical, economic, political, and social contexts, and social action related to these issues.

ELEANOR F. GIL-KASHIWABARA is a doctoral candidate in clinical psychology at Pacific University, School of Professional Psychology in Forest Grove, OR. Her primary clinical and research interests are issues related to women of color. Other related areas of interest include cultural competence in addressing the mental health needs of ethnic minority populations. Her doctoral dissertation research explores Latina acculturative experiences. Ms. Gil-Kashiwabara is a student member of the Association for Women in Psychology (AWP) and has presented on various feminist psychology issues at recent AWP conferences.

JENNIFER M. HILLMAN is Assistant Professor of Psychology at Pennsylvania State University, Berks–Lehigh Valley College in Reading, Pennsylvania. Dr. Hillman is a licensed psychologist who has worked to improve the lives of elderly women patients in inpatient, outpatient, and long-term care settings. Her research includes the development of age-specific HIV/ AIDS primary prevention programs, the differential diagnosis between HIV induced dementia and Alzheimer's disease, attitudes toward elderly sexuality, and grandparenting. She has published more than ten articles in journals including *Professional Psychology: Research and Practice* and *Psychotherapy*, and has authored the text, *Clinical Perspectives on Elderly Sexuality*.

LORI M. IRVING is Associate Professor at Washington State University in Vancouver. She serves as the Staffer/Regional Coordinator for the Association for Women in Psychology, and is the Coordinator for a community-based education and activism group, the Columbia River Eating Disorder Network. Dr. Irving has studied the role of social and cultural factors in promoting body dissatisfaction and eating disorders in women since 1985. While her initial work focused on the origins of weight preoccupation and disturbed eating, her recent work emphasizes interventions that promote self-and body-esteem by empowering girls and women to challenge and subvert sociocultural pressures—through media literacy, activism, and advocacy. Dr. Irving's work on eating disorders and on the advantages of a hopeful dispositional style have appeared in numerous journals and edited volumes. Dr. Irving has served as Book Review Editor for *Eating Disorders: The Journal of Treatment and Prevention* and currently serves as Associate Editor for the *Journal of Social and Clinical Psychology*.

INGRID JOHNSTON-ROBLEDO is Assistant Professor in the Psychology Department at the State University of New York, Fredonia. Dr. Johnston-Robledo is a social psychologist. Her areas of expertise are women and poverty, women's health, reproductive health education, and women's experiences with pregnancy, childbirth, postpartum adjustment, and motherhood. She is currently involved in research related to low-income women's childbirth experiences, images of women in *Parenting Magazine*, and parents' experiences with the post-parental period.

TERRY McCANDIES is an assistant professor at Wheaton College. Her research interests include African-American children and adolescents and clinical interventions with low-income and ethnic minority families.

MAUREEN C. McHUGH is Professor of Psychology at Indiana University of Pennsylvania (IUP). She has been teaching Psychology of Women and Human Sexuality since 1975. Her articles and chapters (on feminist methods and violence against women) are included in several Psychology of

Women anthologies. A Fellow of the American Psychological Association (Division 35), she was awarded the Christine Ladd Franklin Award by the Association of Women in Psychology (AWP) for her contributions to feminist psychology. She received the Distinguished Publication Award from the Association for Women in Psychology for a special issue of the Psychology of Women Quarterly on measuring sex role attitudes that she coedited with Irene Frieze. Dr. McHugh served as book review editor for Women and Therapy, 1997–2001. As director of Women's Studies at IUP (1986–1997) she received numerous programming grants. She has worked for the transformation of psychology, the sciences, and the university curriculum.

CAMILLE PRESTON is the James Marshall Public Policy Scholar for the Society for the Psychological Study of Social Issues at the American Psychological Association. She received her Ph.D. in Psychology (Ecological/ Community) at the University of Virginia. Her dissertation research focused on the influence of community resources on police pro-arrest policies for domestic violence. She has collaborated with police departments in New England and Virginia. Dr. Preston has also worked as a certified mediator and mediation trainer in addition to consulting to the Women's Center at the University of Virginia, the Mediation Center at FOCUS, and the local domestic violence shelter.

CAROLE A. RAYBURN is a clinical and consulting psychologist in private practice. Dr. Rayburn is a Fellow of the American Psychological Association (Divisions 12, 13, 29, 31, 35, and 36). She is a feminist therapist and activist, and a researcher in the areas of leadership, women and stress, women clergy, and life choices (agentic and communal). She has also studied body image and comfort with intimacy, mentoring, and spirituality. She has published numerous articles and chapters on these topics. Dr. Rayburn actively encourages girls and women not to allow boys and men to label/ define them, but for them to define themselves.

LEE J. RICHMOND is Professor of Education at Loyola College of Maryland. Dr. Richmond is a counselor who is known for her work in the areas of stress in religious families and clergywomen. She also studies career development and transcultural counseling and European Americans. She is author of the book *SoulWork* (1998).

RENEE N. SARIS is Assistant Professor of Psychological Science at Ball State University in Muncie, Indiana. Dr. Saris is a social psychologist who received her doctoral degree in Experimental Psychology from the University of Rhode Island. In addition to her interest in women's experiences of poverty, she also studies media images and influences (related to health, adolescent development, and sexuality) and the consequences of women's self-objectification.

JOSEPH SPINAZZOLA is Assistant Director of Research at the Trauma Center in the Department of Psychiatry of Boston University School of Medicine. His clinical activities at the Center are primarily focused on understanding and promoting processes of adaptation, resilience and recovery in adolescent and adult women and men who have been exposed to severe interpersonal violence and abuse. Dr. Spinazzola is particularly interested in the complexity of adaptation to trauma as well as the contribution of gender role socialization in promoting a cultural climate that increases girls' vulnerability to objectification, silencing, and victimization and boys' susceptibility to emotional constriction, social disconnection, and perpetration of violence.

VICKI B. STOCKING is Research Director of the Duke University Talent Identification Program (TIP), an organization dedicated to serving the various needs of exceptionally talented young people. Her research follows her interest in promoting the well being of young people, including self-concept formation, self-expression, and adjustment. In addition to her work at TIP, Dr. Stocking holds an adjunct position in Duke's Department of Psychology, where she teaches undergraduate courses on adolescent development. She promotes reflection, self-awareness, and thoughtful activism in her teaching and through the independent projects in which she mentors students, particularly through her work at Duke in instituting learning through community service. The goal she articulates at the beginning of each semester is that Duke students will leave the university and work thoughtfully to improve conditions for adolescents everywhere.

MERIDETH J. TOMLINSON is a doctoral candidate in the Counseling Psychology Program at the University of Maryland and a Pre-Doctoral Intern at the University of Maryland's Counseling Center where she is developing specializations in eating disorders and trauma among women. Her areas of feminist scholarship in psychology include vocational development, feminist pedagogy, and lesbian and bisexual women's psychosocial development.

CAROLYN M. WEST is Assistant Professor of Psychology at the University of Washington, Tacoma. The University of Minnesota's Institute on Domestic Violence in the African-American community recently awarded Dr. West the Outstanding Research Award for 2000. Dr. West's scholarship and clinical work focus on understanding, preventing, and reducing domestic violence. Topics of particular interest to her include partner violence in ethnic minority families, partner violence in same-sex couples, cultural barriers to help-seeking for domestic violence, sexual victimization, and dating violence. She also studies historical images of Black women. Dr. West has published numerous articles in both areas.

MICHELLE K. WILLIAMS is Assistant Professor at the University of Connecticut, with a dual appointment in Psychology and African-American Studies. She teaches courses devoted to African-American psychology, multicultural psychology, and clinical interventions with ethnic minorities. Her research interests include ethnic identity development, multicultural psychology, domestic violence, and sexual violence.

HELEN W. WILSON works in the Department of Psychiatry and Behavioral Sciences at Northwestern University Medical School. Ms. Wilson's feminist scholarship focuses on adolescent girls' perspectives on the constraints to authentic voice and self-representation in the hope that understanding these constraints can contribute to charting a new course for young women in which they are not compelled to silence themselves.